THE SECRETS OF

GETTING RICH

Amazing Ways to Build Your Wealth

THE SECRETS OF

GETTING RICH

Amazing Ways to Build Your Wealth

DAVID J. PEREL
EDITOR OF **THE FRANKLIN PROSPERITY REPORT**

Humanix Books
www.humanixbooks.com

Humanix Books

The Secrets of Getting Rich
Copyright © 2020 by Humanix Books
All rights reserved

Humanix Books, P.O. Box 20989, West Palm Beach, FL 33416, USA
www.humanixboo ks.com | info@humanixbooks.com

Humanix Books is a division of Humanix Publishing, LLC. Its trademark,
consisting of the words "Humanix Books" is registered in the Patent and Trademark
Office and in other countries.

ISBN: 9781630061616 (Hardcover)
ISBN: 9781630061623 (E-book)

Printed in the United States of America

Table of Contents

Save Big Bucks • The Smart Money Move to Make When Your Car Needs a Major Overhaul

Worth Considering • Guide to a Fully Funded Retirement • The 3 Most Important Calculations You Must Make Before Retiring • The Importance of an Emergency Fund

How to Profit from Stuff You've Inherited • Make Money from a DIY Estate Sale • Earn Extra Cash With These 5 Easy Business Ideas • How to Turn Your Social Media Following into Cash • Rent Your Home to Movie Producers for Big Cash • Make Money Blogging • Turn Your Trash into Cash • How to Become a Financial Planner & Earn More • You Can Make Money Mystery Shopping • Become a Startup Investor Like the Sharks on TV • 6 eBay Alternatives to Turn Clutter Into Cash • Need $100K? How to Raise Cash for an Investment • Smart Financial Moves You Can Make Now • 9 Steps to Start a Home-Based Business • Open Your Own Consulting Business

The Best Months to Buy Everything Cheaper • Get Cash Back on Things You'd Buy Anyway • 5 Splurges That Are Worth It • Best Apps for Saving Money on Groceries • The 8 Best Things to Buy at a Thrift Store • When an Extended Warranty is Worth It • Unlocking the Value of Amazon Prime • Buy Jewelry Online Without Getting Ripped Off • Saving Time and Money With Mail-Order Meals • How to Shop at a Warehouse Store Without a Membership • Wine and Spirits for Less $$ During the Holiday Season • Don't Waste Money: How to Eliminate Impulse Buys • Buy Gold and Silver Without Getting Ripped Off • Save Big on Big-Ticket Purchases • Shop Smart by Avoiding Rip-Offs and Scoring the Best Deals • Read This Before You Rely on Other People's Reviews

The 4 Best Ways to Guard Your Digital Data • Protect Your Business Against ID Theft • Why You Should Freeze Your Kid's Credit Now • The Hidden Problem With Gift Cards

Introduction

You don't have to be born rich to grow wealthy. Nor do you have to strike it big in the stock market or invent an app that goes viral. In reality, wealth is the result of the decisions you make every day. Make enough of the right ones, and you'll see the rewards in your bank account.

This guide isn't about pinching pennies or learning how to scrape by with the bare minimum. You don't have to give up your morning latte or drive a 15-year-old car. You simply have to plug the money leaks that are draining your wealth and take advantage of some smart, yet simple, ways to grow your nest egg.

Let's face it: The odds are stacked against the average person. The big money on Wall Street has an advantage. Those investors not only have plenty of money to begin with, they also have access to the best research money can buy. But what about the regular Joes — the ones who don't have a pile of cash sitting in a trust fund?

Fortunately, there are plenty of ways for regular people to grow wealthy, too. And every one of these techniques will work for you, whether you have an MBA from Wharton or a degree from the school of hard knocks.

It doesn't matter if your goal is to stop living from paycheck to paycheck, retire as a multi-millionaire, or simply maximize the income you have, this book is for you.

As famed billionaire Warren Buffett once said, "Do not save what is left after spending; instead spend what is left after saving."

Chapter 1

Credit Cards
and Banking

"IF YOU WOULD KNOW THE VALUE OF MONEY,
GO AND TRY TO BORROW SOME; FOR HE THAT
GOES A BORROWING GOES A SORROWING ..."

Best Places to Park Your Cash

A decade of extremely low interest rates has had a huge effect on traditional banking. Interest paid to depositors has been nearly zero for years, leading a variety of new competitors to try to pick off bank customers by offering more.

Credit unions, brokerages, investing apps, and financial technology firms — everyone seems to want your cash. And they're offering enticing rates to get it. But what do you get and what do you give up bypassing the savings account at your bank?

Here are some of the non-traditional places aside from certificates of deposit and money market accounts you can put your savings, as well as the pros and cons of each.

NON-BANK APPS

One startup that made a big splash recently was Robinhood, an app that offers commission-free stock and mutual fund trades. At one point its founders claimed that the app would start paying 3% on deposits — then they had to backtrack.

The problem was that the money was not FDIC-insured, but instead offered insurance coverage from the brokerage-world equivalent, the Securities Investor Protection Corporation (SIPC).

The SIPC pushed back, saying it wouldn't cover Robinhood depositors in the same way the FDIC covers bank accounts. Its protection is designed to insure customers against losses incurred when their brokerage firms go bankrupt.

In response, Robinhood switched gears, and instead of offering a high-yield checking or savings account, it offered a cash management account. At one point that paid 1.8%.

Other money management startups are offering similar compelling deals. Virtual wealth manager Wealthfront, for instance, has also given similar rates on cash accounts.

These companies do this the same way any brokerage firm might. They take your money and spread it across several banks with which it has partnerships, with no one bank holding more than $250,000. That way your money is FDIC-insured.

Personal Capital, another investment app, offered 1.55% on deposits. Meanwhile, credit information site Credit Karma joined the race to suck up cash, and was offering 1.9% to its clients on a high-yield product. (Rates for all products are subject to change.)

Is It Worth It? If you're already a customer of one of these firms and expect to deposit money there to invest in the relatively short or medium term, sure, it's worth it.

Those types of returns are likely a far better deal than holding cash in your bank savings account where it earns practically nothing, then transferring it to invest later. On the other hand, if you don't plan to become a customer of one of these organizations, it's not necessarily worth your time to switch.

"Traditional brick-and-mortar banks are taking notice" of the rush of non-bank offers, says Brendan Willmann, a certified financial planner. "They are offering more attractive yields on select savings accounts for good customers, but you'll likely have to ask for an alternative to the meager interest rates offered to the masses."

ONLINE BANKS

Online banks have long been the heavyweights of the high-yield world. The idea of putting your cash in a distant vault with no local branch can be off-putting to some, so high yields help offset the hesitance and draw in new clients.

The argument the online banks give is that not having branches means they can pass along operational cost savings to customers in the form of better rates. Bankrate.com listed a number of online banks paying north of 1.8% in a recent survey, for instance.

Minimum deposits in that ranking ran anywhere from zero up to $1,000. Some of the names offering these high rates include firms better known for credit card services, such as American Express and Discover, investment banks such as Goldman Sachs' online brand Marcus, and big global banks Citibank, HSBC, and Barclays.

Is It Worth It? If you're accustomed to banking entirely online, it may be worth it. Watch out for hidden fees, and make sure you can get cash from an ATM without paying for it. Some online banks have no ATM network agreements or only a limited geographical presence. If you have money that you don't need for six months or so, and you can't get a good rate at your regular bank, consider it.

HIGH-YIELD CREDIT UNION ACCOUNTS

Credit unions have long been known for offering high yield checking accounts. Sometimes they're a full percentage point or more above typical rates elsewhere.

Part of the reason credit unions can do this is that they have a lower cost of doing business, because their depositors are the owners of the credit union. Any profits are funneled back into lower lending rates, higher interest on deposits, or simply year-end cash distributions.

Credit unions also typically operate at a smaller scale than banks and have fewer branches. Sticking to their knitting — service to their clients above growth — keeps the credit unions focused on efficiency.

Is It Worth It? The downside of credit unions is that they are not that easy to join. Many are focused on specific groups of employees, such as state university systems, hospitals, or government employees.

However, some credit unions do make it easy to join by allowing you to pay a small fee if you're not a member of the group the credit union is targeted toward. Even so, it isn't the same as walking into a normal bank branch and just opening an account.

If you try to get the high-yield product at a credit union, there are strings here, too. You may have to have a minimum deposit or a certain number of PIN transactions per month. There can be balance caps as well, meaning you won't earn interest above a certain dollar amount in the account. So before you go this route, be sure to read the fine print carefully.

Why You Have 53 Credit Scores
& How It Can Cost You

In today's digital world, you're often identified by unique numbers. You have one driver's license number, one passport number, and one Social Security number. So when it comes to credit scores — possibly the most influential number affecting your life — it's logical that you'd have only one. Logical, but not true — not even close. In reality, you have more credit scores than you'd ever suspect, including some you may never know about.

It's important to understand how credit scores work, because these scores can affect everything from whether you can get a mortgage to the rate you get for a car loan to whether you get hired for a job.

Let's start with the basics: Why are there so many credit scores?

CREDIT REPORTS VERSUS CREDIT SCORES

Your credit history is collected by credit reporting agencies. While there are several, the big three are Equifax, Experian, and TransUnion. They aren't government agencies, but they are regulated by the government.

These companies get reports from lenders, which show the total debt you owe, timeliness of payments, liens, defaults, bankruptcies, etc. This information is then sold to lenders to help them make loan decisions.

Credit files, however, are just information, not evaluations. Two people carrying $5,000 balances can pose very different levels of risk, depending on age, income, credit limit, length of credit history, education, and other factors. How is a lender to know which combination of factors presents the most risk unless individual borrowers can be compared to all borrowers?

Enter analytic companies. These are the companies that create credit scores, and they're totally separate from the credit reporting agencies. The credit scores these companies create are simply a numeric interpretation of the information in your credit file, based on computer models that are designed to detect the likelihood that you will fail to make payments on a loan or default entirely.

WHY ARE THERE SO MANY CREDIT SCORES?

Just as there are several credit reporting agencies, there are also many credit scoring companies, including CoreLogic, Innovis, LexisNexis, and SageStream. But the two biggest, by far, are Fair, Isaac and Company (FICO) and VantageScore.

FICO, considered the gold standard of credit scores, introduced the first credit score in 1989, while VantageScore was developed in 2006 as a collaboration among the big-three credit reporting agencies.

Both companies use a scale of 300 to 850, with scores above 700 considered good and above 800 being excellent. However, FICO also has different models for predicting risk for mortgages, car loans, insurance, bankruptcies, and installment loans, just to name a few.

But there's more — FICO tweaks each model for each of the three credit bureaus. So if you're checking your FICO score, you may get a different number, depending on whether it's coming from Equifax, Experian, or TransUnion.

Another reason for differing scores is that models get altered over the years, but they don't necessarily get adopted at the same time, just as many people use Windows 7 even though Windows 10 is the latest version. So, it turns out that FICO 8 is the most widely used model, even though FICO 9 was introduced in 2014.

Therefore, your FICO score could be different depending on whether it's coming from Equifax, Experian, or TransUnion and whether they're using FICO 8 or FICO 9. If you consider all the various combinations, you probably have 53 different credit scores floating around. And once FICO 9 becomes widely accepted, that number will increase to about 65 — or even more.

That's because some lenders create proprietary scoring models based on information they receive from each credit reporting agency. If you apply for a mortgage, the bank may be using a proprietary credit scoring model it created, which comes up with a credit score number that nobody else uses or will ever see. No wonder there's so much mystery surrounding credit scores!

IS IT WORTH TRACKING YOUR SCORE?

Despite the complex web of possible scores, it's still worth tracking at least one of your key credit scores as a benchmark, which you can monitor through free websites and phone apps like CreditKarma .com, CreditSesame. com, and NerdWallet.com.

Each of these sites pulls weekly updates — with no impact to your credit score — from one or more of the big-three credit reporting agencies. The scores will rarely match each other exactly, which is perfectly fine. The key to look for is the general level, such as whether you're above 700, 750, or 800.

You'll also want to monitor the direction of the changes to your score. CreditKarma makes it easy by charting your scores over the past year. If you have a good credit score — and your score is increasing — nine times out of 10, you'll be in good shape no matter which score is pulled. It may not be perfect odds, but at least it's a specific number. Best Cash-Back Credit Cards

BEST CASH-BACK CREDIT CARDS

Dozens of credit cards offer perks, ranging from points you can trade in for hotel rooms or airline tickets to cash back and discounts at particular stores.

But cash-back cards remain king. They are wildly popular for obvious reasons: They reward you in greenbacks just for using them.

And whether you routinely use your credit cards for everyday purchases, like gas and groceries, or you only use plastic for major purchases or to book family vacations, there's a card out there that will help you get the most green for the way you shop.

Here's a look at some of the best cash-back credit cards available now.

Capital One Savor Rewards Credit Card
https://www.capitalone.com/credit-cards/savor-dining-rewards

- **APR:** 16.74% to 25.74% variable, based on your creditworthiness.
- **Annual Fee:** $0 introductory the first year; $95 after that.

This card offers cardholders unlimited 4% cash back on dining and entertainment charges, 2% cash back on purchases made at grocery stores, and 1% cash back on all other purchases. Moreover, cardholders can get free delivery from over 350,000 restaurants through Postmates Unlimited on orders over $15.

In addition, new cardholders get a $300 one-time cash bonus after spending $3,000 on purchases (balance transfers don't count) in the first three months of opening the account.

This card does carry a $95 annual fee after the first year. In order to make that worthwhile, you'd have to spend at least $2,375 on dining and entertainment or $4,750 on groceries (or some combination of the two).

Discover it Cash Back
https://www.discover.com/credit-cards/cash-back/it-card.html

- **APR:** 14.24% to 25.24% variable.
- **Annual fee:** $0

This card offers 1% cash back on all purchases, plus 5% cash back at different retailers each quarter, like gas stations, grocery stores, restaurants, Amazon, Walmart, and more. There is a maximum of $1,500 in purchases for the quarterly 5% cash back offer, and you have to activate the offer each quarter in order to participate.

But the really neat thing about this card is that Discover will automatically match all the cash back you've earned at the end of your first year. There's no limit to the matching, however, this offer is limited to the first year of the account.

You can redeem your cash back at any time in any amount (no minimum), and the rewards never expire. You can also use your rewards at Amazon, if you prefer.

Another nice feature: Discover offers free alerts that inform you if the company finds your Social Security number on any of thousands of Dark Web sites or when a new credit card, mortgage, car loan, or other account appears on your credit report. And you can freeze your account in seconds to prevent new purchases.

This card also comes with a 0% balance transfer offer for 14 months.

Capital One Quicksilver
https://www.capitalone.com/credit-cards/quicksilver/

- **APR:** 0% intro APR for 15 months; 16.24% - 26.24% variable APR after that.
- **Annual fee:** $0

This credit card lets you earn unlimited 1.5% cash back on every purchase, every day, including groceries, gas, etc. There are no rotating categories or opt-ins needed to earn the cash rewards.

Additionally, there's no limit to how much cash back you can earn, and your cash rewards won't expire as long as you keep your account open. Also, the Quicksilver card gives you a one-time $150 cash bonus if you spend $500 on purchases within three months of opening the account.

The card has a 0% introductory APR on balance transfers for 15 months, but after that, you'll have a variable APR of between 16.24% and 26.24%. And Capital One charges a 3% fee for balance transfers within the first 15 months.

If you travel a lot, you'll be happy to know that the Quicksilver card has no foreign transaction fees.

Bank of America Cash Rewards
https://www.bankofamerica.com/credit-cards/products/cash
-back-credit-card

- **APR:** 0% Introductory APR for 12 billing cycles for purchases, and for any balance transfers made in the first 60 days. Then 16.24% - 26.24% Variable APR on purchases and balance transfers. A 3% fee (minimum $10) applies to balance transfers.
- **Annual fee:** $0

This MasterCard offers 3% cash back in the category of your choice — select from gas, online shopping, dining, travel, drug stores, or home improvement/furnishings — plus 2% cash back at grocery stores and wholesale clubs and 1% cash back on all other purchases.

There is a limit to how much cash you can earn, though. For the 3% and 2% levels, you can only earn cash back on the first $2,500 in combined purchases you make each quarter. After you reach that threshold, you'll earn 1% cash back. The Bank of America Cash Rewards card also offers a $200 online cash rewards bonus after you make at least $1,000 in purchases in the first 90 days after opening the account, and the card has no expiration on rewards.

If you have a Merrill Lynch investment account, you're considered a "preferred rewards" client, and you will get bonus rewards worth 25% to 75% more than regular cardholders.

Chase Freedom Cash Back
https://creditcards.chase.com/freedom-credit-cards/home

- **APR:** 17.24% to 25.99% variable.
- **Annual fee:** $0

The Chase Freedom card is another cash-back-in-a-category card. You get 5% cash back in categories that rotate quarterly. All other purchases earn 1% cash back.

You also earn a $150 Bonus after you spend $500 on purchases in your first three months after opening an account. And you can use your cash back for purchases at Amazon or Apple.

Chase Freedom rewards do not expire, and there is no minimum threshold you have to reach in order to redeem your cash. You also have the option to redeem your rewards for gift cards from more than 150 brands.

American Express Blue Cash Every Day
https://www.americanexpress.com/us/credit-cards/card/
blue-cash-everyday

- **APR:** 0% intro APR on purchases and balance transfers for 15 months, then a variable APR, 15.24% to 26.24%
- **Annual fee:** $0

With this no-annual-fee American Express card, you earn 3% cash back when you shop at U.S. grocery stores (on up to $6,000 in purchases per year). If you spend over $6,000 per year in grocery stores, the reward drops to 1%.

You'll also get 2% cash back at gas stations and select department stores and 1% on all other purchases. The cash back is awarded in the form of Reward Dollars, which can be redeemed as a statement credit.

There's also a $150 bonus after you spend $1,000 in purchases on the card in the first three months after opening the account. The $150 bonus will be a statement credit.

Unlike some American Express cards, you don't have to pay off the balance in full every month. The Blue Cash Every Day card operates more like a Visa, MasterCard, or Discover card, where you can revolve a balance or pay it off in full every month.

U.S. Bank Cash+ Visa Signature Card
https://cashplus.usbank.com

- **APR:** 16.24% to 25.74% variable.
- **Annual fee:** $0

With the U.S. Bank Cash+ Visa card, you select two specialized categories to earn rewards in every quarter. (You can choose a different category each quarter.)

These categories include fast food, TV/internet/streaming, cellphone providers, department stores, home utilities, clothing stores, electronics, sporting goods stores, movies, gyms/fitness centers, furniture stores, and ground transportation. You'll earn 5% cash back on the first $2,000 you spend in those categories that quarter.

You can also choose one everyday category, such as gas stations, grocery stores, or restaurants, in which you will earn 2% cash back. There is no limit to the cash back you can earn in the everyday category. And for all other purchases, you earn 1% cash back.

Rewards can be redeemed anytime online and can be deposited in a U.S. Bank account, as a statement credit, or as a U.S. Bank Rewards Card (prepaid debit card).

This card also comes with a 0% introductory APR for balance transfers for the first 12 months. After that, APR is 16.24% to 25.74% variable.

Citi Double Cash Card
https://www.citi.com/credit-cards/credit-card-details/citi.action?ID=citi-double-cash-credit-card

- **APR:** 15.74% to 25.49% variable.
- **Annual fee:** $0

You can earn 1% cash back on all of your purchases, then an additional 1% as you pay for those purchases with the Citi Double Cash card.

This card has no categories to track or manage, no caps on cash back rewards, and balance transfers get a 0% introductory APR for 18 months. After that the variable APR will be 15.74% to 25.74% based on your credit worthiness.

FINAL THOUGHTS
Remember, any card comes with (a lot of) fine print. Before committing to any new cash-back or other perk-promising credit card, make sure to investigate all of the cards terms and rates. Most banks have a Frequently Asked Questions section that illustrates the terms in plain English.

Note: Credit card rates, terms and conditions are subject to change.

An Annual Credit Card Fee Can Pay Off

You probably receive new credit card offers promising big rewards and perks regularly. But along with those benefits was the not-so-rewarding annual fee that would mark the beginning of my relationship with this proposed shiny new piece of plastic.

One hard and fast rule to abide by is to avoid credit cards that have an annual fee, especially since there are so many great cards available that don't have one.

But you may wonder if those tempting premium cards can ever end up saving you money. So we sat down with a long-time colleague, Kevin Gallegos, vice president of the Phoenix operations for Freedom Debt Relief. He suggested using the following criteria to determine if that new premium credit card is worth it.

KNOW YOUR PRIORITIES.

A card with an annual fee can be worth it if the perks are for things you would pay for anyway.

For instance, enough points for a cross-country airline ticket, Uber credits, waived baggage fees, free roadside assistance, and free foreign transactions may be high on your list of priorities if you tend to travel a lot. However, if you're a homebody, they offer little value to you, no matter how generous they seem to be.

ARE THE BENEFITS UNIQUE?

Are you able to obtain the same rewards elsewhere for less? For example, the American Express platinum card offers a subscription to Shoprunner, a service that offers free two-day shipping at many online retailers. That seems like a valuable benefit since the service normally costs $79 a year, but it isn't worth anything if you don't shop at the retailers that participate with Shoprunner.

Plus, many high-fee credit cards tout benefits like extended warranty coverage on purchases or price matching, but you can get those perks with plenty of credit cards that don't have an annual fee. And you may not even need some benefits, like car rental insurance, which could be offered through your auto insurance policy.

UNDERSTAND YOUR IMPULSES.

Even if you know that you will actually use the rewards you get with the card, remember that you're still spending money to earn them. For many, that means charging everything from groceries and gas to a kid's soccer cleats to rack up points, with the intention of paying the balance in full every month.

However, if you're prone to spending beyond your budget or giving in to impulse shopping, and you can't afford to pay off the balance every month, you will end up paying interest on those purchases, and that negates the value of any rewards you might get. And along with potentially busting your budget, if you don't use the rewards, you'll be paying an annual fee for nothing.

DOES THE MATH WORK?

The last test is determining the true value of the benefits you're certain you'll use. If you know you'll keep your spending in check and pay the balance in full every month, it may make sense to go with the annual-fee card if the value of the benefits adds up to more than the cost of the annual fee.

For example, a friend of mine paid a $95 fee to get a Capital One Venture card, but got 50,000 in airline or hotel points, which translated to a $500 savings on a flight to Europe.

However, even if the analysis works out favorably, and the credit card's benefits are ones that are valuable to you, it's important to check if there are any hidden fees.

For example, some cards charge fees just to redeem mileage points for airline tickets or to book hotels. If those fees reach several hundred dollars, or you can't use the rewards easily (because of blackout dates, for example), the annual-fee card just isn't worth your time . . . or moolah.

Ditch Your Big National Bank to Save $$

In the downtown areas of almost any city or town, you'll see old buildings with towering Grecian columns and huge metal doors. They were once banks. And their architecture was designed to send a clear message: Within these imposing fortresses, your money is safe.

Perhaps that's how Americans came to believe that the bigger the bank, the better. And many of us still think of big national banks as the best places to put our money. At last count, just four banks — JPMorgan Chase, Bank of America, Wells Fargo, and Citibank — held $8.7 trillion in assets, almost as much as the other 5,000 banks combined!

Even after the 2014 fake accounts scandal at Wells Fargo, Wells and its fellow giants continue to dominate retail banking. People still like the big banks' full range of services, extensive branch networks, and state-of-the- art mobile apps and cyber-security features.

But like large retail chains, national banks are facing increasing competition from credit unions, internet banks, and regional banks. Consequently, national banks are falling behind in many categories. These include:

PERSONAL SERVICE

To cut costs, national banks have been closing thousands of branches and slashing their staff. (Bank of America and Chase each plan to add 400 to 500 branches, but only in new markets they are entering.)

At many remaining branches, tellers are being replaced with ATMs, and bank officers only appear on video screens. It's no wonder that national banks ranked last in personal service in a survey of the American Consumer Satisfaction Index.

Better alternative: If you prefer to deal with people you know at your local branch, you may be better off choosing a credit union or a regional or community bank. In the ACSI survey, these smaller institutions received higher scores for personal service.

FEES

National banks generally charge higher fees than other banks. That's especially true for checking accounts. A WalletHub survey found that the average monthly fee at a national bank was $14.96, compared to $6.43 at community banks and $1.65 at credit unions. And to get those fees waived by keeping a minimum balance in your account, you'll probably need to deposit more cash at a national bank: an average of $6,754, versus just $2,650 at community banks.

Better alternative: You can find no-fee checking accounts with no minimum balance requirements at three-quarters of credit unions and about a third of community banks. However, you may have to pay a small membership charge to do business at a credit union.

INTEREST ON SAVINGS

To get the maximum interest on your parked cash, a national bank is seldom the best choice.

One exception: when a national bank is trying to attract new customers, it may offer a bonus payment of $100 to $600 and a high rate of interest. However, this promotional rate is usually in effect for only a few months. And to collect the bonus, you usually must keep a large amount in the account for a longer period.

Better alternative: You can generally get better interest rates with fewer restrictions at online banks (or locally at a credit union). To find out where to get the highest rates, go to BankRate.com or DepositAccounts.com.

The bottom line: If one-stop banking is your priority, a national bank may still be your best bet. But that convenience will cost you either in higher fees, lost interest, or poor service. You can often make your money work better by splitting your dollars between two or more institutions. And thanks to cellphones and digital technology, moving money between accounts has never been easier.

What You Need to Know About Socially Conscious Banking

Following in the footsteps of socially responsible investing and carbon-conscious air travel, a new breed of bankers seeks to connect your money with the greater good while still making a buck.

Socially conscious banking, sometimes called ethical banking, has its roots in Europe. Currently, such banks hold $46.8 billion in assets, a hiccup compared to the $16.5 trillion in all U.S. commercial banks. Yet there are a lot of these types of banks scattered around the country. And while commitment to the socially conscious model varies, nearly all agree on a basic principle of social banking: Make sure your deposits are invested in good things for the community.

"We believe we can change money and banking through the way we bank. Our mission is to provide well-being for people and the planet through the bank," says Stephanie Meade, former senior vice president of marketing and culture at New Resource Bank, which operates in San Francisco and Boulder, Colorado.

As with all banks, money collected from customers is either loaned out or invested. In the case of the big banks, Meade says, generally the money is invested in, say, stocks and bonds. In banks such as New Resource, the deposits are loaned out to what social bankers call the "real" economy — local businesses, such as growers and small-time manufacturers that supply Whole Foods Market, or a medical center that serves low-income communities.

"Our loans are socially conscious, and we tell you where your money is going, which is something the big banks don't do," Meade explains.

New Resource has four defined impact areas: 1) environmental protection, such as solar loans, energy efficiency loans, and green real estate loans; 2) health and wellness; 3) education and empowerment, such as loans to charter schools and nonprofits; and 4) sustainable commerce, which includes companies that local, pay above minimum wage and are sustainable."

Picking among potential borrowers is a rigorous process. "We do a sustainability questionnaire, everything from energy efficiency, governance, mission, to how they treat employees," Meade says.

First Green Bank in Orlando, Fla., started in 2009 during the economic downturn, says Robbie Gossett, assistant vice president and executive assistant to the chairman and founder at the bank. "Many customers across the board were fed up with big banks, and rightly so. Even now, there's a new story every week or so with some bank and its wrongdoing. People just don't want anything to do with them," Gossett says.

What makes social banks different is that they operate on a "triple bottom line," says Gossett, "equally valuing people, the planet, and prosperity. The single bottom line is just making a profit, such as through subprime derivative mortgages, like Wall Street did a few years ago."

First Green Bank tries to find clients who align with its mission. "We have lending products for fuel-efficient vehicles and putting solar panels on your roof," Gossett says.

The experience extends to the bank's branches and community outreach. "As long as we walk the walk, the bank sells itself," Gossett says. "Our branches are built to sustainable standards, our tellers are all personable and involved in the community."

The goal of many social banks is to build trust, ultimately creating customers in underbanked, lower-income neighborhoods, as well as among millennials who prefer a bank focused on social impact initiatives, says Kristin Messerli founder of Cultural Outreach, a Los Angeles-based social banking consultancy.

Social banks can achieve this by creating partnerships with community organizations, then leveraging those relationships to reach new markets.

"The primary goal was to support the community, not solely to profit. Credit unions are like that," says Messerli. "It's a very early concept in some respects."

Insider Tricks to Maximize Your Credit Score

Who hasn't dreamed of having VIP status? Enjoying perks, freebies, and benefits not available to others sounds pretty ideal.

If you'd like some of that VIP treatment for yourself, get ready — because that's the power that an excellent credit score can bring to your financial life.

A sky-high score is like owning a VIP badge, helping secure higher borrowing amounts when needed, lower interest rates on loans and credit cards, and even cheaper insurance premiums, all of which can set you up for long-term financial success.

Fortunately, there are more ways than ever to access and track your credit scores. The FICO score, which is used in 90 percent of lending decisions in the U.S., is available at myFICO.com and from an increasing number of credit card companies and lenders. Websites such as Credit Sesame, Credit Karma, and Quizzle offer different types of scores that are packaged with financial management or credit monitoring tools.

So once you've obtained your score, you may discover it's lower than you'd like. What can you do to become a credit score VIP?

GOOD NEWS, YOU DON'T HAVE TO BE PERFECT

Your FICO score is a three-digit number ranging from 300 to 850. "The higher the number, the lower the risk of defaulting on debt," explains Anthony Sprauve, formerly the senior consumer credit specialist at FICO.

A perfect score of 850 is mathematically possible, but that doesn't need to be the goal. You just want to reach the threshold at which prime benefits kick in. "If you have a score above 720, you're getting the best rates that are available," Sprauve says.

What Makes a Credit Score?

The score is calculated using data from your credit reports at the major credit reporting agencies (also called credit bureaus) Equifax, TransUnion, and Experian. Here's the basic formula:

Payment history: 35% "The single largest component . . . is paying your bills on time, every time," Sprauve says. Any collections and bankruptcies also are considered here.

Amounts owed: 30% This section measures how much of your available credit you're using, including how close you are to your credit card limits, called your credit utilization ratio. "You need to be managing the credit you have responsibly," Sprauve says.

Length of credit history: 15% A longer credit history generally leads to a higher score. The algorithm considers the average age of your accounts, so you typically don't want to open many new cards at once or close old accounts.

Types of credit: 10% You want a mix of credit types, according to Justin Pritchard, author of *The Everything Improve Your Credit Book* and the banking expert at About.com. There's revolving credit (credit cards) and installment accounts (personal loans, auto loans, and mortgages).

New credit: 10% Having too many inquiries, or lenders requesting your credit report, "looks like you're scrambling for credit," Pritchard says. However, you won't be dinged by rate shopping for mortgages, auto loans, or student loans as long as it's within a focused period of time.

What's not considered? Interestingly, your income, employment status, and savings have no effect. And the algorithm does not factor in gender, race, age, or where you live, Sprauve adds. "It merely looks at your past credit behavior as a predictor of your future credit behavior."

FIRST, WHAT NOT TO DO

If your score is less than ideal, it's natural to want to make it right, right now. But don't jump on the first advice you hear. These methods plain don't work, and they could be harmful:

1. **Don't close credit card accounts.** It's one of the worst things you can do for your score, Pritchard says. "You want those old accounts to be around and active." You can streamline which cards you spend with, but keep old accounts open and use them

sporadically (or set up a minor monthly expense) so the issuer doesn't close them.

2. **Don't opt out of receiving credit card offers (unless you want to).** There's a rumor out there that opting out of pre-screened offers increases your credit score, says John Ulzheimer, the credit expert at CreditSesame.com (and formerly of FICO and credit reporting agency Equifax). In reality, nothing happens to your score.

3. **Don't add a consumer statement to your credit report.** The ability to add a personal explanation is a decades-old practice that predates automated underwriting and credit scoring, according to Ulzheimer. "It's an entire waste of time," he says. "Lenders don't generally read that, and credit scoring systems don't consider it."

4. **Don't get snared by "credit repair" scams.** Some agencies charge hefty fees to "clean up" illegal tactics, such as setting up an employer your report, often using identification number to use instead of your Social Security number.

How can you recognize a scam? Promises of quick or guaranteed results are a red flag, Pritchard says. "Improving your credit is a long, slow process." But it needn't be expensive. All the recommended steps are things you can do yourself. If you need support, consider seeking help through the nonprofit National Foundation for Credit Counseling (nfcc.org).

HOW TO GET BACK ON TRACK

Step 1: Download and Review Your Credit Reports. It couldn't be easier: Visit www.annualcreditreport.com, answer some questions about your accounts, then download — for free — your credit report from each credit bureau. You can download all three at once or space them out over the year, which allows you to better monitor changes without ever having to pay for report access.

Fortunately, the reports have become more consumer friendly in recent years, Ulzheimer says. But they are still dense with information, and the layouts differ between the credit bureaus. Here are the four main sections you should check closely on every report:

- **Personal information.** Here, you'll find your birth date and any addresses, phone numbers, and name variations associated with your accounts. "If your identification information is wrong, you could end up with things that don't belong to you," Ulzheimer says.

- **Account information.** This section shows what credit cards, car loans, student loans, and mortgages the bureau has on file for you. Do the accounts listed belong to you? Are the balances and payment history correct? Some reports list any accounts with negative information first; others group by account type. Adverse information here remains on your report for seven years.

- **Collections and public records.** Noted will be accounts turned over to a collection agency and public records such as bankruptcies, tax liens, or court judgments against you. "Obviously, you'd like both those sections to be empty," Ulzheimer says. But if not, are they accurate? (Keep in mind, if you have no collections or negative public records, the sections may not appear at all, so if you don't see them that's not unusual.) Bankruptcies stay on your report for seven to 10 years, depending on which kind you file.

- **Inquiries.** You'll see a list of any organization that has pulled your credit report and when. There are two types: a hard inquiry, which is a result of you actually applying for something, and a soft inquiry, which is for any other reason (you accessing your report or someone sending you offers of credit). "Focus on the hard inquiries," Ulzheimer says. "Make sure someone isn't out there applying for credit under your name." Inquiries remain on your report for two years.

What shouldn't you focus on? Omissions on your credit report, Ulzheimer says. "If you have an account with a lender that's not showing up, it's very unlikely that you're going to be able to force them to report it." Instead, focus your energy on confirming that what's actually there is correct.

Step 2: Correct Any Errors. One action that has an immediate, positive impact on your score is fixing mistakes lurking on your credit reports. If you find an inaccuracy (including items that should have "aged off"), contact the credit bureau with a dispute letter explaining the error and providing backup documentation. You also may want to contact the lender because the credit bureaus depend solely on them to furnish or confirm details.

"Credit reporting agencies have no longer than 45 days to finish their investigation," Ulzheimer says, but rarely does it take that long.

Still, if you're in the process of buying a house, you need errors corrected ASAP. Fortunately, rapid rescoring is an option. "Most mortgage lenders have the ability to provide that documentation directly to the credit reporting agency and have the report corrected in an expedited manner," Ulzheimer explains.

One important note: The strategy of disputing items on your report does not apply to information that is unflattering but accurate. "You can correct misinformation, but you need to accept the negative information," Sprauve says. In fact, it's illegal to knowingly dispute a legitimate entry.

Step 3: Patch Your Personal Weak Spots. The best strategy for improving your credit score depends on what's lowered it in the first place. Here are some common scenarios, with score-raising solutions from the experts:

"I lose track of bills sometimes and end up paying them late." Because payment history is the biggest factor, your score is being abused in the worst way. Start turning things around by organizing your bills:

- **Leverage technology.** Set a reminder for when you need to pay each month, or sign up for your lender to notify you ahead of the due date. You also can pay bills quickly and easily online.
- **Pick your due date.** Would a different date sync better with your payday or make it easier to pay bills all at once? Just ask — many companies offer the ability to shift statement closing dates.
- **Sign up for automatic payments.** You'll be notified by email when your statement is ready, and all you need to do is review it. Payment can be linked to a checking account or credit card. "You can avoid forgetting about bills," Pritchard says, but you still need to track your account balance to ensure funds are there, otherwise you'll just trade late fees for overdraft fees.

"I don't have enough money available to pay by the due date." Not being able to make even the minimum payment "suggests that you have way too much credit card debt relative to the money you make," Ulzheimer says. Stop the presses right now and do the following:

- **Put your cards off-limits.** You shouldn't use credit cards right now. Freeze yours in a container of water or entrust them to a friend or relative.
- **Find credit counseling.** "Some credit card issuers even have in-house programs," Ulzheimer says. If you don't take action now, you're heading down a very unpleasant road toward debt collectors and possibly lawsuits.

"I have overdue payments I just discovered on my credit report."

The later a payment is, the more damage it does. Your score could drop as much as 125 points by being just 60 days late. Do the following:

- **Make contact with the creditor immediately.** "The quickest improvement would be to get current on those payments," Pritchard says. Short of that, see whether you can work out a payment plan. If you can stop them from sending you to collections, you may be able to slow the free fall your score is taking.
- **Confirm your address is correct.** Perhaps you moved recently and overlooked notifying someone? Definitely do that now, and register with the post office to have any mail forwarded.

"I charge my cards near to their limits, but I pay off everything in full each month."

You're doing a good job avoiding interest, and it sounds as if you can afford your spending, but you are sabotaging your score with a high credit utilization ratio. (Your balances are too high in relation to your credit limits.) To bring it down, do the following:

- **Request a higher credit limit (but don't use it).** There probably won't be an inquiry on your report unless you're requesting, say, twice your current limit. Try calling your credit card issuer to ask what they can give without going through the process of underwriting, Ulzheimer suggests.
- **Pay more often.** There's nothing stopping you from making a credit card payment before your statement comes or even several times a month. "Pay once you start getting to 20 or 30 percent of your credit utilization," Pritchard says. Card issuers typically report to the credit bureau just once a month.
- **Apply for another card (but again, don't spend more).** There will be an inquiry added to your report but just with one bureau.

"If by opening a new credit card you're going to change your utilization percentage in a significant way, you will far outweigh any potential impact of one inquiry on one report," Ulzheimer says.

"I charged some large expenses, and they're taking longer to pay off than planned."

What you thought was a short-term situation is dragging on — and dragging your score down. Try these tactics to get a handle on the debt and send your score in the right direction:

- **Give your debt a new home.** "There are ways to move debt around to make it easier to deal with," Ulzheimer says. If you qualify for a card with zero-interest balance transfers, that can be a good temporary option to get your head above water. "Attack the principal balance and get out of that debt rather than floating along with it," he says.
- **Pay off debt with a personal loan.** Unsecured personal loans typically have a lower rate than credit cards but a shorter payback period. You won't save a lot of money, but converting revolving credit card debt to installment debt is considerably better for your credit scores, and you'll have a light at the end of the tunnel.

"I've recently declared bankruptcy and my credit is a mess."

It might be difficult to get credit, but you still have options:

- **Obtain a secured credit card.** You secure the limit by prepaying that amount. Opening a new account will add a hard inquiry to your report and lower the average age of your cards — dings that may lower your score in the short term.
- **Find a co-signer.** "See if you can get a tiny loan and pay that off on time," Pritchard says. Choose a supportive friend or family member with good money habits.
- **Consider a credit builder loan.** Primarily offered by credit unions, its purpose is to feed activity to your credit report, Ulzheimer says. The loaned money is placed in an interest-bearing account. You make monthly repayments to the credit union, and it reports the positive activity to the credit bureaus. At the end of the agreed period, the funds (plus interest) are released to you.
- **Become an authorized user on someone else's account.** This is the best tactic of all, Ulzheimer says, because its effect on

your credit report is miraculous: Without having to apply for an account, the card's entire history is added to your credit report. (Confirm first that the card has a history of being paid on time.)

Making Money Using a Robo-Adviser

A decade ago, entrepreneurs like Jon Stein and Andy Rachleff realized that technology could dramatically cut the cost of investment planning by using sophisticated computer programs to help people manage their portfolios. This would allow trading costs and management fees to be minimized (by using index funds and exchange-traded funds instead of individual stocks, and by having clients do everything electronically, thereby lowering overhead).

To put these ideas into action, Stein and Rachleff founded the pioneer robo-adviser firms Betterment and Wealthfront. Offering no-minimum accounts and rock-bottom fees, they gained a loyal following of tech-savvy young adults.

Now automated investing is attracting people of all ages. Cerulli Associates says robo-advisers currently manage about $220 billion in assets — and that's expected to explode in coming years.

While Betterment and Wealthfront are still around, they now have many competitors. Robo-advisers now come in two types: pure play and hybrid.

PURE-PLAY VS. HYBRID ADVISERS

Robo-investing's original concept was to minimize interaction between clients and humans in order to save time and money. This is the "pure play" model, offered at firms like Wealthfront and TD Ameritrade.

When you open a TD Ameritrade Essential Portfolios account, you fill out a form with your age, family status, financial goals, and how much risk you are willing to take. This data then is processed by a computer program. About 15 minutes later, you receive a recommendation to follow a conservative, moderate, moderate growth, growth, or aggressive strategy. And unless you object, that's what happens.

TD's computers then invest your money according to your portfolio's formula without your involvement. Of course, you are able to check on your portfolio's progress. Whenever you log in, you'll get a "confidence score" that shows you how likely you are to reach your financial goals. And if you go off-track (say, for example, it was recommended that you invest a certain amount each month and you haven't contributed), the website will offer suggestions on how to improve your situation.

All of this happens without a word being spoken. But what if you prefer to get your investment advice from a real person? And what if you want more input on how your money is being managed?

In that case, you'd be better off going to a firm that instead uses the hybrid robo approach. Hybrid firms use computers to do most of the planning and management, but rely on human advisers to provide guidance.

One such hybrid firm is Vanguard Personal Advisor Services. It's also the largest robo operation. With Vanguard PAS, you have an initial video or phone call with a staff adviser to discuss your situation, risk-tolerance and goals. Then that information is run through the firm's computer program. Then you get your investment plan.

You and the adviser then have a second conference to review the plan, and if you identify major problems, Vanguard says the adviser could adjust it. However, unless you have at least $500,000 invested, your relationship with that adviser ends at that point. From then on, various members of Vanguard's adviser pool will review your portfolio, keep you informed of its progress and change its strategies if your circumstances change.

Not surprisingly, a hybrid robo firm almost always charges more — or has a higher account minimum — than a pure play robo-adviser. For example, the annual fee is the same at both TD Ameritrade Essential Portfolios and Vanguard Personal Advisor Services (.03 percent, based on the amount in your account). However, you need to put up at least $50,000 to open an account at Vanguard PAS versus $5,000 at TD's Essential Portfolios.

WHAT ABOUT PERFORMANCE?

Beating the market isn't likely to happen with a robo-adviser. That's because almost all robo firms use index funds as their primary investment vehicle. To increase your net returns, most rely on tax-reduction strategies, like selling poor-performing funds to offset gains from better performers.

So why bother with a robo adviser when you could just buy an index fund on your own? A robo adviser should help you with asset allocation. A robo adviser can also help keep you from emotional trading. By leaving the investment decisions up to a computer program, you don't have to look at your portfolio every day.

That can keep you from trading in and out of stocks every time the market dips or wanes. This can be a big benefit, as studies have repeatedly shown that frequent trading leads to depressed returns.

But Wealthfront is trying to go one better, by offering a product that aims to beat the market, like a hedge fund. In fact, it is trying to duplicate the strategy of the world's largest hedge fund, Bridgewater Associates' All Weather Fund, with its new risk parity fund. This fund is available to people with taxable accounts with $100,000 or more. It invests in stocks, global bonds, real estate investment trusts (REITs), and commodities in a way that is designed to maximize gains and reduce risk.

Also, Wealthfront has a "smart beta" portfolio for people with at least $500,000 to invest. This portfolio is basically an index fund, but instead of weighting stocks according to market cap, it uses other variables to try to minimize risk and boost returns.

CHOOSING THE RIGHT ROBO ADVISER

Before choosing a robo-adviser, consider the following:

- What are the fees charged by the firm? And what (if any) are the added expense ratios for the funds or ETFs in your portfolio?
- If the firm is a basic pure-play robo-adviser, are you comfortable with doing all of your business online? If you have a question, when is support available? How would you feel if you couldn't reach someone during a market crash?
- With a hybrid robo, do you have enough assets to qualify?
- Are you satisfied investing in index funds? If not, does the robo-adviser offer alternatives?

Also keep in mind: If you have a 401(k) from your employer, most robo advisers can't directly manage the money in it. If you want help deciding how to invest your 401(k), check out blooom.com. It's a robo operation that will manage your 401(k) plan for a $10 monthly fee.

Fees, terms and conditions of companies referenced are subject to change.

Words to the Wise

BONUS TIP!
Google Bank Offers No Fees, But Beware

Google is joining the likes of Apple and Facebook in the drive to manage your money. The idea of a Google bank — which you would interact with through the Google Pay smartphone app — is to displace everyday branches.

The lure for many folks may not be the simplicity of paying with the wave of a phone, but the prospect of zero fees. The caveat is that nothing is truly free. Google, like Apple and Facebook (through its Libra digital currency), wants to make money from your spending choices by selling that data to marketers. Look before you leap into tech giant finance products.

BONUS TIP!
Credit Karma Offers High-Yield Savings Account

You may be among the thousands of people who take advantage of Credit Karma's free credit reporting service. The company also wants to be your bank as well — sort of. The company is joining a slew of other fintech firms that now offer high-yield savings accounts.

The money is actually managed by MVB Bank, a West Virginia-based bank, which then distributes it across 800 competing banks nationwide to get the best rates. All those banks would vie for your cash nest egg under the plan. An introductory rate of 2.03% was publicized at launch, but that is subject to change. Check rates at sites such as Bankrate.com or NerdWallet for comparison before moving your savings.

BONUS TIP!
Freeze Your Report at the Fourth Credit Agency

After the giant Equifax security breach, many Americans were urged to freeze their credit reports at the three major credit bureaus — Equifax, Experian, and TransUnion. Financial planners also suggest that people reach out to a fourth, lesser-known agency and do the same thing: Innovis.

The Columbus, Ohio, company doesn't issue credit reports in the same way as big three, nor does it offer a credit score. But Innovis does track individual credit data in order to help banks avoid fraud, and it sells lists of consumers to insurance and credit card companies. You can freeze your credit at Innovis by filling out a form at www.innovis.com or by calling (800) 540-2505.

While you're at it, you can stop those credit card and insurance come-ons by heading over to www.optoutprescreen.com, a site where the major credit bureaus allow you to temporarily or permanently join their "do not solicit" list.

Chapter 2

Saving and
Investing

"MONEY IS OF A PROLIFIC GENERATING
NATURE. MONEY CAN BEGET MONEY,
AND ITS OFFSPRING CAN BEGET MORE."

Save More By Using a Simple Budget Program

If tracking your monthly spending is one of your new year's resolutions, you're not alone. But few people actually make good on that promise over the long term. According to U.S. Bank, 59% of Americans don't keep a formal budget.

Fortunately, there are plenty of online budgeting programs and apps for your smartphone that are easy to use and will ensure you have more money in your bank account every month.

Their main draw is that they can automatically pull in your bank and credit card transactions, reconcile them with your budget, and display the results. We experimented with a number of these programs to see if any seemed likely to help tempt customers into managing their expenses. Here are our results.

TRACKER NO. 1: MINT
www.mint.com

Right away, we were impressed with some of the program's slick features: It generates interesting charts and graphs to show your spending trends. You can see your net worth at a glance, as well as your credit score.

The budgets section left us less enthusiastic, though. First, you'll notice that Mint uses the term "budget" differently than you'd expect. To most people, a budget is a comprehensive list of all projected expense categories, which is then reconciled with actual spending. In Mint, a "budget" is the spending limit for a single category.

Most programs start with a comprehensive budget with many line items, which you fine-tune to your situation. With Mint, by default, all of your spending categories are in an "everything else" section. Then you build your budget line by line, deciding which categories you want to track closely enough to elevate them out of the "everything else" section by creating a budget around them. When you do, that line item turns into a brightly colored bar chart showing you how close to the target you are.

We could see this working well for casual budgeters who want to track just a few spending categories, but it didn't seem comprehensive enough.

In addition, because Mint relies so heavily on your past spending to suggest how much to budget and to track how you're doing, everything feels very backward-looking. Indeed, you can't see or adjust your projected spending for the next month; you must wait until that month arrives. We weren't a fan of this approach, which can feel like trying to clean up a month that is already in progress, versus make a plan for the future.

Bottom Line: Mint is a great resource for a bird's eye view of your overall financial picture — all for free. However, budgeting is one of its weaker elements.

TRACKER NO. 2: YNAB
www.youneedabudget.com

We've heard a lot about YNAB (pronounced "why-nab"), and so had high hopes. Unfortunately, the built-in tutorial is inadequate to explain this complex program. Several times during the setup process, we were perplexed as to what we were supposed to be doing.

Here's why it's confusing: Unlike most budgeting programs, on YNAB, you budget only with money you actually possess. You apply every dollar currently in your bank account to a budget item. When more income arrives, you give those dollars jobs too. This means your budget is always a work in progress.

On the plus side, this philosophy is designed to ensure you don't spend money that you don't have, and it accommodates variable incomes quite well. However, the constant monitoring may be overwhelming to some.

Many of YNAB's fans in the personal finance community have made tutorial videos that are superior to YNAB's explanations. If you want to try YNAB, watch a few of these tutorials on YouTube first. (we recommend those by Nick True of Mapped Out Money.)

YNAB costs $12 a month (or $84 annually) and has a 34-day free trial.

Bottom Line: YNAB is great for hands-on, advanced budgeters who want to join a passionate community of users and don't mind a steep learning curve or paying for a robust service.

TRACKER NO. 3: EVERYDOLLAR PLUS
www.everydollar.com

Dealing with both money and technology can be stressful, and Every-Dollar Plus succeeds in creating a no-stress setup process. The design is tidy and not overwhelming.

As you budget, EveryDollar Plus displays how many dollars you have left to allocate or how many you're over budget. Through this visual nudge, it encourages you to make proactive decisions about your money.

When it's time to reconcile your actual transactions, EveryDollar Plus has a drag-and-drop feature that's easy — even fun — to use.

One unexpected benefit: Because you list your expected income for the month as separate "checks," it can help you realize if a payment you thought you'd received hadn't actually reached your bank account. (This wasn't as apparent with Mint and YNAB.)

As for downsides, EveryDollar Plus (which pulls in your transactions automatically) has a cost of $130 a year (after a 15-day free trial). There is a free version (EveryDollar), which requires you to add transactions yourself. The free version also has ads for Dave Ramsey products and services, as this is his program based on his system.

Bottom Line: A downright pleasure to use, EveryDollar Plus thinks of everything and handles budgeting details well. It is my top pick and the one I plan to continue using after this experiment.

WHAT ABOUT SECURITY?

You may have concerns about a third-party service accessing your bank and credit card records. Of course, nothing is risk-free, but because of public demand, the apps and financial institutions have been forced to work together in recent years to develop strict security precautions.

Now when you enter your bank login and password, you're doing it through a secure portal to your bank. The budget app isn't storing — or even seeing — your credentials.

Furthermore, if you're using these apps to regularly review your transactions, you'd be more likely to notice fraudulent activity and report it in time to claim liability protection. For our money, the relatively low risk is worth the convenience of getting a clearer picture of my financial situation.

However, if you're not comfortable, there is another option: Don't connect your bank accounts. You can enter your transactions manually with EveryDollar and YNAB, but it's not as easy with Mint. Another option, if you use YNAB, is to download a file of your transactions from your bank and import them into that program.

14 Ways to Slash Your Holiday Expenses

The holidays are almost here, and you know what that means: You'll spend a lot of money for all that merriment and joy. In fact, according to a 2018 National Retail Federation survey, the average household will spend $1,007 per person on the winter holidays for gifts, decorations, food, and entertainment. Here's how to cut that budget down to size.

CUT THE COST OF DECORATING

You don't have to keep your house dark during the holidays, but consider these strategies for cutting your decorating expenses:

Upgrade to LED. When it's time to replace a set of holiday lights, switch to LED versions. Costing just a few dollars more than incandescent, LED bulbs use 70% less energy, according to the Department of Energy. That adds up. For example, you may pay $10 in energy to light a tree with incandescent lights through the holiday season, but if you had LED lights, it would cost just you just 27 cents to power.

Prioritize a key spot. Not every space in your home needs to be decked out. Pick one area to focus on, whether it's a festive mantel or a showstopper Christmas tree, and invest in decorating only that area.

Invest in faux holiday flowers. For around the same price as a fresh plant or flower arrangement, you can get high-quality faux versions that will save you money in future years (provided you have space to store them in the off-season). West Elm and Pottery Barn, as well as Amazon, craft stores, and specialty sites, such as Afloral.com.

SLASH FOOD AND DRINK EXPENSES

If you're hosting a holiday meal, ask guests to bring appetizers, sides, and dessert, while you supply the main dish. Or ask them to bring their favorite drink to share, so you can save on alcohol costs.

Take advantage of free turkey and free ham offers from grocery stores during the holidays.

And look for special winter season deals. My local store gives coupons for 20% off your grocery bill (up to $40 back on $200) to each person who gets a flu shot at the store's pharmacy.

SAVE ON GIFTS

Stick to Your List. Before you start, make a list of every type of expense and every gift recipient, so you can set a holiday budget. Then when you go shopping, watch out for impulse buys. The National Retail Federation says that in addition to gifts, shoppers will spend an average of $155 on non-gift purchases for themselves and their families during the holidays. Remember, it's not a good deal if you weren't planning to buy the item in the first place.

Use Honey. Honey is a browser extension that you can download and install to help you save money when shopping online. (A browser extension is like an app for your web browser.)

After you install Honey, simply shop online normally. When you go to check out, Honey will scan the internet to find every working promo code, and with one click, it will apply the best one to the items in your cart. It has other bells and whistles, too, like price history and price drop alerts.

Visit JoinHoney.com to add the browser extension.

Give it a day. When shopping online, put an item in your cart, then log out. If you have an account with the store, sometimes you will get an email the next day offering you free shipping or a discount on that item.

Shop late. If you won't see a loved one until after the holidays, wait until the after-Christmas sales to buy that person's gift.

Use CamelCamelCamel.com When Shopping on Amazon. This website can get you serious savings when holiday shopping on Amazon. Just paste the link for any Amazon product page into the search bar at CamelCamelCamel, and the site will show you a historical graph of the item's price going back years (or as long as it's been on Amazon).

Perusing these charts makes it clear that Amazon is calibrating its prices constantly, with surprisingly large jumps at times. And CamelCamelCamel indicates not just if an item's price has gone up or down recently, but also what its highest, lowest, and average historical prices are.

Such intel is way more useful than the limited price notifications that Amazon itself provides. Amazon shows you price changes, but only for items in your cart, and only since the last time you logged in. And once you see the notification, it disappears forever.

You can also use CamelCamelCamel to outsmart Amazon holiday "sales" that really aren't good deals. Check the historical price charts to see if the current discounted price really is a good bargain. If it's not, you can then set up an email alert with CamelCamelCamel for the site to notify you if and when an item's price drops below an amount you set.

Use Smartphone App: ShopSavvy. A smartphone app can make in-person shopping more efficient. ShopSavvy does just that.

Here's how it works: Scan an item's bar code using the app, and it will show you the latest prices at major stores online, as well as local physical stores in your area. (It mostly returns online results though, in my experience.)

Because ShopSavvy works by scanning a physical item in front of you, it works best when you are considering an item in a brick-and-mortar retail store.

If ShopSavvy finds you a better price online, you don't even have to finish the purchase on your phone. The app saves the history of any products you've looked up, so you can complete the purchase from your home computer if you'd like.

ENTERTAINMENT

Switch up traditions. If your current holiday rituals are straining your budget, consider forming new ones that are more wallet-friendly. Some ideas: walking or driving around the neighborhood admiring holiday decorations, watching a particular holiday movie together, decorating a gingerbread house together, or making a special family recipe.

Draft a rough holiday itinerary. Entertainment costs add up fast, especially if you have a large group. Instead of getting talked into yet another expensive trip to a professional performance of Handel's Messiah, pick up a local events calendar to see if there are lower-cost options. Oftentimes, local holiday fairs and performances are free or low-cost.

Spend time, not money. Bring out those puzzles and board games from the back of the closet. Walk a local trail or play a game in your own backyard. It doesn't much matter what you do; the point is to hang out together.

Facts About Switching to a
Cheap Cell Phone to Save

When you first hear about low-cost mobile phone plans, your initial reaction may be one of skepticism. When you hear how much lower your cell phone bill could be, it sounds probably too good to be true.

How things change. After learning about these cheap plans (technically called mobile virtual network operators, or MVNOs) and speaking with several people already using them, we may be changing our tune. Here's a primer on how MVNOs work and the basic pros and cons to consider if you're looking to save big bucks on your phone bill.

WHAT ARE MVNOS?

Let's start with what they are not. MVNOs are not Verizon, AT&T, Sprint, or T-Mobile, the four major mobile networks in the U.S. However, MVNOs are dependent on these big players. MVNOs essentially ride the coattails of the major networks, renting bandwidth on their networks rather than building their own.

Some MVNOs have access to multiple networks, and some rely on just one. Because they are renting bandwidth from the Big Four, their customers have lower priority access to that bandwidth than the network's own direct customers. Consequently, some MVNOs may slow your speed once you hit a threshold or during high-usage times.

MVNOs may also be called alternative mobile carriers or wireless resellers.

WHAT ARE THE ADVANTAGES OF USING AN MVNO?

Far and away, the main advantage is cost. People getting cell phone service through an MVNO pay less — a lot less.

As an example, one MVNO subscriber told us that he used to pay $90 a month for Verizon service. Now he uses an MVNO called Ting and pays between $24 and $30 every month. (It's variable because Ting charges at the end of the month, based on how much texting, calling, and downloading you actually do.)

Another says she wasn't paying a lot for cell service to begin with — $30 a month for a simple flip phone on AT&T — but she was able to save money and upgrade to a smartphone by switching to an MVNO. She ended up paying $125 a year (just over $10 a month) for service from Tracfone. This plan, which includes 1,500 voice minutes, 1,500 texts, and 1.5 GB of data, which she says more than meets her needs.

If you don't use a ton of cellular data, or you can shift the bulk of your data usage to times when you are connected to a WiFi network (which doesn't count toward data limits), you can save substantially with an MVNO.

WHAT ARE THE TRADE-OFFS WITH MVNOS?

Of course, those cost savings have to come with some sacrifice. A few limitations of MVNOs are:

- **Coverage issues.** On an MVNO, your coverage is only as good as the host network's coverage. Therefore, it makes sense to choose an MVNO running on a network with good coverage in your area. In highly populated areas, almost all four major networks are solid, but some plans may have poorer coverage in very rural areas.
- **Device hassles.** Not all phones have the right hardware to switch to any MVNO network. Fortunately, most MVNO websites make it easy to check compatibility. It's as simple as typing your phone's IMEI number into a field. (The website will walk you through how to find this number in your phone settings.) Even if your phone isn't currently compatible, some phones can be made compatible by swapping out your SIM card with a new one the MVNO sends you.
- **You may need to watch your usage.** Many plans have caps on cellular data in exchange for rock-bottom pricing. If you go over the limit, you may experience a slowdown or be charged more. However, the people I know who are on MVNOs say this has not been an issue. To save the most money, set your phone to allow WiFi connection whenever it's around.
- **Advance payments.** Some MVNOs, such as Mint Mobile and Tracfone, ask you to pay for months of service in advance in exchange for deep discounts. If you're not able to pay up front, your MVNO choices may be limited.
- **Customer service varies.** With dozens of MVNO plans to choose from, customer service will naturally vary. However, MVNOs on

the whole have higher ratings in this area than the major networks. In the latest Consumer Reports survey, for example, Consumer Cellular, Google Fi, and Ting (all MVNOs) ranked highest for customer satisfaction and support, while AT&T, Sprint, and Verizon ranked the lowest.

IF YOU'RE CONSIDERING A SWITCH

Has the tremendous savings potential of MNVOs tempted you to look at options? First, decide whether you want to keep your current phone or get a new one. Your device is one of the biggest factors that determine which MVNOs you can join.

Then, track down your last few cellphone bills. Look at how much data, voice calling, and texting you typically do. Then head to WhistleOut.com/CellPhones to fill out the search form to see the list of MVNO plans to consider.

How to Stream TV Shows and Movies for Less

You might think it's easy to save money when you forsake cable TV for streaming services. But if you aren't careful, you can end up spending more on streaming than even the most generous cable TV package costs.

And if you're paying for streaming services on top of a cable or satellite TV subscription? Then you have even more reason to try to cut your entertainment costs.

Here are ways to save on streaming services — a mix of deal-hunting and common sense. But first, let's go over some of the major streaming players, what you get from each, and how much they cost.

WHAT YOU'RE PAYING FOR:
SOME OF THE MAIN STREAMING SERVICES
Netflix:

What You Get: Access to 3,800 movies and 1,700 TV shows, all without ads. That library includes licensed content from other studios plus Netflix's acclaimed original programming. However, live TV is not available, and non-Netflix TV shows are typically past seasons (no currently airing episodes).

What It Costs: Netflix memberships go by the number of screens you stream at one time. You'll pay $8.99/month for one screen, $12.99 for two screens, and $15.99 for four screens.

Amazon Prime Video:

What You Get: Prime Video has a massive library of more than 12,700 movies and 2,000 TV shows that you can stream for free. Amazon shows some advertisements, mostly for its own original content.

What It Costs: If you're a Prime member, Amazon Prime Video is already included. (The current cost of Amazon Prime is $119/year or $12.99 a month.) Or you can subscribe to Prime Video as a stand-alone service (without joining the larger Amazon Prime) for $8.99 per month. You can also subscribe to some a la carte channels, such as Starz and HBO for additional charges.

Hulu:

What You Get: Hulu's library includes 1,600 movies and 1,800 TV shows. Many are currently airing TV shows from networks like NBC and Fox, which are available the day after they air. You can also get live TV through Hulu for an upcharge.

What It Costs: Hulu pricing has just two variables: whether you are OK with watching commercials or not, and whether you want to add live TV. So there are four plan levels: The basic Hulu costs $5.99 per month and includes ads. The ad-free version is $11.99 a month. Hulu (with ads) plus live TV costs $44.99 a month, and Hulu (no ads) plus live TV costs $50.99 a month.

8 WAYS TO SAVE ON STREAMING SERVICES

1. Don't buy more content than you need.

There are only so many hours in a day, and it's impossible to watch all the programs available. Take an honest look at your average week, and calculate how many hours you have (or even want) to spend watching TV and movies.

Furthermore, many programs are duplicated between the providers, so one streaming service may be enough. For instance, there at one point there were 47 TV shows that were available on all three major streaming services, and 530 movies that on both Hulu and Amazon Prime Video. To find out where a given show is available for streaming, consult the excellent website ReelGood.com.

2. Don't get sucked in by one blockbuster show.

That's exactly what the streaming services want to happen. Did you just have to watch House of Cards, but don't see much else on Netlfix that appealed to you? Buying it on DVD is a one time cost, which in the end would have cost you less than the monthly recurring fee.

3. Put your subscription on hold.

A little-known feature of some streaming providers is the ability to pause your subscription without cancelling outright. If you have a busy time coming up when you know you won't have much time to watch TV, take advantage of this feature. On Hulu, you can pause up to 12 weeks, and during that time, you won't be billed.

4. Trial hop.

Netflix, Hulu, and Amazon Prime Video all offer 30-day free trials so you can try before you buy. CBS All Access and HBO Now also offer 7-day free trials. If you cycled through just these five options, that's three and a half months of streaming for free.

5. Bundle with your cellphone or music streaming plan.

Some cell phone carried over discounts on streaming plans. T-Mobile plans have offered a subscription to Netflix (which Netflix plan you get depends on which wireless plan you chose), and AT&T has previously included an HBO subscription.

And music streaming service Spotify offered a free basic Hulu subscription.

6. Stream with your library card.

Did you know that some public and college/university libraries provide access to streaming services? The catch is, they aren't Netflix, Hulu, or Amazon Prime Video.

Both Kanopy and Hoopla — are quite serviceable. You are limited to four movies/TV episodes per month on each service. However, Kanopy has a section called Kanopy Kids, with curated children's content that is unlimited.

7. Get cash-back credit card rewards for streaming.

The most generous at one point was the American Express Blue Cash Preferred Card, which gave an impressive 6% cash back on streaming services (as well as grocery purchases up to $6,000). It does have a $95 annual fee. But at least for the first year, that can be offset by the $300 bonus you get after spending $1,000 in the first 3 months.

8. Pay for a full year at once.

Sometimes you can save when you commit to a full year of service and pay in advance. For instance, Amazon Prime (which includes Prime Video) is just $119 when you pay annually versus $155.88 if you pay in monthly installments.

Rates, terms and services subject to change.

13 Ways to Lower Your Cell Phone Bill

The average American cell phone bill is now over $150 a month, according to a 2018 J.D. Power study. The precise figure is $157. That's up from $149 in 2017. That means the average American household is now paying approximately $1,884 each year for cell phone service.

How does your cellphone bill compare? If you'd like to bring it down, here are 13 options to consider:

CHECK FOR AFFILIATION DISCOUNTS THROUGH YOUR EMPLOYER

If you are part of a large company or organization, such as a corporation, government agency, non-profit, or educational institution, your employer may have already negotiated a discount for you.

Consult your human resources representative or employee manual. Alternatively, you can check for employee discounts yourself online. You can find the discount by Googling "[your carrier] AND [your organization] discount." Getting the discount on your bill may be as easy as entering your work email address into a web form.

CLAIM YOUR MILITARY OR
FIRST RESPONDER DISCOUNT

If you are a first responder, veteran, Gold Star family, or active duty military (including National Guard and Reserve), you may be eligible for generous discounts on your family's cell phone plan.

Verizon's discount for military members and first responders is 15%. T-Mobile offers 20% to 50% off, depending on the number of lines in your plan.

AT&T customers can save 25% off each line. And Sprint offers 50% off additional family lines. Find out how to enroll by calling your mobile carrier or searching Google for "military discount [your wireless provider]."

CASH IN ON YOUR SENIOR STATUS

Over age 55? Your cell phone carrier may have special discounts for you. For example, T-Mobile offered two lines for $70 per month with unlimited talk, text, and data for people over 55. If your carrier doesn't have a plan for seniors, see if AARP members get a discount. It may be worth it to join AARP if your savings more than covers the cost of membership.

SWITCH TO A PLAN THAT OFFERS
ENTERTAINMENT EXTRAS

Almost all the major plans are throwing in streaming services as incentives and bonuses these days.

Do the math. Even if switching plans or providers keeps your bill amount the same, you could still come out ahead if it lowers your entertainment bills.

DOWNSHIFT YOUR DATA ALLOWANCE

If you're currently on an unlimited plan, check to see how much data you're actually using each month. If it's less than 5 GB (gigabytes), you may be able to switch to a cheaper plan without making any changes to your habits.

RELOCATE TO A LOWER-TAX STATE

Contemplating a move? Look up the cell phone tax rates of any states you're considering. (The Tax Foundation tracks them on its website at TaxFoundation.org. Search the site for "mobile taxes.") For instance,

NerdWallet found that a move from Illinois to Wisconsin could save over $100 in annual cell phone taxes alone.

SIGN UP FOR AUTO-PAY
You can save an additional $5 to $10 a month if you allow your wireless carrier to automatically charge your bill to your bank account, credit card, or debit card each month.

ASK YOUR KIDS TO PAY THEIR SHARE
If your family plan includes one or more adult children, you aren't alone: About half of kids over 18 (49%) are still on their family's cell phone plan, according to a poll commissioned by NerdWallet. But if your child isn't contributing at all to that bill, you may want to have a chat. Many young adults stay on their parents' plan, but pay their share, or a portion they can afford.

NEGOTIATE WITH YOUR CARRIER
Threatening to leave is the classic tactic for getting a bill lowered. Of course, it does require some research beforehand and negotiation skills.

Before you call your carrier, find out what it would cost to another carrier and if there are any switching fees, discounts, or extra benefits. Armed with the new, better price, call your carrier and ask to speak to someone in the Customer Retention Department. Say you're thinking of switching carriers in order to lower your bill.

When you get the Retention rep on the line, ask if they can offer you a better deal. If they can't beat the offer you have, you can always switch.

OR HIRE SOMEONE TO DO IT
Yes, there are bill negotiation services. Here's how they work: You send the bill negotiation company a copy of your latest bill. The company will then call your carrier — including waiting on hold and being transferred between departments — and try to negotiate a lower rate for you. If they are successful, the company gets a cut of what you save. Two examples are BillFixers (BillFixers.com) and BillShark (BillShark.com).

SKIP THE PHONE INSURANCE
Most studies find that "mobile phone protection" (also known as insurance) usually costs more in the long run than just paying for damage when it happens. Plus, there's a good chance you'll never need it.

Nearly half (49%) of phone owners have never broken or lost their cell phones, according to a study commissioned by Verizon. Phone insurance runs from $5 to $17 a month.

TRY A MIX-AND-MATCH PLAN

Some of the people in your family may need more data and services than others. (And don't assume it's always the kids needing more. Retired folks might be traveling and require more data.) Verizon and Sprint have offered some type of mix-and-match pricing. It always pays to ask and compare.

CONSIDER A SMALLER PLAN

Have you heard of Cricket, h2o, or Unreal Mobile? These small cell phone providers use the same networks as the big guys (they just rent the band-width rather than owning it), but often have cheaper plans, and they may also have caps on data and speeds.

If you don't need all the bells and whistles, you could save hundreds of dollars every year. There are dozens of these plans, called mobile virtual network operators, or MVNOs for short. Get the full list by searching "MVNO" at the comparison website WhistleOut.com.

Rates, terms and conditions referenced are subject to change.

Lazy Ways to Plug Money Leaks Around Your House

So you want to save money in your household budget, but you don't want to upend your whole lifestyle to do it? No problem. It's entirely possible, but you have to be strategic. The secret is to target recurring expenses rather than individual purchases. That way, the effect multiplies over time. Here are some ideas to get you started:

FOOD
Buy more of fewer items

Next time you shop for groceries, it's likely that something you buy regularly will be on sale. When that happens and the item is non-perishable, grab a few more than you need. Next time, a different item will be on sale, and you can stock up on that one. Over time, you'll build a fully stocked pantry, while buying food only when it's on sale.

Savings: $160 a month, for a family of four

Try these tricks to make food last longer.

It's estimated that American households waste $1,500 worth of food each year on average. Much of that loss is spoilage, so extending the life of your food can make a big difference in curbing your waste. Try these tricks:

- Keep broccoli, kale, and asparagus crisp by storing them upright in an inch of water in your fridge. (If the greens are already limp, you can even revive them with the same method.)
- Store mushrooms in a paper bag to gain several days of freshness.
- Use a bread box for your bread, bagels, muffins, and cookies. And if you have bread that has gone stale (but not yet moldy), run it under your faucet for a few seconds and place it in an oven that's heating up. It'll be good as new in about 10 minutes.
- Explore the features of your fridge: Mine has colder sections, as well as higher and lower humidity sections for different types of produce. Placing your food in the right environment will extend its freshness.

Savings: $125 a month

YOUR HOUSEHOLD PRODUCTS
Ask for household products as gifts

Now, we don't mean to suggest that you request toilet paper in your Christmas stocking. I'm simply recognizing that loved ones will typically give you gifts several times a year, and often they are desperate for ideas.

Think about the products you currently buy that would also be pleasant to receive as gifts — items like natural soaps, perfume, candles, body wash, tea or coffee, makeup, lip balms, and warm socks. If someone asks what you'd like for your next birthday, why not suggest one of these items? If no one asks, consider dropping a hint.

If it works, you'll spend less on toiletries and household items and probably receive nicer versions than what you'd buy yourself.

Savings: $10 per month

Put your recurring product needs on auto-delivery

We're a huge fan of auto-delivery services, such as those offered by Amazon, Target, and many other retailers. Typically, you receive 5 percent to 15 percent off the regular price in exchange for setting up a recurring order.

You can get auto-deliveries from Chewy.com for most of our pet needs (food and prescriptions). And our fridge water filter comes from Amazon like clockwork every six months, which is also a helpful reminder to do that maintenance task. Done right, auto-deliveries become a double savings of money and time.

Savings: 5 percent to 15 percent off any items you buy regularly

Your Entertainment

Cancel just one premium channel subscription or streaming service

Sure, individually these don't cost a ton ($5.99 to $19.99 a month). But if you're signed up for multiple services, you may be overspending on entertainment, not to mention paying for more movies and TV programs than any human could ever consume.

Consider how many of the following you have right now: Netflix, Hulu, Amazon Prime, Disney Plus, YouTube Red, HBO, Starz, Showtime, and Cinemax. Do you still need all of them? Pick the one service or channel you use the least, cancel it, and pocket the savings.

Savings: $6 to $20 a month

YOUR ENERGY
Let a programmable thermostat do the work.

Programmable thermostats allow you to set different indoor temperatures for different times of day, useful for saving energy when your home is unoccupied or everyone is sleeping. Yet a surprising 71 percent of American households that have programmable thermostats don't use them. Are you one of them? Consider taking a crack at programming it today: Space heating and cooling are the largest energy expense for most households.

Savings: $180 a year

Clean your refrigerator's condenser coils.

Though you can't see them, the coils are a critical part of how your refrigerator keeps its cool. When coils are covered in dust and debris, they can't release heat as easily, making the fridge work even harder. You can shave 10 percent off the electricity your fridge uses by cleaning the coils just twice a year, or every three months if you have pets.

All it takes is your vacuum's crevice tool and a coil cleaning brush, available for about $15 on Amazon. (For safety, be sure to unplug the fridge or turn off power to it at the breaker before you start.)

Savings: $5 to $10 per month

Getting Paid for Stuff You Planned to Toss

B efore you add that empty ink cartridge or cosmetics bottle to the trash, consider this: there are several recycling programs that not only give you the satisfaction of helping the environment, but can line your pockets with a little green, too. Check out the following:

INK CARTRIDGES

If you're a frequent Staples shopper, you may be able to save a few bucks and clean out your office.

How it works — Spend at least $30 on ink or toner, then bring the used printer cartridge to the store (or request a shipping label from the Staples website), and you'll get $2 in Staples Rewards. You must recycle the cartridge within 180 days of buying the $30 in ink or toner, but you don't necessarily have to recycle that exact cartridge. Office Depot has a similar recycling program, which also offers a $2 reward.

COSMETICS

Kiehl's recycling rewards program lets you recycle empty cosmetics containers for stamps that can add up to free products.

How it works — Bring in an empty full-sized Kiehl's cosmetic or fragrance container, and you will receive a stamp. Once you have collected 10 stamps, you are eligible for your pick of a travel-size item, with a dollar value of up $11. Kiehls.com has the details. Cosmetics company MAC has a similar program, which offers consumers a free lipstick of their choice after recycling six empty MAC product containers. See MACcosmetics.com for details.

HANGERS

Wire clothes hangers can't be tossed into traditional municipal recycling bins because their hooks can cause damage to the sorting system. But many dry cleaners like ZIPS in the Baltimore-Washington, D.C., area, will happily take back any unwanted or excess metal or wire hangers you may be holding onto. Some may even offer you a small compensation.

CLOTHING

Several national and branded clothing merchants offer rewards for clothes that you have outgrown or no longer use. Through its Clothes the Loop program, The North Face will give you a $10 reward toward your next purchase of $100 or more at any The North Face store or outlet when you bring in your unwanted clothes and shoes for recycling. The recycled clothes can be any brand, in any condition.

You can also drop off worn-out clothes or shoes at any American Eagle and receive a text coupon for $5 off a new pair of AEO jeans. And for every bag of clothing (new, outdated, torn, or never worn) you take to clothing retailer H&M, you can get a voucher for 15 percent off your next purchase.

TECHNOLOGY

Electronics retailers including Target, Best Buy, Staples, Apple, and Verizon offer their own trade-in programs to reward you for recycling your unwanted electronics. Some offer store credit or credit toward an upgrade, while others provide gift cards.

Another option is Gazelle.com. Just log on and enter the details of the device you want to trade in. Gazelle will provide you with a purchase price, and if you're satisfied with the offer, you print a prepaid shipping label and send the item to Gazelle.

Another option for recycling old smartphones is to use them for a different purpose. For example, Android phones can become Google Assistant-ready speakers. Or download a book to your phone and use it as an e-reader. You can also simply use an old smartphone as an alarm or white noise machine (just download an app).

Program terms and conditions subject to change.

How to Eliminate Waste and Give New Life to Old Things

According to the Food and Agriculture Organization of the United Nations, roughly one-third of the food produced for human consumption is wasted each year. Yet much of that food can be repurposed. And food isn't the only thing we waste. A lot of household items that fill our trash cans every day can easily be reused if you know how. Ready to think outside the bin? Try these ways to eliminate waste from your household:

USED COFFEE GROUNDS, TEA LEAVES

Sure, you can add these to a compost pile, but if you haven't set one up yet, just add the coffee grounds or tea leaves directly to your plant soil as a fertilizer. Most sources recommend mixing it into the soil a bit rather than spreading it on top. You can also add used tea bags to potted plants between the soil and the bottom drainage layer. They will help retain water, and some nutrients will seep in.

TAKEOUT CONTAINERS

Takeout meals may eliminate the work of meal preparation, but they also generate a lot of containers. You can use the wide containers as travel pet bowls for long walks or hikes with your pet, or use the deep containers to rinse salt from pup's paws in the winter.

EXTRA GREENS AND HERBS

Try making pesto from leftover greens or wilting fresh herbs. The traditional combination is basil, pine nuts, garlic, and parmesan. You can use everything from beet greens to parsley, dandelion greens, broccoli, cilantro, and more. Just blend the greens with nuts, olive oil, garlic, salt, pepper and an aged, hard cheese.

Not planning to use your pesto right away? Store it in an ice cube tray and freeze until you're ready to toss with some hot pasta.

SMARTPHONES

We recently discovered a fantastic way to use discarded smartphones as security cameras. If you have an old iPhone or Android device with a working camera, check out the Presence app (presencepro.com) for instructions on how to set it up. Even though your old phone isn't connected to a cellular network any more, it can still connect to WiFi, so you can still use apps on it.

You could set up a camera at a relative's vacation home, or use one to keep an eye on the dog when you're away. Similarly, my turn an old smartphone into a white noise machine to help a new baby sleep. Simply download a white noise app.

DRYER SHEETS

After the sheet has done its job with the laundry, it can be used for dusting and polishing glass screens. It's also great at cleaning dust and pet hair from baseboards. The anti-static residue will keep them clean longer.

CEREAL BOXES

Drawer organizers are expensive, and they don't always match the dimensions you need. Are you in in reorganization mode? Collect empty cereal boxes, then use a box cutter or X-ACTO knife to trim the bottom to the exact height of my drawer. They're great for storing rubber bands, paper clips, extra pens, buttons, and loose change. The bottoms of cardboard half-gallon milk cartons work well for this purpose, too. Similarly, you can use old shoe boxes to organize socks, bras, and underwear in dresser drawers.

PAPER TOWEL ROLLS, TOILET PAPER ROLLS

The average American family uses two rolls of paper towels and two rolls of toilet paper per week. That's a lot of empty tubes. But you can switch to a "tubeless" brand of toilet paper that works great. Or, if you're sticking with a traditional brand, use empty rolls as small toy organizers for kids, to keep cords free of tangles in storage, or as unique small gift boxes (simply fold the ends in).

You could even use them in the garden. Put them around your brussels sprout seedlings to protect them from cabbage worms. Some gardeners cut them down to use as small seed pots for starter plants.

FIREPLACE ASHES

Salt is great for melting snow and ice but it can be expensive and doesn't work well below 20 degrees. Instead, sprinkle ashes from your fireplace over slippery spots to melt ice and create traction.

GREETING CARDS

Hate to part with fancy greeting cards, especially ones adorned with decorative glitter and sequins? Cut them up to make gift tags. Some people cut them into small circles and string them onto thread or twine for a festive garland.

ALUMINUM FOIL

Lightly used aluminum foil makes the perfect toy ball for a cat (twist ties and bread bag clips work well, too). And don't forget the box: The long, skinny ones that hold foil have a sturdy inner tube and useful cutting edge — try using it as storage for loose ribbons or rolls of washi tape (a paperlike tape used in craft projects).

EVERYTHING ELSE

Have something else you think might have another use? Try searching Pinterest for "[item] recycling" to get loads of creative reuse ideas.

And if you have household items that could find new life in someone else's house, search Facebook for a local Buy Nothing group (in the search field, enter "Buy Nothing [your city or neighborhood]"). Giving away things to your neighbors doesn't save you money immediately, but joining a Buy Nothing group can connect you with people who may give away things you need in the future.

11 Ways to Cut the Cost of Attending a Wedding

Receiving a wedding invitation can spur a mix of emotions. You're excited for the couple and honored to be included in their special day. But the high cost of attending a wedding isn't cheap.

Statistics from a 2018 Bankrate survey, indicate that Americans now spend an average of $628 to attend the wedding of a friend or family member. Of course, that's an average, so if travel is involved, you will likely spend a good deal more.

If these amounts are beyond your budget, you can save money by declining. (It's an invitation to a party, not a court summons, after all.) Wedding planning website The Knot estimates that 25 percent of invited guests RSVP with regrets. It's even higher (35 percent) for destination weddings. Make it clear you are delighted for the couple, and participate with enthusiasm in every other aspect of the festivities.

If you decide to join the celebration, you can still attend and keep costs reasonable at the same time. Here's how.

TRAVEL

1. Make it an adults-only trip (even if kids are allowed)

Yes, your munchkins would look adorable in the photos. But when travel is involved, transporting a whole brood can be prohibitively expensive, not to mention stressful. Consider leaving the kids with relatives, or bringing just your youngest or oldest, as appropriate.

2. Skip the rental car

Before you book a pricey vehicle by the day, study the wedding itinerary. Oftentimes, ceremonies and receptions are held close together, or if not, transportation for guests is provided between the two. It's possible that hailing a ride as needed (taxi, Uber, or a friend or relative) would meet your needs for less than the cost of renting a car. Plus, you'll be able to fully enjoy the open bar.

3. Get a group airfare quote

If you have at least 10 people traveling to the same destination, this could be an option. Check individual airline programs. Some, like Alaska Airlines, may not require your group to be on the same flight or even leave from the same city.

4. Monitor airfare changes

Weddings usually provide a lot of notice, sometimes a year or more. Set up an alert with Kayak, SkyScanner, or AirfareWatchdog to receive an email when airfare prices drop.

LODGINGS
5. Rent a house instead of booking a hotel
It's common for a block of discounted hotel rooms to be set aside for wedding guests. But finding a house to rent with other attendees may be an even better deal.

Houses are often cheaper on a per-room basis, and with a kitchen at your disposal, you can eliminate a few expensive meals out. Check out Airbnb, VRBO, and HomeAway for options.

PRESENTS
6. Gift the couple your services
You don't have to be a professional artisan to do this (though, if you are, obviously offer that service). A few examples of potential cash-free gifts you might offer include:

- Pet-sitting for the couple during their honeymoon. (For a week-long trip, that makes a very generous wedding present. In my area, dog-sitting costs between $50 and $75 a night.)
- Baking sweets for a dessert table, or, if you're ambitious, the wedding cake.
- Building the couple an arbor to marry under or place behind their sweet-heart table.
- Offering your home as a venue.
- Officiating the ceremony, if it's non-religious.
- Serving as a wedding planner or day-of coordinator.
- Picking up and transporting items to the wedding and taking gifts back to the couple's home.

7. Buy gifts off-registry
Check Amazon or other retailers to see if they sell identical products. Most registries allow you to mark that you purchased the gift elsewhere. Be sure to do that so the couple doesn't get duplicates.

8. Gift within your budget
A more modest gift is perfectly fine, especially if you've incurred high expenses to get there.

ATTIRE
9. Shop your closet

Unless you're in the wedding party, there are no rules for what to wear, so there's no reason to buy a new outfit if money is tight.

For women, find a dress you've only worn once or twice, and give it new life by having a seamstress change the length or add lace embellishments. For men, pull out your staple suit, and buy just a new tie or pocket square to freshen your look.

10. Shop someone else's closet

At online marketplaces Tradesy and Poshmark, you can buy gently-used apparel for significantly less than retail. Or go old-school and ask a friend or family member if they want to swap.

11. Rent and return

Men often rent tuxes for special occasions; why shouldn't women do the same with formalwear? In fact, they do. Subscription services like Rent the Runway let you borrow a designer ensemble at a huge discount, and they take care of dry cleaning, too.

8 Cool Wedding Trends That Can Save You Money

You don't have to look far to find some of the crazy nuptial trends out there right now. Our favorites so far? Donut walls. Colored smoke bombs. Alpaca petting zoos.

But not all wedding trends are so off-beat. We've come across a few that demonstrate a rare convergence: an idea that is in vogue, yet budget-friendly.

In short, these are the trends the wedding industry hopes will fade away. We're sharing them here in hopes that they become new standards for the sake of every newly married couple's bank account:

ALL-IN-ONE VENUES

At all-in-one venues, the wedding ceremony and reception occur on the same property, usually in different areas, and the venue typically includes a catering facility on-site. It increasingly applies to locations that have lodging on-site as well.

All-in-one venues offer tremendous convenience for those planning a wedding, but the concrete savings is in transportation between locations. Paying to move guests from one location to another — whether you choose a limousine, trolley, or charter bus — can add up.

Savings: Up to $4,000

SMALLER BRIDAL PARTIES

Massive bridal parties may look great in pictures, but they can add significantly to wedding costs. Similar to the way cutting a guest list saves money in several places, trimming the number of attendants saves on flowers, hair and makeup, and attendant gifts. If a couple was planning to cover the formalwear costs for bridesmaids and groomsmen, as some do, they'll save even more.

Savings: $250 per attendant

RSVP POSTCARDS

This just seems like a smart idea: Instead of two extra pieces in your wedding invitation, the RSVP card and its envelope, just have one piece formatted as a postcard. You'll save on paper (no extra envelope) and postage (postcards are 12 cents cheaper to mail). Online stationery provider Minted (Minted.com) even has an all-in-one invitation design with a perforated RSVP card that guests can tear off and return.

Savings: $200 per 100 invitations

NAKED CAKES

For the uninitiated, these are normal layered cakes, minus the traditional final covering of buttercream frosting or fondant. They can be entirely "naked" or have a bit of frosting, but with most of the cake texture showing through.

Naked cakes are controversial in the baking world, with some bakers dead set against them. If that's your position too, you can still take advantage of the minimalist cake trend by ordering a simply frosted cake, which costs $7 per serving or less. It's relatively easy to add your own decorations — such as fresh flowers, greenery, a fun topper, or brightly colored fruit — for less than it costs to have a pastry chef apply sugar flowers, gold dust, or hand-painted art.

Savings: $300 for a 100-person wedding

POCKET SQUARES

When stylish pocket squares (rather than boutonnières) are the accessory of choice for the groom, groomsmen, and fathers of the bride and groom, the savings on the florist bill can be substantial. Pocket squares can also double as part of the groomsmen's gifts. You can order them on Amazon or sew your own.

Savings: $300

SINGLE-STEM BOUQUETS

Single-stem bouquets are the minimalist trend coming to flowers, and they also mean cost savings. Instead of armfuls of blooms, bridesmaids can carry one striking, substantial stem embellished with greenery.

Savings: $50 per bouquet

RENTED FINERY

It's official: Borrowing clothes has gone mainstream. The number of subscription services that allow you to wear and return high-end clothing has ballooned. It was only a matter of time before the model spread to the wedding industry.

Rent the Runway (RentTheRunway.com/bridal) offers a service for both brides and bridesmaids to borrow attire short-term. However, the bride-focused items are geared to casual weddings and other events like the bridal shower and rehearsal dinner. For bridal gowns, you'll want to check out Borrowing Magnolia (Borrowing-Magnolia.com), which is exclusively focused on formal wedding dresses. You can also rent jewelry costing tens of thousands of dollars for just a few hundred from the service Adorn (Adorn.com).

Savings: Up to 85 percent on attire and 98 percent on jewelry

WEDDING HASHTAGS

If you've seen instructions at weddings to share photos on Instagram, followed by some nonsense words after a pound sign (#), you've likely seen a wedding hashtag in action. Hashtags are simply a way for guests to share pictures they take on social media so others can find them easily. When guests share a photo and include the hashtag in their post, the bride and groom can easily collect these images later. If enough people participate and their photos are decent, couples may be able to save money by not having a photographer present for the whole day.

Savings: $500

How to Cut the Cost of Divorce

Think a $50,000 wedding is expensive? That can be peanuts com-
pared to the tab for ending a marriage, especially if the divorce
involves litigation.

The tab for a typical litigated divorce in the United States is about
$20,000 to $30,000 per side. However, if the case goes to trial, that cost
can double or triple. And in litigation, there are costs that can't be
measured in dollars and cents, like the emotional damage to children
from battling parents.

So it's no wonder that people who are planning to divorce are
increasingly seeking less costly alternatives, like mediation, doing it
themselves, and/or a collaborative divorce.

Unlike litigation, these methods seek to arrive at a settlement that's
fair for both sides without going to court. Yet each method is likely
to work only if both spouses are willing to work together. Here's the
skinny on each approach.

ALTERNATIVES TO LITIGATION
1. Do-It-Yourself Divorce

This is the least expensive route. It works best for simple, uncon-
tested divorces and requires that you do all the negotiating and
paperwork on your own. But before you decide to try it, consider
whether you have a lot of assets and/or shared debts. Also, do you
and your partner agree about how to split your property? And
do you have children you're still supporting? If so, you'll need to
agree on custody terms as well as who will cover which child-related expenses.

If you can reach agreement on these issues, a do-it-yourself divorce
can make sense. It's generally not a complex procedure. Court-levied
document filing fees are the only required costs, running from about
$50 to $500.

You can find articles that will help you understand the process on
websites like divorcenet.com or on the state's family court website.
Divorce forms for various states can be bought online. Completecase
.com offers them with a package of support services for $299. You

also may be able to obtain the forms at no cost on the website of your state's family court system.

However, a divorce is far more complex if you own a business, have real estate, or have issues related to custody and child-related expenses. In these cases, you're probably better off having an attorney prepare the documents. Even with a simple divorce, you may want to consider having an attorney look over the documents after you've filled them out, because mistakes could lead to serious problems later.

2. Mediation

If you and your spouse can compromise and want to save money, mediation may be your best course. This method pushes the partners to work together to reach an out-of-court settlement. But unlike litigation, the mediation process can take place without attorneys and avoids hostility or pressure.

The negotiations are directed by a neutral and impartial party, the mediator. While this person should be knowledgeable about divorce procedures and law, he or she doesn't have to be a lawyer. In fact, many mediators have degrees in psychology, which can be very useful.

In each session, the mediator will encourage you and your spouse to talk to each other and put your individual needs and concerns on the table. And you're both required to disclose all details of your finances.

The mediator's job is to move the discussions along. When the talks stall over an issue, a good mediator knows how to bridge differences between the parties and move on to the next step. Several mediation sessions may be needed. When a settlement is reached, an attorney prepares the divorce documents and takes them through the legal system.

Because of the minimal involvement of lawyers and courts, mediation costs much less than litigation. The cost depends on the complexity of the divorce, but usually ranges from about $2,000 to $8,000, shared between the spouses.

Another advantage: Mediators can tell you in advance approximately how much you'll end up paying. Some even offer flat-rate package deals. That's almost unheard of in litigation, where most attorneys only state their hourly fees and require you to pay an upfront retainer of several thousand dollars. But more cash is due when the attorney's bills exceed the retainer. And because the lawyer's work-load is open-ended, so is the divorce's total price tag.

3. COLLABORATIVE DIVORCE

Collaborative divorce is a hybrid method, combining elements of mediation and litigation. It allows you and your spouse to be represented in the negotiations by your own attorneys. However, in a collaborative divorce, getting the top dollar isn't anyone's objective.

Denise Tamir of The Fair Divorce in Miami is a lawyer who specializes in mediation and collaborative divorce. She says collaborative divorce attorneys are trained to "look more holistically at the family unit and decide what's best for the particular family."

In addition, attorneys for the two spouses typically bring in a neutral psychologist and a financial expert (often a forensic accountant) to work with them. Together with you and your spouse, this team then goes into negotiating sessions to hammer out a fair out-of-court settlement. Each session typically runs two to three hours.

Tamir notes that collaborative divorce isn't cheap. In Florida, she says an easy case will run about $12,500, while a difficult one can cost from $40,000 to $70,000 (total, not per side).

And large payments must be paid upfront, since all of the professionals involved require retainers to cover their fees. However, Tamir notes that the total bill still is far less than litigation. For one thing, the two spouses split expenses other than their attorneys' bills. And many court fees are avoided, since the proceedings don't involve a judge.

Save Money While Tracing
Your Family History

Being fascinated with one's family history is a common experience. As the number of candles on your birthday cake grows, so can your desire to root around your family's ancestral garden. Armed with dozens of sticky notes, names scribbled on the backs of envelopes, and boxes of old family photos, you may find yourself turning to the internet.

The cliché that "if it's not on the World Wide Web it doesn't exist" holds a lot of truth for amateur genealogists. You can point and click your way to birth, marriage and death records, obituary notices, old yearbook photos and more. You can also go down a few costly rabbit holes if you're not careful.

In 2012, Deb Mulder of Grand Rapids, Michigan, learned that the hard way. To map out the course her ancestors took to immigrate to the U.S., Deb purchased a home DNA testing kit. Her hope was she'd gain insight into her own ethnic recipe and perhaps find some new distant cousins with whom she could swap information to build each other's trees. However, it wasn't until after spending $100 for a test kit and reviewing her results did Deb realize the item she bought led her down the wrong path.

The burgeoning genealogist had fallen victim to a scam. And that's easier to do than you might expect because the internet is home to scores of sites promising access to a host of ancestral information that's yours for the taking. But there's a catch: There's usually a fee. And while plenty of reputable sites charge for membership (billed monthly, annually or one-time based on the site), it's easy to be confused and accidentally waste money either buying the wrong product that can't be returned or paying for information that's available for free.

Thankfully, Deb sat down with us to share her experiences. Here's what we learned about protecting your pocketbook while traipsing back through time.

1. YOU DON'T NEED MULTIPLE MEMBERSHIPS
Nearly all genealogical sites dive into the same pool of information to cull what they call ancestor 'hints' and 'research matches.' If you've paid for a membership to MyHeritage, Ancestry, etc., you're set. Despite the marketing, jittering leaves and other attractive icons, there isn't a hidden well of records available to just one genealogical site that others also can't access.

2. DON'T FORGET ABOUT FREEBIES
Before committing to annual fees (that can surge as high as $389/year) for access to Newspapers.com, Ancestry.com and similar sites, surf around free resources like FamilySearch.org and Google News (news.google.com). In many instances, you can find the same — or

more — information without your budget feeling the pinch of several pricey memberships.

The same goes for deciphering DNA test results. GedMatch.com offers many free tools, including one that lets you upload your results and compare one — or many — DNA matches. The easy-to-digest format lets you hone in on potential relatives whose genetic makeup may resemble yours and even provides email addresses (if the user agrees) to make a connection and swap genealogical research.

3. All DNA Tests Are Not Created Equal

Ancestry.com, 23andMe.com and FamilyTreeDNA.com offer the largest and most reliable home DNA testing kits currently available. Prices range from $99 to $566 depending on the company and type of information you hope to uncover. But because the type of information and the way you access it varies greatly, you could waste money purchasing a test for the wrong reason or that doesn't yield your desired result.

Ancestry's DNA test proved to be the most effective. Their match results are user-friendly and (at the DNA tester's discretion) allow users to view potential shared surnames in each others' trees and see if there are any shared matches between them.

FamilyTreeDNA's Family Finder test is a bit more limited. It matches you with possible relatives up to six generations. But, the yDNA (tracks DNA passed from father to son and can only be taken by males) and mtDNA (tracks DNA passed from mother to child) tests are invaluable to ancestor hunters looking to track a specific limb of their family's tree. These advanced tests will only identify DNA matches along the specific DNA strand (y or mt) tested, so don't expect broad stroke match results.

But its specificity means you won't waste your precious time trying to determine which one of your 64 fourth great-grandparents is shared with a match. Matches stemming from an mtDNA test are related via your mother's mother's mother and so on. yDNA test results are the same for a father's father's father, etc.

The trait that predisposes your face to flushing when drinking alcohol or being lactose intolerant and more can be uncovered via 23andMe.com's test, which is the only one currently approved by the FDA for consumer use to identify medical issues. But the site's reporting hampers deciphering matches and identifying shared matches, making it less genealogy-friendly than its rivals.

4. Ask for Samples

Before committing your hard-earned dollars to any membership or DNA test, take advantage of the free trial membership or ask customer service for a sample results report. You'll get a better sense if the information resulting from your financial commitment is worth the monetary and time splurge. Any DNA test site that won't offer a sample report could have something to hide and is one you probably should avoid.

5. Ask for References

The lure of tracing your ancestral roots can be hard to ignore. And may tempt you to elicit the help of local genealogists in foreign towns and cities. Before sending money via PayPal (a preferred method for many) or international money order, ask for references and samples of the type of research results you can expect. And make sure to obtain a written quote that specifies the scope of the project, including time, results, whether you'll receive digital or hard copies of records, etc.

6. Watch Your Bottom Line

It's easy to lose track of the money spent on memberships, DNA tests, etc. when you're in hot pursuit of an ancestor. Setting a budget and tracking expenses ensure that your hobby doesn't jeopardize your financial health.

10 Ways to Instantly Improve Your Finances

You've sworn to yourself that this was the year you were going to get a handle on that mounting credit card debt, save more money, build up your retirement nest egg, and help your kids or grandkids pay for college.

But maybe you're still trying to figure out what to do first to make your finances better. Here's the good news — it's not too late and it's not that hard. In fact, according to several nationally recognized financial experts, there are many ways to instantly improve your finances. Here are 10 of the most recommended "first steps" to consider:

1. Start with a phone call. For the price of a phone call, you could end up saving thousands by renegotiating your debt, says Neale Godfrey, a No. 1 New York Times best-selling author who has written 27 books empowering families to take charge of their financial lives. Godfrey, a former bank president, says you can call to get your interest rates lowered or stretch out payments on credit card debt, mortgages, and student loans. "You don't want to wait for them to call you. You want to be proactive," she says. "If your interest rate is 15 percent and you reduce it to 7 percent, right there you are saving thousands of dollars." And don't worry about those student loans you still haven't paid off. "You can negotiate student loans. People think you can't, but you can."

2. Carry an index card in your pocket or purse. Write down what you're buying every day or use your debit card to track what you're spending, notes Godfrey, who used to help families with their finances during appearances on Oprah. "Compare your debit card to your spouse's and at the end of the month see what you really spent. When you are accountable to somebody else and doing it together, all of a sudden it's a challenge . . . and we love challenges."

3. Take advantage of free credit reports. Be sure to check your credit score as often as possible, not just for errors. Godfrey says there might be something small on your credit report that you forgot to pay off that is affecting your score. Take care of it right away and watch your score improve.

4. Start gifting now. "If you're going to die with an estate, why would you leave that for your heirs to be really hurt by that," Godfrey notes. "Look into gifting, things like 529 college savings for kids and grandkids. You can put a lot of money in that now. You get the tax benefit and so do they." Godfrey said most people don't realize that a 529 account can be transferred within a family, among siblings, or even given to a niece or nephew. It also can be used for accredited vocational schools or even by the parents if they want to go to graduate school.

5. Don't rush to pay off your mortgage early. If you're choosing between building up your retirement account or putting an extra $200 a month or so toward paying off your mortgage, go with boosting your 401(k), says Christina Povenmire, a certified financial planner and founder of CMP Financial Planning in Columbus, Ohio. "Sometimes people are obsessed with paying off their mortgage but you don't want to forgo putting money in the 401(k) to pay off the mortgage, especially if you have a nice low interest rate." And don't forget that your mortgage interest is tax deductible.

6. Be smart about "found" money. Your boss gave you a bonus or a raise. Your Aunt Sally left you something in her will. You got a decent tax refund. They're all examples of "found" money, a windfall you may not have been expecting, explains Povenmire. Once again, she recommends putting at least part of that into your retirement savings instead of your checking account where you would spend it all.

7. Buy a coffeemaker and a mug. It's not necessarily the major unforeseen expenses that come along that derail us — it's all the little daily spending decisions. You've heard the advice a million times before, most likely, but have you really put it into action? If you want to avoid that "drip, drip method of spending," as Godfrey puts it, buy a coffeemaker and skip the daily Starbucks trip. Ditch your expensive cable bill for a cheap Netflix subscription and a digital antenna. Keep the car parked and walk or bike for short trips around the neighborhood. As Franklin wrote, "Beware of little expenses: a small leak will sink a great ship."

8. Ask for help. Find an expert and trustworthy financial adviser who puts your interests first, suggests Stephen F. Lovell, president of Lovell Wealth Legacy in San Francisco and Walnut Creek, California. "You need someone who understands all the upsides and all the pitfalls," he says.

9. Keep count. "Learn about investment costs," Lovell reminds investors. "You have mainly three costs — the cost of an adviser, management fee, and trading cost. Don't diminish the importance of investment costs, because they diminish your wealth." Taxes also can impact your return on investment, so find out how investments are taxed so you can increase your after-tax gain.

10. Know your options. There are many different types of investments for different financial needs and for different times in your life. "Don't neglect the full array of available investments," Lovell cautions. "Relying only on stocks, bonds, and cash puts you at a disadvantage."

3 Types of Bills That Frequently Have Errors

Everyone and every company makes mistakes sometimes, but there's no reason you should pay for them. It's too easy to accept a bill, invoice, or receipt without scrutinizing it. Sure, most are computer-calculated, but there can still be human errors, as nearly every bill depends on input from a person at some point in the process.

Ideally, you should check all of your bills and receipts for errors, but if you have to prioritize your attention, focus on the following three, which tend to be the ones most likely to have errors.

HEALTHCARE BILLS

For medical bills, always request an itemized statement to see a detailed breakdown of all charges. Look at it next to the Explanation of Benefits (EOB) from your insurance company. Examine the bill for these common errors:

- **Incorrect patient information.** Check all your personal information, including name, address, ID number, and insurance provider. A digit may be wrong in your member ID number. Your name may be misspelled. Or the doctor or lab may have incorrect insurance information on file.
- **Incorrect billing codes.** Each line item should include its Current Procedural Terminology (CPT) code. If any descriptions don't make sense, look up the CPT code at https://coder.aapc.com/ to see what the charge is for.
- **Duplicate charges.** Look for services or treatments you received once but were billed for twice.
- **Charges for extras that weren't used.** Situations change rapidly in the hospital. A medication, test, or treatment may have been approved, then become unnecessary. Make sure you weren't billed in that situation.
- **Incorrect quantities.** Look at quantities for both medications and supplies. Are they accurate?

- **Incorrect lengths of time.** Some physicians bill for their time in small increments, such as five or 15 minutes. Does the time on the bill match how much time the doctor actually spent with you?
- **Overcharges for in-network services.** Compare the figures on the bill from the doctor or lab to the EOB from the insurance company to ensure that the amounts match.
- **Incorrect dates of service.** This is particularly important to check if it's a hospital bill. You don't want to be billed for an extra day in the hospital.

GROCERY RECEIPTS

After grocery shopping and checking out, always scan your receipt for errors. If you find one, simply request a refund. Errors you're likely to find on a grocery receipt include:

- **Sale prices not reflected.** This includes "buy one, get one free" deals and items that were marked on sale in the store, but didn't ring up that way. You should get the price as marked, even if it was incorrect.
- **Tax charged on non-taxable items.** State laws differ on which grocery items are eligible for state (and local) sales tax. Familiarize yourself with your state's list, available on your state's department of revenue website.

CREDIT CARD BILLS

Sometimes if you've exchanged or returned an item, you can be incorrectly charged. This is just one common instance of your credit card bill having an inaccuracy. Mistakes to look for on a credit card bill include:

- Purchases you don't remember making.
- Charges for items or services you purchased, but never received.
- Recurring bills for services you've canceled.
- Missing or misapplied payments or credits.

IF YOU FIND AN ERROR

Once you uncover a mistake, address it as soon as possible with the company. If it's a major issue involving a lot of money, consider calling, then sending written communication. The Federal Trade Commission has a generic sample letter for disputing billing errors. Go to ftc.gov and search "billing error." It's the first result.

6 Insurance Policies You Can Do Without

FINAL EXPENSE INSURANCE: WHAT THE SALESMAN DOESN'T SAY

Why? For the benefits they provide, final expense policies are actually very expensive. That's because these policies are generally sold to anyone, regardless of their medical condition. And having unhealthy people in the pool means higher prices for everyone.

Still, few people die soon after buying final expense insurance. (In fact, many policies don't even pay benefits if the policyholder passes away within the first two years). And with most policies, customers must pay premiums each month for the rest of their lives. That could be a long time. On average, a 65-year-old man will reach age 83, while a woman will live past age 86.

Maintaining those payments could be especially difficult if you have a financial emergency. Some policies let you borrow against the policy's cash value to keep making your premium payments. But that can't be done with cheaper policies that don't build cash value.

Fortunately, there are better ways to get the same benefits as final expense insurance. If you're healthy, consider buying a small term-life policy. That should give you a bigger payout for a lower price.

Alternatively, just keep putting an extra $50 or $100 a month into your emergency fund or a separate savings account. In a short time, you'll have enough money to cover a modest funeral. More importantly, if there is an emergency while you are living, you'll be able to draw on that money. If you don't use it, there will be funds to cover your funeral costs. Either way, your kids won't have to bail you out.

Final expense insurance isn't the only kind of insurance to avoid. Here are some others:

ACCIDENTAL DEATH AND DISMEMBERMENT

While TV news constantly features reports about casualties from car crashes, storms, and other tragedies, your odds of dying or being seriously injured in an accident are quite low. According to the National Safety

Council, you have only a 1 in 1,656 chance of dying in an accident. You're far more likely (a 1 in 7 chance) to die from cancer or heart disease.

However, an accidental death policy doesn't pay if you die of a disease or an illness — and you don't get to choose how you are going to die. So to be sure that you'll leave money to your survivors, you're better off having a life insurance policy that pays regardless of how you pass away. One exception: If you can't qualify for a regular life insurance policy for medical reasons, an accidental death policy may be of some benefit.

FLIGHT INSURANCE

If there's any type of insurance that's least likely to pay off, this is probably it. Your lifetime odds of dying in a plane crash are approximately 1 in 8,000. And consider this: More than 90 percent of plane-related fatalities involve private planes, not commercial airlines. So if you don't bother to get special insurance to cross the street (about a 1 in 700 chance of death), why shell out $10 for flight insurance every time you buy a plane ticket?

Note: We're not talking about trip cancellation insurance, which reimburses the costs of canceling or postponing a trip.

MORTGAGE OR CREDIT CARD LIFE INSURANCE

These forms of insurance promise to pay off your home mortgage or credit cards if you have balances when you die.

That sounds good, but even if your survivors don't have to deal with those debts, they still will have to deal with other debts, plus funeral expenses. Again, a life insurance policy is a much better deal. It typically pays much more and lets your survivors use the money for whatever they need.

LIFE INSURANCE ON A CHILD

The main point of life insurance is to replace the income the insured person was bringing in. If a child isn't contributing to the family's finances, there's no reason to have such a policy. Instead, parents should increase the amount of their own life insurance policies. That way, the child will be financially protected if the parent passes away (a more likely scenario).

What about using a child's policy as a way to save for college, by building up cash value that can be collected when the child turns 18?

That's a costly way to save for college, because life insurance policies have high fees and the entire investment doesn't go toward college (in other words, if you pay premiums of $250 a month, some of that goes toward the cash value of the policy, and some of that premium just goes to the life insurance company).

On top of that, when you withdraw money from a cash value insurance policy, it is taxed. It's far better to put the money into a tax-free 529 college savings account. Go to www.savingforcollege.com for more information.

SPECIFIC DISEASE INSURANCE

A lot of people fear getting cancer. But if you have medical insurance, treatments for cancer and other diseases are already covered.

Also, it isn't possible to buy a disease-linked policy once you have the condition. And since 70 percent of Americans never get cancer, getting a cancer policy won't pay for most people.

TIP: HOW TO KEEP FROM OVER INSURING

We all want financial protection against potential catastrophes, but there is a psychological tendency to see risk levels as much greater than they really are. And when the chances of encountering a specific risk are infinitesimal, buying specialized insurance is a poor gamble.

That's why narrowly focused policies tend to be among the biggest profit-makers for the insurance companies — and the worst deals for individuals. To keep from falling into this trap, be sure you have enough of the general types of insurance, like homeowners, renters, medical, disability, and life that will protect your finances in most situations.

Another general rule: It can be overly costly to have the insurance company assume 100 percent of the risk. For example, one of the top ways to overpay for insurance is to choose the smallest deductible. But if you can afford to pay some of the potential damages out of pocket, your premiums will be far lower. And that can add up to significant savings over time.

The bottom line: It's financial folly to try to insure against every worst-case scenario. So even though I live in the number-one place in the country for lightning strikes — Florida — you won't find me buying lightning insurance. (Odds of being killed by lightning in the U.S.: 1 in 174,426). However, also don't go walking around in thunderstorms!

Protect Your Business With These Key Insurance Policies

Business owners should have several layers of insurance to protect not only their income, but their family and business partners too. To that end, one of the most important insurance policies a business owner can purchase is commercial general liability (CGL).

CGL provides financial protection in case your business causes injury or damage to a person or property, adjusted based on the type of business and perceived risk. (In other words, a designer or consultant needs less coverage than a building contractor or a firm with a fleet of company vehicles on the road.)

The best way to determine your commercial general liability coverage amount needs, and to gauge how that impacts your bottom line, is to have up to three different insurance agents audit your needs and provide quotes to compare coverages and annual premiums.

Beyond CGL, however, there's another type of policy you may want to consider — especially if the continued success (and very existence) of your company depends heavily on one revenue-generating person, or a handful of top performers.

Indeed, when thinking about all the ways to protect a business — and the individuals who depend on that business for their financial well-being — key person life insurance is one of the best investments that a small business can make, says Richard Reich, president of Intramark Insurance Services in Glendale, California, and a nationally licensed life and disability insurance broker.

You might assume that "key person" means the business owner, but it can be anyone who is instrumental in the day-to-day business operation or the company's revenue stream. "That may be the founder, managing director, or a top sales person who generates significant revenue for the company," Reich says.

Similar to personal life insurance policies that provide a monetary benefit to named beneficiaries in the event of a person's death, key person life insurance allows a company to purchase an insurance policy on a specific individual who is instrumental in running the business. The difference is the beneficiary component. Reich says instead of an individual, like a spouse or child, being named as the beneficiary, the company is the beneficiary and receives the cash value of the policy.

Deciding how much key person life insurance to purchase requires crunching a few numbers. Reich says the most straightforward method to calculate how much key person life insurance you need is multiplying the key person's salary by between five and seven. For example, a key person whose salary is currently $100,000 would warrant a minimum $500,000 policy and a maximum $700,000 policy.

However, there are some other things to consider that could drive the policy coverage — and thus its price tag — up or down. "Take into account the amount of time, salary, and resources required to replace that individual and for the replacement to achieve the same contribution or earning level, the amount of money the individual typically generates for the business in a given timeframe, and the costs that may be incurred following that individual's death," Reich says.

When you are shopping for key employee coverage, remember that loyalty can be a major plus when it comes to insurance. It may be tempting to shop for different coverage with different insurance agents, especially if one offers a one-time discount to transfer an existing policy or purchase a new policy, but having one agent write the key employee coverage policy, another write the policy for the business's liability coverage, and yet another write the policy for, say, disability insurance can create costly overlaps and/or gaps in coverage.

"Dealing with multiple agents and insurance companies increases the likelihood you'll pay for the same coverage twice or not have the coverage you thought you did in the event you need to file a claim," says Jonathan G. Stein, a consumer attorney and former insurance adjuster in Elk Grove, California.

A better approach is to package all insurance policies together to fill the gaps. "You have to shop around to find an agent who can, and will, handle all business policies, but doing so is possible and will save headaches down the road," Stein says.

In addition to avoiding overlaps and gaps, you might even save a little, too. Most insurance companies offer discounts to bundle coverage. So if you purchase your commercial auto policy and your commercial general liability policy from the same company, you may end up paying a lower overall annual premium than purchasing those from two separate companies.

When It's Time to 'Break Up' With Your Insurance Agent

When you first started seeing your insurance agent, he or she probably swept you off your feet, courting you with promises of customer service, undivided attention, and a happy wallet. But sometimes, once you're a fullfledged paying customer, your once-attentive suitor loses interest.

It can happen for many reasons, and, likely, it's not personal. Perhaps your agent's business grew beyond his or her ability to manage it all. Also, just like a romantic relationship, an agent can become complacent and take you for granted — and in that case, something important like a renewal or a chance to save you money on your rates can slip through the cracks.

An isolated mistake or some inattentiveness is probably forgivable. But how do you know whether you should sever ties? "An agent should be helpful, knowledgeable, and always put the client's interests first," says Liran Hirschkorn, founder of ChooseTerm.com. "If your gut tells you this isn't the case, run in the other direction." Other clues it's time to make a change:

You feel pressured. Your agent should be there to answer questions and provide you with information that will be helpful for you to make a decision about insurance, but should never pressure you. "If you're being put on the spot to make a decision, you need to fire your agent," Hirschkorn says.

The phone goes silent. "Customer service is very important in the agent-client relationship," Hirschkorn says. "If after purchasing a policy you can't ever get the agent on the phone, it's time to shop for a new agent."

Your rates keep rising. You shouldn't receive rate increases without at least an explanation from your agent or without the offer to review coverage and discounts to manage rates, says Ronny C. Jetmore who was with Jetmore Insurance Group Inc., in Lusby, Md.

Your agent is stingy. Jetmore says a good agent who values his or her clients isn't afraid to refer you to someone else when he or she can't insure a particular item (artwork, jewelry, boat, all-terrain vehicle, classic car, etc.) very well.

The agent is pushy about other products. "Your home and auto insurance agent should not constantly push another type of insurance down your throat after you have made it clear you are not interested," Jetmore says.

Your agent refuses to think out of the box. Usually, companies can be reasoned with on various items regarding a rate or a claim, but sometimes agents won't do this, Jetmore says. If that's the case, move on to someone who will perform the due diligence you deserve as a paying customer.

How to Make Money and Benefit Society Too

The film "Wall Street" starred Michael Douglas as the arrogant Gordon Gekko who was modeled after the real-life corporate raiders of the 1980s.

These investors would take over a company with the promise of making it more efficient. But what they really did was close plants and fire employees in order to quickly trim costs. Then they would turn around and sell their stock for a fast profit and walk away. The weakened firm was then left to die.

In the film, Gekko orchestrates such a takeover in order to enrich himself, regardless of the damage to the company and its employees. He has the audacity to tell the shareholders there is nothing wrong with what he's doing. In a famous speech, he says, "The point is, ladies and gentlemen, that greed — for lack of a better word — is good. Greed is right, greed works."

But many people in the audience at the time were repulsed by that rationale. These were working people with strong ethics. Thanks to their new 401(k) retirement accounts, they had recently become stockholders. And they wondered why an investor couldn't make money without hurting people — or the planet — in the process.

It's not surprising that just three years later, Domini Impact Investments opened the first mutual fund dedicated to following socially responsible investment standards.

THE EVOLUTION OF SOCIALLY RESPONSIBLE INVESTING

At first, Domini and other early socially responsible funds simply avoided the stocks of companies that engaged in what they deemed to be "destructive" activities, like tobacco, weapons, defense contracting, alcoholic beverages, and gambling casinos. But boycotting such socially incorrect stocks proved to be a costly mistake, as many were big winners during the booming 1990s.

For years afterward, socially responsible investing was ridiculed on Wall Street as a foolish strategy. Serious investors only considered a company's bottom line. The only thing "do-gooder" investors got for their idealism was lower returns.

But that changed around 2008, when deceptive and illegal activities brought down Lehman Brothers and many players in the mortgage and financial industries. Suddenly, corporate behavior became a relevant factor.

The subsequent financial crisis left much of the investing public disgusted with Wall Street and its disregard for values. Many people — especially young investors — got out of the stock market altogether. But others thought there was still a chance to turn investing into a force for good. Out of this climate came the concept for a new and improved form of socially responsible investing.

THE RISE OF SUSTAINABLE INVESTING

This new type of investing — sustainable (or impact) investing — focuses on identifying companies that make a positive impact on society and are managed responsibly.

Its key component is a numerical rating a firm receives for its performance on environmental, social, and governance issues (ESG). For example, the avoidance of fossil fuels and pollution boosts a company's environmental score. Good labor or community relations hikes its score on social matters, while limits on executive compensation can help its governance score.

Combining high ESG scores with certain financial parameters yields a list of responsible companies with good earnings prospects. The idea is that by putting your money into these companies, you can invest in a socially responsible way without having to make financial sacrifices.

And increasingly, companies with high ESG scores are seen as having lower risk.

Sharon French of AIG says a low governance score kept Volkswagen stock out of one of her firm's ETFs before the automaker was implicated in a scandal over the doctoring of emissions data. And Harvard professor Michael Porter wrote that companies with high ESG scores are "generally better-run, more profitable, and enjoy associated cost savings."

SOME WAYS TO ENGAGE IN SUSTAINABLE INVESTING

Mutual Fund Companies Offering Sustainable Funds:
- Pax World (www.paxworld.com)
- Calvert Investments (www.calvert.com)
- Domini Impact Investments (www.domini.com)
- Vanguard (www.vanguard.com)

General ESG-Based ETFs:
- MSCI KLD 400 Social Index Fund (DSI)
- MSCI USA ESG (SUSA)

Low Carbon ETFs:
- MSCI ACWI Low Carbon Target ETF (CRBN)
- SPDR MSCI ACWI Low Carbon Target ETF (LOWC)

Fossil Fuel-Free ETFs:
- SPDR S&P 500 Fossil Fuel Reserves-Free (SPYX)
- ETHO Climate Leadership US ETF (ETHO)

Women-Based ETFs:
- SPDR SSGA Gender Diversity Index ETF (SHE)
- Barclays Women in Leadership ETN (WIL)

To check out a fund's ESG standing, Morningstar now provides sustainability ratings for more than 20,000 funds. This data is available at http://global.morningstar.com/SustainableInvesting.

SUSTAINABLE INVESTING CHOICES

So if you want to invest sustainably, where should you put your money?

Mutual funds that use ESG in their evaluation processes are an easy choice. They prescreen the stocks or bonds in their portfolios to ensure they are from companies with high ESG scores and are financially strong. They also provide diversification.

But the bigger question is whether you should choose between actively managed or passively managed sustainable funds. Passively managed funds are those that invest in all the stocks in an index, and they tend to have lower fees and outperform actively managed funds. Like regular index funds, sustainable index funds simply track the performance of a group of stocks or bonds; the only difference is that these stocks or bonds have high ESG scores.

And there is no shortage of such indexes these days. Some are groups of high-scoring large-cap, small-cap, or international stocks. Others consist of companies with good records on a particular issue or cause, like having women in leadership positions.

As you might expect, both types are offered by sustainable mutual fund families, like Calvert and Pax World. But fund giant Vanguard also has its own sustainable index fund: the Vanguard FTSE Social Index Fund.

You can also buy sustainable index ETFs, which are traded like stocks. And the number of sustainable or impact ETFs has been exploding, as ETF issuers look for new products to market to millennials. (Indeed, a Bank of America survey found that three-quarters of millennials are interested in sustainable indexing).

As a result, you can buy an ETF that mimics the S&P 500, but eliminates those companies with low ESG scores. Alternatively, you can choose an ETF with a mix of companies that don't deal in fossil fuels, or whose products have a low level of carbon emissions (see the sidebar).

FINDING A SUSTAINABLE INVESTMENT THAT MATCHES YOUR PRIORITIES

Investing in sustainable funds of any type can be tricky. There is no single standard for fund managers to determine a company's sustainability status. Some funds pledge to follow the United Nations Principles for Responsible Investment (https://www.unpri.org/about). However, others do not.

In addition, the acceptability of a company's actions may change. For example, any utility connected to nuclear power was long considered off-limits as a sustainable investment. But Jon Hale, who heads Morningstar's Sustainability division, says because of nuclear power's "ultra-low carbon intensity," it may be time to rethink that blanket exclusion.

Also, sustainable versions of the S&P 500 or other conventional indexes may put performance ahead of social impact; some contain the stocks of companies with questionable ethical histories, like Wells Fargo.

And of course, wherever there is a diverse mix of companies in a sustainable fund, the collection may not coincide with your own social priorities.

To bridge this gap, Ethan Powell of Impact Shares has come up with an innovative solution. His firm will soon come out with a line of custom ETFs, where the stocks in each match the specific goals of a nonprofit organization. For example, a civil rights ETF could match the goals of a national civil rights organization or an affordable housing ETF could be associated with a group that provides homes for low-income people.

Creating these funds will be a collaborative process. First, each partner group will list several social objectives that it wants to promote. Using ESG data, the Wilshire 5000 Stock Index will then be screened for companies with outstanding records in those areas. From them, Wilshire analysts will select the stocks with the best potential to outperform financially to put into the fund.

Powell expects three to six such ETFs to be on the market by the end of the year. (For more information, go to www.impactshares.org). He says this model will dispel any doubts about a fund's suitability. Why? Because having the brand of the leading nonprofit in a social cause will signal that the ETF's investment mix has the group's seal of approval.

If that isn't enough incentive, Impact Shares (itself a nonprofit) will donate its advisory fee to the ETF's namesake. That means that besides investing in sustainable for-profit companies, the ETF buyer will also be supporting the nonprofit group that he or she admires.

For investors interested in bringing about social change, that could be the ultimate sales pitch!

Investing With Your Conscience and Still Making Money

Some people love the idea of investing solely in companies that share their values. While difficult at a granular level, mutual funds and advisers who invest with values in mind attempt to achieve a balance using tools that screen out certain types of companies on a variety of social aspects, such as tobacco, alcohol, defense, or unacceptable labor practices in developing countries.

Some screens focus on specifically religious grounds, while others rely on consensus among investors on what makes a corporation a "good citizen" and thus investable from a social standpoint. Screens can vary dramatically in intent and effect, but all attempt to weed out companies that fail to meet a basic set of acceptable practices.

Demand has grown for such screens. Nearly 18 percent of the $36.8 trillion in assets under management tracked by Cerulli Associates is invested using socially responsible investing (SRI) methods, according to the Forum for Sustainable and Responsible Investment (USSIF).

But does it make sense to vote with your investment dollars? Advisers are split on the issue, yet recent research supports the idea that — at a minimum — you increasingly are less likely to pay a penalty for picking only stocks that adhere to your vision of good corporate behavior. "As an adviser, I bought into a lot of the myth about sustainable investing — that returns are going to be lower. But there are studies showing that's not true," says Tom Nowak, a certified financial planner.

Since 1995, for instance, funds tracked by USSIF posted a compound annual growth rate of 13.1 percent, the group concluded in its 2014 report. The S&P 500 with dividends reinvested returned 9.45 percent during that period.

Increasingly, too, large investors are leaning toward SRI as a strategy, Nowak points out. "The 2014 USSIF report shows one institutional dollar out of six is screened. It used to be one in nine, so that's a significant jump," Nowak says. "What do the institutional investors know that ordinary investors don't?"

Nowak cautions investors interested in SRI to avoid index funds, since they automatically include stocks that socially conscious investors would find objectionable. Rather, he says, find an adviser with low fees to help you build a screen that fits your objectives at a lower cost. "Low fees are appropriate and diversification is important," Nowak says. "Will they be successful? In 20 years we'll see, but I'm no longer of the view that sustainable investing is necessarily going to do poorly."

Not all advisers think the effort to prune your investing choices based on your morals is worth the effort. One problem facing many investors, particularly young people, is that they want to invest their values, yet they don't act the same way when it comes to their own spending, says Stephanie Genkin, an independent fee-only financial planner in New York.

"Many young people and novice investors don't want to give their IRA dollars to Philip Morris, ExxonMobil, BP, Monsanto and other companies they perceive are bad for our health and the environment — that makes it almost impossible to invest in a large-cap fund, which is one of the building blocks of any portfolio," Genkin says. "I ask these same folks if they have an iPhone or any Apple products and whether they shop at H&M or at other fast-fashion retailers, because these companies have less-than-stellar labor records in their factories in developing countries."

In addition, it can be hard to understand what SRI even means to a mutual fund that uses the concept to market itself, Genkin notes. "In many cases, there's a lack of transparency beyond the top 10 holdings, and it's very hard for even the most diligent investor to find a solid match of values," she says.

Genkin instead tells clients to put money into index funds that generate a market return, pick a few individual stocks that fit their values, and then donate a portion of their investment profits to favored causes. Alternatively, investors can avoid single stocks they really don't like. If those same stocks are small portions of a large index or mutual fund the investor owns, their impact on return is minimal.

There's a case to be made, too, that people shouldn't bother with social screening strategies at all. That's because avoiding ownership of "sin stocks" isn't going to make a difference to anyone but you in the end, says Paul Ruedi, a registered investment adviser.

"Mutual funds own shares from secondary market, for the most part. Shunning stocks of companies you do not admire might make you feel better but neither helps nor hurts the companies," Ruedi says.

It's more effective, Ruedi argues, simply to make more money and donate more to charity. He goes further, suggesting buying so-called sin stocks because they often are great value investments. "Value stocks have had returns well in excess of growth stocks, 4 percent to 5 percent per year or more over time," he says. "So better to buy these companies, hope for stronger returns, and donate more to your cause."

Slash the Cost of Pet Care

Any pet lover knows there's nothing like the unconditional love of a furry family member. And because you love your bundle of fur, you want to provide him or her with the very best healthcare possible. But that care comes at a cost. According to pet insurance company PetPlan, the average pet household spends between $769 and $1,400 annually on routine pet care. And for unexpected care, the average bill can range anywhere from $800 to $1,500.

Whether you have a chronically ill animal or a mischievous one who eats greasy leftovers, you could find yourself on the receiving end of a hefty pet healthcare bill. And those exorbitant costs — chronic or emergent — can leave pet parents facing the unbearable reality of having to compromise their pet's care — or even life — because of financial limitations.

Has your family talked about purchasing insurance for a pet, but opted to not spend the approximate $600 per year? Having insurance may help defray some of the costs of care for a dog with chronic health issues.

CHANGE THE TYPE OF VISIT
A routine visit to your veterinarian may be billed differently than a "recheck." If you have a pet with a chronic condition, ask your practice if they have recheck options for the animal to be seen for the same condition several times a year.

USE VET SCHOOLS
Check to see if any vet schools in your area offer discounted services. Cornell University College of Veterinary Medicine, for example, offers veterinary services to the public at a greatly discounted cost than typical practices and animal hospitals. The care is provided by board-certified veterinarians, residents, and interns who collaborate (with heavy oversight from the certified professionals) to provide diagnosis and treatment.

But programs like Cornell's also typically provide routine services like vaccinations, medicine re-checks, etc., at prices that are much lower than those of a typical vet practice. Similar programs can be found at the University of Tennessee, University of Minnesota, and Iowa State.

SHOP AROUND

Pet stores like Petco and PetSupermarket offer clinics that can significantly cut the cost of vaccines, fecal testing, and microchipping your pet.

USE TECHNOLOGY

If your pet has a chronic condition, you may be able to email photos and/or videos to your veterinarian to show a flare up of a condition that's been previously treated. This may allow the vet to determine treatment in some cases without you having to take your pet to the office.

GET PRESCRIPTIONS ELSEWHERE

You don't have to fill your pet's prescriptions at the vet. Your local pharmacy may be able to fill your pet's prescriptions.

JOIN A STUDY

Ask about opportunities to take part in clinical studies through your vet clinic. Doing so means things like your pet's bloodwork, diagnostic tests, and future medication could be free of cost.

VOICE CONCERNS

Lastly, speak up. Your vet should be someone you can speak frankly with. If affording a service or diagnostic test is problematic, ask your vet if there are any alternatives. He or she may have other creative options or practice-specific programs to offset or reduce the cost of care without lessening the commitment to your beloved animal companion's well-being.

Words to the Wise

BONUS TIP!

Services to Manage Bills for Elderly Relatives

If you have an aging relative and worry about him or her falling behind on bills or getting scammed, it might be time to bring in a professional to watch over the accounts. Two companies — SilverBills and EverSafe — now offer concierge bill payment services that manage bill payments for senior citizens.

These services can even watch for erratic behavior that might signal cognitive decline or tip off a caring relative that a scammer has gotten between grandma and her bank account. EverSafe, for instance, will watch bank accounts, investment accounts, credit cards, and credit reports for signs of trouble and alert a trusted relative to take action.

BONUS TIP!
Here's Exactly How Much Savings You Need . . .

How much money do you really need in the bank to feel safe? Research says . . .not that much. A low-income household benefits just by having $2,467 in the bank. So say Jorge Sabat and Emily Gallagher, two economists who worked on the concept for a recently published paper. Compare that to financial advisers and authors who recommend three months, six months, or more in cash as a safety net. If you're not sure what to think, perhaps aim for that research-backed number as your first goal, then consider padding it until you've saved three to six months of living expenses.

BONUS TIP!
Keep Streaming Costs Down

For a long time, many cord-cutters found entertainment easy and cheap just by canceling cable and signing up for Netflix instead. All that is changing fast. A flood of new streaming offerings from Disney, Apple, NBC, and others means many consumers could effectively be rebuilding an expensive cable package piecemeal, and even paying more than before. In addition, monthly fees for the mainstays, such as Hulu, PlayStation Vue, SlingTV, and Netflix, have gone up.

One strategy for keeping it all in check is to set a family budget for streaming, including music streaming fees. Then carefully comb over the offerings to find the choices that best fit your needs and jettison the rest. Remember, too, that some, such as Amazon, will sell you single shows or seasons. If all you want is a movie once or twice a month, no need to subscribe to a whole catalog of shows you won't watch.

Chapter 3

Save Big
on Cars

"A MAN MAY, IF HE KNOWS NOT HOW TO SAVE AS
HE GETS, KEEP HIS NOSE TO THE GRINDSTONE."

Buying an Electric Car
Could Save You $1,600 per Year

A few years ago, all-electric cars were unusual on the road, something to be pointed out. Now there are dozens of models available, from cheap city runabouts to full-fledged luxury sedans and high-end sports cars.

While most still lean toward the ugly-cute subcompact look, and car chargers remain few and far between, it's beginning to feel like we're near a tipping point. The union head at Hyundai, for instance, called electric cars "evil," citing a potential 70 percent decline in auto manufacturing jobs if car makers abandon gasoline engines en masse.

They will be cheaper and simpler to make, for sure, and they are likely to be cheaper and simpler to maintain, too. Tough times for auto workers and the repair shops, but for the consumer, it means electric is probably cheaper to buy and run than the fossil-fuel ride you grew up with.

But are they really cheaper to own and drive?

First of all, there is still a popular federal credit worth between $2,500 and $7,500 on qualifying all-electric cars. How much of a credit you get depends on the size of the battery (among other things), and only plug-in models qualify. Hybrids

There is no phaseout on the consumer side, but dealers will not be able to offer the break to buyers after a manufacturer sells its 200,000th electric car in the country. That was nearly the entire fleet of EVs sold by all manufacturers combined in 2017, so many automakers are nowhere near that ceiling yet. But things change fast. Many manufacturers have gone full-scale into electric in anticipation of demand.

You have to buy a new car to get the tax credit, and it's non-refundable, so if you owe zero taxes you get no money back from Uncle Sam. Prices for new cars mostly fall between $32,000 and $40,000 before the tax credit is applied.

As for running the car, one study in 2007 estimated the electricity cost to be the equivalent of paying 75 cents per gallon for gas, if you assume 8.5 cents per kilowatt hour compared to a traditional engine vehicle that gets 25 miles to the gallon. That's on the low side, however. The average kilowatt hour now costs 13.3 cents.

A lot depends on exactly when you charge your car — many systems charge less for power at night and far more when grid demand is peaking during the day and during heat waves.

"Electricity prices state-to-state differ by as much as 319 percent, so it's important to take in state-specific electricity costs and the typical distance driven in each state to make a fair comparison," says Mia Yamauchi, marketing manager for Volta Charging, which is building a free electric vehicle charging network across the country.

Generally, she says, electrics cost about $100 a month less to operate than gasoline vehicles, and it's cheaper by at least some amount in all 50 states. Wyoming is cheapest, with annualized savings of $1,602, and Oklahoma rounds out the top 10 at $1,409 in savings.

As for the driving experience, that's a mixed bag, says electric car owner Bennett Lauber in Washington, D.C. Lauber bought a used 2013 Ford Focus with a range of 70 miles. Advertised range isn't necessarily a reliable number, he warns.

"The range varies depending upon the outside temperature," he says. "In the summer, it has been as high as 90 miles and in the deep winter as low as 40. The heater can pull 20 miles off, while the AC about 10- to 15-mile reduction."

What results is "range anxiety," Lauber says, from not being able to properly estimate when you will need a charge and how to get it.

"Spontaneity is gone, and you have to plan most of your driving based upon your current charge, and the availability of chargers near your destination," he says.

Lauber doesn't miss oil changes, though. However, he has to remind himself to rotate his tires since auto shop visits are less regular.

"It's fun to get oil change coupons from all of the vendors you take the car to for any work," he says. "It really proves they don't read things."

4 Wrong Assumptions About Car Insurance That Can Cost You

Trying to make sense of car insurance policies can be frustrating. Add to that the fact that people often make faulty assumptions about insurance, and you have a potential for unwanted costs and unpleasant surprises down the road. To help, we've identified the truth about four common misconceptions:

Costly Assumption No. 1: Auto insurance rates automatically go down as you get older. The truth: "Age is an important factor in annual car insurance premiums," says Keith Moore, CEO of CoverHound.com, an auto insurance comparison site. And like other factors, including gender, miles driven daily, and region where you reside, age is used to gauge the likelihood that the insured will make a claim in the future.

But there is no firm rule that once a member of your household (your child, younger brother living with you, etc.) hits a certain age — often thought to be 25 — the cost of car insurance will decrease.

"While people under 25 are statistically more likely to get into an accident, each company handles the impact of age on the price of the policy differently," Moore says. "Some carriers may offer a pricing break at age 21, 23, or 30."

Because there's no way to alter a birthday, take advantage of other ways to reduce car insurance premium costs. "There are a variety of other ways to receive discounts on your policy, such as bundling a homeowners or renters policy with your auto coverage, paying your premium in full, or even choosing to receive paperless billing," Moore says. Ask your insurer about all discounts you may qualify for.

Costly Assumption No. 2: Going to a direct insurance company like Geico or Progressive is always less expensive than using a local agent. The truth: Moore says it's true that direct companies like Geico and Progressive don't employ agents while writing the insurance policies they sell (rather than having another company write their policies) and can offer less costly options than the other guys. By not incurring agent commission fees, these companies spend less to offer a similar product as their competitors.

"But that does not necessarily mean the savings will be passed on to you," Moore points out. "Many direct auto insurance carriers will use those savings to spend more on marketing their brand and product." Without the benefit of local agents marketing for them, direct carriers may need to spend a bit extra on national advertising and marketing to create brand awareness.

In addition, the pricing algorithms that dictate the price of car policies can be wide-ranging. As a result, Moore says the typical driver can expect to see a large span in price for a given policy. "As long as you are comfortable working with a local agent and a direct carrier, it's always best to shop all available policies to ensure you receive the best price and policy for you."

Costly Assumption No. 3: Comprehensive coverage covers theft of your vehicle and all items contained within. The truth: "Comprehensive coverage of an auto insurance policy only covers items physically attached to your vehicle," Moore says. That means a stereo or GPS device that's factory installed is covered in the event it's stolen or vandalized.

But items not factory installed such as iPods, tablets, clothes, designer sunglasses, and CDs stolen from your car or damaged in an accident will not be covered by a car insurance policy. "Those would typically be covered if there is a homeowners or renters policy in place," Moore says.

Costly Assumption No. 4: You can't switch car insurance carriers until your current policy expires. The truth: Being unhappy with the level of customer service, price, or handling of a claim can leave you unsatisfied with your car insurance company. But did you know you can drive out of a policy you no longer love? Because they want to keep your business, insurance companies guard this little-known secret that you're not bound to an auto insurance policy for the full term of six or 12 months.

The truth is, you can cancel a policy at any time — for instance, if shopping around turns up comparable coverage for less money, Moore says. However, your current carrier may charge a fee (often 10 percent) on any unused premium. "For instance, after three months of coverage, if you cancel a $600 six-month car insurance policy, you may be subject to a $30 fee."

Moore suggests when shopping for car insurance, in addition to comparing apples to apples on items like deductibles, coverage limits, annual premiums, etc., make sure to ask your current — and prospective — carrier about any fees and penalty charges. These may offset the potential savings stemming from switching your coverage.

How to Get a Great Deal on a New Car

Buying a new car is a big emotional and financial investment, so naturally, you want to get the best deal. But that isn't always so easy, and with pricing designed to confuse, it can be difficult even to know what a good deal actually is.

In order to feel confident asking for the lowest possible price and to be able to avoid the temptation of enticing sales tactics, here's everything you need to know to negotiate the best possible price on a new car like a pro.

BEWARE OF ONLINE PRICES

Sites like Edmunds.com, Kelley Blue Book, NADAGuides.com and others let you put in a vehicle's make, model, and features to discover the average price consumers paid for a particular car in your area.

Some of these services also give you the manufacturer's suggested retail price and dealer invoice cost. And almost all of them offer some sort of "negotiated" price that seems like a great deal. You can simply print out the "negotiated" price and take it to the dealer to supposedly buy your car at a discount.

But many of these car buying services are operated by the same company — TrueCar, and quite often, the average price consumers pay isn't necessarily the best price you could get for a car.

The most important point to remember is that TrueCar gets paid by the dealers. So while the site seems to be oriented toward consumers, it is actually in business to serve the dealers (i.e., help them acquire new customers), not help consumers score a shaved-down sticker price.

So how do you get the best deal?

FORGET FAIR PRICE, AVERAGE PRICE, AND INVOICE COST

First, don't be fooled by terms that make it seem like you're getting a discount when you aren't. "Fair price," "average price paid," and "true value" are just marketing terms. They don't have any generally accepted meaning in the industry. And they aren't likely to be the best price you can get.

What's more, knowing the dealer's invoice cost — once a good measure of what dealers paid for a car — is equally as useless. Most people think a dealer's profit is the difference between the invoice cost and the price the consumer pays.

Not true.

Dealers get secret incentives from the auto manufacturers based on their ability to meet certain sales targets. When a dealer meets those targets, the manufacturer may give the dealership an extra $500 or $1,000 in profit per car.

That's why dealers will gladly sell one or two cars in a given month at a loss if those sales end up helping them meet their manufacturer sales targets.

That means your goal isn't to find out the invoice price of a car and get a price as close to (or below) that as possible. Your goal is just to get the best possible price you can get.

HOW TO NEGOTIATE A BETTER DEAL

To do that, shop in the last week of the month. That's when dealers that haven't met their sales targets are angling to do whatever they can to meet them — including sell you a car at a steep discount.

Next, use the free online car buying tools and dealers' websites to check local dealer inventories for the car you're interested in. Make a list of a half dozen dealerships that have the car you want in stock.

Then call the internet sales managers from these dealerships and tell them the car you want (be specific on the model and the options). Be sure to mention that you plan to buy at the end of the month. And ask if they will give you a complete itemized price, including all the documentation fees, freight fees, motor vehicle fees, taxes, etc., by phone or email. Give them a deadline, say by the next morning.

Be sure to mention that you are contacting several dealers with the same pitch and that you plan to call all of them back to offer them a chance to beat the best price you get.

When you get the offers, call all of the dealers back and ask them if they can beat the best out-the-door offer you got. Whichever dealer offers the best price is the one you choose. However, before you go in to buy the car, make sure you get written confirmation of the price in detail, including all the taxes and extras. Make it clear that you don't plan to pay a penny over total all-inclusive cost the dealer quoted you.

AVOID DISTRACTIONS

Always talk in terms of total out-the-door price of the car. Don't get distracted by talk of monthly payments or pre-incentive prices. Simply say you want a bottom-line figure that includes everything.

SEPARATE OLD FROM NEW

Dealers love to talk about how your trade-in will lower the cost of the new car. But don't be fooled by this smoke-and-mirrors tactic. It's always best to negotiate the sale of your trade-in separately from the price of the new car.

That's because dealers will sometimes inflate the trade-in value they offer you in an effort to hide the fact that they're bumping up the cost of the new car.

And consider selling your old car yourself. Consumers who do this typically get more for their cars anyway.

BE PREPARED TO WALK AWAY

It's easy to become emotionally invested in a potential new car. After all, you've done a lot of shopping, price comparing, etc. But remember there are dozens — even hundreds — of terrific new cars out there. Even if you can't get a great price on the one you've got your heart set on, there's likely another one that will be just as good, if not better.

Importantly, you don't want to get locked into overpaying or being pressured to commit to a loan that's not in your budget just because you "love" the car.

WATCH OUT FOR EXTRAS

Even after you've agreed on a price, some dealers will try to boost their bottom lines with extras. Don't fall for it.

Avoid buying aftermarket accessories, like tire maintenance packages, rust-proofing, and the like from the dealer. Those things almost always can be found cheaper elsewhere.

For example, we found a set of four manufacturer floor mats for $125 (including tax and shipping) on Amazon. Those same mats would cost $169 plus tax from the dealer. And off-brand floor mats (which I'd be fine with) would cost a mere $79 for a full set.

AVOID THE FINANCING TRAP

While most of us focus on getting the best price for a car, Sonia Steinway, president of Outside Financial, taught us there's money — a lot of it — to be saved on financing.

Steinway says that consumers who shop around for car financing are usually able to get a better interest rate than they could get from the dealership. That's because dealers have no obligation to show buyers the rates they qualify for, and they typically don't choose to share that info.

Why? Because many of the banks and lenders dealers work with compensate them for originating loans. And the financial institution passes that compensation cost on to consumers in the form of fees built into the loan. Steinway told me the average markup on a loan package arranged through a dealer for a new car is $1,717.

To get the best rate, check with your current banking institutions (not just where you have your checking account, but also where you have credit cards and other loans). Consider joining a credit union, too. They typically have ultra-low car loan rates. And shop around at online banks just for comparison.

Remember, dealers are free to select the rate from a lender that gives them the most opportunity to profit from markups. But when you get your own financing, whether through your bank, credit union, or a lender platform like Outside Financial, you can compare all of your options at your leisure, without the added stress and pressure that comes from sitting in the back office of a dealership. Doing so can save you as much as $3,000 on the total cost of your new car.

Plus, there is the added bonus that you will spend a LOT less time at the dealership, sidestepping the loan application, approval, and processing process.

$mart Moves for Buying a Car Online

It's hard to imagine waking up and thinking, "You know what I'd love to do today? Test drive a dozen cars at several dealerships, spend hours negotiating prices with various salespeople, then spend a few more hours filling out paperwork before taking ownership of my new vehicle!"

Indeed, the 2016 Beepi Consumer Automotive Index reveals that 52% of Americans feel anxious when visiting a car dealership, while 61% feel like they're going to be taken advantage of at some point during the process.

No wonder online car buying is such an enticing alternative. You can sit in your jammies on the couch, surf a few apps, easily comparing features and prices, then have a vehicle delivered right to your home.

But is buying a car from companies such as Carvana or Vroom really as fool-proof as ordering a pizza? "Online car buying can be very convenient, and you don't have to worry about haggling," says LeeAnn Shattuck, aka The Car Chick, who owns a personal car buying service. "However, there are a lot of pitfalls that car shoppers need to watch out for."

PITFALL 1: NO TEST DRIVES

More often than not, when it comes to online car buying, you won't even see the vehicle, let alone have the opportunity to test drive it, before committing to a purchase.

"Test-driving a car is a critical part of purchasing any vehicle, because once you buy it, you'll need to keep it for five to 10 years, or you'll take a hit financially," says Lauren Fix, an automotive analyst, ASE-certified technician, and race car driver. "There are some factors that you simply can't determine online, such as seating comfort. That's a top priority for most people, and a vehicle will not get more comfortable the longer you own it."

The second most critical factor is visibility — being able to see out the front, back, and corners clearly. You'll also want to ensure your practical needs are met, such as having enough storage space for golf clubs and luggage, or being able to get car seats in and out easily for weekends with your grandchildren.

Fix says those are all things you'll never be able to get from reading reviews online, because we're all built differently and have different preferences.

Potential workaround: "Nothing replaces the experience of a test drive," confirms Fix. So if you're truly committed to an online purchase, you'll want to head to a dealership to test drive the vehicle you intend to purchase first. Make sure you drive the exact model and trim level you want to buy.

PITFALL 2: UNKNOWN CONDITION

Since online car buying companies are selling used, not new, vehicles, there's no telling what condition the car will be in upon arrival.

"Some of these vehicles are sourced from rental car fleets, which can get pretty beat up, cosmetically," says Shattuck, noting that wear in upholstery, dings, chips, dents, and scratches won't show up in the online pictures. "Some have been smoked in, have worn tires, or have fluids that need to be changed. You just don't know how it's been taken care of."

Not to mention, it could also have a branded title, such as a lemon law buyback.

Potential workaround: Step one is to look at the CARFAX Report, even though Shattuck warns it doesn't always tell the whole story. Next, have an appointment lined up with a certified independent car mechanic to inspect the vehicle within a day or two of taking possession. "Most of the online car buying companies offer a three-day return policy, so you could theoretically buy the car, get it inspected, then return it if the mechanic finds problems, or if the cosmetic condition isn't acceptable to you," says Shattuck.

Of course, you'll be time-crunched and could face a "return shipping" fee if you decide to send it back. Plus, if you got a bank loan to purchase the vehicle, and you return it, you may have to jump through some hoops to get the bank to cancel the loan.

PITFALL 3: CONFUSING TECHNOLOGY

If it's been half a decade or more since your last vehicle purchase, then you'll probably be shocked by all of the gadgets available these days. For instance, backup cameras are now standard on all U.S. vehicles manufactured after May 1, 2018. Many makes and models also offer advanced safety features, such as blind-spot detection, lane-departure warning, automatic emergency braking with forward-collision alert, adaptive cruise control, and even facial recognition software to measure a driver's alertness.

A test drive with a knowledgeable salesperson can show you how to use everything. But you won't get that by buying online.

"Good luck taking your online purchase to your local dealership for a run through of the technology," says Sarah Lee Marks, an independent car concierge and private fleet manager who also serves as an AARP Driver Safety instructor. "Since they didn't sell you the car, they won't be motivated to give you a hands-on demonstration. There's no relationship there."

Potential workaround: Sign up for Smart DriverTEK, a free 90-minute AARP workshop that teaches seniors all about these safety features.

"Two-thirds of the people who show up are there to learn about the technology before they car shop, while the other third is there because they bought a car and have tons of questions about how all this stuff works," says Marks. "But you'll still want to get a feel for what to expect in your own vehicle, such as if you'll feel a vibration in the seat or steering wheel, what each alert sounds like, and any visual cues."

How to Shop for Auto Insurance and Save Big Bucks

Shopping around is by far the best way to cut your car insurance costs. In fact, one study found that drivers who compared prices saved an average of $358 on their annual premiums.

But shopping around can be far more confusing and time-consuming than the Geico commercial might have you believe, because it can be tough to determine how much insurance you need. Here's how to figure that out.

DECIPHERING THE THREE NUMBERS

Car insurance includes three types of coverage: liability, collision, and comprehensive. Liability covers injuries or damage that you cause. The amount of coverage is typically expressed as a three-number combination, like 100-300-500. The first number (100) is for bodily injury liability. It's the maximum amount the policy will pay for the medical bills of someone you injure in an accident (in this example, $100,000).

The second number (300) is the limit of combined bodily injury awards that are covered when several people are injured in the same accident (in this example, $300,000). The third number (500) is the maximum for repairs to other cars and property that you damage in an accident (in this example, $500,000).

100-300-500 is the standard level of liability coverage and works for most middle-income people. However, it may not be enough if you own valuable assets. That's because if you cause a serious accident, damage awards could exceed your coverage, and the injured people could sue you for more, putting your home or investments at risk.

To avoid that possibility, choose higher coverage (like 250-500-100) or add an umbrella liability policy (for $1 million or more of additional protection).

Don't settle for your state's minimum level of liability coverage; it's almost always inadequate. And don't skimp on liability coverage if you have teen drivers in your household, since they're more likely to be involved in an accident.

COMPREHENSIVE AND COLLISION

Collision and comprehensive coverage are designed to protect your own vehicle. Collision covers accident-related damage, while comprehensive covers damage stemming from other incidents and theft. These coverages are optional, and if you have an older car with no loans outstanding, you may not need them.

With these coverages, you simply choose the size of your deductible (the amount that you pay out of pocket if you make a claim). The easiest way to save money is by taking a larger deductible. Rate-comparison site TheZebra.com reports that a $1,000 deductible on comprehensive and collision (rather than a $500 one) can lower a typical premium by $159.

Another option is personal injury or medical coverage. Some states with no-fault insurance require personal injury coverage. But if your state doesn't, and you have other medical insurance and mostly drive alone, you probably don't need any. However, if you regularly transport people other than family members, some added medical coverage could be worthwhile.

Finally, there is uninsured and underinsured motorist coverage. Even if this coverage isn't required by your state, adding it isn't very expensive (usually $100 or less per year) and the cost could be well worth it. Having it means that if a driver without sufficient liability insurance hits you, you'll still be able to collect.

HOW TO GET THE BEST DEAL

Comparison shopping isn't quite as easy as going online for airfares or hotel prices. That's because insurance rates and requirements vary from state to state. Also, many insurers won't cooperate with websites that give quotes from multiple companies.

However, one website provides estimated prices for almost 200 companies: TheZebra.com. The Zebra uses the rate-setting formulas these companies file with the various states.

If you want actual prices, Compare.com is another good choice. It gets its data by dealing directly with a smaller assortment of insurance firms.

Other websites, like Everquote.com, take your information and give it to various insurers. The companies then contact you to give you their quotes.

Of course, some insurers try to entice you to go to their own websites (or call them by phone) for a quote. The downside: Once they have your personal information, you're likely to get numerous follow-up calls or emails seeking your business.

An alternative is to use an independent insurance agent who represents several companies. This way, you enter your information once and the agent helps you compare quotes. One such agency that operates nationwide is InsuranceBrokersGroup.com. It promises to give online quotes in just 5 minutes.

MORE CONSIDERATIONS

Remember, you may also be eligible for discounts beyond the stated rates, especially if you've taken a safe driving course, belong to a certain group, or drive infrequently. So be sure to ask if you qualify.

Also keep in mind that rates aren't the only things to consider. You also need to be sure that an insurer is financially stable. You can check insurance company ratings at WeissRatings.com.

You also want to be sure that the company has a good record for processing claims. One way to find out is to check the number of complaints filed against the firm with your state insurance commissioner.

The Smart Money Move to Make When Your Car Needs a Major Overhaul

Shake, rattle, and roll. No, you're not listening to the oldies station on your commute — that's the sound your car is making without the radio on. Again. Maybe it's finally time for a new car (or, more accurately, new to you because a used car is always a more prudent investment).

"When deciding whether to keep one's car, there are a number of factors to consider, as this decision is one of personal taste as well as a business decision," says Steve Smyth, COO of Smyth Automotive, a privately held automotive aftermarket parts company. According to experts, your answers to the following questions should indicate whether you ought to press ahead with a repair or make the decision to replace:

1. Is the cost of repairs greater than the value of the vehicle? The most costly repairs are those involving the transmission or drivetrain (i.e., engine and shifting). For example, if the Kelley Blue Book value of the vehicle is only $3,000 yet your transmission goes out and you'll also need new tires soon, you're looking at a potential $2,500 repair bill, Smyth says. At that point, the math leans toward replacement, although you'll want to get the actual repair estimate and not just rely on a guess.

2. What's its current condition and repair history? If your vehicle has become a safety hazard — or has left you stranded somewhere in one or two instances over the past six months to a year — you may want to evaluate. If the underbody is badly rusted or if there is extensive body damage that causes the vehicle to be unsafe or out of the State Highway Patrol's defined "safe inspected" operating condition, these repairs will add up quickly, Smyth points out.

3. Is it still under the manufacturer's drive-train warranty? This is a no-brainer, but keep the vehicle until it's out of warranty because most of your repairs are covered until this point at no or little cost to you. Even if the repair is outside the scope of the warranty, it likely still makes financial sense to hold on to the car until the end of the warranty period.

4. Is your vehicle paid off? This is where the math of vehicle ownership becomes important. So many people will segue from one car payment to another, even rolling over old car debt into a new loan in a maddening snowball. (After all, do you really want to be paying for some heap in a junkyard today, years after you last sat behind its wheel?)

Owning a car may be a necessity in this day and age, but what's not required is overpaying for a depreciating asset. If you're buying vehicles that don't last at least three to six years beyond the date they are paid off, you're likely buying more car than you actually need and you're not adequately maintaining the vehicle along the way to help you stretch its useful life beyond the payment period.

Not that you should keep a dangerous wreck at this point, depending on your answers to questions 1 and 2 — but if the car isn't paid off yet, err on the side of repair, assuming you likely owe more than the car (especially in a state of disrepair) is worth.

If you do determine it's time to shop for a vehicle, choose used and aim for a traditionally reliable make and model. Certain cars, such as Honda, Volkswagen, Mazda, and Toyota, are known for having high resale values because these cars have proved over the years to have high-mileage capabilities with minimal repairs over time, Smyth says. (For 2014, Kelley Blue Book named Toyota as the brand that holds its resale value best, with Lexus topping the luxury segment.)

Words to the Wise

BONUS TIP!
Car Prices Are Higher, But You Can Still Score a Good Deal

If you're on the way to buying a new car soon, prepare for some sticker shock. The average cost of a new vehicle is $36,902, reports car-comparison site Edmunds.com. That's up 17% from 2013. Blame fancy new technology. Cars are safer than ever before, but all those sensors and cameras drive up the cost of a new vehicle.

An ordinary base-price car now costs an average of $25,200. An SUV will run you $34,400 on average, and a pickup truck costs an average of $47,200, according to Edmunds.

Take heart, though. An oversupply of SUVs means that dealers are more likely to discount a new car if you haggle. Sales of the popular vehicles rose 1.9% in the first half of 2019, down from 13.2% growth in the same period last year. They're sitting on dealer lots longer, too. If car loan rates stay low, there are deals to be made.

BONUS TIP!
Before You Let Someone Borrow the Car..

Is your vehicle covered if you let a family member or friend borrow it? Well, it actually varies by policy and insurance carrier. You'll want to find out from your insurance company before handing over your keys, Moore suggests. There are some typical coverage situations, though.

Generally, liability car insurance follows a driver, not a car. Therefore, in most instances, no matter what car you — or anyone else who has liability car insurance — drive, the policy likely covers damages up to the stated coverage limits. Comprehensive and collision coverage, meanwhile, is tied directly to a vehicle, not a driver. Moore says that portion of a policy's coverage should provide protection against any damages to your vehicle. If in doubt, ask.

Bonus Tip!
Cut Your Internet Costs

Competition between internet providers has never been stronger, but it can be a hassle to switch services. You may be locked into a contract, or you may wonder whether the new service will really be fast enough and reliable enough for your needs.

Here's a trick for getting a better deal without having to switch providers. Find a competitor who is offering a teaser rate or better deal. Call your current internet service provider and ask to speak to someone in the customer retention department. Say, "I'm thinking of switching to XYZ provider because I can get a better deal. Can you offer me a better rate if I stay?" Oftentimes, that will do the trick.

Bonus Tip!
An Easy Way to Slash Your Energy Bill

You can knock anywhere from 5 to 30 percent off your power bill by doing an energy audit, a close examination of your appliances, energy use, and insulation quality around your home. Many local power providers will do what's called a "walkthrough" audit for free, though the check will be mostly a cursory examination of your appliances and windows. If you want someone to get down in your crawl space with equipment to look for air leaks, that can run from a couple hundred bucks and up to $650 a visit. Or you can do a home energy audit on your owns using a checklist at energy.gov/energysaver (click on "Weatherize" for more).

Beware of companies offering free energy audits; They mostly are looking for a chance to sell you insulation or expensive new heating and cooling systems.

Chapter 4

Health Care

"THE BEST DOCTOR GIVES
THE LEAST MEDICINES."

Getting the Most Out of Medicare Benefits

The date you retire and the day you start Medicare are unlikely to coincide. Many Americans retire early, and many others choose to wait to collect Social Security. For Social Security, waiting to file can be a benefit, but with Medicare, waiting to enroll can cost you.

To confuse matters, there are different levels of Medicare coverage to consider. And in some cases, you have to make choices when you first enroll that you may not need or use until later in life. Let's address some key questions about enrolling in Medicare.

DO I NEED TO DO SOMETHING TO ENROLL?

Are you already on Social Security? Or will you be collecting Social Security benefits at least four months before you turn 65? If so, you don't have to take any action. You will be automatically enrolled in Medicare Part A, free hospital coverage, and Part B, a monthly premium you pay for doctor visits.

WHAT IF I'M TURNING 65 AND NOT COLLECTING SOCIAL SECURITY?

If you're about to turn 65 and not yet collecting Social Security, you have to enroll yourself. You can enroll during your Initial Enrollment Period, which is any time during the three months before, the month of, and the three months after you turn 65.

Alternatively, you can enroll during a Special Enrollment Period if you were covered by your own or a spouse's work insurance plan. In that case, you have eight months to sign up after you lose your employer-based group health insurance.

Finally, if you missed either of these enrollment periods, you can sign up during the General Enrollment Period (GEP), which is January 1 to March 31 of every year.

MUST I TAKE PART B COVERAGE?

Some folks might not need the doctor visit coverage from Medicare Part B right away because they're covered through a working spouse's plan, because they're still working, or because they have VA benefits. So it's optional.

WHAT HAPPENS IF I DON'T TAKE PART B?

You can enroll later in Part B, but it will cost you more. Expect a 10 percent higher monthly premium for each 12-month period you wait.

CAN I CHOOSE TO ADD PART B AT ANY TIME?

No, if you didn't take Part B when you first signed up, you won't be able to enroll until the first three months of the year, and coverage won't start until July 1. Wait two years and that's a 20 percent higher cost, waiting three years will cost you 30 percent more, and so on. And that additional premium cost is forever — not just in the year you sign up. So consider if a permanent 30 percent bump in monthly Part B premiums is worth it compared to saving today from your cheaper workplace plan?

WHAT'S NOT COVERED BY MEDICARE?

Essentially, Medicare covers most doctor visits and services or supplies that are needed to diagnose your condition. Exceptions include long-term care, dental care, eye exams for glasses, dentures, cosmetic surgery, acupuncture, hearing aids, and routine foot care. Remember, you will have deductibles, coinsurance, and copayments as well.

WHAT IS PART C AND DO I NEED IT?

To make matters even more confusing, Part C is not a supplement to Parts A and B. It replaces them. Part C, also called Medicare Advantage, is a private insurance plan that is an alternative to traditional Medicare.

WHY WOULD I CHOOSE PART C INSTEAD?

Some people prefer Part C instead of Parts A and B because it's cheaper and/or because Medicare Advantage (Part C) typically offers more benefits, such as dental and vision coverage, and greater choice of doctors.

CAN I CHANGE MY MIND LATER ON PART C COVERAGE?

Besides having to shop around to see if Part C is a good fit for you, there are limits on enrollment periods. Your window to choose a Medicare Advantage plan is the three months before you turn

65, the month you turn 65, plus the three months after, totaling seven months.

If you want to move from original Medicare to a Medicare Advantage plan (Part C) later on, the enrollment period is Oct. 15 to Dec. 7. To switch between competing Advantage plans, the enrollment period is Jan. 1 to March 31.

WHAT'S THE RISK OF MOVING TO TRADITIONAL MEDICARE LATER ON IN RETIREMENT?

Mostly it's the Part B delay penalty. Putting off Part B now to choose a Medicare Advantage plan (Part C) would still require you to pay a higher Part B premium later if you decide to move to traditional Medicare and elect Part B doctor visit coverage.

DO I NEED PART D, MEDICARE PRESCRIPTION DRUG COVERAGE?

Drug coverage is optional under Medicare and comes with a premium. Most Medicare Advantage plans offer prescription drug coverage. If you choose traditional Medicare, you can pay for Part D coverage or simply skip the plan altogether and pay for drugs yourself.

IS THERE A PENALTY FOR DECIDING LATER ON TO TAKE PART D?

As with Part B, there is a cost to waiting to take Part D, roughly 1 percent more on base drug prices set by Medicare nationally for each month you wait. Of course, that's an extra 1 percent for the rest of your life on drug prices that also tend to rise every year.

This penalty kicks in if you go more than 63 days without coverage elsewhere, say from a Medicare Advantage plan, an employer, a union, or other coverage with comparable pricing.

Alternative Health Remedies
That Are — and Aren't — Worth It

When most people have a health issue, they call the doctor. However, increasingly people are taking chances on a health remedies they discover online — such as coconut oil for a skin rash. Of course, not every health remedy works. But because of the internet, we have access to so many ideas and products that other people swear by. Aren't at least some of them legitimate? If so, which ones?

We put these questions to Paul Offit, MD, a professor at the University of Pennsylvania and Children's Hospital of Philadelphia. He regularly writes books and articles for the general public on medicine.

The problem, he explained, is evidence. There just isn't solid proof for many remedies, because the alternative medicine industry isn't required to provide it. "If this was regulated in the same manner that the pharmaceutical industry is, then you'd have to prove that it worked," he says.

Nonetheless, we wanted to know what he thought of some common health remedies (and some products) advertised online. He shared which are worth your time and money to try.

REIKI

The claim: A Reiki session, during which a practitioner places their hands lightly on or over the body, can reduce pain and speed healing from illness or injury.

The verdict: Worth it. "I think you can learn to release your own cortisol, which can affect your immune system," Offit says. Many hospitals are starting to include Reiki as a complement to standard care.

MAGNETIC BRACELETS

The claim: Magnets draw the iron in your red blood cells, increasing blood flow and promoting healing.

The verdict: Not worth it. "The flaw in that logic is that the iron in your red blood cells is not magnetizable," Offit says. "It's built on a false premise."

CHICKEN SOUP

The claim: When you have a cold, eating chicken soup will make you feel better faster.

The verdict: Worth it. "Yes, chicken soup is of value," Offit says. Ongoing research hopes to identify exactly why. Studies have shown that chicken soup improves the flow of nasal mucus better than plain hot water, and that the soup helps the tiny hairs in the nose (cilia) work better. Other findings indicate that the common soup ingredients of garlic, onions, and ginger have antiviral properties.

DRY BODY BRUSHING

The claim: Using a soft but firm brush daily on the skin will stimulate the lymphatic system, improve circulation, help exfoliate, clean pores and reduce cellulite.

The verdict: Not worth it. "When you hear that you're going to, in any way, affect your lymphatic drainage by something that you do to your skin — it's absurd," Offit says.

DUCT TAPE

The claim: Covering a wart with duct tape for a few days is as effective as cryotherapy (a dermatologist freezing off the wart with liquid nitrogen).

The verdict: Worth it. Warts aren't a medical emergency, and you probably already have the duct tape. "It has some biological basis in fact," Offit says of the remedy. "It probably has something to do with drying associated with the duct tape."

ALKALINE WATER

The claim: Water with a pH higher than normal drinking water can neutralize acid in the body, slowing the aging process and preventing chronic diseases.

The verdict: Not worth it. The human body works very hard to keep itself at a constant pH of roughly 7.2, Offit says. "You could drink all the alkaline you want. That's not going to change the pH in your bloodstream."

MELATONIN

The claim: The hormone melatonin can treat sleep disorders when taken as a supplement.

The verdict: Worth it. Offit generally doesn't recommend vitamins and supplements, but he says melatonin is one of the few that "meets manufacturing and labeling standards, and that actually has good data," he says.

ESSENTIAL OILS

The claim: Distilled from plant leaves, roots, and flowers, essential oils improve immunity, speed illness recovery, treat skin problems, and balance hormones.

The verdict: Not worth it. "I would put that in the unlikely category," Offit says. "The way to boost your immunity is to just eat healthy foods."

HYPNOTHERAPY

The claim: Hypnosis changes your perception of pain and help you change habits.

The verdict: Worth it. Offit says that perception change can be powerful. "You can perceive smoking as being more distasteful than you had before," he says. Studies also indicate that hypnotherapy is effective for treating symptoms of irritable bowel syndrome and reducing hot flashes in postmenopausal women.

Words to the Wise

BONUS TIP!
A Quick Way to Slash In-Hospital Healthcare Costs ...

Hospitals are now required to publish their costs of services online, offering price tags for specific services in detail. Nevertheless, healthcare experts note that the price quotes you might find are likely the highest possible charge, not necessarily what you would be assessed or have to pay.

Insurance companies regularly get big discounts for agreed-upon services, and most hospitals will negotiate a favorable payment plan for any costs that are not covered by insurance.

If you get a large bill, first contact your insurance company and ask if the payments from their side are complete. (Oftentimes, the itemized bill shows this to be the case.) Should the remaining balance seem unmanageable, don't ignore it. Call the hospital billing department and ask for a payment arrangement. A full year to pay with no interest charge is a common response.

Bonus Tip!
Before You Fill That Prescription . . .

The next time you have to fill a prescription, check with your insurance company's website before you head to the drugstore. That's because Express Scripts and CVS Caremark, companies which provide pharmacy benefit management to lots of health plans, recently dropped coverage for 90 drugs.

As a result, you might go to pick up your regular prescription and find that the price has shot up dramatically.

You have options, though. One is to ask your doctor to prescribe another drug, one that is covered and also treats your condition. It might be a generic or simply a cheaper competing non-generic.

You also can try transferring your prescription to one of the deep discount providers, such as Costco. Another strategy is to ask the pharmacist if there is a coupon offer, such as from GoodRX, so you can sidestep insurance altogether.

Finally, many drug companies will lower drug costs if you petition for a break based on your ability to pay. Don't skip your prescription in any case. Some pharmacists will issue you a short-term supply of a week's pills at a lower cost if you need time to strategize a way to buy the full supply you need.

Chapter 5

Your Home

"A HOUSE IS NOT A HOME UNLESS IT
CONTAINS FOOD AND FIRE FOR THE
MIND AS WELL AS THE BODY."

Home Inspection Tips
That Save You Money

Hiring a home inspector is a common part of the homebuying process. They promise to help you avoid everything from leaks and drips to mold and shaky foundations. But that protection can cost anywhere from a few hundred dollars to $1,000 or more, depending on the size and location of the property. So before you hire a home inspector, it's important to know exactly what you're getting.

Home inspectors aren't regulated by federal guidelines. Each state has its own licensing and/or certification requirements. That puts the onus on you to find a reputable inspector. Start by choosing an inspector who is not recommended by your realtor. Inspectors recommended by realtors often go easy on the flaws. Next, verify the inspector's references. Finally, review the items that will be covered during the inspection. They should include:

LEAKY WALLS AND VALVES

Inspectors typically look for evidence of past water damage, but they can't see things hidden in walls. That means there could still be a slow leak inside a wall that won't be seen unless the drywall is removed. In addition, if a seller turns off a valve, that can mask a leak, too.

"We generally do not operate things like valves or other devices," explains Welmoed Sisson, a home inspector at Inspections by Bob in Maryland. So an inspector won't turn on water that's shut off at the meter or valve. In most instances, an inspector only runs enough water to ascertain whether or not the fixture drains properly and the drain plug is functional.

MOLD

Inspectors can take air samples in different rooms and send them to a lab to see if you have mold. Because you can't see inside walls, this test is crucial, especially in southern areas where the climate is warm and humid.

THE ROOF

Home inspectors often rely on the age of the roof to determine how long they think it will last. They rarely walk around a roof to obtain a first-hand look. And Sisson cautions that age isn't indicative of workmanship. A roof might be rated to last 30 years, but if a contractor cut corners when installing, it could leak a few years after installation.

CENTRAL AIR CONDITIONING

If you're buying a home during chilly months, an inspector cannot test the A/C. That's because running an air conditioning unit at an outdoor temperature of 65 degrees or less can damage the unit.

BUILDING CODES

Unfortunately, many home inspectors are not versed on current building codes, mostly because those vary by municipality. Make sure the inspector you choose is aware of health-specific code risks, like deck railing heights or spindle spacing.

DIY IMPROVEMENTS

Home improvements completed with low-quality materials or not installed properly aren't typically on a home inspector's checklist. So if the basement is finished without proper permits, or electrical wiring isn't installed to code, you could face an expensive, unexpected renovation.

AGING APPLIANCES

A home inspector might not test all the features of an appliance. In fact, they rarely run a washing machine or dishwasher cycle. Ask your inspector to check the water dispenser on the fridge, the washing machine, dryer, microwave, oven, and dishwasher.

Another tip: Check the model numbers of appliances and Google them to find when they manufactured and to read reviews. That will give you an idea of when you may need to replace them.

CRACKED SEWAGE AND DRAINAGE PIPES

A typical home inspection is limited to what is visible and accessible, meaning that cracks in underground or buried pipes and drain lines would go undetected. It may be worth it to pay more for a camera inspection.

DAMP PORCHES, DECKS, AND BALCONIES

Decks and balconies are common sources of costly leaks, according to Bill Leys, owner of Division 7 Waterproofing Consultants and a deck inspector in San Luis Obispo, California. "Many homeowners don't understand the cost of damage can surge to $100,000 from a leaky deck or balcony. There's also the potential of serious safety issues and risk of collapse." Ask your inspector to check these areas for possible damage.

Bottom line: Consider having a contractor inspect areas you're concerned about, such as wiring or the roof, in addition to having a home inspection.

When Renting is a Better Financial Move Than Buying

It's the American dream, but is owning a house always a good financial idea?

For many, home values are skyrocketing, sending already high property taxes soaring. Consider if your property tax obligation is basically the equivalent of buying a new economy car straight off the dealer's lot or paying for a year of college at a public university. When you keep in mind that you'll have to foot that hefty bill as long as you see yourself staying in your house, you may begin to wonder, "Is it even worth it to own a home?"

At first, it sounds like a joke to sell and rent, but coupled with the costs of homeowners insurance, maintenance, and upkeep, your real estate investment may be taking an ever-increasing chunk of your income. Is it time to ask if it's the best use of your money?

Kara Stachel, a real estate attorney and owner of a title company with offices in Florida and Pennsylvania, suggests that it's important not to buy into the myth that owning a home is definitely a solid financial move.

"Renting is not always more expensive than buying," she said. "Depending on where you live or are looking to live, there are instances where renting may actually be less expensive than having a mortgage and all the other expenses that come with it."

Before making a decision either way, run the numbers. Certainly the best decision will depend on your unique situation. However, there are a few times when renting (even temporarily) can undeniably be the better option.

Consider the following situations:

YOU'RE NOT ROOTED.

Anna Keisler, CFP, an associate adviser with SG Financial Advisors in metro Atlanta, Georgia, notes that it's smart to rent if you'll soon make a life change that will involve moving. Maybe you're on the verge of retirement and considering relocating. Or you're looking to relocate for a new job or to live closer to family.

Before committing to 30 years' ownership of a white picket fence, Keisler recommends trying out the new area with the flexibility of a lease. That way, you can get to know the area and decide where you might like to buy, while still having the freedom to move at the end of your lease (or cancel it if necessary). Renting gives you a chance to try out different neighborhoods until you are comfortable with a specific area to put down roots.

In a similar situation, it can also make sense to rent if you know you plan to move in a few years. For example, say you may be planning to relocate to after a child moves out of the house or finishes school. In addition to saving a boatload of money by renting, you would also have the flexibility of knowing that you can pack up and leave quickly at the end of a lease versus waiting for your house to sell.

This may make sense especially if real estate values in your area appreciate slowly. Make sure you have your home valued by a realtor and the market, not the town assessor, to get an idea of what your appreciation has been in the time you've owned it.

What's more, it's possible your home's value may not be expected to increase significantly in the next several years, depending on the economic outlook for the area. Meanwhile, you'd be paying a significant amount in taxes and insurance.

YOU'RE BI-ZIP CODE.

The lure of more pleasant weather or being closer to grandkids may find you considering dual residency in two or more areas. But instead of paying maintenance, taxes, and other costs on properties you'll occupy part-time, it might make sense to rent in one or both locations.

In this instance, renting can bring peace of mind, too. There are no worries that your pipes will burst during a harsh northern winter while you're toasty warm out West. You won't have to wonder if the yard on one property is being maintained while you're living in another. Additionally, you won't have to bear the costs of any repairs on properties you don't own either.

While it will be a challenge living for the next four years in a place that lacks some of the homey touches you like, the sting of temporarily renting will be overshadowed by the thousands you might save during your stint as lessees.

These Home Improvements
Offer the Biggest Payoffs

Are you looking to sell your house soon? Or simply protect it from weather events and day to day wear? It's wise to consider what investments have the biggest returns. What home improvements are likely to pay for themselves when a house is sold?

According to Remodeling magazine's latest Cost Versus Value Report, of 29 common remodeling projects that it examined, the one that brought the top return was adding fiberglass insulation to an attic (bringing a 107 percent return). The runner up: Replacing a wooden front door with a new steel one (77 percent).

That news surprised us, as the common knowledge says that the best way to increase a house's value is by doing major kitchen or bathroom upgrades. However, these remodels received relatively low scores, recouping only about two-thirds of their costs. (New windows ranked higher — returning about three-quarters of their investment.)

Of course, housing markets differ greatly. What's in demand in Florida may not be in Alaska, so these national averages should be taken with a grain of salt. But if you're thinking about selling your house in the near future, here are some guidelines on which home improvements make the most sense:

1. Consider improvements that add to your home's curb appeal.
Justin Riordan of Spade and Archer Design stages homes for sale in
Seattle, Portland, and Palm Springs. He says today's buyers typically
see about two dozen photos of a home online before visiting it. For
that reason, he says curb appeal now includes anything that can be
captured on camera and makes the home seem more inviting.

Riordan says improvements that boost curb appeal are especially important in hot housing markets. But in a market where sales are depressed,
he concedes that buyers are usually less concerned about a home's appearance and more concerned that everything is in good working order.

2. Know the demographics of buyers in your area.
This advice comes from Amy Chorew, director of education for Better Homes and Gardens Realty and a Connecticut realtor. She says
middle-aged buyers with big budgets often want a turnkey house that
requires minimal changes. If that's your target buyer, she says investing in significant kitchen and bath renovations may bring the biggest
payoff. On the other hand, young buyers may be looking for a house
that can handle a growing family. To meet their needs, Chorew advises projects that result in more usable space, like adding a bedroom or
finishing a basement or laundry room.

3. Know your neighborhood.
To be competitive, your home needs to have features that are in line
with other homes in the area. Chorew recommends getting a professional analysis of homes that have recently sold in your neighborhood. That will help you decide what is worth adding.

4. Keep up with the latest trends.
Buyers are easily put off by a house that looks dated. That's why your
real estate agent should be keeping up with the latest trends.

For example, blue bathrooms are now the rage; homes with them
are reportedly selling for $5,400 more than expected. To find out for
yourself what are the current hits with homebuyers, check websites
like www.hgtv.com, www.houzz.com, www.bhg.com, or www.pinter-
est.com. But since trends change, it's wise to avoid radical styles or
color schemes that could quickly go out of fashion.

5. Don't ignore the home's infrastructure.

Riordan says one reason new front doors and windows tend to be good investments is that they lower a home's operating costs, while adding to its visual appeal. Similarly, Chorew reports demand is high for homes with green features like energy-efficient appliances and smart features, like interactive thermostats.

6. Minor fixes can have major payoffs.

Don't think you have to spend a lot for an improvement to pay off; even inexpensive ones can have a huge impact. Some of the most cost-effective can be interior or exterior painting (in neutral colors), refinishing floors and installing new light fixtures. And rather than do a full kitchen or bathroom renovation, just replacing cabinet doors or putting in granite countertops can do wonders.

Of course, the biggest home sales season doesn't officially begin until the spring. But now is the perfect time to contract for improvements to get your home ready for sale. By doing the work over the next few months, your home can be ready to go on the market as soon as the snow melts!

When to Choose a High or Low Deductible

It's a fact of life that homes deteriorate as they age. From plumbing to heating and air conditioning, components eventually fail, often causing significant damage. And it's easy for such accidents to drain your finances.

Homeowner's insurance is the way to protect against that. However, it's easy to overpay for a policy. How? By insisting on one with a low deductible.

Indeed, Professor Justin Sydnor of the University of Wisconsin studied 50,000 homeowner's policies issued by a major insurer. Although the company offered a $1,000 deductible, most of the customers opted to pay an extra $100 to lower the deductible to $500. But few got any of that money back. The low deductible ended up costing more than four times what it was worth!

CAUTION: MAKING A CLAIM CAN BE RISKY

Why did so many customers make that losing bet? Sydnor thinks they simply overestimated their odds of having an in-home accident. During the year he tracked, only 5 percent of the group filed any claim.

But that may not be the whole story. It's possible that while more people had accidents, many decided not to file claims for their damages. They may have opted to pay for damages out of pocket because they feared getting into hot water with their insurance company.

Say a pipe inside your house leaks, causing $6,000 in damage. Because your policy has a deductible of $4,800, you to put in a claim and collect $1,200. While this may seem standard, an insurance adjuster we consulted said that would be foolish. She warned that could lead your insurer to raise your premiums — or drop you as a customer.

Independent insurance agent David Shaffer of Walnut Creek, California, thinks that may be an overreaction; he's never seen a company refuse to renew a homeowner's policy after just one claim. But he warns that if you make more than one claim every 10 years, watch out. Shaffer says insurers are then likely to drastically hike your rates or refuse to renew your policy. (The specific actions vary by company and state.)

We checked on that with insurance industry spokesperson Loretta Worters. She denied that any 10-year standard exists. But she confirmed that having frequent or unusually large claims could lead to those penalties.

It's much the same with car insurance. Putting in one claim for an accident may or may not put you on the road to higher rates. (Some companies even offer "accident forgiveness" on a first accident to customers with good driving records.)

But making several claims almost always brands you as a bad risk and means paying much higher premiums.

And once you've made multiple claims against your auto or homeowner's policy, don't expect to get significantly lower rates by switching to a competing insurer. Property insurers have set up a giant database that allows them to easily share claims information with each other. That means there's little chance that other companies will be unaware of your previous claims history.

Buying a Vacation Home
Without Wasting Money

As summer winds down, your thoughts may be turning to trying to get out of town for that last vacation while the weather is still nice. Do you have a favorite spot, somewhere you return to, that you might think of investing in as a you towards retirement?

Nearly 6 percent of Americans have a second home. And demand for vacation homes remains strong. Last year, nearly a million were sold in the U.S. at a median price of $192,000. The National Association of Realtors reports that baby boomers at or near retirement were the largest group of buyers.

It's not hard to understand why. When you're working, you typically get only two to six weeks off per year. If you hold the vacation home for seven years, your total time in the house will amount to between 14 and 42 weeks. And that assumes that you spend every vacation there. Of course, retirees have unlimited vacation time. So in theory, they should be able to get more use out of a second home.

BEFORE YOU BUY . . .

That is often the case — but not always. Many retirees buy a home by the beach or in the mountains, with the idea of spending time there with their children and grandchildren. However, it often becomes increasingly difficult for families with children to get away, especially if a job transfer takes them to a different part of the country.

When that happens, the retirees often decide to shorten their time at the second home and instead visit the children and grandchildren where they live. Then, as they get older, these retirees may have to cut back on travel entirely. Either way, the second home may get used less and less. So be sure it will be someplace that you and/or your whole family will enjoy for some time to come.

Remember, too, that regardless of the amount of time you spend in it, a vacation home's expenses don't stop. Besides mortgage payments (if the house isn't purchased for cash), the owner must pay property taxes, insurance, utilities, repairs, and general maintenance. Depending on where the home is, these costs can total $2,500 a month or more. If you're retired and also have to pay your primary home's expenses, that can really strain your budget, so be sure you can afford the second home.

Some people offset the expenses by renting out the vacation home when it's unused. Rental websites like homeaway.com and airbnb.com make that easy. However, demand for rentals varies. Consider whether the home you're looking at is near a ski area or a major metropolitan destination, for example.

Also, don't assume that your vacation property will pay for itself through appreciation. During the housing crash of eight years ago, home values in prime vacation areas like Florida and Arizona actually plummeted in value.

But not buying doesn't mean you'll have to forget about summers in your destination of choice. In searching for a place to rent, look for choices that will cost you less than buying and maintaining a house year round. That can be a wonderful alternative if the costs don't work out for your finances.

Pros and Cons of Paying Off Your Mortgage Early

One of the largest line items in most household budgets is a home mortgage. And the chance to crack that tough nut by paying off a mortgage early is an opportunity many homeowners would love to have. But experts say it might not be the savviest financial option.

There are pros and cons to paying off a mortgage early or sticking with it, making monthly payments for the duration of a loan. That said, here are reasons you may want to pay it off sooner rather than later:

1. The tax deduction isn't as valuable as many think.
One of the main reasons people think a mortgage shouldn't be paid early is the loss of an income tax deduction. Experts have some startling counterpoints to this thinking.

"The only way to get the tax deduction is if you itemize it on your taxes," says Sam Farrington, a financial planner at Sound Mind Financial Planning in Omaha, Nebraska.

According to an analysis by Congressional Research Service, only 32 percent of American's itemize, so unless you're part of the itemizing crowd, the deduction argument doesn't hold water.

The Tax Cuts and Jobs Act also revised the mortgage interest deduction for many people, depending on income and marital status.

If you do itemize, Farrington says the mortgage deduction might not be worth it. If your mortgage has a balance of $200,000 and an interest rate of 5 percent, Farrington says in the past you'd pay around $10,000 in interest.

If you happen to be in the 25 percent tax bracket, you can deduct 25 percent of the $10,000 worth of interest on your taxes, which comes to $2,500.

"If you didn't have a mortgage, you'd have to pay the IRS taxes on the $10,000 you can no longer deduct, which means you're sending Uncle Sam an extra $2,500 at tax time," explains Farrington.

You have to ask yourself what's a better scenario. Paying the bank $10,000 of interest in order to deduct $2,500 off your tax bill (you're in the hole $7,500) or keeping the $10,000 and paying Uncle Sam $2,500 (you wind up ahead $7,500).

If you have a mortgage and can take the deduction, by all means do it. "But, the argument to keep the mortgage in order to receive a deduction isn't a good one," says Farrington.

2. You might not get better returns by investing.
Farrington says another popular argument for not paying off a house is there may be better returns to be had investing the money you'd use to pay off a mortgage. "While this may be true from time to time, the market is an unknown, cautions Farrington. It's just as possible for the market to experience a surge as it is a significant loss.

"However, paying your mortgage off is a guaranteed return on your money based on the interest rate you're paying," Farrington says.

3. A factor not always figured in: peace of mind.
The ability to make different decisions with less financial risk comes from not having a mortgage. Maybe you don't like your current job and have always wanted to go back to school, switch careers, or start your own business. With the largest expense in most household budgets a non-factor, those decisions are easier and not nearly as risky.

"Paying off a mortgage can also provide some level of asset protection when it comes to claiming Medicaid for long-term care, depending on the state," says Curt Sheldon, CFP, president and lead planner, C.L. Sheldon & Company, LLC, in Alexandria, Va.

WHY YOU MAY WANT THAT MORTGAGE

Financial independence doesn't just mean having the income to cover your normal expenses. It means having the ability to absorb large expenses or spend money on desires, too — i.e., having the liquidity to absorb financial shocks and planned outlays.

And if your income is almost entirely annuitized, either through wages or in retirement through a pension or Social Security, then spending down income and assets to pay off the mortgage can be a mistake in the long run, Sheldon says.

If you put yourself in a limited liquidity situation, you may have to take out a reverse mortgage or home equity line of credit to pay for unexpected expenses or to do something like take a big trip with the grandchildren. "These options are expensive," Sheldon adds.

Shop for a Home with Resale Value in Mind to Make More Money

Satisfying your "must-have" checklist is important when shopping for a new home. Does it have enough bedrooms? Is it in a neighborhood you like? But what many forget is perhaps the most important question of all: When the time comes, would you be able to sell it easily?

"I counsel my buyers that it's important to do all you can to buy a home that has the potential to be sold," says Rob Levy, a principal broker with Keller Williams Realty Professionals in Portland, Ore. and Palm Springs, Calif. "That way, if they must sell their home right in the middle of the next recession or have to move quickly due to loss of job or relocation, (they won't be stuck)."

That means looking at the house with a dispassionate, critical eye. Flaws you think you can "live with" or overlook because the home is otherwise perfect for you could be a deal-breaker to the next potential buyer. There are several key features you should consider to stack the deck in your favor when it's time to sell.

- **Don't build (or buy) your dream house.** When opting for new construction, home buyers need to exercise caution and enforce a strict budget related to optional finishes, extras, and add-ons. "Too frequently, a buyer will add unnecessary finishes that not only fail to add to the bottom line, but can take away from the overall improved value," says Bob Gordon, Realtor with Re/Max Alliance in Boulder, Colo. If you build, keep an eye toward resale and the percent of the cost of upgrades you'll be able to recoup when you sell.

- **Assess the homeowners association.** The stringent rules, approval process for property upgrades or improvements, and fees or assessments can reduce your resale value, says Ron Rovtar, a Realtor with Front Range Real Estate, Ltd., in Denver, Colo.

- **Keep score.** Good HERS, Energy Star, or LEEDS ratings or certifications will continue to be of importance to the millennial generation and beyond, Rovtar points out. Millennials already account for 31 percent of U.S. homebuyers and that number will only increase over the next decade. "Buying a home with a good Home Energy Rating System score or a widely accepted energy efficiency certification can really help sell a home down the road," he says.

- **Learn the easements.** Even though you own a parcel of land, the town or local utility company may have rights to the property via an easement or right of way. If that's the case, the town or utility is able to dictate what can — and cannot — be done to the land. And while the inability to plant trees or place a shed on the easement might not deter you from purchasing the property, it could dissuade someone you hope to someday sell to.

- **Avoid shoddy craftsmanship.** Rovtar suggests visiting the local code enforcement office before signing a purchase offer. "Home construction and improvement projects, like a new deck or a finished basement, done without all required permits might not have been completed properly," he says. And while that might not matter to you, it could be a sticking point to someone interested in buying your house when you're ready to sell.

- **Be wary of master bedrooms not on the ground floor.** During the next 17 years, 10,000 people a day will turn 65. And as we age, climbing and descending stairs to get to and from a bedroom can be hard on tired knees and other joints. "This makes a master bedroom on the main floor or a single-level home a good choice to protect resale value," Levy says.
- **Learn the ecological and/or regional issues.** A dream home can quickly become a nightmare to sell because of environmental or ecological issues, says Rovtar. For instance, "fracking in the region has been scaring away buyers and negatively affecting home values," he says. Other potential pitfalls to investigate before buying include if a manufacturing factory or plant is — or was once — on or near the premises. Plants that still operate can emit offensive odors that turn off potential buyers; and those that are closed down, and possibly even gone, may have contaminated the soil. The same goes for former gas stations that may have left behind leaky fuel or oil tanks in the ground. Expansive soil — it expands when wet and contracts when dry — can cause serious problems with foundations. Rovtar says a good real estate agent should be able to help you identify these types of local problems.
- **Watch where the sun rises.** The orientation of the house can greatly impact its resale value, Levy says. For instance, having a driveway with a southern exposure in a snowy area means less shoveling and ice build-up in the winter — it's not something you need to disclose, but a savvy buyer may ask (and you may indeed need to sell in the winter). A yard facing west can get too hot in warm, sunny climates. "You have to think of the house's orientation and the climate to maximize resale value," Levy says.
- **View the property from all available angles.** Having a park or open space next door is an obvious benefit. But, park or not, Levy also suggests taking a look at your potential property from above before buying to assess how views can impact your resale value. Google Earth and several real estate Internet sites like Zillow or Trulia offer a bird's-eye view of a property for free. "You may be surprised by what you see from that vantage point," says Levy. This perspective may reveal a nearby eyesore, congested intersection, or other factors that can lower resale value.

Increase Your Home's Appeal
On a Budget

Whether you're selling your home or just want to spruce it up, landscaping is a great way to improve your property value. Homes with leafy surroundings have been shown to command higher prices and sell more quickly than those without.

To find out which upgrades are the most advantageous, we spoke to Rick Campbell, co-author of *Landscaping Makes Cents: Smart Investments That Increase Your Property Value*, and owner and president of Gnome Landscapes, Design, Masonry & Maintenance in Falmouth, Maine. His five top recommendations:

1. **Consult a landscape designer.** The DIY route can be fun if you have years to experiment through trial and error. But when you need results right away, involve a professional. A landscape designer will explain what elements of your yard have value already and what plants work best with your home's sun exposure and architectural style. "When you have a cohesive design," Campbell says, "it's going to increase the property value even more."

2. **Tend to your steps.** If your front or back steps have seen better days, don't think buyers and visitors won't notice. If replacement is necessary, opt for stone steps (granite, basalt, slate, bluestone) over brick ones, which require high-cost masonry expertise to install. "Granite is really forever," Campbell says. The material is affordable and solid, so water won't have a chance to get in and do damage, he adds.

3. **Choose annuals.** These flowers live just one year, but they stay in bloom for longer than perennials, which return year after year. Annuals also are less expensive when buying established plants. "If you want to sell your house [this] year, buy annuals, not perennials," Campbell suggests.

4. **Think patio, not deck.** Most families want an outdoor space to enjoy a meal and watch the kids play, Campbell says. Rather than installing a deck, a structure typically built of wood, he suggests a patio made of brick, concrete, or cobblestone

pavers. "A patio is less maintenance and less expense initially," Campbell says. "If you have a choice, a patio is going to be a better buy."

5. **Got time? Plant saplings.** Despite what you've heard, money does grow on trees, Campbell says. According to data collected by the U.S. Department of Agriculture, each large tree in the front yard increases a home's sale price by 1 percent. However, transplanting a fully grown tree can cost thousands of dollars. Instead, plant young trees for a fraction of the cost and give them time to grow — about three years to establish root systems and flourish, Campbell says.

Speed Up Your Homeowners Insurance Claims

You never know when a disaster will strike — whether it's theft, damage, or weather related. But when it does, the priority is to restore your life. A home inventory documents your contents and the value of your possessions to help expedite the claims process.

"When someone is affected by a property loss, whether damage or theft, they have a lot to think about," says Karen R. O'Neil, spokeswoman for The Hanover Insurance Group. "Having a detailed inventory alleviates one major concern for the insured and allows the adjuster to start pricing new items right away." Additionally, it's often hard to remember what you had in the event of a catastrophic loss like a fire after the fact.

There are two keys to a good home inventory: item descriptions and proof of ownership. For electronics or appliances, that means serial numbers, make and model, along with receipts or warranty information. For collector's items or jewelry, appraisals are recommended. "Make sure to include anything you would want to replicate in the event of a loss," O'Neil says. In addition to items like electronics, furniture, and artwork, think about a collection of high-value pocketbooks, sports equipment, and china.

Some compile their inventory room by room. Others start with the most valuable items and move on. O'Neil suggests including images and/or video with your list. "As they say, a picture is worth a thousand words." she says.

Keeping your inventory current is key. Do it when you move, during a remodel if you're upgrading furniture and electronics, too, or a set time of year.

Keep your inventory in a safe place, away from home — with a family member or in a safe-deposit box. Save an electronic copy on a cloud-based server such as Google Drive or a home inventory website, that is accessible in an emergency. Your agent also may keep a copy of your home inventory in your file.

O'Neil says home inventories are a great tool for evaluating coverage. "Many homeowners don't realize the value of their possessions before going through the exercise of listing items for an inventory," she says.

7 Ways to Save on Realtor Commissions

The standard commission that sellers pay for most residential properties is 5 to 7 percent, with a cooperating broker (representing a buyer) receiving half of that amount. That's a lot — especially if it's a home you're taking a loss on, or barely eking out a gain.

What a lot of sellers mistakenly assume, however, is that the commission is set in stone. Not all Realtors will haggle, but real estate commissions are indeed flexible. You just need to know when to negotiate, and how to recognize when a cheaper rate actually means "cut-rate service."

"Although I negotiate my commission on a regular basis with my clients, I do believe the worst mistake a home seller can make is selecting a Realtor based on the lowest fee and highest sales price," says Barry Miller, a Realtor and owner of Buy Homes Denver Realty.

If you want to sell your property quickly and at top dollar, you should consider at least talking to a licensed Realtor who will make the investment of time in your listing. "That includes heavily marketing the property in the best possible manner," says Janet Lawless Christ, the top-producing Realtor at Coldwell Banker Previews International in Rancho Santa Fe, Calif.

That marketing, which is part of the commission paid at closing, includes photography, video, signage, print advertising, printed collateral material, intense digital advertising, on-site parties, caravans, open houses, and many more facets. "That all costs money, and the listing agent pays those costs with reimbursement coming out of their commission once the property successfully closes escrow," Christ points out.

That doesn't mean you can't whittle down the commission price a bit. And even a little bit can make a big difference. If you sell your house for $200,000, shaving 1 percent off the commission rate nets you $2,000 more.

Here's how you can get the biggest bang for your commission buck, Miller says, without compromising the level of service or risking your home sitting in inventory longer than necessary.

1. **Act fast.** Commission discussions and negotiations should occur before signing a contract with a Realtor. In fact, asking about commission rates and talking about the possibility to negotiate the rate is one of the first things you should discuss with a Realtor.

2. **Know who you're negotiating with.** Most negotiated commission rates have to be approved by the firm the agent is affiliated with. Ask your agent if it's possible to schedule a commission negotiation meeting that includes their boss or the decision-maker at the real estate firm you're dealing with.

3. **Crunch your numbers in advance.** Instead of simply asking for a "lower" rate, walk into the negotiations with a number you're willing to pay. That way you'll look like a confident professional rather than someone simply looking for a deal.

4. **Two deals are better than one.** If you're in the market to buy a house, using the same agent may help you land a lower commission rate. Frances Dawson, a Realtor at Prudential Carolinas in Charlotte, N.C., says the easiest way to successfully negotiate a lower commission is if your listing agent is the one credited with selling you a new home.

   "Even if the client is moving from/to another area or state, it's a regular practice to research and refer my client to an appropriate Realtor in the second location. That Realtor will typically agree to pay me a referral fee, which is very common in the industry," Dawson says. "If my client allows me to assist with both transactions in any way, I can certainly modify the commission."

5. **Offer your services.** You may be able to justify a lower commission rate by tapping into some of your own talents and strengths. If you have (or can shoot) high-quality photos of your home that show off its assets, offer them to your Realtor for promotional material and online listings. That can save a Realtor the expense of hiring a professional photographer.

   The same goes for wording on literature. No one knows your home better than you, so if you're a whiz with words, suggests putting together and printing out a bulleted list of your home's standout features, upgrades, etc., that can be handed out during showings and open houses.

6. **Ask about package options.** Many Realtors have different commission rates for varying service packages. Some packages may provide more seller "hand holding," a greater amount of marketing, etc. And while you will get what you pay for, you may be able to sell your house even after paying for fewer bells and whistles, especially if you can fulfill some of the "added" or extra duties yourself.

7. **Ask about hourly rates.** In some instances, real estate agents may agree to work on a set hourly rate, rather than a flat fee or fee based on commission. If your housing market is hot and your house is pristine, this may be an option. You do have to carefully calculate your potential costs, however — ask your Realtor for an estimate of hours he or she thinks will be needed for your listing to make sure this is the most economical option.

Maximize the Profit From Your Home Sale

The U.S. foreclosure rates are the lowest they've been in eight years, according to S&P/Case-Shiller. And while monthly gains are slowing, U.S. home prices appear to be rebounding, nearing mid-2004 levels. That has homeowners hoping to recoup some of their real estate investment by planting a "For Sale" sign in their front yard. Whether you're only considering selling your home or have it already on the market, these strategies will help you squeeze every possible penny from your property.

1. Let buyers know what's coming.

"Coming Soon" for-sale signs are a new trend aimed at generating buzz about an upcoming listing. "Putting a 'Coming Soon' sign on the front lawn gets people excited about the home before the listing is live and anyone can go in the property," says Steven Gendel, a Realtor and owner of Keller Williams Realty Inc. in Livingston, N.J. This can speed up the sale of a home as well as increase the number of offers, giving sellers more leverage to negotiate for a premium asking price.

"Soon-to-be buyers can increase traffic around the house by having a garage sale," suggests Kelly Hager, CEO, Kelly Hager Group Real Estate Services in St. Louis. "Shoppers will see the bright, colorful 'Coming Soon' sign in the yard." Collaborate with neighbors on a street wide garage sale to expose your property to even more potential buyers.

2. Invest in creative options.

In addition to targeting your home to residential consumer buyers, explore nontraditional markets, too. For example, the investor market, which Edmund Bogen, Realtor at Estates & Fine Homes LLC in Boca Raton, FL, says is currently booming. "Your local market may be producing a higher profit on income property than residential," he says.

To determine whether your abode might be attractive to investors, find out what similar properties are being rented at in your area. "Calculate the annual gross rent and divide that number by 10 to 12 percent, the average premium investors would expect to pay for income property, and you may land a higher asking price than you'd expect from a residential transaction."

3. Set the stage.

Hager says the golden rule of receiving the maximum sales price of a home is staging that home to sell. And that oversize sofa, 70-inch flat-screen TV, overflowing pantry, or litter box odor all break the staging rule. "Less is always more when it comes to furniture, knickknacks, etc.," Hager says.

And clear out personal things like pictures of your family, refrigerator decorations, dog beds, and toys or countertop items. Potential buyers need to visualize your house as their home, and your great-grandmother's wedding photos in your hall or your child's artwork hanging on the fridge — as cute as it may seem to you — could distract or hinder that visualization. "Decluttering and depersonalizing helps the home 'live better' than comparable properties, which typically leads to better offers," Hager adds.

4. Lighten up.

Following up on the last tip, you'll also want to take down heavy curtain and window treatments, open the shades or blinds, and trim landscaping away from windows to allow as much natural light as possible to come into your home. "That makes the home feel larger than what the actual square footage is," Hager says. "When the home feels larger than it truly is, we have seen sellers get closer to their asking price than with a home that doesn't feel as big and bright."

That's because when potential buyers compare a home with natural light, which feels open and bright, to another home with less natural light, they are more likely to feel the dim or dark house is smaller and not worth the asking price.

5. Clean up.

Hiring a professional cleaning crew to arrive days before the listing goes live can help get top dollar for your home. "Homeowners rarely see the dirt that accumulates on air vents, along the molding, on bathroom tile, and inside the oven and refrigerator," says Bob Gordon, Realtor, Re/Max Alliance in Boulder, Colo. "But buyers notice this immediately."

When your home sparkles, buyers assume the "bones" (foundation, roof, underlayment, etc.) are well-maintained, too. "An extremely clean home gives the buyers peace of mind that the entire house has been maintained very well," Hager explains.

6. Assess add-ons.

Exclude furniture, appliances, and other personal property from the total price of the home and have sellers write a separate check for these add-ons. On paper, this creates a lower home value, which results in sellers paying less transfer tax and buyers facing lower property tax.

7. Appear exclusive.

Gordon has found the strategy of underpricing the property, then collecting multiple offers, is an effective path to creating demand and maximized profits. It's aided by Realtors adding a sellers' request to the listing that states "all offers to be reviewed on Monday, bring your highest and best."

This can reduce back-and-forth price haggling because buyers who worry they may be in a bidding war will generally offer their best price upfront. "Multiple offers generally ensue on well-priced or un-derpriced houses, causing the seller to net better than list price with backup offers being quite frequent to boot," Gordon says.

8. Double dip.

Using the same Realtor to sell and buy is one of the easiest ways to squeeze a bit more out of your home sale. In most cases, Hager says the agent will agree to a reduced commission to sell your house if they have the chance to earn commission on your upcoming home purchase.

Hidden Listings Can Offer
Best Value for House Purchase

For most of us, searching for a home today means scrolling through convenient online listings. However, properties may be available that do not appear on your real estate agent's multiple listing service, or MLS. Instead, the homes are shared with a select few clients and contacts of one agent or brokerage in what could be referred to as "dark pools," to borrow a term from Wall Street.

These hidden properties can be hard to locate and even harder to define. Called pocket listings, coming-soon listings, office exclusives, or off-MLS listings, the one thing they have in common is exclusivity.

"The nature of pocket listings is secretive," says Katie Johnson, general counsel for the National Association of Realtors. "It is to withhold it from general distribution." She characterizes pocket list-ings primarily as a marketing strategy. The goal can be to generate buzz before listing on the MLS or to sell the property outside that system entirely.

The pocket-listing tactic can come into play for various reasons, she says. A seller may want to start the ball rolling but is not ready for people to see the home, if for example renovations are in progress. He or she could have a strong desire for privacy, not wanting photos of personal spaces broadcast far and wide. Those with expensive possessions may have security concerns about strangers touring the home. A seller might want to gauge the demand or the asking price before deciding to sell. Still others are concerned about minimizing the number of days a property is on the market.

Whatever the reason, pocket listings can be an opportunity for buyers. Typically, sellers want to expose their property to the widest possible audience in order to obtain the highest selling price.

In a pocket listing, however, there are fewer competitors, so prices can be lower. "If you are not getting full market exposure, the seller is potentially not going to get the best price," Johnson says. "That's a benefit to the buyer — getting it at a good deal."

To find your dream home among pocket listings, try the following tactics:

Interview agents about their connections. When you're meeting with agents you're considering, "ask what kind of resources they have," Johnson says. "In some areas, networks of agents have gotten together privately to share these listings." They can operate in various ways: word of mouth, password-protected websites, or even closed Facebook groups. Find out whether the agent belongs to — or is aware of — such networks.

Target agents specializing in luxury homes. Concerns over privacy "pertain mostly to high-end properties," Johnson says, so this type of agent will have more access to clientele who might favor a pocket listing.

Get your foot in the door through current public listings. One strategy is to find an MLS-listed home that is close to your specifications. After asking the agent smart, specific questions about the property, explain why you can't make an offer right now. Then ask whether he or she happens to have any pocket listings that are similar.

If you already have an agent, inquire whether there are hidden properties available. If you aren't seeing many options on the MLS, you may be in an area with a high number of pocket listings. (Certain regions of the country have as much as a quarter of for-sale homes marketed this way, according to data from Realtor.org.) Johnson suggests asking your agent, "Is there other inventory out there that I'm not seeing?"

Keep tabs on the neighborhood. The right real estate agent is your best resource to find pocket listings, Johnson says, but there's also no harm in being plugged into the area in which you want to own. If you're noticing activity around a house and it's not showing up on the MLS, "knock on the door and ask them what's going on," she recommends. You just might get a scoop.

Don't abandon the MLS. It's still the place to find the majority of properties that meet your criteria, Johnson says. And if you decide to pursue a pocket listing, it also can be a valuable tool to determine how much of an offer to make.

Read all paperwork carefully to protect yourself. Pocket listings may put you in the situation of sharing an agent with the seller, which is called dual agency. Because such a relationship allows the agent to cash in on a double commission, proceed with caution.

"Most states have laws dealing with dual agencies," Johnson says, noting that the agent should conduct a frank discussion with you about what it means and provide a written disclosure. "They're not going to be able to advise on behalf of both. The clients have to be aware of the lack of representation."

When a Reverse Mortgage Can Help or Hurt Your Finances

When you turn 62, you are eligible to make two very important financial decisions, ones that will set the course for the rest of your life: It's the earliest age at which you can claim Social Security benefits, and it's the minimum age you can qualify for a reverse mortgage.

It's that second one that can cause a lot of confusion and fear. What exactly is a reverse mortgage, and is it safe? The answers to those questions are complex yet not impossible to discern.

A reverse mortgage is a loan against your home that allows you to convert part of your equity into cash, which you can receive as a lump sum or over time. The loan only needs to be repaid once you sell your house, move out of it, or pass away.

As attractive as that may sound, there is a lot to be aware of in the fine print. First, interest is added each month, so the total balance you owe will grow. And while what you have to pay is insured to never exceed the appraised value of your home or the sale price, you are making a commitment that may extend beyond your own finances to your estate after you're gone.

If you've considered a reverse mortgage, you'll want to read this report.

Do I Qualify?

The most common type of reverse mortgage is offered through the Federal Housing Administration's Department of Housing and Urban Development. The HUD-sponsored product is called the home equity conversion mortgage (HECM). Peter Bell, president and CEO of the National Reverse Mortgage Lenders Association, explains that you must:

- Be age 62 or older
- Own your home outright or have a low mortgage balance
- Live in the home as your primary residence
- Not be delinquent on any federal debt, such as student loans or small-business loans
- Participate in reverse mortgage counseling
- Be financially able to cover ongoing home expenses (taxes, insurance, maintenance)

How Much Can I Get?

The amount you're eligible to borrow varies with these factors:
- Your age. The older you are, the more you can borrow. With couples, the age of the younger person is used.
- The current interest rate. The higher the rate, the less you can borrow.
- Home value. The HECM program applies to home values of $625,500 or less. Your home can be worth more, but the reverse mortgage can be taken out only on this amount.
- Your "mandatory obligations." Any existing mortgages on the home must be repaid first, usually with funds from the reverse mortgage. The less you owe on the original mortgage, the more funds are available to you.

The calculations start with a figure called the principal limit factor. Bell explains that the PLF, which is pulled from a table published by HUD, is the "percentage of the homes value you have available."

Here's an example: A couple, 65 years old and 62 years old, owns their $400,000 home outright. They apply for a reverse mortgage when rates are at 5 percent. The age of the younger borrower (62) is matched with an interest rate of 5 percent for a PLF of 0.526. This means they can borrow up to 52.6 percent of their home's $400,000 value, or $210,400. (A 90-year-old widow in the same situation has a higher PLF of 0.660, so she could borrow 66 percent, or $266,400.) If the couple (or the widow) didn't own the home outright, the money available would be decreased by the amount left on the mortgage.

You have four payment options: a lump-sum payment, a line of credit, monthly payments for a set term, or monthly payments for as long as you live in the home. You also can select a combination of these options or change them at a later time for a small fee.

WHEN DO I PAY IT BACK?

Reverse mortgages become due after a "mobility event" (moving, selling) or a "mortality event" (passing away). While most people imagine it's the mortality event that will prevail, "more of them end in a mobility event," Bell says. It's common for borrowers to downsize, relocate to be closer to family, or move to an assisted living center or senior community.

At that point, what's due is the balance of the funds advanced plus the interest accrued. However, you will never have to pay more than the value of your home, even if the loan balance grows to exceed the home's value.

THE DECISION PROCESS: COUNSELING IS KEY

If you're considering a reverse mortgage, you're required to attend counseling with a government-approved agency. "The counseling is there for people to get all the information about reverse mortgages from a third party with no affiliations with any lenders," says Claudia Fehribach, the reverse mortgage manager at DebtHelper.com, a nonprofit counseling agency in West Palm Beach, Fla. (Find HUD-approved counselors and lenders in your area by searching "reverse mortgage lender" and "reverse mortgage counselor" at www.hud.gov.)

Before you schedule counseling, Fehribach recommends speaking with a lender first to make sure you're eligible for a reverse mortgage, as there is typically a fee for the counseling session. It will also help you make the most of the session because of what you will have learned ahead of time.

When you do attend counseling, make sure you have a sense of your home's value — Zillow.com can give you an estimate — an idea of what you'll use the money for, how long you hope to stay in your home, and how you plan to pay taxes and insurance.

Expect the counselor to share how reverse mortgages work, the financial and tax implications, your payment options, the associated costs, and what benefits you may qualify for to lower expenses. The counselor also may ask you a few questions. "It's not a test," she says. "We ask questions to make sure they're getting the information."

Sessions are conducted by phone or in person, and Fehribach's company also performs them via Skype. At the end of the session, you'll receive a certificate to present to your lender. To protect the borrower, a lender may not process an application or incur any charges until they have proof that counseling has occurred.

Above all, Fehribach wants potential mortgagees to realize that making the most of counseling is in their best interest. "It's a tool not only to help them understand the program but also to protect them," she says.

RISKS OF REVERSE MORTGAGES

Getting money from your home without having to sell it may sound ideal, but it's important to know there can be significant risks.

Risk No. 1: You withdraw too much too soon.

It's tempting to go on a spending spree when given access to a large chunk of money. However, withdrawing the funds too fast works against you and limits your future options. "A reverse mortgage works best if the money is drawn out slowly over a long duration of time," Bell says. "The interest accrues at a slower pace and doesn't compound as fast."

To reduce the risk of borrowers taking too much too soon, HUD imposes a limit on withdrawals in the first year (60 percent of your total loan amount). And you can always take less if you don't need it.

Risk No. 2: You borrow in only one spouse's name to qualify for a higher amount (or to be eligible at all).

Because you must be 62 to hold a reverse mortgage, the loan is not an option for couples with someone under that age — unless the younger person's name is removed from the title. Or, if one spouse is significantly older, a couple may remove the younger one from the title to get a higher payout.

When only one borrower is on the loan and that person passes away, the loan becomes due immediately. "It's probably not a good idea to remove one spouse from the title, unless the surviving spouse has other means to pay off the loan," Bell says.

Some lenders will not make loans when there is a non-borrowing spouse involved. "The spouse is protected as long as the spouse is also a borrower," Bell says.

Risk No. 3: You don't have the money to pay for ongoing home costs in addition to your living expenses.

With a reverse mortgage, you still own your home and all the responsibilities that come with it: property taxes, insurance, utilities, and maintenance. Not covering these costs can lead to your home being foreclosed.

TOP QUESTIONS TO ASK

You'll surely have many questions about how the program applies to your situation. Here are some you should be sure to ask.

Ask your counselor: What other options do I have?

Reverse mortgages are not right for everyone. Be sure to consider the other resources you have to meet expenses or other ways to access the equity in your home, such as home equity lines of credit.

How will this affect my estate?

Be sure to ask what financial implications a reverse mortgage will have far into the future. Having a reverse mortgage may lower the amount you can leave behind. "A lot of clients have difficulties in understanding how it's going to affect their heirs," Fehribach says.

Ask your lender: What types of reverse mortgage do you offer?

"Not every lender has the same products," Bell says, noting that there are variations in fixed vs. variable rates and whether you can use the credit again if you pay it back. "It's good to talk to a couple of lenders."

What kind of loan structure would be best for me?

Bell says that consumers tend to favor fixed rates over variable, but they should consider the advantages of each. "In most cases, the variable rate HECM is more advantageous," he says. "You'll have a lower interest rate upfront, and the interest rate is one of the factors in determining how much money you'll get out of the loan."

What fees will I pay?

Standard costs include an origination fee, mortgage insurance premium, appraisal fee, closing costs, plus monthly servicing fees to the lender. Many of these fees are capped by the government and can be financed as part of the mortgage so you don't pay out of pocket.

Ask yourself: How well do I understand reverse mortgages?

Fehribach says many seniors start the process with fundamental misconceptions. "People hear that it's free money the government is giving you," she says. In truth, a reverse mortgage is a loan like any other that must be repaid at a certain point.

What is my long-term plan?

Take a close look at your complete financial picture and ask whether tapping home equity is the best course of action. Are you and your spouse in good health and likely to remain in the home for a while? Do you have other sources of income you can use first? Is what you plan to spend the funds on necessary? "If the reverse mortgage is only going to be a short-term solution, [you're] going to have problems down the road," Bell says.

5 Ways to Cut Costs on
Your Next Painting Project

A fresh coat of paint may well be the quickest and most economical way to spruce up your home. Whether you choose a bold color for an accent wall, a soothing pastel for a bedroom, or a noncommittal neutral for the powder room, the improvement can be dramatic ... without breaking the bank.

Beverley Kruskol, a general contractor in Los Angeles and owner of M.Y. Pacific Building, which specializes in high-end painting, offers these tips for homeowners looking to save money while applying a fresh coat to their abodes:

- **Do your homework.** Many times homeowners go to the store and ask how many coats to apply. Remember, these stores make their money by how much they can sell you, so it benefits them to automatically say, "Three coats." In reality, you may not need that much. Do some research on your own to be sure, and consider trying a coat less than suggested if the store's advice seems excessive. (You can always head back for more paint if it turns out you need it.)
- **Get a sample.** Once you've decided on the color, get a quarter-gallon can of the paint and a cheap brush. Go home and put it on the wall in a couple of places — first to see how you like the color in the room because it can look very different from the color chart, and second, to see how many coats you'll need. This process will cost only about $15 and can save a whole lot of heartache and money in the long run.
- **Prime your walls.** Prepping walls and priming is very important. When covering dark colors, always put a prime coat on the complete area that is going to be painted. Then you should only need two coats. When buying extremely dark colors for painting, save money by using a tinted primer or a gray primer. This also will cut down on the amount of coats needed on the painted surfaces.
- **Scope out your stucco.** Exterior paint is different from interior paint, and one of the biggest factors when considering exterior paint is the condition of the stucco (one of the most common exterior surfaces). If your stucco has not been painted for a number of years, priming the surface can save a great deal of money — that's because non-primed stucco surfaces will absorb paint, increasing the total number of coats required.
- **Price the paint.** The biggest misconception is that the more expensive the paint, the better it is. Wrong! All paints are basically the same, although many expensive products will claim a difference in the coverage. Paint rarely, if ever, goes on sale. However, some specialty stores (specific paint brands) are starting to offer coupon discounts with a minimum purchase.

How to Save Money When Paying Someone for Work Around the House

We all have items on our to-do lists that make us cringe. Whether it's scouring the bathroom, mowing the lawn, or walking the dog in two feet of snow, we all have icky tasks we wish we didn't have to perform. Typically, we do them ourselves because we think it saves us money.

But does it? As it turns out, not always. The answer lies in comparing the money you'd spend with what your time is worth. You can determine this by your hourly rate. If your hourly rate is less than what you'd pay someone else to do the task, it may be worth it to do it yourself. But if not, go ahead and pay someone else. This is one instance when spending can actually save you money!

How to determine your hourly rate? One of the simplest ways is to take your annual salary and divide it by the number of hours you work. For instance, working 40 hours a week and grossing $52,000 a year breaks down to a rate of $25 per hour.

Next, consider what you'd do with the time you gain by paying someone else to perform the task. Then if you can, calculate the value that added time has to you. For instance, would you devote those precious hours to working and increasing your annual income? Would you start training for a 5K? Would you make dinner instead of ordering out? It's nearly impossible to put an exact number on those gained hours, but if they bring in extra income or save you money, it's worth adding those figures to your hourly rate.

Now that you know what your time is worth, simply compare that to the cost of hiring someone to do those unpleasant tasks. For instance:

CLEANING THE HOUSE

Using the above example, if your hourly rate is $25, and you dedicate five hours per week to dusting, vacuuming, and polishing the house, you're essentially "spending" $125 a week to perform that chore yourself. Call local cleaning services and see if they can beat that. Sometimes they will send a crew of two or three people and be able to get your house sparkling for less than your hourly rate, and faster, too!

Hint: When you call around, ask if the price differs based on the frequency of the cleanings. Many cleaning services will charge you less if you have them come weekly or bi-weekly instead of monthly.

LAWN AND YARD CARE

Most lawn care services charge a flat rate per visit for lawn cutting, plus additional fees for extra services like leaf-blowing or seasonal clean-ups. According to Homeadvisor.com, the average lawn mowing prices range from about $30 to $80 per mow, though, of course, it depends on the size of the lot and what other services are needed. Using the $25 hourly rate example, it may or may not be worth it to hire someone for this service.

DOG WALKING

According to Angie's List, dog walkers charge about $15 to $20 per 20-minute walk. However, as is the case with any task, rates vary by region, size and age of the dog. For instance, DoggieWalker.com, located in Arlington, Virginia, charges $35.5 per hour (for a monthly package of 30 minutes/5 days a week). In many areas the cost will be much lower. However, paying someone to soak up the sun and green space with Rover means you miss out on the bonding and de-stressing time spent with your pooch.

SNOW REMOVAL

The exact price you'd pay a contractor to plow your driveway depends on the area's size and if you want to pay by the plow or sign a seasonal contract (and pay up front) for someone to plow as many times as necessary within the season. HomeAdvisor.com says the national average for snow removal (using a plow on a truck) runs $30 to $50 per visit, and sidewalk shoveling runs $25 to $75 per hour. If you opt to pay for a season of a snow-free driveway, the average cost is $350 to $450.

Obviously, if you reside in the South, you can do without this service. But anyone in an area that sees significant amounts of the white stuff from November to April should take a long look at retiring that shovel. A modest double driveway (that fits two cars) can take an hour or two to clear, depending on the weight and amount of snow, especially after the municipality plows drive past and pack several extra inches at the end of your drive.

At our average $25/hour rate, a homeowner could devote $50 of his time (and those two valuable hours) shoveling to accomplish what outsourcing can do in 15 minutes or less, and for much less moolah.

Save Big On Your Monthly Home Costs

As the old saying goes, if you want to know what people care about, watch where they spend their money.

If that adage is true, we Americans certainly cherish our homes. The U.S. Bureau of Labor Statistics estimates that the average family of four spends $22,511 — about a quarter of its income — each year on housing costs.

Without a doubt, we love to shower our living spaces with investments in furniture, art, and housewares. What's less delightful are the prices we pay for mortgages, energy, and home maintenance, items that are quite necessary but less tangible. Chances are, you wouldn't mind saving a few dollars on those "operating costs" of your home.

Whether you live in a house or condo, there are always opportunities to trim. We spoke to experts in four key areas to help you root out savings so you can put more money where you want it. You'll learn how to:

- Trim your monthly mortgage payment;
- Tackle energy-saving modifications in the right order;
- Prioritize the one maintenance task that's most effective and costs next to nothing;
- Cut cleaning costs in half while improving your family's health.

Read on for these tips and more.

YOUR MORTGAGE

You signed a stack of documents promising to make a monthly payment for 30 years . . . so you might think there's little you can do to change it now. Fortunately, that's not the case. David Reed, author of Mortgage Confidential and content editor for the mortgage education site tacfi.com, shares some options:

1. Request a cancellation of private mortgage insurance.

If you made a down payment of less than 20 percent on a conventional loan, you're paying for private mortgage insurance in addition to your mortgage itself. However, it's not forever. Your lender is required to terminate the PMI when your principal balance falls to 78 percent of your home's original value, but there's a way to eliminate it even sooner. You can request a PMI cancellation as soon as your balance falls to 80 percent of the home's original value. With PMI rates ranging from 0.3 percent to 1.15 percent of the loan amount, the savings can be substantial.

Here's an example. For a 30-year conventional loan opened with 5 percent down on a $200,000 property, PMI will be included in your mortgage payment. Once the balance falls to 80 percent of the home's original value ($160,000), PMI charges can be eliminated.

Total savings: $114 a month, or $1,368 a year.

2. Make an extra payment, and request a loan recast.

Extra payments are automatically applied to your principal balance, Reed says, but how they affect your loan depends on the type of mortgage you have. "On a fixed-rate mortgage, it just shortens the term," he explains. With an adjustable-rate mortgage, however, it will actually lower your monthly payment starting at the next rate adjustment date (while the term length stays the same). In lender speak, it "recasts" over the remaining loan term.

But here's a secret: This option is available for some fixed-rate mortgages, too. "If the loan has been sold to another lender, you can't modify it at that point," Reed notes. But if it's with the same lender, he says, "you can certainly make the request." Some require a lump-sum payment and a fee of around $250 to recast a loan.

Example: Let's say you are five years into a $160,000 loan paying 5 percent interest. At this point, your balance is likely down to about $147,000 with a monthly payment of approximately $859. Making a $10,000 lump-sum payment (thus lowering the balance to $137,000) and recasting the loan over the remaining length (25 years) can lower your monthly payment to $801.

Total savings: $58 a month, or $696 a year.

3. Appeal your tax assessment if it seems off.

"You don't have to take what you get," Reed says. "You will have a period where you can protest your property tax bill." The county estimates a value based on recent sales in the area, he explains. But if your property is not comparable for some reason (maybe you're at a busier intersection, or your lot is smaller than most in your neighborhood), it might be worthwhile to hire an appraiser to make an assessment for the purposes of protesting your taxable value.

Total savings: Vary by situation.

4. Don't spring for biweekly payment services.

Your lender or a third party may offer them, but the general gist with these programs is you make one extra payment per year, divided by 26 payments to match most people's paycheck schedule. For the convenience, however, you'll be charged a setup fee as well as fees for each transaction.

Why pay for something you can easily do yourself? Just add 1/12 of your mortgage payment to each month's check. "If the mortgage is $1,200 a month, and you pay $1,300 a month, it'd pay down in a similar fashion as a biweekly plan," Reed says. You also could pick a date each year to make a full extra payment, or do it whenever you have spare funds. This approach gives you more flexibility, as well, should you need to skip or delay an extra payment because of a change in circumstances.

Total savings: $414 the first year, $39 each successive year.

YOUR ENERGY BILL

The average family spends $750 per person per year on home energy costs — totaling $3,000 for a household of four. Paul Scheckel, author of *The Homeowner's Energy Handbook*, wants to help Americans trim that number significantly. He says energy efficiency improvements are some of the best investments you can make. "There's always a financial return," he notes.

And unlike investments in stocks or bonds, the "earnings" (your energy cost savings) are taxfree, and you keep benefiting every single year. Plus, it's a hedge for the future: The higher energy costs go, the more your investment pays off. Here's how to save, with a "total savings" estimate for all six steps at the end of the section:

1. Get audited.

Fear not, it has nothing to do with the Internal Revenue Service. Rather, it's something that can put money back in your pocket. A home energy audit is the first step to improving your home's energy efficiency. "It's not a direct energy savings, but it will help you develop a plan for your house," Scheckel says. He recommends checking out Home Performance With Energy Star, a program offered by the U.S. Environmental Protection Agency to connect homeowners with qualified contractors or their local utility to perform home energy audits.

2. Take action — in the right order.

Ready to make energy improvements to your home? You might be surprised that the first step is not to cover your roof in solar panels. "Solar is 'in' and has incentives," Scheckel says, "but you will have much longer-term savings by reducing your energy requirements."

How do you do that? "The biggest bang for your buck is around air sealing," he explains. "That means sealing up drafts around windows and things that go up through the roof and the ceiling."

After air-leakage control, next up is adding insulation, Scheckel says. "Once you've reduced the energy requirement of the home, then you can look at getting a new heating system or getting a new hot water system." At that point, he explains, your newly efficient home will require a smaller system — yet another savings.

What's the impact of all these changes? Alterations you can do on your own, such as sealing cracks with caulk or spray foam, can net you approximately 5 percent energy savings, Scheckel says.

The next level involves working with a contractor to execute a more detailed plan. "If you follow the instructions of your average home performance contractor, you can achieve between 10 to 20 percent energy savings," Scheckel says. Beyond that, you could administer a deep energy retrofit of your home. It would cost a bundle, but this comprehensive approach can produce as much as a whopping 80 percent decrease in energy costs.

3. Skip the CFLs and buy LEDs.

Some folks procrastinated on installing the "curly" compact fluorescent light (CFL) bulbs because of the hassles associated with disposal. (They contain a small amount of mercury and have to be recycled at particular facilities.) Fortunately, there's an even better bulb available now: the light-emitting diode, or LED, which uses 75 percent less energy than an incandescent bulb and lasts 35 to 50 times longer. They have rapidly supplanted CFL bulbs as the recommended lighting choice.

"Go straight to LEDs," Scheckel says. "LED light quality is great, and they don't have that disposal issue." He recommends replacing old incandescent bulbs right away, even if they're still functional. For fluorescent lights in your home, it's OK to wait for them to burn out before replacing with LEDs.

4. Maximize efficiency-adding opportunities.

Another strategy is to use your existing maintenance schedule to find ways to go deeper with efficiency. In other words, any time you are repairing or replacing a component of your home, see what can be done to improve energy efficiency in the same area. Replacing your roof, re-siding the house, or renovating a room are examples of these opportunities. "You might as well go deep while you can," Scheckel says, noting that some opportunities only come around every few decades. As you'd expect, working with a qualified contractor is key to identifying the potential. "You need some guidance so you don't cover up an opportunity with a less than perfect repair," he says.

5. Try out new technology.

Scheckel recommends a cool gadget called a controlled power strip. "It senses when your computer is on, and it turns on all your peripheral equipment." When the computer is off, he says, it disconnects the power to related items such as modems, printers, fax machines, and office lights. It's great for entertainment centers, too, where items like the cable box, DVD player, and gaming console can be plugged into the power strip along with a television. "A lot of game systems use a lot of power in standby mode," Scheckel says. One popular model is called the Smart Strip.

6. Explore an energy-improvement mortgage.

Loans to complete energy efficiency projects aren't widely promoted, Scheckel says, but they exist. "You have to go through an energy audit process to prove that your bills are a certain amount," he adds. It could be well worth the effort.

Total savings: $150 a year with a do-it-yourself approach, $600 a year by working with a qualified contractor, or $2,400 a year by performing a deep energy retrofit.

Your Home Maintenance

Of course, the central purpose of maintenance is to save money by preventing large, costly repairs and extending the life of your home's systems. But are some tasks more important than others? And how much yearly investment is required to stop major problems? To find out, we spoke to home improvement expert Danny Lipford, host of the nationally syndicated TV and radio program Today's Homeowner With Danny Lipford. Here's how to stretch your home maintenance budget further:

1. For the most impact, clean items regularly.

It's the No. 1 maintenance chore you should tackle to prevent problems, Lipford says. That's great news because it's also one of the least expensive. Target your siding, doors, gutters, sidewalks, and driveway for cleaning, and drain your hot water heater once a year to flush out sediment that can accumulate inside. In the same vein, replace the air filters in your heating and cooling system every one to three months. "It's basic things that make the most difference," he says.

2. Lubricate, lubricate, lubricate.

"You've got a lot of moving parts in a house," Lipford says, which is why lubrication is right behind cleaning in terms of bang for the buck. He suggests that you walk around your home and lubricate everything that moves: doors, locks, gates, and the garage door. Items will last much longer and make less noise. You could do this only once a year, he says, "and be smarter than just about everybody in the neighborhood."

3. Invest the right amount to get protective benefits.

Maintenance costs differ for each home, especially depending on its age. But as a general guideline, Lipford suggests $500 to start. "That would buy a lot of paint, cleaning goods, all the filters you would need, a little bit of caulk, and a little bit of 'this, that, and the other,'" he says. "The wise use of $500 . . . would go a long way to adequately maintaining your home every year."

4. Get a discount on all your materials.

Check out www.giftcardgranny.com to compare the best discounts on gift cards to the big-box home improvement stores. At this writing, Lowe's gift cards are available at 9.5 percent off face value, and Home Depot cards are discounted 9 percent. (Another option, Cardpool.com, which features only no-expiration cards.)

5. Find a helping hand.

No one says you have to slog through every maintenance task yourself; a handyman can be a great solution for chores you dislike or can't physically do. In fact, the demand for these services is higher than ever, Lipford says.

While it is an added cost, handymen have the skills and tools to get projects done quickly: "A good handyman can do an amazing amount of work in a two-to three-hour period." Rates vary by region, but many handymen have a $75 minimum charge, plus a $25 to $50 per-hour rate, Lipford says.

6. Lower the cost of HVAC inspections.

Because heating, ventilation, and air-conditioning systems require regular checkups by a licensed professional, one approach to saving is to sign a long-term maintenance contract. You prepay a certain amount to cover a number of years' maintenance, making the cost per visit lower. You also may receive a discount on parts. Lipford thinks these contracts can be a good idea and a money saver, as long as they're with a quality servicing company. (Plus, they usually handle scheduling, too, giving you one less task to remember.)

7. Account for home costs in your emergency fund.

You know it's a good idea to have a cushion in case of job loss or other financial emergency. Lipford suggests including funds for home repairs there, too. "But nobody ever does it — we always wait and max out our credit cards," he says. In a way, home repairs are easier to plan for than other emergencies because every component of your home has an estimated life expectancy. "The smart homeowner is always going to be budgeting for replacement and knows how long things are going to last," Lipford says.

Total savings: At least $1,500 if you can prevent one major ($2,000-plus) repair a year with $500 of maintenance.

YOUR HOUSECLEANING

The average family of four spends $230 a year on cleaning products. Organic Housekeeping author Ellen Sandbeck thinks that's way too much. Cut your cleaning expenses by half or more with these tips and sweep up big savings:

1. Reduce specialized cleaners.

"People are buying way too large a variety of cleaning products," Sandbeck says. "Every time you buy a product, you're buying the product and the packaging and the advertising." Not only are products for every unique surface expensive, but they're also unnecessary.

The key to successful cleaning, Sandbeck says, is to focus on what you're trying to remove (grease, mineral deposits, biological mess) and choose your cleaning agent accordingly. She does make three exceptions to the no-specialization rule: dishwashing detergent, liquid dish soap, and laundry detergent. "Those are the only things I buy that are for one use. Other than that, everything is interchangeable," Sandbeck says.

2. Use less cleaning product for better results.

"You can use way less detergent than you think you can," Sandbeck notes. In the case of laundry detergent, she says using too much not only wastes money but also makes the clothes rougher and more prone to attracting dirt. As an increasing number of households upgrade to high-efficiency appliances, the problem compounds. "When you're not using as much water, you have to cut way down on detergent," she says.

3. Ditch plug-in fragrance emitters.

"There is not an air freshener on this planet that actually makes your air cleaner," Sandbeck says. And many of these products emit potentially toxic or hazardous chemicals that put babies, pets, or sensitive individuals at risk. Cut the danger and the expense by burning an unscented candle or spraying a mixture of equal parts water and vinegar into the air to dispel odors. To add pleasant aromas, pour some vanilla extract onto a cotton ball or heat cinnamon sticks, cloves, or lemon slices in a saucepan with water. Growing herbs or houseplants, which emit fragrance and clean the air, may be the best solution of all.

Total savings: $115 a year.

Higher Deductible = Lower Rates

Of course, you have little control over accidents. But you often get a choice of deductibles on insurance policies. And while property and auto insurers penalize people who make serial claims, they reward customers who take out high deductibles. Consider the following example.

These days, even a minor fender-bender can result in more than $500 of car damage. That means if you have a $500 deductible, you're likely to put in a claim after almost any accident.

However, with a $1,000 deductible, it won't pay for you to make a claim unless you have a more serious accident (which shouldn't happen very often). That's why auto policies with high deductibles can offer significant savings.

The same is true of homeowner's policies. Homes with high values get the biggest price cuts; in California, Shaffer says taking a $5,000 deductible (rather than $500) on a high-end policy can save up to $1,500 in premiums. And those savings repeat every year.

On the other hand, a lower deductible only pays off when you make a claim. Furthermore, it usually takes several claims to recover its higher cost. The problem of course is that making multiple claims could backfire.

For this reason, David Shaffer advises that you use property insurance only to protect against catastrophic losses (those you can't afford to absorb). He recommends taking the highest deductible available on a homeowner's policy — and never less than $5,000. If your insurer only offers policies with smaller deductibles, he recommends that you shop around for another.

Words to the Wise

BONUS TIP!
Looking Online to See What Your Home Is Worth

Who doesn't occasionally check the value of their home online? And, of course, you come away either shocked at how much your humble abode has appreciated or shocked at how low the price seems vs. the neighbor's beaten-up shack of a place.

Whether you believe your home's online valuation or not, it's getting close to being right in most places around the country. Zillow, the online real estate listing service, held an international competition among data scientists to improve its signature online price guess, the Zestimate. Four thousand teams in 91 countries entered, and the winner was announced in January 2019.

The bottom line: Your Zestimate used to be off by a margin of error of 14%. Now it's down to 4.5%, and that error margin is forecast to fall below 4% soon. Still, says Zillow, get a real estate pro to do actual comparisons that take into account your home and its condition vs. local homes of similar size and age.

Bonus Tip!
Why That Fixer-Upper Doesn't Pay Off

Thinking of flipping a home for fun and profit, or just buying the most rundown house on a nice block for an instant equity win? Consider the numbers carefully. A new survey finds that most fixer-uppers are as costly as buying a home in move-in condition — once you realistically calculate the cost of the renovation.

Porch.com, a home improvement website, asked 1,069 U.S. homeowners about the costs of their new homes. The move-in ready buyers paid $250,000 on average, and the fixer-uppers paid on average $50,000 less. But the fixer-upper buyers then spent the extra $50,000 and sometimes more to get their homes ready to move in. And 40% of the fixer-uppers blew their budget, spending on average of $76,000 on repairs and improvements.

Chapter 6

Retirement

"HE THAT GETS ALL HE CAN HONESTLY, AND SAVES
ALL HE CAN, WILL CERTAINLY BECOME RICH."

What to Consider Before Choosing Where to Retire

Your kids are long gone, you've officially earned your gold watch for years of dedicated service to your previous employer, and now it's time to live life on your own terms. If you're considering relocating to chase sunshine (or your grandchildren), here's what to consider before making a big move.

Just because you've vacationed somewhere and fallen in love with it doesn't necessarily mean you'll feel at home there long-term.

"I suggest first renting a home in any city you're considering moving to for a few months," says Robert Kalin, a realtor with Keller Williams Luxury Homes in Palm Springs, California. "Try wintering there to get to know the various neighborhoods, cultural offerings, traffic patterns, medical facilities, and more. You want to remove the 'vacation' mindset, where everything seems perfect, and really experience it as a local."

While you're doing your on-the-ground research, some things to pay particular attention to include:

1. LOCATION, LOCATION, LOCATION

"For older boomers and the silent generation, between ages 64 and 93, one of the top reasons to relocate to a new city or neighborhood is to be closer to friends and family," says Jessica Lautz, vice president of demographics and behavioral insights for the National Association of Realtors. But just because a city like San Francisco is right for your techie son and his young family, doesn't mean it'll be right for you.

What you may not notice while visiting them is how inconvenient it is to get groceries, how awful the traffic is, or how expensive housing is. Make sure the city you're considering relocating to fits your lifestyle first. You may not end up spending as much family time as you envisioned, so you need to enjoy the city itself without putting pressure on your loved ones to fill the void of leaving your previous home behind.

2. AFFORDABILITY

While younger buyers may be more apt to throw caution to the wind when it comes to their budget, retirees need to remember they are in a different stage of life.

"Rightfully so, the second-most important decision older home buyers focus on is the affordability of homes," says Lautz. "They understand that they are on a limited income now, usually without a steady income, and are relying on their savings."

Be firm on your budget and don't get sidetracked looking at higher price tags — your savings account needs to last as long as you do.

3. ACCESS TO MEDICAL CARE

If you have a chronic medical condition, choosing a city with first-rate physicians, specialists, and convenient hospitals is a wise decision. If you don't know anyone who can provide referrals, look for physician reviews on websites such as Healthgrades and Vitals.

You'll also want to make sure these doctors are in your network. And since your healthcare insurance or program, such as Medicare, may change if you leave the state (and premiums may increase or decrease accordingly), it's a good idea to research that ahead of time.

4. TAXES AND INVESTING

Moving to a state with no income taxes might seem like a great idea, but the state's lost revenue is usually a tradeoff for higher property and sales taxes.

"If you sell your current home for a profit, chances are you'll get hit with capital gains taxes," says Tyler Martin, a CPA who owns Financial You, LLC. "And speaking of profit, what will you do with that influx of assets? Will you reinvest that money if you select a less expensive house for retirement? It's important to seek expert advice from a financial planner and update your estate planning documents."

5. PROPERTY SIZE

Oftentimes, retirement relocations include downsizing. After all, who wants to spend their golden years mowing a huge lawn and cleaning a big house?

"You can't have an emotional attachment to everything you own," says Kalin, "so know your non-negotiables." For instance, if you can't part with your grandmother's dining room hutch, fine. But how about that piano nobody has touched in decades? Also, get to know the housing market in the neighborhoods you're considering. Are they experiencing an inventory shortage? Are there affordable homes in that area that meet your needs?

6. EXTRA EXPENSES.

You don't want to end up cash poor in a fun new city, so be sure to research and budget for hidden costs. For instance, will you need to fly back to your hometown periodically to visit family? Are you further from a major airport, which will drive up the cost of airfare for your vacations? Will you need to purchase flood insurance? Is there an HOA in your new neighborhood?

7. FITTING IN.

No matter where you decide to relocate, prepare yourself for a breaking-in period. It takes time to find a new social circle, so be patient. Some ways to help expedite the process include choosing a city that offers the level of diversity you want, is compatible with your political stance, and offers the types of leisure activities you crave. Joining a cycling group or book club ensures you have one interest in common right off the bat.

An Easy Estate Planning Move With Massive Benefits

More than a decade ago, actor Kimberly Williams-Paisley didn't realize the opportunities to talk with her mother were dwindling. She imagined that at some point in the future she'd hear her mother's voice and reaction when she'd learn she would be a grandmother, relish sharing laughs with her mom over the phone for years to come, and enjoy catching up on life's little things mothers and daughters so often chat about.

But in 2005, Kimberly's mother, Linda, then 62, was diagnosed with primary progressive aphasia, a degenerative brain disease caused by Alzheimer's that robs a person of the ability to communicate. And along with sadness, anger, and denial, Williams-Paisley was filled with regret that she and her mother missed out on some important conversations every family must have.

PLANNING TO LOSE YOUR VOICE

"No one wants to think of their own demise," Williams-Paisley says. But as her mother's condition progressed, and long-term care became a necessity in 2012, she, along with her father and siblings, realized that the family was ill-prepared. They were unaware of what Linda's wishes and expectations for her care might be.

Linda ultimately succumbed to Alzheimer's disease in 2016 after battling it for more than a decade. "I wish we would have known to ask what my mother's wishes were when we had the chance to ask," she says. "We didn't want to offend her and didn't even know what questions we should have asked. We should have planned ahead."

Williams-Paisley acknowledges these conversations can be tough to navigate. And not having that conversation has filled the mom of two with regret. "We've tried to make the very best decisions for her and guessed what she'd want in a long-term care facility. But I regret we didn't pinpoint more. If I knew how important that information can be down the road, I would have pressed harder."

The Williams family has vowed to prevent future generations from living with similar regret. Kimberly and her siblings have talked to their father to fully understand his wishes in the event he requires any sort of medical care, and the Paisleys have made their own plans.

"My husband and I planned out everything we could think of," she says. "I know it's uncomfortable to think of your own mortality, especially when retirement or golden years may be a few decades away. But the fact is, none of us really ever knows what will happen. I don't know if what happened to my mom will happen to me or if I might be in an accident that leaves me needing care long before I'm elderly."

She also wrote a letter to her sons and husband she hopes they'll never have to read. "It says it's OK to move me from my home and gives them permission to make decisions for me," she says. "It's a letter that I wish I had from my mom."

Taking control through planning was liberating for Kimberly. "It's empowering to take charge of something that can have such a big impact on you as well as those you love," she says. "After what we went through with my mother, thankfully, my dad detailed all of his intentions and discussed the locations of important documents, accounts, etc. Now we know exactly what to do and have all the tools to do it, should we have to."

WHAT YOU NEED TO DO

Regardless of your age or health, it's never too early to talk to your family about the location of certain documents, banks, insurance policies, investment accounts, and legal and financial contacts. Doing so will ease the emotional toll should a health crisis arise or your independence decline.

Hire a lawyer to draw up a health proxy and detailed medical directive to help your family navigate medical situations and long-term care. This is in addition to your will and/or trust.

Your spouse, children, and/or person named as your healthcare proxy or who has legal power of attorney should know where to find these original documents and should have copies of their own to expedite your care and financial matters in a health crisis.

Create a file that includes the following items:

- Your birth certificate
- Driver's license or state identification card (if you do not have a license)
- Social Security card
- Medicare/Medicaid/insurance coverage card along with any supplemental coverage cards
- All insurance policies (life, homeowners, vehicle, etc.)
- Organ donor card/information (if not included on driver's license)
- Military records
- Marriage certificate or divorce agreement
- Living will, medical directives, and/or durable power of attorney
- Credit cards (if you keep the cards in your wallet, simply write that on a piece of paper)
- A list of your regular recurring bills and any outstanding debts (monthly utilities, loans, etc.)
- Mortgage records/deeds
- Automobile loans or titles
- Post office box information if you have one
- Will and, if applicable, trust
- Safe-deposit box location and key along with a list of the contents and names of anyone who has access to it
- Any letter of instruction listing personal property not disposed of by a will and wishes for distribution
- Receipts and appraisals for valuables
- List of banks and financial institutions where you have accounts, loans, CDs, annuities, retirement funds, etc., including account numbers

- Past tax returns that you've filed or a note about where past returns are located
- Burial plots and desired funeral arrangements

You should also share the contact information for the following people, as appropriate:

- Primary care doctor
- Clergy members
- Attorney, financial planner, tax adviser, broker, and/or anyone else with knowledge of or control over trusts, wills, and finances
- Beneficiaries
- Bank account, loan, and credit card contacts
- Insurance agents

How your family shares this information can be as unique as the individuals involved. Google Docs and DropBox are easy ways to share a spreadsheet and scanned documents containing pertinent information with several family members.

No matter if you opt for hard copies or virtual ones, the most important thing is sharing this information with your loved ones.

"This conversation can be one of the most important ones you'll ever have," says Williams-Paisley.

The Best Retirement Plan in America Is One You Probably Aren't Using

Want to retire with a nice cushy nest egg that will support you for decades? You're not alone.

And if you're like most people, you're probably using a tax-advantaged retirement vehicle, such as an IRA, 401(k), 403(b), SEP-IRA, or Roth IRA, to boost your savings. But what if the best place to save for retirement is not an IRA at all, but your health savings account (HSA)?

It's not obvious, but it turns out that HSAs, which accompany high-deductible healthcare plans and allow you to sock away up $3,550 for an individual or up to $7,100 for a family (plus $1,000 if you're over 55) annually, are great retirement savings vehicles. That's because HSAs are not only funded with pre-tax dollars, the withdrawals are not taxed either, as long as you follow certain rules.

"HSAs are a unicorn in the tax code, allowing a valuable deduction for contributions, tax-free growth, and tax avoidance on the back end if expenses are for medical costs," explains John Gjertsen, a senior wealth advisor at BlueSky Wealth Advisors in New Bern, North Carolina.

Indeed, no other retirement savings vehicle offers all three benefits. Traditional IRAs and 401(k)s allow you to get a tax deduction for your contributions (provided you meet the income and maximum contribution limits), but you have to pay taxes on the withdrawals.

Roth IRAs allow you to withdraw your savings tax-free, but they are funded with money you've already paid taxes on.

Moreover, the money you contribute to an HSA is deducted before Social Security and Medicare taxes whereas money you contribute to a 401(k) is still subject to those taxes.

A LONG-TERM SAVINGS VEHICLE

An HSA is designed to be used for healthcare expenses that aren't covered by the high-deductible health insurance plan it accompanies. But there is no law that says money in an HSA must be used in the year it was invested. Unlike a flexible spending account, an HSA is not a use-it-or-lose-it savings vehicle.

That means you can let the money in your HSA grow for decades. And like an IRA or 401(k), you can invest the money in your HSA. It doesn't have to sit in a money market account.

What if you don't have high healthcare costs? You should still max out your HSA contribution.

For one, health costs are no joke, and they typically rise with age. Fidelity Investments estimated that the average couple over the age of 65 will spend $285,000 on health expenses in retirement (as of 2019). That money will have to come from somewhere.

What's more, even if you remain healthy into retirement and never have high medical costs, you can use the money from your HSA to pay for your Medicare Parts B, C, and D premiums after age 65, as well as long-term care insurance costs and premiums (with some limits).

You can also let the money in your HSA grow and leave it to your spouse when you die or simply withdraw the money and use it for non-medical expenses. If you withdraw the money, you will have to pay taxes on it (and a penalty if you're under age 65), but then it functions just like a traditional IRA.

And remember, medical expenses don't just mean doctor's office visits or expensive drugs. Qualified medical expenses include things like eyeglasses, hearing aids, psychotherapy, dental care, imaging expenses, acupuncture, weight loss programs, and more.

"HSAs are advantageous for people who are heading into their prime earning years and thinking about retirement. With HSAs, you can make tax-free deposits into your accounts every year, lowering your tax bills," says Bill Sweetnam, legislative and regulatory director for the Employers Council on Flexible Compensation, a national nonprofit that advocates for tax-advantaged benefit programs.

EVEN MORE BENEFITS OF HSAS

HSAs also let you escape the minimum distribution requirements associated with other tax-advantaged retirement plans.

IRAs and 401(k)s require that participants take distributions as early as age 70½ [depending on when you were born], regardless of whether you need the funds or not, says Josh Trubow at Sensible Financial Planning in Waltham, Massachusetts. "With an HSA, you can leave the balance of the account to grow tax-free until it is needed."

HOW TO GET AN HSA

The main requirement for opening an HSA is having a high-deductible health insurance plan.

With these types of plans, the deductibles are typically quite high — often $5,000 to $10,000 for a family plan — so if you currently have a lot of healthcare expenses, you'll have to either use money from your HSA to fund them (which would be depleting your HSA) or pay for them with after-tax dollars.

Most high-deductible health insurance plans come with HSA custodians attached, although you aren't required to use that company. You can open an HSA account on your own nearly anywhere, including a bank, credit union, or brokerage firm, such as Charles Schwab, Fidelity, or TD Ameritrade.

Where you open your account can matter. Some custodians will have limited investment choices, like a workplace 401(k), while a big investment company, such as Fidelity, will allow you far more flexibility and also likely lower investment costs.

If you're late to the game, don't worry. There is a neat quirk in the law that gives you a one-time opportunity to fund an HSA account with the money you've socked away in an IRA. Doing so lets you convert money that will be subject to required minimum distributions and taxes upon withdrawal into totally tax-free money for the future.

There are some limits, however. First, you must still be covered by a high-deductible health insurance plan at the time of the conversion. Second, the amount you're allowed to convert is equal to the amount you're allowed to contribute to an HSA, so $7,100 for a family or $3,550 for an individual (plus $1,000 if you're over 55).

Deduction limits and other details are subject to change annually.

Expand Your 401(k) Investment Choices While Still Employed

When you leave an employer, it's common to roll over your 401(k) balance to an IRA. But did you know that sometimes you can make this move while still employed?

If you ask most people, they'll tell you that of the basic rules of 401(k) plans, one of them has always been: Don't touch the money until you retire or change jobs.

The reason? Although in certain cases, current employees can qualify for a hardship withdrawal or a loan from their 401(k) plans, generally, it's a bad idea to take out funds early. You will likely pay penalties and income taxes on the withdrawal, not to mention the fact that you will rob yourself of the ability to grow your nest egg over time.

However, some 401(k) plans have a loophole that allows you to pull out your money without any of those downsides, while still remaining an employee of the company that sponsors the plan. It's called an in-service rollover, in-service distribution, or in-service withdrawal.

The catch is that you can't take out the money and spend it, but rather you can use it to set up a self-directed individual retirement account (IRA). Why would you want to do that? There are a few advantages, most of which have to do with gaining flexibility and control:

ADDITIONAL INVESTMENT OPTIONS

Many 401(k) plans don't offer a wide variety of investment vehicles. Typically, you'll just find mutual funds, and even then, you may not have the ability to invest in say, a gold fund or a healthcare sector fund.

Shifting money into a self-directed IRA gives you access to a greater number of choices. You can opt for different funds than the ones available in your employer's plan, or stocks, bonds, managed investment accounts, REITs (real estate investment trusts), or even options.

If you have a favorite stock you want to own for the long haul, an individual IRA gives you the opportunity to do so, whereas a 401(k) typically won't.

POTENTIALLY LOWER FEES

Does your employer's plan have above-average expenses? Find out by reading the annual disclosure statement that every 401(k) plan is required to send participants. If the fees are higher than about 1 percent, you may be able to save money by rolling funds over to an IRA and choosing investments with lower fees, like index funds.

FLEXIBLE BENEFICIARY OPTIONS

As you know, your named beneficiary is the person who will inherit your assets when you pass away. By law, your spouse, if you have one, is the default beneficiary on 401(k) accounts. For you to name anyone else, your spouse must sign a waiver approving the move.

With IRAs, you can typically name any beneficiary without these extra steps and signatures. Different IRA custodians have different rules surrounding beneficiaries, however, so check on the new custodian's rules before making a move.

UNINTERRUPTED ACCESS

Did you know that some 401(k) plans can limit access to your money for days, weeks, or even months? It's true. This is called a blackout period, and it typically happens when an employer is making major changes to the plan, such as switching to a new administrator or changing the investment options.

Assets in an IRA, on the other hand, are totally under your control and not subject to blackout periods.

Before You Make the Switch, Read This

Of course, there are some downsides to switching money out of a 401(k), too. Some 401(k) plans allow you to take a loan from your account; IRAs do not. This could come in handy if you have kids attending college or might want to take a loan to buy a house.

And if you hope to take an early retirement, know that most 401(k) plans allow you to withdraw your money starting at age 55 without penalty. IRAs require you to wait until age 59 1/2 to start withdrawing, or else pay a 10 percent penalty.

How to Find Out If You're Eligible

Because not all 401(k) plans offer the option of in-service rollovers, your first step should be to find out if yours does. Usually your employer's human resources department is a good place to start.

If your 401(k) plan does allow them, ask the following questions before making a move:

- Will I be able to continue contributing to the employer-sponsored 401(k) plan? Some employers place a temporary ban on further contributions after an in-service rollover or distribution. This gap could negatively impact your ability to continue saving for retirement — at least in the short term.
- What are the age requirements for in-service rollovers? Some plans offer them starting at age 55. Others have no age requirement.
- Is all the money in my account available for an in-service rollover? Some plans allow you to remove only a certain percentage of your assets for an in-service distribution. Others have different rules for money you deferred from your paycheck versus money the company contributed on your behalf. Sometimes your age and length of employment determine whether or not the funds are available for in-service rollovers.
- Is there a limit on how many in-service rollovers I can take, or how much money I can roll over? Some plans have a maximum number of in-service rollovers per year or a minimum amount that must be taken out each time.

Consider a Longevity Annuity to Prevent Running Out of Money

Do you have a family member with dementia or another condition requiring around-the-clock care? The cost can easily be about $100,000 per year.

Some families may be fortunate enough able to pick up that tab. But not everyone can afford that. As you know, Social Security payments keep coming throughout your lifetime. But retirement savings do not provide a continuous income stream. And people are living longer. A 65-year-old man now has a 10 percent chance of living to age 98, while a 65-year-old woman has a 10 percent chance of making it to 100!

Of course, many people who live past 85 have major health problems or require a nursing home stay. So you want to be sure you don't deplete your retirement savings.

Fortunately, there is a way to guarantee extra income for your octogenarian years (and beyond). It's called a deferred income annuity, also known as a longevity annuity.

HOW A DEFERRED INCOME ANNUITY WORKS

With an immediate annuity, you give a sum of money to an insurance company. In exchange, you get a stream of monthly payments that begins immediately and continues for the rest of your life. A deferred annuity is the same except the monthly payments don't begin until years later. And the longer you delay taking those payments, the bigger they'll be.

For example, say you're a single man and at 66, you buy a $100,000 deferred annuity that doesn't begin to pay out until you're 85. You then receive fixed monthly payments of about $4,141 — a much higher payout than you'd get from an immediate annuity. And those payments continue until you die. That's a 5.2 percent average annual return if you live to age 90. (The return goes up if you live longer.)

So is it worth it to buy a deferred annuity? Citing historical data, financial planner Michael Kitces says you would do much better by simply invest ing in stocks. However, stock market returns aren't guaranteed. Deferred income annuities are; they're backed by the issuing insurance company.

Variable or index annuities are hybrid alternatives that offer some guaranteed income plus the possibility of higher returns from investments. But the bonus payments are dependent on the stock market, and these annuities are often loaded with hidden charges.

Warnings about that have led have many people to avoid buying annuities of any type. In fact, only $2.2 billion of deferred income annuities were sold last year. That's tiny compared to other retirement-oriented products.

QLACs: DEFERRED INCOME ANNUITIES WITH TAX BENEFITS

However, there can be a place for an annuity in your retirement plan, especially if you, like many people, don't have a pension. To make annuities more available to people, the government approved a special kind of deferred income annuity: the Qualified Longevity Annuity Contract (QLAC). You can only buy one with funds in a tax-deferred retirement savings account, such as a traditional IRA or a 401(k).

QLACs were designed to be as simple as possible. That means they lack the bells and whistles that many variable annuities have. That's good because bells and whistles have often been used to hide charges and confuse customers.

Even better: QLACs have special tax benefits. Buying one doesn't trigger income taxes. And QLACs are exempt from the retired minimum distributions that retirees must take from retirement accounts after age 70½.

About 10 insurance companies now offer QLACs. These companies must follow these rules in order to offer the tax benefits of a QLAC:

- The monthly payment amount must be clearly stated. It reflects interest rates at the time of purchase and the age when you start taking payments.
- Account values are free of required minimum distributions until you are 85
- The seller gets a one-time commission (usually about 3 percent).
- Taking payments early is not allowed, and the annuity has no cash value.

- Add-on options are generally limited to a death benefit (which allows your heirs to recover the original premium, minus any payouts) or an inflation-adjustment feature
- A joint life QLAC also provides lifetime income to a surviving spouse.

You can only put up to 25 percent of the your IRA or 401k or $135,000 (whichever is less) in a QLAC.

COMPARING AND ACCESSING QLACs

These uniform standards make it easy to compare QLACs from different insurers. BlueprintIncome.com posts price quotes from various annuity providers. It also provides ratings information for those insurance companies. Blueprint Income Vice President Lauren Minches says rates and ratings are all the data you need to make a good QLAC choice.

What if you don't have a large sum to invest? You can instead open one QLAC with a small amount and later repeat that process. Having multiple QLACs also keeps your money from being locked in at a single interest rate.

Unfortunately, few QLACs are currently available in 401(k) or similar employer plans. That's because companies are concerned about their liability if a QLAC insurer becomes insolvent.

If the $135,000 limit for QLAC contributions won't provide enough income to meet your needs, you can consider also buying a regular deferred income annuity. If you're concerned about the possibility of outliving your money, having both could be worth the extra cost!

Quit Your Job Slowly and Ease into Retirement

The transition from full employment to retirement can be harsh for many. Instead, stepping down to a part-time role or transitioning to a different career can keep you busy and keep the income coming in a bit longer.

"I start each retirement conversation with a simple question: 'Does your vision of retirement involve a rocking chair on a porch?'" says Ryan Miyamoto, a certified financial planner in, California.

For most people, a rocking chair is not realistic. Today, retirees are gradually transitioning to retirement, whether by doing part-time work, consulting, mentoring or volunteering just to stay busy.

Many employers are happy to have retiring employees stay on part-time, whether to do a slightly different job or simply to train their replacements. "It all starts by asking," says Miyamoto. "You'd be surprised by how impressed your employer may be with your loyalty."

Stepping down slowly worked for Terry Feinberg, who worked as a consultant in Gilroy, Calif. Feinberg was a partner in a small 12-employee marketing firm. He sold his portion of the business to his partners and became a consultant where he got got some clients through contacts and some through Upwork, a freelancing website.

At that point he achieved his goal of working between two and four hours a day.

Carol Gee, a professor at Emory University in Atlanta, made a complete career change as retirement loomed.

"All my life I worked positions that would continue to generate income. Once I retired, I wanted to realize my lifelong dream of writing," says Gee. "So after serving over 21 years wearing camouflage and combat boots in the Air Force and Air Force Reserves and close to 28 years as an educator at the university level, two months short of age 62, I was ready."

Gee became a freelance writer, a shift she made before leaving the university life.

The transition part of easing into retirement can trip you up, says Joan Marie Gagnon, who worked as a certified financial planner and CPA and is the author of "Journal Your Way to Retirement."

"Many people think they will not have any issues with retirement, but from my experience, it can take two to five years for people to adjust to retirement," Gagnon says. "If retirement isn't what they expected, I have seen health issues pop up, even depression."

Reducing your hours slowly will help if that is an option, Gagnon says. Many employers do not want to lose an employee's expertise overnight, so a slow and steady retreat can be a better option for both employer and employee.

Learning something new is also great for the brain, so there are health benefits along with anything new, Gagnon says. "Transitions are tough for some people. Everyone reacts differently. Some people hibernate, while others over-volunteer. Knowing how you handle transitions is important," she says.

The other key item is how people feel about work as they wind down their career, says Bill Ryon, who has worked as an investment adviser in Dover, Delaware. "Some feel great, while others feel very stressed and tired and will need at least a year off before they can even entertain the idea of going back to work," he says.

While working on the numbers with clients, Ryan says it was common for him to get the "please say yes that I can retire" look.

"It's a very emotional time for people and they can often feel very unsure about what their future holds," he says. "This is where solid planning, which could include a part-time job, can help provide some certainty and something to refer to for support when feeling uneasy about the years ahead."

Carisa Miklusak, a careers expert and the CEO of job recruiting website Tilr.com, says many retirees find they're not fully prepared financially to retire, or they enjoy working, but aren't interested in keeping up the 9-to 5 grind.

"Part time and gig work can be a great way to earn some extra income in retirement, keep your mind sharp, or even just to get out of the house and socialize with others," she says.

"The reality is that people are living longer than ever before and, with that, comes retirement periods that are upward of 20 years. Most of us didn't plan for that, so even working a few days a month or a few hours a week can really help retirees supplement their nest eggs," Miklusak says.

What can you do? Some of the most popular jobs for retirees include driving for Uber or Amazon, hotel concierge, banquet serving, house sitting, pet sitting, landscaping, data entry, teacher's aide, retail work, or even seasonal work designing or delivering gift baskets. Or if you prefer work that engages your brain, try preparing taxes or doing consulting.

Facts About Funeral Insurance

Few people are comfortable talking about their mortality. The mere thought of "the end" turns a person into an anxious puddle of sweat.

But the thought of purchasing funeral insurance to remove the possibility that our loved ones will have to bear any financial burden when we pass can spark a conversation into what exactly that means. You may wonder, is funeral insurance something you need — or want?

To best understand the nuances of this tailored policy, we sat down with Anthony Martin, owner of Choice Mutual, the largest funeral insurance website in the world. As an exclusive specialist in funeral insurance, he was able to expertly answer the array of questions we threw his way. Here's what we learned about this option to fund your final resting spot.

WHAT IS FUNERAL INSURANCE?

In many ways, it looks like ordinary life insurance. However, there is one glaring difference: the amount of coverage.

In general, burial insurance tops out at $25,000 to $30,000 and is earmarked specifically to cover the cost of cremation, burial, funerals, etc. Any additional funds can be used at the discretion of the beneficiary, but the initial death benefit paid on a burial insurance policy is designed to pay for a person's funeral. Preneed insurance policies are also available to cover specific funeral and burial costs and are paid direct to the funeral home, crematorium, etc. versus a family member beneficiary.

Life insurance policy coverages can be much higher — into the hundreds of thousands and beyond. And the benefits from these policies can be used not only for funerals, but also to pay off any debts, medical expenses, etc., left behind by the deceased as well as be an income stream for survivors

DO I REALLY NEED FUNERAL INSURANCE?

You need funeral insurance if you currently don't have the cash or other life insurance policies on hand to cover your final expenses should you pass away tomorrow. An annual review of your day-today expenses and current life insurance policies and the current cost of a funeral will help you determine if you need a specific funeral insurance policy.

Remember, assets such as investments or bank accounts may not suffice because they may have to go through the probate process, which can take months. A funeral must be funded right away.

How Much Might I Need?

To crunch this number, decide if you want to be buried or cremated. A traditional burial typically costs between $7,000 to $10,000, while a typical cremation service will cost anywhere from $1,500 to $5,000, according to a report from the National Funeral Directors Association.

If you're looking for a basic service, you'll need a smaller policy than one that will cover a service with lots of bells and whistles. To best hone in on this cost, survey five to seven funeral homes in your area to understand the services they provide and any associated pricing.

What Type of Policy Do I Need?

For starters, the term funeral insurance is merely a marketing term and may also be frequently referred to as final expense insurance or burial insurance. All three terms mean the same thing.

Funeral insurance, burial insurance, and final expense insurance all refer to a small face-value whole-life policy that has very limited — to no — underwriting. You don't want to purchase a term life policy to cover final expenses because it will one day expire. Whole life policies don't expire at any age, so they are guaranteed to be there to cover your final expenses, whenever that coverage is needed.

Can I Afford the Policy I Want?

Figure out how much you can allocate to this expense. Then choose a policy that has a payment that fits in your budget. Do that by asking yourself: Can I comfortably afford the monthly payment all 12 months of the year? Will I have to drop the coverage due to an unexpected event, such as car trouble or a washer breaking down?

If you answer "yes" to both of these questions, you're all set. Otherwise, you may have to buy less coverage. Remember, some coverage, even though it's less than you would like, is much better than a bigger policy that you are unsure you can afford maintaining over the long term.

HOW SHOULD I BEGIN SHOPPING?

The single most important step here is to identify the appropriate agency to work with. You want to look for an independent agency that specializes in funeral insurance and represents at least 10 different insurance companies (the more the better) to ensure you receive the best possible price and policy versus the one an insurance company employee favors.

They will compare offers from all the insurance companies they represent to find you the best deal. Funeral insurance has a lot of underwriting nuances, which is why you'll want to work with an agency that specializes in this type of insurance. An expert in this field will be able to identify which insurance companies view your health the best because that results in lower premiums.

Before signing on the dotted line, make sure to ask the following questions:

- How long have you been in business?
- Do you deal with other lines of insurance?
- Do you have any online reviews I can read?
- Why should I work with you?

You can buy directly from the insurer or through an agency. If you buy direct from the insurer, you might pay more because of their policy restrictions.

Insurers who sell direct only offer guaranteed issue policies that have no medical underwriting. So they don't ask health questions or assess your health in any way. That means a non-smoker with tip-top blood pressure and a healthy weight will pay the same rate as an overweight smoker with diagnosed hypertension and diabetes.

These policies also typically have a two-year waiting period built in. During this time, the insurer will not pay out a death benefit if you should pass away. They will, however, refund any premiums paid, plus interest.

On the flip side, insurance agencies are licensed by various insurance companies to sell their products. It's through them that you will find the lowest cost funeral insurance. Agencies have access to funeral insurance policies that have health questions which ultimately can cost much less and offer immediate coverage. Agencies also often have access to no health question policies if that is something you need or want.

Once you find a qualified agency, get approved as soon as possible. While you may be in tip-top shape today, sadly that's not a guarantee.

And you don't want to leave your loved ones holding the bag for a pricey burial they can't afford.

The Right Way to Prepare a Living Will

If you've ever been wheeled into a surgical suite, chances are you've been asked if you have a living will or handed one to review and sign. Sometimes you get it the day before; sometimes it's thrust upon your nearest loved one as you slip into a hospital gown.

Yet that short form is a bare-bones document at best, one designed to protect the hospital's finances, not you and your family. Here's the living will you really need and the best way to set it up, according to lawyers and patient advocates.

1. Always read the basic legal form well in advance.

Most U.S. states provide bare-bones, state-mandated living will forms, and most, if not all, are posted online, said Stuart Shiffman, a retired judge and law professor in Springfield, Illinois. "Attorneys generally use these forms as a starting point and then tailor the form to specific client needs," Shiffman said.

You can find your state's living will at Estate.FindLaw.com. The website of AARP also maintains a state-by-state living will database, or you could search for your state name online plus "living will" or "advance directive" to find the current form.

2. A form is no substitute for thoughtful planning.

Chances are, you won't be physically or mentally capable of making a complex medical decision in real time. That's why you need to name a surrogate in advance and why you have to make your wishes clear to that person.

"Signing a generic two-page directive — the Iowa statutory form is only two sentences! — is not only meaningless to the patient, it provides no guidance to the potential decision-maker if the patient lacks decision-making capacity down the line," says Jo Kline Cebuhar, author of "The Practical Guide to Health Care Advance Directives."

Be careful with default options on forms, which can result in a Do Not Resuscitate (DNR) order on your record, meaning no life-prolonging measures of any kind will be undertaken.

"Most of the forms and laws concerning advance care planning in America were crafted in the 1970s and 1980s. They were never respectful of patient autonomy by their very nature, but now they are also completely out of touch with the complex healthcare environment we all live in," Cebuhar says.

3. Make sure your directive names names.

There will be a lot of people involved if you are incapacitated. You must make key decisions early, counsels Cebuhar, and communicate those decisions in advance.

"In order to be effective, any healthcare advance directive needs to include the appointment of a substitute decision-maker, a process for shared decision-making with healthcare professionals in a variety of situations, and specific instructions in the event of a 'triggering event,' such as a terminal condition, irreversible unconsciousness, or late-stage dementia," Cebuhar says.

"Achieving health literacy, fully considering the process of medical decision-making, and communicating one's specific directives for care is crucial to maintaining patient autonomy in any medical situation, whether it involves preventive, elective, emergency, or end-of-life care," she says. "It is better to speak with your loved ones about your wishes and have no written directive at all than to have one that does not reflect your true preferences for care."

4. Consider getting a lawyer.

While the generic templates you find online are likely to be adequate, that doesn't mean they'll be effective. If you hired a lawyer for your will regarding assets, get him or her involved in your living will too.

"Working with an attorney will be more costly, but it is generally well worth it, considering that if and when this document is needed, you will not be capable of clarifying your intentions or fixing any mistakes," says Anthony D. Criscuolo, a certified financial planner and portfolio manager with Palisades Hudson Financial Group in Fort Lauderdale, Florida.

"You should have a competent attorney draft the documents to ensure they meet state law, express your intentions clearly, and are consistent with your other estate planning documents," Criscuolo says.

You might want your living will to address specific topics, such as pain management, the use of prolonged life support, resuscitation, and organ donation, he says.

5. Update it

Medical technologies change over time, and so might your views. "Like traditional wills, living wills need to be updated regularly. These updates may reflect changes in opinion, circumstances, or even available medical treatment. You should also be sure to update your living will if you move, as legal requirements can vary between states," Criscuolo says.

6. Make your intentions simple and clear

It's important for a living will to consider all medical outcomes, but it's equally important that your doctor understands what you want and why, says Amy J. Fanzlaw, an elder law and estate planning attorney in Boca Raton, Florida.

"While I agree it is important that a person's desires be reduced to writing so they can be implemented, longer and more detailed isn't always better. Medical professionals' time is often limited, particularly in an emergency situation, and you want their time spent on your healthcare, not on trying to decipher a written document," says Fanzlaw.

Talk to your family members and make sure they fully understand what you want, then put it in writing succinctly, she says.

"Most state-specific living will forms have a section for additional instructions; if your particular state does not have such a section, add one," says Fanzlaw. "In this section, insert clear and concise directions about the care you want in case you cannot verbally communicate with your doctor."

Standard Retirement Rules Can Cost You a Fortune

Rules of thumb are useful for getting started on retirement planning, but really only for getting started, say, when you are in your 20s and just opening a 401(k).

Later, when you have to make concrete choices with consequences, you should be much more certain of what you're doing.

Fidelity Investments has a retirement savings rule to help you keep tabs on your retirement progress. Like all good rules of thumb, it's simple: have 10 times your expected final year's salary saved up by age 67.

Say you are 51 this year. You need about six times your salary in savings right now, according to the Fidelity guidelines. The next checkpoint is 55, when you'll need seven times your salary and so on, every five years until retirement age.

What's missing from the rule is that your money must be prudently invested in order to reach your goals. Almost no one can save enough cash from work income to build $500,000 or $700,000 without the power of compounding, and that means owning stocks and bonds.

Later, when retirement starts, there's another common rule of thumb, but it's one that will get many retirees into trouble, the so-called 4 percent rule.

THE 4 PERCENT RULE — DOES IT STILL WORK?

Developed in the 1990s during a period of relatively normal interest rates, the 4 percent rule is dead easy — and possibly deadly to your planning.

Here's how it works: According to the rule, you can take out 4 percent of your savings each year in retirement, adjusting annually for the rate of inflation and assuming inflation is 2 percent.

In this scenario, if you have $250,000 and take out 4 percent, that's $10,000 you can spend without worry. The next year, take $10,200 and so on. You increase your withdrawals with the inflation rate to keep up with the cost of living over time, though doing so is optional.

This rule worked for a long time because interest rates on CDs and money markets over decades averaged about 4 percent. A portfolio that was half in stocks and half in bonds reliably produced enough income that retirees could relax and forget about it for up to 33 years, essentially their remaining life span.

So what's wrong with the 4 percent rule now? Interest rates are very low, under 2.5 percent. If you spend 4 percent annually, but only "put back" 2.5 percent, your money won't last nearly as long. Many advisers now recommend 3 percent withdrawal rates instead.

In fact, researchers Michael Finke, Wade Pfau, and David Blanchett found in 2013 that the "failure rate" of the 4 percent rule — how often the rule fails to work — was 57 percent. The failure rate in the 1990s was just 6 percent, a more reassuring number for sure.

What a "failure rate" means is that more than half the people who use the rule now will find they have run out of money before a three-decade period ends. Rather than certainty, the rule has become a coin flip for many.

DIVIDEND STOCKS: A REASONABLE ALTERNATIVE?

Looking for alternatives, investors have gone heavily into dividend-paying stocks, increasing the unpredictability of their portfolios. Company managements can cut dividends long before they could default on bonds. Moreover, stocks are more volatile than bonds.

The Federal Reserve has suggested that the target benchmark interest rate will rise steadily during the remainder of the year. Yet that assumption is based on the idea that the U.S. economy is on a sustainable trajectory toward growth.

Historically, however, it's unlikely that we can go much longer without a recession — our last one, the Great Recession, ended in June 2009. The average expansion, the period between recessions, is about 39 months or a little more than three years. We're in our eighth year of expansion now.

Add into that the aging baby boomer population in the United States. The fact is slower economic growth is more likely as the boomers consume less. So you end up in a situation in which it becomes very hard to "normalize" rates back to something like a steady 4 percent.

As Finke, Pfau, and Blanchett concluded, the 4 percent rule is not a rule so much as a "historical anomaly" that is not likely to be repeated.

WHAT TO DO

You can manage your spending in retirement just by assuming a lower withdrawal rate than 4 percent, and by being conservative for the first five years. Many retirees overspend early in retirement on new cars and travel.

Or you can use other tools and rules of thumb. One tool is the CoRI calculator online at BlackRock.com/cori, which you can use to figure out what amount to withdraw year by year. The calculator finds the likely return on bonds using your age. It then suggests a target withdrawal amount for the year.

One alternative rule is the "feel free" rule, developed by actuary R. EvanInglis, a senior vice president at Nuveen Asset Management. Here, you divide your age (or the younger of you or a spouse's age) by 20.

For instance, if you are 60, then the withdrawal amount is 3 percent. If you are 70, take 3.5 percent. This rule is automatically more conservative early on so more money stays invested, allowing you to increase withdrawals as you get older.

Finally, avoid the temptation to buy an annuity that tracks the stock market, called a fixed index annuity, because it has high fees and commissions.

Rather, adviser Allan Roth suggests that you put most of your money into long-term CDs and invest the difference into a low-cost S&P 500 fund, such as an index fund.

For instance, Roth told Barron's, if you have $10,000, put $7,200 into a CD at about 3.5 percent. At that rate you would expect to get $10,000 back at the end of 10 years.

Put the remaining $2,800 into the index fund. Over 10 years, that money is likely to double in value to $5,600, suggesting a steady annual return of 5.65 percent a year.

"You get your $10,000 back, plus what the stock investment has grown to, and you can't lose," Roth said. Plus, the CD portion under $250,000 is backed by the FDIC.

Try Working for Your Old Employer in Retirement

Imagine this: a job you don't have to interview for, where you know exactly what to expect and where your expertise is respected and highly valued. Sound too good to be true? Not at all — it's called being a boomerang retiree.

The term is new, but the concept is not. A boomerang retiree is any worker, who, after a period of time in retirement, rejoins the same employer from which they retired. The work can take many forms, from freelance to full time and everything in between.

Retirees looking for a lighter workload can make excellent members of an organization's "flexible workforce" — workers who are called in when needed.

That was the case for Jane Moss a retired elementary school teacher in Southern California. For several years after retiring, she taught as a substitute teacher at her former school, but she only took prearranged assignments — meaning no last-minute, early morning phone calls.

David Hackney a semi-retired college professor in southern New Jersey, was in a similar position. He taught two classes per semester at the university from which he retired in 2015. After just one semester of taking it easy, he found himself missing the interactions with students and asked to return to teaching.

But he had one condition: "I wanted to be certain I wasn't keeping a young person from a position," he says.

The university assured Hackney that that wasn't the case, so he helped fill holes in his department's course schedule on a per semester basis as a senior adjunct professor.

A "three-quarter time" setup worked for Roxann Wetlaufer, an IT tech specialist who lived near Tucson, Arizona. She returned to her former employer, a nonprofit hospital system, in 2015, after taking an early retirement package.

When she retired, she knew coming back part time might be a possibility, but there were no guarantees. But just five months after Wetlaufer retired, the hospital called to offer her a new position at 30 hours a week. The new job wasn't a permanent position, but given the projects the hospital had, Wetlaufer knew she'd be around for a while.

Plus, the position came with a nice bonus: As a part-timer, she was never on-call for technical emergencies outside of normal hours.

There are boomerang stories of retirees returning to full-time work, too. Jennifer Hirsch, who from outside of Madison, Wisconsin, accepted an early retirement package in 2015, but her employer wasn't able to fill her executive editor position after several months of searching.

Hirsch was open to re-joining the team in some capacity, but freelancing was against the stipulations of her retirement package. Returning as a full-time employee to her former position, however, was allowed . . . so she did.

HOW TO POSITION YOURSELF FOR BOOMERANG OPPORTUNITIES

Nearing retirement? Lay the groundwork for a boomerang arrangement by doing this:

Learn what rules you'll have to follow.

Get your hands on an employee handbook before you retire and read about all the policies of your pension or retirement plan. This is the ultimate authority on what you can and cannot do.

Look for information on how the organization handles rehires, and if it mentions them, rehired retirees (sometimes known as retired annuitants in pension documents).

Typical requirements include a valid break of employment, meaning a certain length of time in retirement with no commitment (written or verbal) that you'll be rehired later.

There may also be annual limits on how much money you can earn or how many hours you can work. These vary widely. For example, Hackney, the university professor, is prohibited from teaching any more than six credits (two classes) by his pension plan.

Clearly communicate your reasons for retirement.

Hirsch, the executive editor who returned to full time work, says she made it very clear to her co-workers that her decision to retire early was a hard one to make and that it was in large measure about exploring her own life goals.

"I made sure they knew my decision was not about disliking the job or disliking the company," she says.

Even if you do have misgivings about the organization or management, be diplomatic. Things may change over time. New managers may come in, the company may even undergo a merger or buyout, and the culture could change.

If you've already retired, use these strategies to pursue a successful comeback:

Know what it means for your Social Security benefits.

Heading back to work may affect your ability to collect Social Security benefits or the amount of your payments.

Social Security has an earnings test, and it applies if you begin collecting Social Security benefits before you reach full retirement age and you earn more than $16,920 this year. Full retirement age is between age 65 and 67, depending on your birth year.

If you earn more than the $16,920 limit, Social Security will withhold $1 for every $2 you earn over that amount. But there is a silver lining: When you reach your full retirement age, you will start getting back the Social Security benefits that were withheld for exceeding the earnings limit. How? Your monthly payment will be bumped up from then on. While it will take up to 15 years to fully recover the benefits you lost, that money will come in handy in later years!

Let people know you're interested.
Of the boomerang retirees interviewed here, all made it clear upon leaving their jobs that they would be open to returning.

Moss, the elementary school teacher, signed up to be on the substitute list and told all her friends at the school she'd be happy to return in that capacity. David called the department chair directly to say he'd like to come back if possible.

Stay in touch with former bosses and colleagues.
You may not like the idea that you have to keep networking even after you retire, but if you want to sow the seeds for a possible return, it's the easiest way to lay the groundwork.

Hirsch's return happened in large part due to a friendly lunch. So accept social invitations from old colleagues whenever you can, and extend some of your own. These simple steps can keep you in the loop and when a need arises, you'll be top of mind.

What to Do When Your Adult Child Asks for Money

Are you helping to support an adult child who hasn't been able to achieve financial independence? You're not alone. Many people in their 50s and 60s find themselves in the same situation. The odds are even higher if your child is pursuing a career where money isn't the primary reward.

Take Joshua, the 25-year-old son of Miami residents Joe and Sue. When he was 18, Joshua moved to Israel to pursue advanced studies. He continues to study in Israel full time. His only income is the small stipend he receives from his kollel (seminary).

A few years ago, Joshua married an Israeli woman, Sarah. The couple quickly had their first child and settled into a small apartment near Joshua's kollel.

Then, Joshua and Sarah had their second child and saw a three-bedroom condo for sale in a nearby town that would be perfect for their growing family. But with Joshua's meager salary, they can't qualify for a mortgage. So he asked his parents if they could lend him $350,000 to buy the place.

WHY MILLENNIALS CAN'T MAKE IT ON THEIR OWN

There's no shortage of financial challenges facing young adults today. Millions struggle with the burden of college loans. (Most members of the Class of 2016 owe $37,000 or more). About one in three young adults is a boomerang kid, living with his or her parents.

It's true that some millennials are content to "mooch" off their parents indefinitely. California psychiatrist Mark Goulston told me this happens primarily in wealthy families, where parents never stressed about the need for children to become self-reliant.

However, most millennials don't want to be perpetual dependents; they are just the victims of bad timing. They entered the job market just as the economy went into a tailspin a decade ago. Since then, they've lost more jobs and wages than any other age group.

Many are itching to move on with their lives. But because they lack collateral, a good credit record or a high-paying job, banks are reluctant to give them loans. So they turn to the Bank of Mom and Dad. Or they ask parents to co-sign a commercial loan or mortgage to enable them to qualify.

SHOULD YOU RISK YOUR RETIREMENT FOR YOUR KIDS?

But losing a substantial chunk of your retirement savings could have serious consequences. That was what Joe and Sue's financial planner told them when they turned to her for advice.

She warned that making this loan would leave Joe and Sue dangerously short of cash reserves — both now and in retirement. Diana also was skeptical that Joshua would be able to pay back the loan. And without those dollars to supplement their Social Security income, Joe and Sue would probably have to sell their own home.

As a parent, it can be difficult to turn down a child who desperately needs money to jump-start his or her life. However, if you're in this boat, it's important not to let your emotions keep you from making a sound financial decision. Since you know your own children better than anyone else, ask yourself: Will your son or daughter use the money wisely? Will he or she stop after one request or come back for more money?

Also, if your son or daughter falls behind on loan payments, are you prepared to foreclose on the mortgage or repossess their assets? And if you co-sign on a loan, are you prepared to pay back the full amount if your child defaults?

ANNOUNCING YOUR DECISION

Then there's the problem of communicating your decision to your son or daughter. Consider this advice: If you decide to go ahead with a loan or an investment deal, don't just seal the deal with a handshake.

Instead, formalize it with a legal contract. That will help ensure that your money is spent in the intended way. It also will make it clear there are serious penalties if the contract terms are not followed. (You later can drop the penalties if you want). In the case of a loan, you also should charge market interest. That will avoid tax problems.

Your son or daughter may protest that requiring a contract shows a lack of trust in them. But Dr. Mark Goulston, author of *Talking to Crazy: How to Deal with the Irrational and Impossible People in Your Life*, disagrees. He suggests that you respond along these lines:

"I've learned the importance of contracts from dealing with people that I never should have made agreements with. I'm not trying to punish you; I just insist on learning from the lessons life has taught me. And one lesson is that you need to be prepared if something doesn't work out."

- If you decide that you can't afford to come up with the money, you may face a confrontation with your son or daughter, an angry outburst, or even a threat never to talk to you again. But don't let these reactions stop you from saying "no."

To soften the blow, say that you made your decision only after consulting with a financial planner. This shows you cared enough to properly consider your child's request. It also provides a convenient scapegoat to shield you from some of the blame.

It also may be worth pointing out to your son or daughter that it's in their own interest that you not run out of money in retirement. The reason? Because if that happens, they'll have to support you!

5 Ways to Mess Up Your 401(k)

Ah, a new job. You get a fresh parking pass, a cubicle to call home, and the inevitable stack of benefit forms to fill out, including ones to set up a 401(k). And getting your retirement plan choices right matters.

Retirement experts around the country share the mistakes they witness people making in these well-meaning HR confabs and to offer their advice on how to avoid them.

MISTAKE No. 1: NOT REALLY INVESTING

Cash is not an investment. Over time, it loses purchasing power due to inflation. That's why you need stocks, bonds, and other investments in your retirement plan.

"Leaving retirement plans in cash, especially in the current low interest rate environment, will ensure disappointment as you reach retirement because you miss the opportunity to grow your assets, and you see your funds destroyed by inflation," says Jamie Ebersole, a certified financial planner in Wellesley Hills, Mass.

Consider using a target date fund instead, which manages a mix of stocks and bonds for you based on your age, and automatically adjusts your exposure over time.

MISTAKE No. 2: NOT INVESTING ENOUGH

Some company plans automatically put their employees at an initial low percentage 401(k) savings rate. It's meant to get you started, but that savings figure usually is not nearly high enough.

If your company starts you off with a 3 percent investment in its retirement plan, stop and think: Is 3 percent going to get you where you need to be in 20 years? Is it even enough to qualify for the company match? Instead, figure out the maximum you can sock away, and do that.

MISTAKE NO. 3: PAYING FAR TOO MUCH TO INVEST

Investing is not expensive, but fund managers can be. Investment fees of 1 percent or more for a typical mutual fund mean you will pay $100 per year for an investment of $10,000. A better bet: An index fund that matches the performance of the S&P 500. These funds have ultra-low expenses, and they typically perform better than managed mutual funds.

MISTAKE NO. 4: BORROWING FROM YOUR FUTURE

Think you can do better things with your money than put it in the stock market? The data says you won't. In fact, taking a loan out of your retirement plan is a demonstrable loser.

Say you want to borrow $25,000 from your 401(k) to buy a home. Assuming your cost is 4.5 percent over 10 years and you have to give up your average 8.8 percent return on those funds in your 401(k), you won't come out ahead.

Says Ryan McGuinness, a financial adviser in Illinois. "If you left the $25,000 invested, it would have grown to $206,000 over 25 years. Taking out the loan, even after paying it back with interest, only grows to $168,000."

It's also high risk. If you quit or get laid off before paying off the loan, it immediately comes due. And if you can't pay it off, it will be subject to a 10 percent penalty plus taxes on the gains.

MISTAKE NO. 5: DIVERSIFYING INCORRECTLY

The reason you own a wide variety of stocks is to reduce the risk of any one stock going south and sinking your retirement. Yet many times people load up on a stock or fund that has done well recently. Or they own mostly their own employer's stock.

Concentration in a small number of companies increases your risk, but the other extreme can be a problem too. "One way people fumble 401(k) choices is by choosing to invest in equal amounts across all available funds. They figure it gives them diversification," says Stephanie Genkin, a certified financial planner in Brooklyn, N.Y. "Having an equal weight in bonds, emerging markets, and large cap stocks, for instance, doesn't make sense."

Asset allocation matters, but so does understanding the proper use of each type of investment. "You'll want to determine the amount of each asset based on your time horizon, risk tolerance, and ability to take risk," adds Genkin. "It's like baking a cake. You wouldn't put in sugar, salt, and baking powder in equal measures."

Two Great Places to Retire in Mexico

Why retire in the U.S. when you can enjoy a low-cost, warm lifestyle south of the border? Many Americans agree, which is why Mexico is already the most popular country for U.S. expats. Reportedly, about a million live there.

And it's easy to see why. Mexico's low cost of living and proximity to the United States make it a natural destination. Making it even more alluring to American retirees: Social Security and pension income isn't subject to Mexican taxes.

And getting permission to live in Mexico as a non-working resident is pretty easy: You just need to show monthly income of about $1,250 or own real estate in Mexico valued at about $167,000.

Mexico's attractions for retirees include its unique cuisine, an IN-APAM discount card for residents over 60, and fabulous beaches on its east and west coasts. But if your idea of retirement isn't sitting on the beach, here are two locations in central Mexico that are worth checking out — and not just because they share some of the world's best weather, although both places are at high elevations and have an average annual temperature of about 70 degrees.

SAN MIGUEL DE ALLENDE (SMA)

This picturesque small city about 170 miles north of Mexico City was founded in 1542 and retains its Spanish flavor. San Miguel de Allende's historical central area features a classic towered church along with cobblestoned streets and gardens that flower year-round. And few cities have its array of baroque architecture. That led UNESCO to declare San Miguel de Allende a World Heritage Site in 2008.

But American artists and writers discovered SMA's charms decades earlier. Over the years, many settled there, and today, San Miguel is home to about 10,000 Americans. As a result, it boasts an active expat community (with many English-language clubs, publications, and events) and a vibrant arts scene.

John Scherber is a writer who moved from Minnesota to SMA in 2007. He was enthusiastic about the city's advantages for American residents. He describes them in detail in his book *Living in San Miguel: The Heart of the Matter*, available at his website www.sanmiguelallendebooks.com. John said San Miguel is the perfect place for retirees to try "new and exciting things they may not have felt free to do before."

Although many gated communities have sprung up outside the city's center, Scherber saw no need to live in one. He believed they're mainly for part-time residents who don't want to leave their property unattended. He said he and his wife never had any trouble with crime in their open neighborhood. In fact, Scherber says that crime in Mexico is vastly exaggerated by the U.S. media. He claims almost all violence is concentrated in the drug trade and a few distant trouble spots, which are easy to avoid.

Scherber also had no problem with San Miguel's medical care. He was happy with his bilingual personal physician. And while he admitted that SMA's hospitals aren't equipped for some complicated procedures, these can be handled in the larger city of Querétaro (less than an hour away) or Mexico City (a 3 1/2 hour drive).

As for housing, Scherber said prices are comparable to Mexico's beach towns, with what he calls "a fine house in a good neighborhood" going for between $300,000 and $400,000. Long-term home rentals start at about $1,200 a month; condos are less.

But other living costs are a real bargain. Annual property taxes on Scherber's 4,000-square-foot home was $197, and his combined utility bills came in at under $100 per month — including internet!

CUERNAVACA

For those who prefer to be closer to Mexico City, a good alternative is Cuernavaca. Located just 56 miles south of the capital, it is also a colonial city and is in a lush valley ringed by mountains. However, unlike San Miguel, its central area has yet to be fully restored.

Cuernavaca had a building boom following the 1985 earthquake in Mexico City, so it now has many apartments for rent. That may account for rental prices that are lower than those in SMA (according to numbeo.com). Otherwise, the cost of living in both places is similar.

Because it is much larger than SMA, Cuernavaca offers more advanced medical facilities, better shopping, and other big-city amenities. Cuernavaca also has many foreign university students studying Spanish and a community of expat retirees.

Cuernavaca's state of Morelos has experienced a wave of gang-related violence. But local expats have said it didn't affect them. They also noted that Cuernavaca's overall crime rate is far lower than many U.S. cities.

The bottom line: If you like the idea of spending your retirement in Mexico, either San Miguel de Allende or Cuernavaca could make a great home base!

Protect Yourself From a Pension Going Bust

For millions of Americans, a pension remains a solid "third leg" of the retirement stool after Social Security and personal savings. And while nearly all pension plans are backed by the federal government, pensions can fail. Then what do you do?

First, here are some facts to keep in mind: When a private pension plan goes under, the government does step in to assume at least part of the liability.

Corporations pay premiums to a government agency, the Pension Benefit Guaranty Corp. Just like any insurer, the agency pays out if a bankruptcy damages the viability of the plan. A striking example of this occurred in 2005, when United Airlines won the right to default on its pension obligations, resulting in the biggest-ever pension failure, with $7.4 billion in claims.

The federal government expects up to 173 multi-employer pension plans to run out of money over the coming decade. Some are large and some are small, but in every case, there is a risk that employees will receive less than they expected from a federally rescued plan.

In number terms, the government guarantees up to specific monthly payments by age if your plan fails and is turned over to the agency. In 2015, for instance, a 70-year-old could expect up to $8,318 per month, while a 62-year-old would have gotten up to $3,959.

If your plan goes bust, and the payout is less than you had budgeted or planned for, you'll be left scrambling to rethink your retirement strategy. "If someone fears that their pension will fail, they should plan their retirement accordingly and plan as if that source of income will not be there," says David C. Jozefiak, a certified financial planner in Sterling Heights, Michigan. "They will need to make sure they have sufficient income from other sources to meet or exceed their expenses. They must also account for inflation and how much more their expenses may be 20, 30, or more years into retirement."

One way is to delay receiving Social Security payments, which increases the monthly payments by about 8 percent a year up to the ultimate retirement age of 70. Delaying retirement and saving more is a help (obviously), as well as reducing expenses sooner and paying off debts, such as a mortgage.

Most important, all near-retirees should "practice" living on their eventual retirement income well ahead of the actual start of retirement, Jozefiak says. "Six months or more prior I have them begin living on that reduced income — the extra income gets saved," he explains.

"I have found they will try very hard and be willing to make sacrifices if necessary to try to make it work," he says. "Ultimately, they will be able to decide for themselves whether it is going to work, which makes my conversation a lot easier on either moving forward or discussing alternatives."

One such alternative might be tapping into other assets to make up the gap. Chances are, the largest single investment you own after a pension and Social Security payments will be your home. If your mortgage is paid up, a good course of action might be to unlock some of that value, says Donald L. Reichert, a chartered financial consultant in Greenville, South Carolina.

"If someone had some real concerns about the prospect that a pension plan might fail, they have a couple of simple choices," Reichert says. "Consider selling the home to the children and renting it back on a long-term lease, or either refinancing the home to pull a block of equity out or selling the home and renting something."

The equity cash could be used to purchase a single-premium immediate annuity on one or both of the spouses. "Depending on age, the guaranteed rate of return on the equity used to purchase the annuity would more than likely be substantially higher than the payments on the line of credit on the borrowed amount or on the monthly rent expense," Reichert says. "The older the annuitant, the higher the payout rate on the principal."

5 Post-Retirement Careers Worth Considering

For years, you dreamed of settling into a fun, relaxing retirement. But for any number of reasons — boredom, financial necessity, or a yearning to embark on a second career path — you found yourself hoping to return to the workforce.

As you submit your resumé for open positions, you can't help but wonder: Are there companies willing to embrace older workers?

"Many older job seekers know age discrimination, although tough to prove, is a fact of life," says Kerry Hannon, career and retirement expert, and author of *Love Your Job: The New Rules for Career Happiness, What's Next? Finding Your Passion and Your Dream Job in Your Forties, Fifties,* and *Beyond and Great Jobs for Everyone 50+*. "But increasingly they're finding jobs at smaller organizations — nonprofits, startups, trade associations and niche educational programs. Typically, these employers operate with a spare staff and depend on the experience and expertise that comes with age."

By 2050, according to Pew Research projections, about one in five Americans will be over 65, up from 13 percent of the U.S. population now. "This demographic shift is already creating new opportunities for workers of all ages," Hannon says. "These are jobs and services people in their 50s and 60s can do to cater to those in their 70s, 80s, and 90s living longer, healthier lives." Hannon shares five career opportunities to consider:

1. HEALTH CARE

The aging population and longer life expectancies are spurring a wide range of healthcare-related jobs. In fact, for the period 2012 to 2022, the U.S. Bureau of Labor Statistics projects that industries related to healthcare will generate 5 million new jobs.

Look for jobs at public and private hospitals, nursing and residential care facilities, and individual and family services. Specific jobs to explore in the sector include dietitian and nutritionist, personal and home healthcare aide, registered nurse or licensed/practical nurse, nurse practitioner, school nurse, paramedical examiner (screening individuals applying for life or healthcare insurance), skincare specialist, and medical equipment sales.

2. Financial Services

As boomers slide into their retirement years, they're increasingly seeking help with managing their money, whether it's bill paying, estate planning, or choosing the right insurance policy.

Moreover, as traditional employer-provided pensions are being replaced by 401(k)s and similar plans, demand is on the rise among all age groups for experts who can make sense of retirement investment.

"Little wonder that the Bureau of Labor Statistics predicts job growth in the financial activities arena to rise about 10 percent in the next decade," Hannon says. Jobs to explore include accountant, personal financial adviser, insurance broker, retirement coach, bookkeeper, financial manager, and tax preparer.

3. Move Manager

For those downsizing to smaller quarters — usually an apartment or retirement community — a move manager can coordinate all aspects of a move and configure the setup of the new home.

For instance, as part of the service, a manager can assess what can be sold, donated, or given to friends and family, and may be in charge of shopping for new furniture that suits the new home, or organizing and running an estate or yard sale.

For more information on courses and certification, contact the National Association of Senior Move Managers (www.nasmm.org).

For leads on jobs, stop by real estate offices and visit retirement and assisted-living communities to ask about their future residents' needs.

4. Patient Advocate

Some advocates tackle billing mistakes and insurance coverage rejections. Others might help in choosing doctors, offer guidance in treatment choices, assist in locating a specialist or hospital, go with patients to doctor appointments and keep track of prescriptions.

Job opportunities might include working on staff as an advocate or patient navigator at a hospital. Nurses, social workers, medical professionals, and insurance experts are in high demand for these positions. No licenses are required, but there are credential programs available.

5. FITNESS TRAINER

If you're fit, you can share that with others. Trainers teach group classes and one-on-one sessions.

"Aqua aerobics is one growing specialty, as is 'accessible' yoga, which adapts techniques for people with chronic illness and disabilities," Hannon explains. "Instructors tweak traditional yoga positions for people who are in a chair or wheelchair or have other physical issues."

Certification isn't required by law, but most fitness clubs demand it; an understanding of physiology, proper exercise practices, and an ability to judge a client's fitness level is essential.

Guide to a Fully Funded Retirement

We've all heard the dismal retirement statistics for the millions of baby boomers now hitting their mid-60s. By one measure, nearly half the boomers are "at risk" of not having enough income in retirement.

The Employee Benefit Research Institute reports that 47.2 percent of the oldest boomers are in danger of running short, while for younger near-retirees, it's 43.7 percent. Unsurprisingly, more than 70 percent of lower-income households are projected to have retirement shortfalls, but even 41.6 percent of middle-income households are "at risk."

Retirement income is a tough problem, one beset by many unknowns: your longevity, your health, the performance of investments, and the economy. Unless you have several million dollars free and clear today (very few people do), the question of retirement income is a serious one.

Looking for answers, Franklin Prosperity Report spoke to financial planners and advisers around the country. They offered up a lot of considering the question of funding retirement.

MISTAKE NO. 1: AIMING FOR A NUMBER WITHOUT UNDERSTANDING REALITY

A lot of the focus on retirement saving in the past few years has been on reaching the "number" you need to retire. However, that can be a trap, says Kris Carroll, a chartered financial analyst at Carroll Financial Associates in Charlotte, North Carolina.

"A lot of retirees and near-retirees look at their investments too frequently and get focused on the total amount, sometimes on a daily basis. That's a lot of emotional capital tied up in the daily random moves that investment markets tend to make," Carroll says. "You'll be a happier person if you look less often."

Yet the real trouble is focusing on a single number that you need to hit or have hit in order to retire in the first place. For example, you might think $1 million is enough to retire comfortably and enjoy your lifestyle.

"When are you most likely to hit the goal? Typically, it will be after a big move up in the stock market," Carroll says. "So let's say you hit your $1 million goal at the end of 1999. You tell your boss to 'take this job and shove it' and walk out to enjoy your retirement. During your first three years of retirement, the stock market goes down each year, and three years later, you are thinking about going back to work."

Moreover, research has shown that when equity values are higher, the sustainable withdrawal from a diversified portfolio is lower, Carroll says. "It is easier to delay retirement by one year than to go back to work three years later. Give yourself some room for error," Carroll says. "I'm not calling for another bear market, but I wouldn't risk my livelihood betting that it won't happen."

MISTAKE NO. 2: FAR TOO ROSY PROJECTIONS

If you plan conservatively and carefully, you can live out the retirement of your dreams and live a rich, rewarding life along the way, says Elle Kaplan founding partner of LexION Capital Management in New York. Big assumptions can get you into a lot of trouble down the line.

You'd never get in a car without an idea of your endpoint and think, "I hope I just end up in the right place," Kaplan explains. You would, of course, carefully choose your destination and the best route to get there. Your financial life is no different, Kaplan says: You need a retirement road map that is customized to fit your individual situation and goals.

"Every assumption you make should be extremely conservative," Kaplan says. "Plan like you'll live to be 100, and make contingency plans for everything. Your plan should take into account all the factors that might affect you in retirement, like each and every one of your anticipated expenses, what you'll be receiving in Social Security, what kind of investment risks you're able to tolerate, and so on.

"Your savings become your paycheck and must last the rest of your life," she adds. It's easy to find ways to spend extra money but much more difficult to deal with a shortfall."

MISTAKE NO. 3: CONFUSING YOUR FUTURE WITH YOUR PARENTS' PAST

Boomers need to know this is not their parents' retirement, says Tom Scanlon, a certified financial planner in Manchester, Connecticut. "Many of our parents had a pension plan when they retired. Now pensions are mostly limited to federal, state, and municipal workers. Boomers that want a fully funded retirement need to know they are on their own," he says.

That means having planned, saved, and invested to have that fully funded retirement by taking advantage of a 401(k) plan and both traditional and Roth individual retirement accounts. Along with Social Security, private retirement funds will provide a basis for retirement income, Scanlon says.

If the plan is funded correctly, many retirees are better off waiting until full retirement age before collecting Social Security, Scanlon advises. Additionally, they should consider downsizing their large homes sooner rather than later because it will cut down on monthly living expenses. "They should also consider working part time during retirement. The extra income will be nice to have, but staying active and engaged is a huge benefit," Scanlon says.

MISTAKE NO. 4: PUTTING ALL YOUR RETIREMENT PLAN EGGS IN ONE TAX BASKET

Americans pay a lot of taxes during their working years — Social Security and Medicare taxes, income taxes at the state and federal levels, real estate and investment taxes, and so on. Some of those taxes can be deferred and some not, so the key to a strong retirement income is being able to control those tax rates.

Retirement savers thus should seriously consider opening a Roth IRA, says Michael Clark, a certified financial planner in Orlando, Florida. Have some money in a tax-deferred account such as an IRA or 401(k), Clark says, and some in a Roth, which is tax-free because you made the original contribution with already taxed income.

"We have all heard we should diversify our investments. Believe it or not, it's the exact same thing with your future tax liability," Clark explains. "When you use both Roth and pre-tax accounts, you are diversifying the taxes that you are going to have to pay in the future. You are going to have some taxable accounts, and you are going to have some tax-free accounts. This will give you options in retirement."

If tax rates are high in a given year, Clark continues, then you can take tax-free distributions from your Roth instead. If halfway through retirement your tax rates drop (say you move to a state with no income tax), you can take taxable distributions from your tax-deferred accounts.

"Having both accounts will allow you to play around with your tax bracket," he explains.

MISTAKE NO. 5: ASSUMING A RULE OF THUMB APPLIES TO YOU

A lot of financial advisers assume that a retiree's spending will go up by the rate of inflation, yet a J.P. Morgan study found that many costs such as clothing and meals go down and really only medical spending consistently rose, says Neil Brown, a certified financial planner in West Columbia, South Carolina. "Their spending did not go up as much as people assumed. Your health care is going to rise, and your other spending is going to fall," Brown says. "If you don't spend as much, the amount you need to save will be lower."

The longstanding rule of thumb was to spend no more than 4 percent of your portfolio annually if you wanted the money to last. But in today's near-zero-interest-rate world, that is now more realistically 3 percent. There are other things you can do to manage spending, like moving to a tax-friendly state for retirees and delaying Social Security.

"You can add 10 to 20 percent to Social Security with planning. It can add two or three years to your retirement planning," Brown says. "If you have other assets, it's usually a good decision to delay Social Security."

Asset allocation matters, too. "If you don't need a lot of risk to meet your goal, you don't need a lot of equities," he says. "Don't under-save and retire early and then take on a risky portfolio because you didn't have the discipline to reach your goals during your working years."

Nevertheless, as you get older, equities can play a growing role, Brown says. "Be conservative in the first year you retire, but add 1 or 2 percent in equities as you age. If you have a big loss early, it hurts more than having a big loss later," he says.

MISTAKE NO. 6: IGNORING WHAT MAY BE YOUR SINGLE GREATEST ASSET, YOUR HOME

Most people have heard of a home equity conversion mortgage, often called a reverse mortgage. But few realize how powerful it can be as a standing credit line, says Bill Parker, a CPA and reverse mortgage specialist at Wallick & Volk mortgage bankers in Scottsdale, Arizona.

"One of my favorite uses is when one spouse has taken out a single-person pension payment, set up a home equity conversion mortgage early, let it grow at government-guaranteed rates, and then we use it to supplement the income of the surviving spouse when the pension receiver passes away," Parker says.

The key is that, by federal law, the unused portion of the credit line grows at the same interest rate of the loan. You could compound interest over several years until you really need the cash flow later on. "Over 15 years, a $200,000 line of credit can grow to $400,000, and it's guaranteed by the government. Unlike a home equity line of credit, the value of your house has nothing to do with it," Parker says.

"I think over time planners are going to start using it as a planning tool," he says. "Imagine if you could avoid taking out Social Security and instead use the line of credit, then at age 70 get full Social Security benefits. This will help millions."

MISTAKE NO. 7: MAKING TOO MANY DECISIONS IN A SHORT PERIOD OF TIME

One of the problems facing near-retirees is "decision fatigue," says Douglas Goldstein, a certified financial planner and co-author of

Rich as a King: How the Wisdom of Chess Can Make You a Grandmaster of Investing. In short, they try to make too many decisions in a short period of time — even in a single day — and wind up making poor choices.

You run into this tactic in everyday life, Goldstein points out. "Car salesmen are trained to walk you through a series of decisions in which you are likely to choose the default, like worthless anti-rust coating." The brain simply turns off as fatigue builds. The same thing can happen with investment and retirement planning, Goldstein warns. When people make too many decisions late in the day, for instance, they tend to be too conservative.

In the case of investors, they when they should be investing for growth. A good financial planner will not force too many decisions on an investor too quickly for precisely this reason. "A retirement plan is a great tool, but make your investment decisions when you're fresh the next day," he says.

The 3 Most Important Calculations You Must Make Before Retiring

We all have financial goals. Paying the mortgage is an obvious one, as well as keeping up with utilities and grocery bills. Medium term, we tend to think of paying off a car or saving for our kids to attend college. But here's the thing: Those weekly and monthly financial targets are minor concerns if you let them distract you from the truly important thing: retirement.

Indeed, retiring on time and in good financial condition is truly the first and most important money-related goal you should have, no matter what your age. When you're in your prime income-earning years, you have options — but once you've hit retirement, if you're not already positioned to pay for your living expenses, your back is against the wall.

To start the planning process, everyone faces the same three simple questions. They require a bit of math to help each of us find a reasonable, applicable answer to our own situation. Here, then, are the three most important calculations you must make in order to retire comfortably:

1. HOW MUCH SHOULD I SAVE?

This is a tricky question. Not everyone earns the same salary, nor does everyone have the same expenses, now or in retirement.

While you cannot easily change how much you earn, it is easy to control how long you save. Ultimately, time is like rocket fuel for savers. At a market rate of 7 percent, a saver who puts away $5,000 a year for 40 years will retire with around $1.1 million. A person who starts later, leaving just 20 years to save, has to put away a lot more money to get the same ending figure — $25,000 a year, every year.

So to catch up, our late-blooming saver can reach the same goal by either saving more or earning more on his or her money. In our example, over 20 years, if you save just $5,000 a year and want to reach that same end result, you'll need to figure out a way to earn about 20 percent on your money (which admittedly would involve a lot of risk). Really, the older you start seriously saving, the more you'll need to save while balancing your threshold for risk with the potential rewards.

All these gains are fueled by compounding. When you put aside money, it earns interest over time. That interest in turn is added to your principal, where it begins to earn interest on itself, over and over, above and beyond any money you add.

Compounding drives the entire financial world, from simple bank loans to credit cards and everything between. The helpful calculation you'll need is the "rule of 72." If you know the interest rate you expect to earn, divide that into 72. The result is the number of years it will take for your savings to double in value.

Example: The rate of return on, say, a real estate investment fund is 9 percent. Divide 9 into 72 to get 8. Thus, earning 9 percent, your money will double in eight years.

2. HOW MUCH WILL I NEED?

People love big round numbers. In retirement terms, we tend to think of $1 million as a goal, irrespective of the underlying realities of our cost of living, inflation, and other factors. A million bucks might be enough for you to live well in retirement. But it could just as easily be too much or far too little. Investment firms like to simplify things by talking about multiples of your current income. Benefits consultant Aon Hewitt, for instance, came up with 11 times your final pay at age 65.

So if you make $85,000 a year that last year, Hewitt figures you need $935,000. Of course, if you retire early, the number is higher, and if you leave work later, it's lower.

Chad Nehring, a certified financial planner in Appleton, Wis., prefers a slightly more precise number. "Generally, after-tax retirement should equal your after-tax working income times 0.75, adding 0.05 for each five years you are under the age of 70," Nehring explains (since younger retirees are more active, travel more, and thus spend more). "For example, if you retire at age 65, then 0.80 is the percentage to use."

Example: Your after-tax income is $65,000. You decide to retire at age 65. Your after-tax retirement income should be $52,000.

3. HOW LONG WILL IT LAST?

The average retired worker in 2013 took home $15,228 in Social Security payments. If you expect your investments to earn 4 percent in retirement, you will need $920,000 to make up the gap in the above scenario.

Nehring cautions, however, that taxes and inflation also figure into your retirement income. You might need more than a 4 percent return, or simply more cash at the start, if you live long in retirement or have higher-than-expected taxes.

Example: Subtracting $15,228 from $52,000 equals $36,772. A portfolio of $920,000 throwing off 4 percent as an income stream (simply doing an ordinary calculation of 4 percent of $920,000) produces $36,800.

Words to the Wise

BONUS TIP!
The Importance of an Emergency Fund

Just 4 in 10 Americans could cover an unexpected $1,000 expense. That means millions of us are just one hospital stay or car breakdown away from broke. According to a Bankrate survey of 1,000 people in January, most would resort to borrowing at a high rate of interest to cover the extra spending.

A separate WalletHub survey of 500 people found that 1 in 3 Americans is afraid that a single large purchase will mean maxing out existing credit cards. What's more, they defined as "large" as an expense above $100.

One way to reduce your risk is to adjust your tax withholding. If you get a refund every year, reduce the amount withheld from your paycheck, then set up an automated investment into your savings account for the same amount (or more). Set up reminders to automatically increase that amount by 10 percent every six months. You likely won't miss the money, and most importantly, you'll be beefing up your emergency fund.

Chapter 7

Alternative
Income

"BY FAILING TO PREPARE,
YOU ARE PREPARING TO FAIL."

How to Profit from Stuff You've Inherited

When a loved one dies, you not only have to deal with your grief, you also have to deal with their belongings. There will surely be some items you'll want to keep, but there's bound to be others you want to get rid of, and if you're smart, you can make money from them.

How? You'll typically have too much for a garage sale, and many items are too bulky for eBay and too valuable to give away. Enter estate sales.

While most people think of estate sales as the liquidation of expensive homes, jewelry, and heirlooms, it's better to think of them as high-level garage sales. Indeed, they're not only useful when trying to get rid of other people's stuff, but your own as well. Experts say the motivations for holding an estate sale are typically one of the Four Ds: downsizing, divorce, debt, and death. Because estate sales involve many things for sale, and potentially of high value, you'll likely want to hire a professional firm to organize, advertise, and appraise the belongings.

To make sure the liquidation agent is reputable, check with the Better Business Bureau or scan online reviews. Unfortunately, there are no national licensing, ethics, or insurance regulations and no central repository for complaints. What's more, many liquidators have no formal training, which means anyone can get into the business. Reputable agents should offer to do a free walk-through assessment.

Once you find a qualified business, everything in your home being offered for sale is tagged with a price. This is why you may also see estate sales called "tag" sales. However, the owner or family cannot attend the sale, so before you open the doors to the public, be sure all of the tagged items are things other family members don't want.

From there, it's like an organized garage sale. Potential buyers show up and use a sign-in sheet or take a number to keep the sale orderly and determine who can enter and purchase items at any given time.

Estate sales are usually scheduled to take from one to three days. As the sale progresses, prices are reduced to try to clear out unsold inventory. At the end of the sale, anything unsold is normally purchased by the estate-sale firm — but for just pennies on the dollar. The good news is that if you're really trying to get rid of it, at least you'll have a guaranteed buyer.

GOING ONCE, GOING TWICE, SOLD!

If the thought of having people traipsing through your home isn't appealing, you can hire a firm to hold an auction. With this method, you get two choices: online or gallery.

An online auction means the stuff stays in your home, but a firm will take up to three days to catalogue and price everything and perhaps 20 to 30 days to market the event. Once that's done, an online auction is held, normally lasting from one to two weeks. The biggest benefit is that you have the entire world as potential buyers — not just locals. Also, competition means bidding wars can break out, and you may receive much more than expected for some items.

A gallery auction means your things get moved to the agent's location, which will later host a live auction. However, there's usually additional costs for the company to relocate your things.

Whether online or gallery, you'll generally get more things sold — and at higher prices — than you would with an on-site estate sale. Another benefit of either style of auction is that there are licensing, ethics, bonding, and insurance requirements for auctions in most states.

No matter which method you choose to dispose of your stuff, you'll have to pay hefty fees. Liquidation agents usually take between 30% and 40% of all proceeds. So if the sale brings in $20,000, you'll receive between $12,000 and $14,000.

ARE THE FEES WORTH IT? IT DEPENDS.

Estate sales run by professionals usually net better overall results. Professionals are trained in holding sales and usually have large networks of followers and collectors. The more they sell — and the more money they receive — the more they make. So they have a strong incentive to sell everything at the highest price. However, if you don't have a lot of things for sale, you may consider doing it yourself.

Make Money from a DIY Estate Sale

In today's online world, it's easy to host your own estate sale. These make the most sense if you have just a few potentially valuable items.

Advertising is free on Craigslist and Facebook. You can also use websites like EstateSales.net and EstateSales.org, which allow you to list your estate sale.

The most difficult part is the appraisal. If it's easily identifiable by a brand and model number, such as a Nikon D850 camera, look at completed eBay auctions to get an idea of what it's worth. However, if you have unique pieces such as art, jewelry, antiques, or exotic rugs, get a professional appraiser. You'd hate to discover you sold a Picasso painting for $10. It's happened before.

Here's an estate sale checklist to help:

THE DAY BEFORE:
- **Stage the house:** Common items should be grouped together and placed in the room in which they would be used. For example, all the kitchen utensils should stay in the kitchen.
- **Set up tables:** Smaller items should be neatly displayed on tables throughout the house, but also have a table at checkout for people to stack up their items while paying.
- **Clear a path:** Crowded rooms and hallways can create chaos when people are just milling around. Map out how that allows people to move through every room, and set up signs along the way to keep things moving in the right direction.
- **Go to the bank:** You'll need plenty of cash, especially smaller bills, to make change.

SALE DAY:
- **Manage the crowd:** If the sales starts at 9:00, you can be sure people will start arriving by 7:00 (seasoned buyers may show up the day before). Don't let anyone in early, and limit the number of people going through the house at any one time.
- **Control the exits:** There should be one door for going in and out. Block off other exits.

- **Use a receipt book:** If you're the estate trustee you'll need to account for every sale, and keeping records can head off potential disputes with buyers.
- **Take a deep breath:** Planned correctly, an estate sale should draw 100 to 200 people, or more. You need to be mentally prepared to deal with the crowd, and you need to be emotionally prepared to see strangers pawing through the merchandise. Buyers don't have a personal connection to your family. So while some of their actions or questions may seem rude, remember, it's just business.

CLOSING UP SHOP:

- **Disposal:** Schedule purchase pickups and removal of all leftover items.
- **Clean up:** Take down any posted signage in the house and neighborhood.
- **Take a break:** Put your feet up and count your cash!

Earn Extra Cash With These 5 Easy Business Ideas

Maybe your goal for the coming years is to start earning a little extra cash to help supplement your Social Security check and retirement accounts. Or perhaps you're looking to create a new career with more freedom and flexibility.

There's never been a better time to explore entrepreneurship. According to a Gallup study, about 57 million Americans, or 36% of U.S. workers, are now involved in the gig economy. And if this trend keeps growing at its current pace, more than half of the U.S. workforce will participate in it by 2027.

While entrepreneurship may sound exciting, the upfront investment required to get started can be a deterrent. Thankfully, you don't always have to spend money to make money. In fact, there are plenty of businesses that cost next-to-nothing to start.

What's more, you don't have to become an Uber driver or Amazon package delivery person to get your piece of the entrepreneurship pie.

Actually, there are plenty of options to choose from, depending on your interests, lifestyle and skill set.

One of the following real-life examples might be a great fit — or you can use these ideas as a jumping off point for your own venture:

1. STUDENT TUTORING

Are you a former schoolteacher, or do you just love passing your knowledge on to the next generation? Student tutoring is a low-cost business idea that's perfect for anyone who's strong in academics.

"All you need is an expertise in a specific subject and a bit of money to put out some targeted social media ads for marketing," says Shaan Patel, founder and CEO of Prep Expert. "There is no other major overhead to contend with, and with referrals from happy customers, you can cut down your marketing costs even further."

2. PRINT ON DEMAND

You know that cute mug donning your granddaughter's picture? It likely came from a print-on-demand (POD) site, which takes your designs and prints them on T-shirts, hoodies, mugs and other gear to sell. The best part? The products are only printed when a customer wants to buy one, meaning there's no waste, little risk, and the costs are low.

"POD sites handle the printing, shipping, payments, customer service and returns," explains Becca Whitestone, a side hustle expert, online entrepreneur, and founder of the blog Boost My Budget. "All you have to do is upload your digital file to the platform, write a description, and set your price. This means there's no inventory piling up in your living room."

She says there are free graphic design programs — such as Canva and GIMP — that you can use to create your designs. And POD sites don't require any money upfront; they simply take a royalty out of sales.

While there are dozens of different POD sites out there (such as Zazzle, Teespring, and Redbubble), Whitestone prefers Amazon's print on demand platform, called Merch by Amazon, because you get access to Amazon's enormous customer base.

3. BLOGGING

Do you have a deep wealth of knowledge about a particular topic? Share your wisdom with the world through blogging.

"I started a financial independence and entrepreneurship blog in the summer of 2018 and have made little investment in the site since its founding," says Riley Adams, a licensed CPA who founded Young and the Invested.

His initial investment of about $1,500 covered a domain name, hosting, and web development expenses. And now that site traffic is growing, Adams has begun to find ways to monetize it. He's now making around $1,000 month through ads and affiliate links that drive revenue.

"With time, I'll need to invest more in content development, but only for the sake of improving my revenue with additional site traffic," he concludes.

4. FREELANCING AND CONSULTING

Anyone who spent their career as a writer, editor, designer, or photographer knows that freelancing was always an option if you didn't desire the safety net of a corporate salary and benefits. Retirement can be the perfect time to explore this avenue.

"Find a customer, provide the service, and get paid," says Nick Loper of Side Hustle Nation. "There's no inventory to buy, no audience to build, and you probably don't even need a website to get started."

Websites like Fiverr and UpWork allow you to bid on projects or list your services so interested parties can find and hire you (the platforms take a cut of your earnings, of course). Or you can find clients on your own and keep all the profits for yourself.

This path works especially well if you have a strong network. Other backgrounds also work well in freelancing and consulting business models, such as accountants, event planners, virtual assistants, translators, and more.

5. RESELLING FREE GOODS

One man's trash is another man's treasure — and there's no shortage of local Facebook groups and re-sell apps that provide such opportunities. Apps such as Offer Up, LetGo, and Craigslist, and online marketplaces like Swip Swap and Facebook Marketplace, all have "free" sections that could mean cash in your pocket.

"Every morning, check these platforms, scan for free items that hold value, such as couches, appliances, and electronics," says Joe Staiber, CEO and founder of Staiber Consulting, who funded his entire startup using the money he made reselling items in college. "You then contact the person behind the listing and schedule a date for pickup."

Alternatively, if you enjoy perusing garage sales and thrift stores, it's easy to negotiate a great deal, then resell it for more money later if you have the storage space.

How to Turn Your Social Media Following Into Cash

You might roll your eyes at the persistent stream of hashtags that punctuate my social media streams. And while everything from selfies to pictures of meals to your dog's favorite chew toy appear to be just personal expressions, scores of savvy social media users have figured out how to turn those tweets and tags into passive revenue streams.

In fact, Statista estimates that the influence marketing industry will reach $2.6 billion by next year. Clearly, if you're aggressive and dedicated, it is possible to turn your social media skills into a well-paying career.

However, that level of income requires consistent effort and unwavering dedication. So not everyone will be able to make a career out of being a social media influencer. But even if you're not quite ready to quit your day job and start making videos for your own YouTube channel, there are plenty of ways you can earn some extra bucks if you have a decent following on social media.

BECOME A BRAND AMBASSADOR

One great way is to reach out to brands in your niche or interest area to see if they might be interested in using you as a brand ambassador for a company or product.

In this role, you can receive freebies and even earn cash once you can prove your engagement creates actual sales.

Instagram micro-influencer, Christina Maria Chrysanthou (@ TheChristinaMaria) suggests reaching out to brands that have products you currently do — or might — use on a regular basis. She says it's much easier to churn out new content (that could turn into commission for you) for products you already like and know well.

It's also better for the company (because you're already a fan) and easier for you to be able to take new photos of yourself with the product.

For example, she wears workout clothing all day every day and is a fan of one brand's specific type of leggings. When she became a brand ambassador for these leggings, she received a discount on that brand's clothing, which enabled her to buy more of the company's leggings.

That means she's typically wearing them in the pictures she posts, whether she's at lunch with her pals or specifically promoting a new style she's trying out.

When she posts as a brand ambassador, she tries to always advertise the brand by directing followers to a link to purchase the leggings. She then receives a percentage of the sale.

Along with the potential for a cash commission, a brand ambassador role can yield free swag too. Shaunda Necole, a brand ambassador in Las Vegas, Nevada, says she receives an average of five new outfits each month and says she's usually able to select the items she prefers.

PROMOTE LIKE A PRO

How do you go about getting a brand ambassador gig? Start by creating a media kit that details the demographics of your followers, your level of engagement with them, and the platform(s) you use (Instagram, Facebook, Twitter, etc.).

Then craft a custom email to the company that describes your niche, your reach, and shows how you can create content for the brand and use your followers to boost the company's engagement and sales. Be sure to explain all the reasons why you are uniquely qualified to be a good ambassador for that particular product or brand.

The best way to contact companies? You can direct message them on Instagram or do some research on the company's website to find the email address of their influencer marketing manager.

Or consider joining a network, such as Klear (www.klear.com) or Brandwatch (www.brandwatch.com). These platforms are basically clearinghouses that connect social media influencers with companies that are looking to boost their influence marketing programs.

THE RIGHT WAY TO USE HASHTAGS

If you want to attract a company's interest without directly contacting it, simply include a relevant hashtag in all of your posts, recommends Necole. This way, the company can see that you're already a fan and can gauge the interest of your followers, too.

But you have to make sure the hashtags are really specific to your post. Using generalized hashtags that don't call out brand names (such as "girl," "holiday," or "fun") won't work for you, as they are too broad, and your post will get lost in a sea of thousands of other off-topic posts.

Any post on Instagram or Twitter should include a hashtag with the brand name shown in the photo and any specific hashtag or tag line that the brand is currently promoting. You can find that information in the company's bio or marketing materials on its website or social media site.

Doing this helps you get a social media marketer's attention. Many companies have dedicated staff devoted to monitoring the company's social media engagement, which includes users who tag them in posts.

You can also use some hashtags that represent your niche, but try to be as specific as you can, using tags that describe exactly what is going on in your photo.

For ideas, you can search for hashtags in your niche on Instagram by going to the hashtag search and clicking on one you are considering. You'll see many similar and suggested hashtags that will relate to the same audience. Necole says she might use up to 20 hashtags in one Instagram post's caption.

To enhance the appearance of your hashtags, break them up into neat paragraphs. Putting hashtags at the end of a post with line breaks makes them more visually pleasing to your audience and keeps them from detracting from your post.

Another trick: Ask your audience questions in the hashtags. For instance, use #Doyoulovethisdeal instead of simply #deal. This will boost your engagement with your followers, which is what you need to attract corporate eyeballs.

THE KEY INGREDIENT

There's no need to wait until you have tens of thousands of followers to get started either. The most important thing for piquing a company's interest is having an audience that engages with your content.

Even if you only have 500 to 1,000 followers, if your audience is engaged with your content (clicking through to links you post, retweeting your tweets, etc.), brands will see you as a legitimate influencer.

Just be sure to create posts that are authentic, attention-grabbing, and offer something for your followers. Before you know it, you'll be making money from your social media platforms.

Rent Your Home to Movie Producers for Big Cash

Whether you have a cute bungalow in the city, or a Victorian house nestled in a remote corner of town with trees draped in Spanish moss, your home could be turned into a surprising income stream . . . and become a famous movie star!

Across America, television, feature film, and commercial film crews are using McMansions, log cabins, lofts, farmhouses, and more in their productions. And those properties are almost always privately owned by homeowners just like you who rent to camera crews for filming.

While the bragging rights are cool, the money is even better. Renting your home to a production crew can net anywhere from $1,000 to $5,000 or more a day, depending on location, size, features, and how the property will be used (exterior only, just one room, etc.). But you have to be willing to allow actors and directors to invade your space and tinker with it as they see fit.

GETTING YOUR HOME NOTICED

To see your home in lights, you need to grab the attention of a location scout who is connected to the production industry.

Eric Johnson, the founder of a creative studio called You Betcha, which produces branding videos and other short-form media projects, says location scouts are usually used by the production companies to find locations.

Most scouts pull potential sites from databases like Set Scouter (www. setscouter.com) or CinemaScout (ca.reel-scout.com). You can also contact your local film office or tourism board.

To get noticed by a scout, take professional (or professional quality) photos of the property, highlighting its charm, uniqueness, amenities, etc., and post them on one or more location database sites. In your listing, document how the property is laid out and the characteristics that the property offers.

You must be the property owner to list it on Set Scouter (as is the case with most databases and tourism boards). There is no cost to list your space, and you keep 100% of your negotiated rental rate. Set Scouter is paid directly by the production team.

The information and types of projects in these databases varies. For instance, Set Scouter specializes in smaller productions (commercials, music videos, and branded content). An average production is 12 hours, with a cast and crew of about 15 people.

Set Scouter collects mandatory security deposits from the filmmaker for any minor damages. When agreeing to use of your home via Set Scouter, your home is also covered by the production company's insurance policy.

But before you list your home as a potential filming location, it's a good idea to speak with an insurance agent to see what's required of you and the film crew to ensure that you're covered in the event of an accident.

HOW THE PROS DO IT

Real Estate analyst, Emile L'Eplattenier's photogenic loft in Brooklyn has garnered a lot of attention from location scouts over the years. Although he's been approached many times for shoots, he's only agreed to a handful, because there are many things to consider if you want to have your home featured in a film.

Here's what he says you need to know if you're gearing up to turn your abode into a star.

1. Get it in writing.

The only law that applies to most shoots is Murphy's Law. Anything that can go wrong will go wrong. That shoot that the location scout said would be done in six hours might not be done for 12 hours. For indie projects, almost everyone promises the moon, and almost no one can back it up. Worse, delays are very common, so you may have spent a night in a Motel 6 for no reason. So if you want to limit your inconvenience, put your requirements in writing.

In addition, most shoots will require their own props and lighting. That means your furniture — all of your furniture — will more than likely be moved. Make sure you stipulate how your furniture should be handled in writing as well.

Clean up should be spelled out, too — unless you want to spend the next afternoon scraping gaffer's tape off your hardwood floors.

2. Try to get paid (at least partially) in advance.
This is especially important for low-budget or independent film productions. In some instances, a production company might drag its feet to pay contractors they don't think they'll work with again. That means your check goes to the bottom of the priority pile as soon as any budget issues arise.

3. Ask how large the crew will be.
Since even photo shoots can have crews of a dozen or more people, it's important that you ask just how many people will be traipsing through your home and for how long. Maybe you're fine with a dozen people going through your home, but not 50 or more.

4. Make sure the production company has insurance.
Even though you know what your insurance will — or will not — cover, or you're covered through a database like SetScouter, it's smart to know what the crew's insurance will cover.

Damages are not uncommon even if the crew is extra careful. Those college filmmakers might sure seem nice, but will they be able to pay for any damages they do to your property?

5. Make sure your neighbors know.
Since those six-hour shoots can easily become 13-hour shoots, make sure your neighbors know what's happening and discuss with them how they might be impacted by lights, generator noise, the sounds of a large crew next door, etc., especially late at night.

THE BENEFITS
While it might not be enough to fund your child's college education, if your home becomes the backdrop (or main character) in a production, you can collect a few extra bucks and enjoy seeing your house made famous.

Remember, films are expensive to put together, and producers expect to pay well for the locations that they use. L'Eplattenier says the reputable filmmakers he's worked with are all extremely careful and considerate of the locations they enter and often provide limited hassle.

Make Money Blogging

Anyone can have a blog these days. With just $100, you can get a domain name and hosting for a full year. That's a pretty low barrier to entry, making blogs seem like a great, low-risk way to earn money. But how much can you actually make?

Perhaps you've heard wild tales of people earning thousands of dollars a month with their blogs. Nick Eubanks says his blog was earning $8,000 a month at its peak. At that time, he was working about 30 hours a month on it. The blog focused on search engine optimization techniques (a topic in tremendous demand), and he sold it a few years ago for $100,000.

But such experiences are rare. The majority of bloggers earn much less, especially at the beginning. Blogging advice site ProBlogger recently collected earnings information from 1,500 of its readers. The majority of these bloggers, 53 percent, earn less than $100 a month from their blogs, and 10 percent make nothing at all. That's not great, but there is a bright spot: 9 percent of bloggers surveyed earn between $1,000 and $9,999 a month, and 4 percent earn over $10,000 per month!

HOW TO MAKE MONEY BLOGGING

Here are the most common money-making tactics for bloggers. Successful bloggers typically rely on a combination of these revenue sources:

Run ads on your blog.

These include banner ads, pop-up ads, and ads nestled in the copy. Bloggers get paid for the total number of page views (times that page is viewed by visitors) or clickthroughs. Some bloggers sell ads on their sites, and others simply rent out the space to an ad network that fills it with ads tailored to the blog's topic.

Sell services related to your blog's topic.

These can include consulting, one-on-one coaching, speaking, training programs, etc. For almost any blog topic, there is someone willing to pay for advice on that subject.

For example, Donna Smallin Kuper runs a blog called Unclutter .com, which helps people organize their lives. She told me that her blog led to her becoming a spokesperson for several products in that area. "The real money from my blog comes from having a media presence," she said.

Embrace affiliate marketing.

This is a more subtle type of advertising. Instead of a display ad, you endorse a product by mentioning it in one of your blog posts and include a link to the business or product. If any sales are generated by your readers clicking the link and making a purchase, you get a percentage of that sale.

For example, Donna refers her readers to a decluttering course that costs $89. It's taught by another expert, but that person gives her half the fee for making the referral. Lots of bloggers participate in Amazon's affiliate marketing program, which pays up to 10 percent of the sale, depending on the item category.

Sell products.

Examples of digital products include ebooks and online courses. When he had his blog, Nick offered an online course for $150 (3,500 people bought it).

Physical products are an option, too, the most common one being books. One blogger we met named Abigail Perry runs a personal finance blog called IPickUpPennies.net. In 2016, she self-published a book on frugality for people who have depression and earned residuals of $544 from it in 2017.

Write sponsored posts.

A sponsored post is one that another business pays you to write. It's similar to affiliate marketing, but you're writing a full post instead of a brief mention. You'll want to keep sponsored posts to a minimum to keep your readers' trust. Because these posts are online advertising, they are regulated by the Federal Trade Commission. Be sure to peruse the FTC's "Guides Concerning the Use of Endorsements and Testimonials in Advertising" for guidance on staying within the law.

OTHER WAYS BLOGGING CAN EARN YOU MONEY

Of course, there are indirect ways blogs can pay off, too. If you are blogging about topics related to your profession, it may improve your reputation, which can help you to get a raise or land a better-paying job.

Another path is to start blogging for businesses, writing posts that appear on their websites' blogs. This can pay anywhere from a few dollars to hundreds of dollars per post. The easiest way to get these gigs is by targeting businesses that line up with the topic area of your own blog.

The verdict: Starting a blog probably won't make you rich, but it could be a way to earn some solid side money while exploring a topic you're interested in.

Turn Your Trash into Cash

Chances are, you know your home could use a little decluttering, but you're not sure where or how to get started. Or, you've had the sad and sentimental task of cleaning out a loved one's house after their passing and stood in front of a lifetime of collected belongings wondering, "Now what?"

One thing to keep in mind that getting rid of stuff isn't a black and white issue. What one person deems invaluable, another is eager to toss in a dumpster. Decluttering can lead to tears, arguments, and mental and physical exhaustion.

To spare families the stress, confusion, and temptation to close the door and walk away from a pile of clutter, we asked Kelly Juhasz, a fine art and estate appraiser and an accredited member of the International Society of Appraisers (ISA), based in Chicago, for some advice. Our goal was to understand how to best clear out clutter without tossing away anything of value, while also figuring out how to get most money for any items you might choose to sell.

Here's what we learned.

DON'T GO IT ALONE.

Before you begin selecting things to get rid of, talk to family members. This process can be touchy, but you might find that some objects that you didn't realize held special meaning to people.

This not only aids in making decisions, it also helps you convey respect and empathy to family members. Remember, downsizing is an emotional experience. Sometimes, it's not about the "stuff" at all but more about the relationships and family stories.

GROUP OBJECTS THAT YOU THINK MAY HOLD VALUE.

The next step is making sure no one accidentally does away with something of value, without understanding its worth. Juhasz suggests before making any piles or scheduling a dumpster delivery, look for signatures, markings, craftsmanship, and uniqueness.

Objects that hold value are judged on many characteristics including historical importance tied to an individual or an event, rarity, desirability (current style trends), condition, authenticity, provenance, and intrinsic quality. If you think there are items in the home of value, gather any documentation you may have on them and write down any family stories you remember about them (where you got them, when, what the occasion was). Provenance, the place of origin or the record of ownership, can be used to help authenticate an object and assist in its valuation.

Armed with all these facts, you can now begin to get a valuation of the item to know how to best distribute it.

WORK WITH A QUALIFIED APPRAISER.

You don't want to be one who sells the old master painting in the garage sale for $8 and then see it go up for auction for $1 million the following year. And you can search online or shop around antique sales, etc., to understand an item's value. But that's not always reliable.

So for this special grouping of objects, you can also work with a qualified appraiser such as a member of the International Society of Appraisers (ISA). You'll pay for an appraisal, but a qualified appraiser has specialized education plus experience in working in the specific markets for the property. So you're sure to know exactly what you have, whether or not it's worth selling, and should you part with it, the price to put on a tag.

CREATE FOUR PILES.

After sorting out items that may hold special value, separate the rest of your belongings into four piles: keep, sell, donate, and throw away.

This will help you stay organized and speed up the process of getting rid of stuff that is costing you time and money.

Remember, if you donate any items, keep the receipts for those that are worth up to $250 and written acknowledgment from the charity for donations worth more than $250 to use for your taxes. And don't be shy about throwing away items you believe have no worth and are taking up valuable space.

SEPARATE EMOTION FROM FACT.

When forming those piles, ask yourself: Does it improve your life? Does it really hold sentimental value? Would it be hard to replace? If the answer to those questions is no, it's time for that item to go and possibly turn it into extra cash.

PERFORM A CLOSET MAKEOVER.

If you're simply looking to turn some of your clutter into cash or be able to stand in your closet, garage, or basement, ask yourself, "Have I worn/ used/picked up this in the past two years?" If the answer is no, get rid of it!

GETTING RID OF STUFF THE EASY WAY

Yard sales are always a fun time to get to know your neighbors and sell unwanted items. But it can be time-consuming and sometimes leave you with more work than profit. So if you're lacking spare time, turn to technology to sell your items.

Facebook or eBay's marketplace are options to sell your goods from the comfort of your own home. Other outlets to sell (many times with lower fees than eBay) include Bonanza, Mercari, eBid, and Poshmark. Be sure to factor in the cost of your time to list the item, manage the listing, pack, and ship it.

Auction companies will happily sell everything and anything for you, from antiques to paper towel holders (yes, even those!). However, auction companies really only make sense for high-value assets (antiques, artwork, collectibles, etc.). Otherwise, the commission fees eat up too much of your profits.

Finally, remember to stay calm. It sounds easier than it might feel in the moment, but try to remember to keep cool. If needed, take a step back and take a break from decluttering for a day or two. Or enlist the help of a trusted pal who isn't emotionally invested in the items in your closet or your grandmother's china cabinet. And be patient with yourself. You're clearing out years (or a lifetime) of clutter, and that's no easy feat!

How to Become a Financial Planner & Earn More

Chuck Rylant first got interested in the excitement of finance after watching the movie Quicksilver, starring Kevin Bacon as a stockbroker turned bicycle messenger. Chuck wanted to become a stockbroker, but he didn't have enough money to go to college at age 18, so he went to the police academy instead.

Chuck performed well on the force and got along with his colleagues. As it stood, things were looking more Lethal Weapon than Wall Street. But he just couldn't shake the finance bug.

While still a police officer, Chuck decided to go to school part time to get a bachelor's degree. All the while, he was doing informal financial planning for other cops "over the hood of a car at 3 a.m." He was good at it, and wanted to keep going.

Several years after getting his bachelor's degree, Chuck obtained a master's degree, then completed certifications to officially become a financial planner. He stayed on the force as he built his business and client roster, but after a few years, he was able to leave to do financial planning full time. He's had a successful financial planning practice ever since.

Ever consider becoming a financial planner yourself? If so, read on.

IS IT RIGHT FOR YOU?
A financial planning career might be for you if:

You are perceptive and have good communication skills.
Chuck learned quickly that money arguments between couples are often relationship arguments in disguise. A savvy financial planner must know techniques to navigate these often tricky waters.

You like flexibility.
Financial planners, especially those with their own practices, typically have more control over their hours than other financial professionals,

and they have more control over the types of clients they work with, too. It's also the kind of career that can be continued on either a part time or full-time basis well into retirement.

You like to be in demand.

Financial planning is a burgeoning field, according to the Bureau of Labor Statistics, which projects job growth of 30 percent for financial planners between 2014 and 2024 ("much faster than average," the agency says). Furthermore, the supply of planners is not expected to keep up with that need, due to the number of established planners nearing retirement.

You want a career where experience is an asset.

If financial planning isn't your first occupation, experts say you should at least have knowledge of other industries and the working world in general to succeed in this area. More importantly, you should've encountered and overcome real-life money challenges of your own — what Chuck calls "the life experience to deal with humans and human problems."

You like to help people.

A sincere desire to help others is essential, according to Chuck. He told me that good financial planning is mostly listening to the clients and their needs, and doing what's right for them. It's a rare career where you can earn large sums of money as well as make other people's lives better, but the latter should be your motivation.

STEPS TO BECOMING A FINANCIAL PLANNER

OK, we're going to level with you here. Unlike accountants, lawyers, and real estate agents, the title of "financial planner" has little regulation surrounding it. It's a dirty little secret of the industry that nearly anyone can put out a shingle with little training or experience.

That's a big problem for the millions of Americans who rely on advice from such individuals. Of course there are plenty of good, hard-working, highly qualified people in the business, too, and you can become one of them by following these steps:

1. Obtain a college degree.

The profession doesn't require it by law, but a bachelor's degree (ideally in finance, but it can be any field of study) gives you a distinct edge — not to mention experience and contacts — and it is increasingly preferred by employers.

2. Gain experience in the field.

Entry-level planning jobs may be advertised using titles like "paraplanner," "junior financial adviser," or "financial adviser associate." One avenue is to join a financial institution such as Ameriprise Financial or Wells Fargo Advisors. These companies recruit constantly for new advisers and offer robust training programs that pay a salary while you learn the ropes.

However, be aware that they are sales-focused, and you'll be expected to lean heavily on the institution's products in your recommendations.

An alternative path is to pursue employment at independent firms or fee-only firms, which have fewer — or no — conflicts of interest, depending on the firm. These firms also offer internships and entry-level positions, albeit in smaller numbers than the larger institutions and usually to those who have completed their coursework to become a certified financial planner (more on that below).

3. Take exams to become licensed.

Financial planners provide advice in numerous facets of a client's financial life, and some of those areas require specific licenses. For example, advisers who sell insurance need to be licensed by their state and as an accredited adviser in insurance. Those who sell investments must pass the FINRA Series 7 and Series 66 exams. Many firms expect you to obtain these licenses within five to six months of hire.

4. Demonstrate your expertise with a further credential.

Gaining certification — especially the certified financial planner (CFP) designation, the highest standard available for financial planners — offers you not only more education but also experience, contacts in the field, and marketing opportunities for your business.

Becoming a CFP requires taking specialized coursework, passing an exam, and keeping up with continuing education requirements. The six-hour exam is challenging, with a 64 percent pass rate in 2016, so a high-quality training program is essential.

Choose the format that works best for you: traditional classroom-based instruction, online courses, or self-paced study. Well-regarded training programs include those from JR Financial Group (jrfinancialgroup.com), College for Financial Planning (cffpinfo. com), or The American College of Financial Services (theamer- icancollege.edu). Your local university may also offer a certificate program that can prepare you for the rigorous exam, and many fi- nancial firms (especially independent and fee-only firms) recruit directly from these programs.

Depending on the nature of your business, other credential op- tions — such as personal financial specialist (PFS), chartered finan- cial consultant (ChFC), or chartered financial analyst (CFA) — may make sense, too.

You Can Make Money Mystery Shopping

In today's world of online review sites and customer surveys, mys- tery shopping seems downright quaint.

You'd think that paying someone to physically walk into a store and evaluate it would be unnecessary for a business. Yet mystery shopping remains relevant. The difference comes down to quality. Most online customer feedback skews negative, naturally, and it's unfocused.

That's why companies looking for objective, reliable feedback still turn to mystery shoppers. It's a way for the folks in charge to find out what's really going on in exactly the areas they're interested in.

Everyone still mystery shops, including airlines, cruise lines, casinos, nightclubs, restaurants, grocery stores, bowling alleys, movie theaters, urgent care centers, fitness centers, golf courses, and country clubs.

With all this mystery shopping still going on, it made us wonder how much an individual mystery shopper could cash in. Can a person earn a decent sum by mystery shopping as a side gig or even a full-time job? Who is a good fit? What are the best strategies to make it work financially?

THE IDEAL CANDIDATE

Getting paid to eat, shop, and play sounds like a great gig, but it is a job with real responsibilities and challenges. It's not a free ride, and it's not for everyone. Mystery shopping is best for those with:

- **A flexible schedule.** Many shops request evaluations at specific times of day or days of the week, and reports usually are due within 24 hours. These constraints make mystery shopping a natural fit for retired individuals who have more flexibility and free time. However, Mike shared with me that shoppers of every age are sorely needed in the industry.

- **Comfort with technology.** Much of the process is online, from the listings of assignments to the reports you file. Some mystery shoppers are asked to test a company's mobile app functionality in stores and restaurants.
- **Writing skills.** Reports regularly ask for narrative descriptions in addition to yes or no questions. Your writing should be both clear and error-free.
- **A great memory — or the ability to take notes discreetly.** Every interaction has to be documented, including the names of all individuals. Wait times need to be tracked, and you must remember as many details about the experience as possible.
- **A bit of cash to float.** The industry operates on a reimbursement model, meaning you have to put out some of your money first (or carry charges on your credit card) before you're repaid.
- **Role-playing skills.** Sometimes mystery shoppers are given specific roles to play ("a couple looking at engagement rings" or "a woman buying a mattress for her new home"), and they need to be convincing.

HOW MUCH CAN YOU EARN?

Unlike some careers, mystery shoppers aren't obligated to work a certain number of hours or take certain assignments. You can choose to do as many or as few shops as you like, day by day. That means your income is highly variable and entirely depends on how much time and effort you devote.

Nearly all assignments are paid with a flat fee, with reimbursement for any purchase you are required to make. The average fee is between $10 and $20 per assignment, but can go as high as several hundred dollars for more exclusive assignments. For fine dining, you may be compensated not with money but with a generous reimbursement allowance.

Taking into account travel time, doing the shopping, and submitting your report, the consensus is the work averages $10/hour, plus regularly getting meals, clothing, car maintenance, and entertainment experiences for free.

IS IT WORTH IT?

You won't get rich from mystery shopping unless you start your own company. (You might consider that after you get some experience and if you enjoy the work. The barriers to entry are low for mom-and-pop operations.)

Can you live entirely off mystery shopping? Probably not. But it might be a great option for a retiree with higher-than-anticipated expenses or when Social Security isn't enough.

Part-time workers could use mystery shopping to pick up a little more money with less commitment than a full-time job.

Can you make a career of it? Perhaps an encore career or a flexible side business if you find that you're good at it. Freelancers or other workers already in the "gig economy" (Uber, Airbnb, and the like) could add mystery shopping to their list of options for work.

It also can pay off if you're looking for a hobby, but you'd prefer something that pays rather than costs you money.

The flexibility of the work also should figure into your calculations. You might use mystery shopping to achieve a specific financial goal on your terms, such as putting a little extra toward a mortgage or buying a special gift.

5 WAYS TO EARN HIGHER RATES

There are ways to make mystery shopping more profitable. The best shoppers do this:

1. Don't get scammed by fake companies.

Mystery shopping scams have become a problem in recent years, but it's relatively easy to avoid them. Sign up as an "independent contractor member" with MSPA-NA (Mystery Shopping Providers Association of North America). It's the trade association for the industry, and the de facto clearinghouse for legitimate companies.

The association's opportunity board lists assignments from the 150 or so vetted member companies. Never pay anyone to get access to listings. And beware of any assignment offers you get from a company out of the blue. Legitimate firms have an application process to go through first.

2. Combine shopping assignments.

The savviest mystery shoppers will figure out multiple shops along a route to stack their earnings and spread out the costs of travel and time. At the upper echelon, shoppers might construct an entire vacation where airfare, valet, meals, drinks, and rounds of golf all are comped. At mysteryshopforum.com, novice and experienced mystery shoppers compare notes and share more such strategies.

3. Stick with it.

Mystery shoppers have to "pay their dues" with less interesting shops before they can graduate to better (and better-paying) assignments. During this time, you'll gather the information you need to discover what types of assignments you're good at and enjoy.

4. Build your reputation.

Most mystery shopping companies have a way of scoring their shoppers. Pay attention to feedback if they offer it. The dream assignments — fine dining, rounds of golf, Caribbean cruises — are out there, but they're reserved for experienced shoppers who consistently maintain positive ratings in the system. Consider getting training and certification from MSPA-NA to improve your chances further.

5. Mystery shop with credit cards that pay you.

A sneaky trick: Get yourself a credit card that gives cash-back rewards. If you can get at least 2 percent back on all the purchases you make as a shopper, you can eke out a little bonus cash for yourself.

Become a Startup Investor
Like the Sharks on TV

If you've ever dreamed of being an entrepreneur, you're probably familiar with the TV show Shark Tank. In each program, four entrepreneurs face several "sharks," rich and successful business people who, if impressed with the entrepreneur's presentation, will invest in his or her business.

Normally, the presentation starts with the entrepreneur introducing his or her new product. The entrepreneurs are highly enthusiastic and typically describe their products as "revolutionary breakthroughs" that will either uniquely solve a common problem or blow away similar solutions that are currently on the market. The entrepreneur then demonstrates how the product works, passes out samples for the sharks try for themselves, and the entrepreneur concludes by saying there is no doubt this product has huge sales potential. All that's needed is for one or more sharks to invest the requested amount so the entrepreneur can produce and distribute the product on a large scale, and everyone involved will make big money.

The hard-nosed sharks are not easily impressed. Their usual response is skepticism. The leading skeptic, bald-headed shark Kevin O'Leary, also known as "Mr. Wonderful." Still, there are always a few products that impress, and one or more deals are made.

Shark Tank's executive producer says at least half of the entrepreneurs who appear on the show leave empty-handed. But it's important to realize that if the sharks usually say no, it's not because they're mean people. It's simply because anyone who invests in startup companies must be very selective.

Why? Because startups are one of the highest-risk investments you can make. True, if a startup becomes the next Facebook or Starbucks, the investors backing it stand to make millions. But the odds of that happening are slim. The fact is that most startups fail. And when that happens, their investors end up with nothing.

Because of that, it's always been tough for entrepreneurs to find funding. And lately, this task has become even harder. That's because a major funding source — venture capital — now concentrates on high-growth, high-tech firms. That's keeping many other businesses from getting off the ground.

THE BIG CHANGE THAT OPENS STARTUP INVESTMENT DOORS TO YOU

To boost the flow of dollars to new companies, the federal government has decided to let more individuals invest in startups. For 83 years, this was a privilege allowed only to wealthy people like the sharks. But that recently changed. Now, some startup companies can accept investment cash from anyone through a new system called equity crowdfunding.

You've probably heard of crowdfunding. Artists and nonprofits use it to raise money for projects through websites like Kickstarter. But with typical crowdfunding, all that contributors get in return is a T-shirt or similar token of appreciation. Equity crowdfunding also raises funds via the internet. The difference is that your money then buys you an equity stake in a startup company. That means you share in the gains if the company turns out to be the next Google. And that could be far more valuable than a T-shirt! So let's say you want to invest in a promising startup through equity crowdfunding. Where do you begin?

Of course, you'll want to find out about the company's business model, strategy, and competitive advantages. Unfortunately, with equity crowdfunding, there are no Shark Tank-type presentations. In fact, companies aren't even allowed to advertise or solicit investors directly.

That's why you first need to visit a funding portal. It's a one-stop website that lets you consider several startups that are seeking investors. At some portals, you can also invest in those companies. To locate a funding portal, Google "equity crowdfunding" to discover different platforms.

We recently went to the portal www.wefunder.com, and one startup offering caught our eye. It was a media production house called Legion M, with the slogan, "The First Hollywood Studio Owned by Fans."

By reading Legion M's profile, we learned quite a bit about the firm, its objectives, and its staff. we were particularly impressed by the qualifications of co-founders Phil Scanlan and Jeff Annison. They both won Emmy Awards and had previous experience in starting companies and raising venture capital.

We also found that Legion M has "signed partnerships with some of the coolest and most creative companies on the planet" to create new projects. However, no specific projects were yet disclosed.

As for financial information, the company said it had raised about $650,000. It's selling shares to investors for $7 each, with a minimum purchase of $100. That means Legion M still must raise a lot more money before it can take on major projects. And we couldn't find any clues regarding how long it will take for the firm to turn a profit.

Certainly, you can access much more detailed information about a public company with a track record. Then you can examine quarterly sales and profits, SEC filings, reports by investment analysts, the performance of its stock, etc. But when you're dealing with a startup, you're basically in uncharted territory. You're essentially betting that the firm has a great money-making concept and that its staff will be able to bring it to reality.

Legion M's founders compare their quest to launching a moonshot. That's a pretty good analogy. Being aboard a startup at takeoff is exciting (even for investors). However, the ride doesn't always end with a triumph. It could also crash.

IS EQUITY CROWDFUNDING FOR YOU?

Ordinary people were long excluded from startup investing for some good reasons. For one, people without deep pockets may not be able to wait for years to get a return on their investment. And like a lottery, the prospect of a huge return in a startup could lead a non-wealthy person to put in too much money in one investment that may not pay off.

Government regulators still worry about these dangers. That's why anyone who invests in a business through equity crowdfunding is only allowed to put in a limited amount of money.

The government also won't let you jump in and out of a startup like you can with a stock. Crowdfunding investors are forbidden from selling their shares in a startup for at least a year. That's intended to keep people from trying to flip shares for a quick profit.

Another reason to be wary of investing this way is because businesses that use equity crowdfunding may suffer from having no venture capitalists as shareholders. When they are heavily invested in a startup, venture capitalists closely monitor the firm's progress and make sure that it is being run efficiently. Ordinary investors lack that expertise, which means you could be investing in a business that's going downhill without the outside oversight to reveal that.

CROWDFUNDING NOT ALWAYS
GREAT FOR THE COMPANY

Companies that choose to raise funds through equity crowdfunding also face strict regulations. One regulation prevents a firm from raising more than $1 million per year from non-wealthy investors. This could end up convincing many entrepreneurs to bypass equity crowdfunding and pursue wealthy ("accredited") investors instead, according to a new report from MIT's Sloan School of Management.

The MIT report also says businesses may avoid equity crowdfunding because of another rule that requires a crowdfunded company to conduct an initial public offering (IPO) of stock upon reaching more than 500 non-wealthy investors and $25 million in assets. When that happens, a company is subject to costly financial reporting and disclosure requirements.

That's why the MIT report says that crowdfunding may only end up being attractive to ventures that can't raise money any other way. However, crowdfunding may be a good option for businesses that intend to stay small, such as local restaurants, art galleries, and coffee shops.

HOW TO INCREASE YOUR CHANCES OF SUCCESS

If you want to invest in a startup through crowdfunding, follow the example of venture capitalists. They increase their odds of making money by:

Doing a lot of research

Try to verify any claims made about the startup on its funding portal. At least do a Google search of the founder(s) and other key personnel. See if their previous experience is relevant to the business and if members of the management team have different specialties.

Hedging bets

Only invest money that you can afford to lose and that you won't need for at least five years. Remember, a startup investment is illiquid. It's also important to diversify. Rather than sinking all of your money into one firm, divide it among several offerings.

Looking at the big picture

Ask: Is the company involved in a sector that is growing? Are business conditions right? Does its business model and strategy make sense?

Knowing the investment terms

If a company's initial valuation is set too high, you may not make much money if the business is acquired. So find out who's calculating that valuation number (an outside third party is best). Also ask if there are safeguards to keep your shares from being diluted in a future financing deal. If there are none, your stake could get watered down to almost nothing. Then you'd hardly share in the profits.

6 eBay Alternatives to Turn Clutter Into Cash

While auctions website eBay is a dominant force, with more than 60 million unique U.S. visitors each month, sellers often complain about the site's fees, crowded competitive landscape, and declining user base, which is down from 89 million unique visitors in July 2013. It's no wonder high-volume online sellers seek out other platforms to ply their wares. Even someone who sells something only occasionally has multiple options outside eBay.

If you're hoping to profit from items discarded in your fall cleaning efforts, check out these seven eBay alternatives:

1. CraigsList

Surely the most obvious entry on this list, CraigsList is a free and popular platform that is active in most U.S. cities, and allows users to post unlimited items free of charge. Include your contact information (either phone or email) and potential buyers will reach out to you. If you can, experts recommend meeting potential buyers in a public place other than your home, which is good advice (if possible) with all such sites.

2. us.Ebid.net

This is one of the largest auction sites of its kind. It charges casual sellers a 3 percent fee on final sales. The site is a Google Shopping partner, meaning that products listed there enjoy more exposure than some other sites, and has unique technology to allow for rapid uploading of product listings.

3. Bonanza.com

This fixed-price site offers mostly lower-priced, previously owned items. Sellers here enjoy low fees, at 3.5 percent of the final sales price, or a minimum of $0.50.

4. Amazon Marketplace

Similar fees and reach of eBay, Marketplace offers individual sellers a platform for selling their own goods in either auction or fixed price, and charges $0.99 in fees per item sold, plus a percentage that varies on product category.

5. ETSY

This site focuses on new, handcrafted items, as well as quality vintage apparel and home goods. The fees are reasonable and the site is well-done. It's suggested for those who have a collection of appropriate items big enough to support a storefront.

6. ECRATER.COM

This site attracts sellers by promoting the ability to create an online store for no fees, though you will pay a 2.9 percent commission on any sales to buyers that come to you through the site's main marketplace. A unique feature: A button to automatically transfer listings from your eBay store to eCrater's own platform.

Need $100K? How to
Raise Cash for an Investment

Most investors are content to grind it out, taking on as little risk as possible and hoping for a return plus inflation that allows them to come out ahead over decades. But what if a truly impressive short-term investment beckons? You get a chance to double your money or better in a month or two — but only if you have the money to throw at the opportunity.

Who keeps that kind of cash around? Nobody really, but that doesn't mean you can't find it fast and make the new investment. You just have to open your mind a bit to the piles of capital all around. If you need $100,000 in a week or less, here are six methods to consider, starting with the most obvious options first:

1. LIQUIDATE ANOTHER INVESTMENT.

Got a taxable account with stocks in it? If you have been building that account for years, the initial lots will have a low basis and trigger a big capital-gains tax hit. But later lots might be at or above recent prices for the stocks in question. If you can sell those first, the tax hit should be minimized. You can always repurchase them later, possibly at a lower basis.

2. BORROW FROM A BANK.

If you have a home with equity in it, you can set up a low-cost home equity line of credit (not a loan) and use the line to make investments. The bank will only give a certain percentage of your estimated equity, but once you have the line established you can draw on it and repay it at currently low rates. Yes, you're supposed to use that money to improve your home, but the bank is usually less concerned with the ultimate purpose of the line as it is with your ability to repay. If you have solid credit and a good relationship with the bank, you'll probably get approved.

3. BORROW FROM YOUR BROKER.

Margin loans can be had from your broker. Instead of your home as collateral, such loans depend on your investments through the firm. The problem is very high rates, often 6 percent or more. However, online firm Interactive Brokers has very low rates, currently from under 1 percent to just under 2 percent. If you can establish a non-IRA account with a minimum of $10,000, those easy terms can be yours.

4. TAP RETIREMENT ACCOUNTS.

Financial advisers warn clients to never take money out of a long-term retirement plan, with good reason. You'll likely pay a penalty for doing so and the taxes will be due as well. Not, however, if you are taking contributed money out of a Roth IRA open for at least five years. All Roth contributions are post-tax, so there's no tax on withdrawals. There's also no penalty for taking out past contributions (not earnings). You will have to fill out an IRS form later explaining how you met specific conditions, however. Talk with your CPA or account manager before withdrawing from any tax-qualified plan.

If you know what the penalties will be (if any) and the investment remains attractive in comparison, you could borrow against your retirement plan or withdraw and just pay the penalty, says Leslie Bocskor, a hedge fund manager and philanthropist in Las Vegas. "If the trade is that good, the penalty will be meaningless, even the taxes," he says.

5. TAP FRIENDS AND FAMILY.

Before you pull the trigger on borrowing from your retirement savings, do your homework, says Bocskor. Look at all of your options and the upside that might come from the investment at hand. "Maybe there's a sweetheart deal with a right of first refusal. Maybe you could build homes in Las Vegas at $60 or $70 a square foot and they sell for $200 a square foot within three to four years. Maybe a home is being sold short and it's a triple in 90 days," Bocskor says.

You look at your range of sources for money, then you go to your friends and family and show them all of your options, he says. Offer them a percentage of the deal at no risk. "There's plenty of capital out there, so much liquidity. Trillions out there, it's just a matter of crafting the structure for the vehicle that is going to attract capital," Bocskor says. "Money is like water. It's called liquid for a reason. If you dig a ditch, water will move there and create a pool. It's the same thing. You create a space near where capital is flowing and it will flow there."

6. CONSIDER A "HARD MONEY" LENDER.

Do you own a small business with accounts receivable? Collectibles? Anything of measurable, verifiable value? Then you could get a loan in a day or two with a hard-money lender. "You can't think in a regular way and find money — sometimes you've got to really get creative," says Stephen Replin, an attorney and angel lender in Denver, Colorado. "Find the thing that you have that has value." These are bridge loans, meant to last for a year at an interest rate of 10 to 14 percent, plus two to four points in origination, Replin says. A traditional bank would charge 8 percent plus two points, in comparison, he says. "But most of the time you're talking about 45 days out" to finalize the loan. The opportunity likely will have passed.

Investors in a hurry very often have things of value they don't recognize as valuable, Replin points out. "First of all, I take a look at accounts receivable. That debt, if it's legally established, can be used as collateral in 12 seconds for a loan," he says. "I find that accounts receivable is something people overlook."

Business owners can generate fast money a number of ways. "Call up your best customer and ask them to buy a year's worth of your product in advance for a discount. If not immediately, have them pay in 60 days and now you have a receivable," Replin says. The other thing to consider is collectibles. "I know a guy who has a 1961 Chrysler 300G convertible. They made like 300 of them," Replin says. "It's worth $150,000. I would certainly loan $50,000 on it. I could put his car in a secure warehouse or a bonded lot and have the money for him the next day."

Smart Financial Moves You Can Make Now

Countless articles have been written about the mindset of a millionaire. And that's important, because before you can change what you do, you need to reorient how you think.

However, we also know this: Thoughts don't make money. Actions do. So which actions contribute most to financial success? We wanted to find out, so we interviewed five millionaires who have dedicated themselves to helping others achieve financial success, uncovering the strategies they've used to increase income and maximize savings.

Here's the key: You don't need to be a millionaire (yet) to apply these principles to your life. These tactics can benefit anyone's net worth. Let's get started.

INCOME STRATEGIES

There is no one path to securing millionaire-level income, as you'll soon see. Millionaires can own businesses or work as employees, and sometimes both. Some get rich by inventing a product, others by delivering a message. Some are entrepreneurs who build a startup business and sell quickly; others are professionals who cultivate a successful practice for decades before seeking a buyer. Here are their tested income strategies:

1. They seek advice from other successful people.

When getting directions to a destination, it seems obvious you would only trust someone who's been there. In his book *The Millionaire Map*, Jim Stovall maintains that financial success is no different. "I'm a big advocate that you shouldn't take advice from someone who doesn't have what you want," he says.

No matter what your goal — starting a business, becoming a highly paid executive, making a mid-career switch — find someone who has already done it successfully and ask for his or her insight. If direct contact isn't an option (though don't rule it out before trying), seek out the person's books, speeches, and interviews.

2. They build social capital constantly.

Call it networking, mentoring, or simply friendship. Forming relationships and making connections has been sound business advice since Dale Carnegie's landmark 1936 book How to Win Friends & Influence People.

Nearly 80 years later, the concept still is vital to success. Jude Miller Burke, Ph.D., author of The Millionaire Mystique and a business psychologist who studies self-made millionaires (and is one herself), explains that you gain social capital by forming sincere relationships with people you like and care about, then helping those people do their jobs better. "And oftentimes, they return that favor to you," she says, by thinking of you for challenging, unique opportunities, which are often the most lucrative. "To get opportunities, you really have to have social capital. No one's just going to pick you."

3. They always keep going, no matter what.

Perseverance in the face of adversity is a common millionaire behavior. Kim Lavine, author of Mommy Millionaire and inventor of the Wuvit, a spa therapy pillow you heat in the microwave, says that setbacks and struggles are common among business-owner millionaires. "Don't be seduced by the myth of overnight success," she says. To get through the rough patches, just keep making decisions based on integrity and your business plan (or life goals).

Stovall's story is particularly dramatic. As a motivated young athlete, he set his sights on playing for the NFL. Then a routine physical revealed a condition that would eventually rob him of his sight. With his football dreams quashed, he switched gears to weightlifting and won two national championships. Then he founded the Narrative Television Network, which makes programming accessible to the nation's blind and visually impaired. Now a multimillionaire, Stovall is a platform speaker and prolific author. "The adversity does help you focus," he says. "It helps you establish a goal and sacrifice to get there."

4. They affiliate themselves with quality organizations (or create them).

It's true that many millionaires find their path to wealth in owning a business, but it's not a requirement. "There's a lot you can do within an organization to become wealthy," Miller Burke says. "The most important thing is to look at the organization you're in and determine whether it can get you to where you want to go."

How can you tell? Look for stock options, profit sharing, generous 401(k) plans, regular salary increases, and commissions. If you're the person in charge, make sure your organization is a good one. Leah Hoffman, CFP, did just that and it paid off. As she was growing The Hoffman and Hock Group, a private wealth management firm, employee benefits were a priority from day one. Without that support, Hoffman says, "it's hard to keep good, talented people who are very motivated to create success in their lives." She successfully sold the practice to Robert W. Baird & Co. and continues as managing director.

5. They learn effective negotiation techniques.

We'd all like to be more skilled at negotiation, but how to start? Alan Corey, author of *A Million Bucks by 30*, finds this tactic to be effective.

6. Failure Is Part of Success

While it's not a strategy per se, failure is a common element in many millionaire stories, according to Jude Miller Burke. "Failures and detours are part of the road to success," she says. When taking the risks required to build major wealth, "of course you're going to fail once in a while."

Alan Corey earned much of his net worth through real estate. As you might imagine, he experienced a reversal of fortune after the real estate crash of 2008. He has since become a millionaire once more via a different route. "I lost a huge proportion of my wealth and re-created it in the corporate environment," he says.

"People usually fall on an anchor point," he says. "Give an artificially high number, even if you're joking. Come in and say, 'Let's negotiate this million-dollar salary.'"

Another idea is to focus on asking yes or no questions, Corey says. For example, when requesting a raise, he suggests saying to your boss, "I've worked really hard on this project. Did you know that it came in on time and under budget?" And then, follow up with: "I'd like a

$10,000 salary raise. Is that something you can approve in the next two months?" If the answer is no, say you'll check in again in two months, and follow through.

7. They invest only in things they understand.

It's often said that you shouldn't use a financial product or service that you don't understand. Some millionaires apply that strategy in a different sense to their investments. While they fully comprehend how owning shares works, they might not have a deep knowledge of some sectors of the market, so they don't invest heavily there.

For example, Stovall chooses industries that he is more familiar with (energy, real estate) over those he isn't (tech, pharmaceuticals). "I don't personally understand them well enough and they're not my area of interest, but I've seen others get wealthy doing those," he says. "I invest in things I understand. I invest in companies that make sense to me."

8. They take on good debt and some risk.

Both risk and debt can be harmful to your finances. On the other hand, when used properly, they can be instrumental to building wealth. Lavine acknowledges it took her a while to realize that there is good debt and bad debt. "Bad debt is blowing $300 on shoes," she explains. "Good debt is taking out an equity loan on your house (the interest of which you can deduct) and using that to start a business."

When it comes to risk, she maintains that having some money in high-risk investments or endeavors is essential. "Nobody gets rich without opening up to some risk," Lavine says. Hoffman adds that managing risk appropriately also means not becoming overly invested in one area — the simple but powerful concept of diversification. "In 2008, many people owned a tremendous amount of real estate," she says. "That's real risk."

9. They create opportunities by solving other people's problems.

"The whole world's looking for a great idea," Stovall says, "and they trip over one about three times a week." He suggests going through your daily routine to identify a problem you face. Then ask yourself how you could have avoided it. "The answer is a great business idea," he says. "People will give you fame and fortune if you focus on them and solve their problems."

10. They create a vehicle that makes money even when they're not working.

Most of us make money by trading our time for a yearly salary or hourly rate. If you want to break into the next echelon of wealth, you need to think past that formula. "There are a few people who are so talented they can trade their time for money," Stovall says. (Think professional athletes or neurosurgeons.) "But most of us have got to create a vehicle."

For instance, Stovall has written many books, a few of which have been made into movies. Other millionaires invent products (such as Lavine's Wuvit pillow) or services that can be sold over and over again without their input.

11. They plan an exit strategy.

Millionaires often build businesses with the ultimate goal of selling them. "Nobody gets rich running a business; they get rich selling it," Lavine says. For this reason, she recommends that business owners familiarize themselves early on with how companies are valued for sale. "You have to see the reward right at the beginning," she says.

Even if you don't own a business, it's good to contemplate your next move. After all, nothing is forever, and change can bring opportunities for a higher salary and better perks.

SAVINGS STRATEGIES

Ah, life as a millionaire. Surely it involves spending with abandon, right? Wrong. No one becomes wealthy living that way, and once a person puts in the hard work to become a millionaire, the idea is to remain one. Here are 10 key things millionaires do savings-wise to reach and keep a seven-figure net worth:

1. They know where their money goes with a budget.

"The average American has more money go through their hands than it takes to be a millionaire," Stovall says. "They just spend it all." How to combat this tendency? Establish a budget that reflects your income and expenses, then tailor it to funnel money to your real priorities. A recent Gallup survey found that only one-third of Americans do this sort of review and planning. For the millionaires we spoke with, it's a different story. "I've always stayed on a budget," Hoffman says. "As your income grows, people start spending up to that [new] income or beyond that income." Instead, she says to ask yourself what you want and what you need to adjust in your budget to get there. "There's always an answer to that question," she says.

2. They identify a reason to save.

Without a doubt, saving large sums of money involves hard choices. How do millionaires stay motivated? "I've always had a goal in mind," Hoffman says, explaining that she identified a certain amount of wealth she wanted by a set point in time. "You have to plan for that. It doesn't happen by accident." Corey, who made his first million in real estate, thinks about his savings in those terms. "If I can save $30,000, I can put that as a down payment on a house," he says.

3. They invest a portion of their income for the future.

Millionaires designate money that will create more money for them years, perhaps decades, later. Stovall explains the approach simply: "Spend less than you earn. Save and invest the difference." While most of us look at a dollar as something to spend now or save for later, he says that "millionaires see that dollar as an ongoing stream of income for [their] kids and grandkids." He cites his grandfather as saying, "You can have beef once or milk forever."

4. They keep working, even after financial success.

You often hear people joke that when they win the lottery, they'll quit their job first thing. In reality, most millionaires continue to work, even after they amass wealth. Why? They want their wealth to last, and they enjoy work. "When I did 'retire,'" Corey says,

"I found that I was just completely bored, and the way I would entertain myself was to spend money. I need a day job to occupy my time." Hoffman found that continuing to work after selling her financial planning practice increased her satisfaction. "After I didn't have all the business aspects to attend to, I was able to really focus on my clients," she says.

5. They seek professional advice but do some tasks themselves.

While consulting with qualified professionals is always a good idea, you don't need to pay their high hourly rates for everything. "I had an attorney search my trademark, but I filed it myself," says Lavine, who used a free online tutorial offered by the U.S. Patent and Trademark Office to register the trademark for her Wuvit pillow.

6. They spend prudently when launching a business.

"So many people have gotten themselves in trouble from spending so much money at the beginning," Lavine says. "You always have to have cash flow to support your expenses." It's not about cutting corners — it is about finding lower-cost ways to get essential things done, knowing every dollar counts, and not spending indiscriminately thinking the money will roll in soon.

7. They spend with an eye toward savings.

Corey considers the ongoing costs of each item he buys, so he leans toward items with less upkeep. "A more expensive car has more expensive repairs. A more expensive house has a higher heating bill," he says. "I never enjoy something if I know it's costing me a lot of money." Hoffman lets the law of supply and demand work in her favor, by waiting to purchase certain consumer items when prices drop. "I've never been driven to have the newest, biggest, best," she says. "You sit back and wait [for costs to come down]."

8. They don't spend excessively on luxuries.

Lots of us see great shoes or a handbag and think, "I need that." But many millionaires steer clear of such purchases, even for work attire. "I don't think success equates with your wardrobe," Miller Burke says. "When I started at Honeywell, I went to my mom's closet. I think you can look nice and professional without spending a lot of money on clothes."

9. They incorporate their businesses.

Incorporation creates a legal entity and limits your liability to the assets within each business. It separates your businesses from each other and from your personal assets. "I own a golf course," Stovall explains. "Heaven forbid someone should fall and sue us, the most someone could take is my golf course." You don't need to own such an asset to take advantage of this strategy, however; incorporation can protect businesses of any kind from unforeseen events.

10. They are financially smart when looking for a life partner.
But not for the reason you think. Sure, dating and perhaps marrying
someone who loves extravagant vacations and shopping sprees can
affect your ability to save. But you also must consider your own patterns when you start a relationship. Do you spend too much on gifts
and entertainment to win the potential mate? Miller Burke calls this
"the love syndrome," and she says both genders are at risk. "A lot of
people give their money away when they fall in love."

9 Steps to Start a Home-Based Business

Tired of slogging into the office every day? Perhaps you're looking for more flexibility and freedom in your career. Or maybe
you've been downsized or outsourced and aren't sure what your next
professional move is. Regardless of the reason, starting a home-based
business is an option many people are eyeing these days. In fact, more
than half of all businesses are operated from someone's home, according to the most current U.S. Census Bureau data.

But here's the flip side: Fifty-seven percent of home-based businesses
brought in less than $25,000, meaning it's not an instant road to riches.

Far too many people start their business out of absolute desperation,
says Anita Marchesani, Ph.D., a personal and executive coach and licensed
psychologist who specializes in helping home-based and small-business
owners grow their businesses. "They think, 'I need to make money, and
start!' While that approach may sometimes be unavoidable if you've lost
your job and don't have any career prospects, it's best to build yourself a
cushion of cash to increase your chances of success," she says.

That cushion should include having at least six months of household
expenses in the bank, along with enough capital to meet any business
needs such as purchasing equipment and hiring a freelance Web designer. With that, these nine steps will help you start a home-based business:

1. DECIDE ON A BUSINESS MODEL

Do you want to join a multilevel marketing company and take advantage of the low startup costs, built-in training, and high-income potential? Or do you want to pursue a specific interest/skill/ talent you

have, such as being a consultant, speaker, author, trainer, or service provider like a yoga instructor, life coach, or motivational speaker? Before landing your first client or even naming your new endeavor, you must outline all the details of what you want to provide and when, where, and how you want to deliver it to customers, Marchesani says.

2. Determine Your Delivery

Some people start home-based businesses because of the flexibility to work around their family's schedule — this might mean you prefer a business that you can conduct mainly over the phone or Internet. Other people want to get out of the house to meet with clients and customers and only manage the business from the house.

3. Land a Whale

Before giving your two weeks' notice, make sure you have one solid contract client that will pay you enough to allow you to leave your current job and pay the bills while continuing to grow your business, suggests Julie Phillippi-Whitney, who formed her business Phillippi-Whitney Communications LLC at home. This will give you the confidence and the credibility to woo and pursue other clients while keeping food on your table and lights on in your home office.

4. Incorporate

The most important step a new business can take is to incorporate. Incorporating can protect a business owner from personal liability for any injury or damage that may occur during the course of normal business activity, says David Reischer, a New York City attorney and founder of LegalAdvice.com.

5. Do Your Due Diligence

New business owners don't always understand how nuanced the law truly is. "Quite often, laypeople will select boilerplate forms to memorialize a transaction or agreement based on the name or title of the form," Reischer says. However, every legal form exists as a boilerplate for a specific purpose, and selecting the wrong one may result in a completely different legal consequence than the one intended by the parties. Consulting a lawyer, financial adviser, or accountant can help a new business establish a solid foundation with an inexpensive "due diligence" review that assesses whether a company is infringing on existing trademarks. This review also should include reading any licensing and lease agreements. (Unless you actually have the degree and experience, don't play accountant, financial adviser, or lawyer at home. You could end up in hot water with the IRS if you fail to file the right documents, taxes, etc.)

6. HAVE TWO ACCOUNTS

A home-based business needs its own bank accounts to pay for supplies and other expenses. As soon as you have your legal business name and any applicable incorporation papers or documentation (EIN number from the IRS, etc.) that prove you've established a business, you should open a separate bank account. That's where you should deposit all funds and pay bills from. "I also have a tax bank account where I put the percentage of my funds my accountant suggests to make sure I have enough money to pay my quarterly taxes," Phillippi-Whitney says. "Home-based business owners can easily forget that they have to pay their own self-employment tax. That really adds up."

7. GET A LANDLINE

Unless you want clients pestering you day and night on your mobile phone, you need to have a landline. That landline won't drop a call in the middle of an important negotiation. And set ground rules that no one other than you should answer the phone in your home office. "My son answered the phone when he was 3, and a major potential client was calling. That was very unprofessional," Phillippi-Whitney says.

8. TREAT YOUR BUSINESS LIKE A JOB

If you wouldn't take your children into the office with you or show up to an office in your pj's, don't think that's an option once you start your business. Make arrangements for kids to be put in an after-school program several days a week.

9. INVEST IN TECHNOLOGY

From making sure you have the right gadgets like tablets, laptops, and phones to having a top-notch professionally designed website, technological tools will help you perform at your peak. They also tell prospective clients you're a pro. "A good website is a beneficial promotional tool, too," Phillippi-Whitney says. "I also continually update it so that potential clients can see relevant work."

Open Your Own Consulting Business

As more baby boomers hit the traditional retirement age, many are finding they don't want to stop working ... or can't afford to. One popular solution to that dilemma: putting their skills to use as consultants.

If you're considering it but are not sure how to start, here are some steps shared by experts in the consulting field.

1. THINK IT THROUGH

Some who end up failing at consulting approach the enterprise a little too casually. Jennifer Leake, a certified management consultant and owner of Assessment Pros in Roanoke, Va., says the first thing is to remember it's a business, not a hobby. "I think sometimes people don't look at consulting as a real business and go into it with the wrong mindset," she says.

Practically speaking, you have to analyze your own preferred working habits. If you are currently working in a company, decide whether you can go from an office environment to being on your own without colleagues or support staff, says William A. Overlock, a business management consultant from Westbrook, Maine. Consider joining an established consulting firm or partnering with someone if you don't enjoying working on your own, Leake adds.

2. GET YOUR LEGAL DUCKS IN A ROW

Not sure whether you need to incorporate, set up a limited liability corporation, or just be a sole proprietor? Leake says her business is an LLC. "I did it to legally protect personal assets," she says. But she advises checking with an accountant to be sure what is right for your situation.

It's also important to prepare a business plan. If you need help, contact SCORE, which offers free small-business mentoring and advice (www.score. org) — and have money set aside pre-launch. "The ideal situation is you would have two years of income socked away that you could live off of," says John Delmatoff, owner of PathFinder Coaching in Murrieta, California.

3. PICK THE LOW-HANGING FRUIT FIRST

If you're still working, don't burn your bridges, because your last company may be your first consulting client, Delmatoff says. Even those who are already retired should reach out to former employers.

"The easiest way [to get clients] is to start where you used to work and inquire about getting some consulting work there," he says. "Start in an area where you feel most comfortable using your skill set. You may find you don't have to do a lot of cold-calling."

4. OFFER YOUR SERVICES FOR FREE, AT LEAST INITIALLY

You may think it's crazy, but Delmatoff and Leake say a complimentary meeting or coaching session can actually pay off for the consultant and client.

"This discovery session helps because it's nonthreatening. You're not asking for any money," Leake says. "It helps establish rapport. I want to make sure you're a client I want to do business with."

Delmatoff says when he started his business, he offered free coaching for four or five weeks. "Every one of [those clients] was interested, and I converted the freebies to paying clients," he says.

5. PRACTICE YOUR PITCH

Leake, who has a background in sales, management, and training, says, "I have a very high close rate with people who will have a conversation with me." Which leads to one of her most important tips — you have to be able to sell yourself, your skills, and your expertise. "If you're not selling, then nothing is happening and you don't have a business," she says.

6. BE FLEXIBLE

Delmatoff suggests keeping an open mind and let the market drive your business. "What your clients want from you may not exactly square with what you think you have to offer," he says. "I found the counsel I was giving my coaching clients on leadership, personnel, and conflict resolution, all of which I derived from my years as a CEO, were more beneficial than my expertise in advertising and marketing. No one was more surprised than I was. Listen to what your clients are asking for."

7. JOIN A PROFESSIONAL GROUP

Leake is a member of the Institute of Management Consultants, a certifying body and professional association for management consultants and firms with chapters across the United States. She is also active in the local chamber of commerce. Overlock is a member of the Association for Consulting Expertise in Portland, Maine. They all agree that mingling with diverse groups of professionals matters.

8. SET THE RIGHT FEES

Not sure what to charge? Delmatoff says research rates on the Internet, and ask other consultants about their fees. "Find out what the low range is, what the high range is, and try to come in the middle," he notes. "You can always go up, but it's hard to go down."

He increases rates every 18 to 24 months, depending on the project. "Keep your fees moving consistent with the marketplace," Delmatoff recommends.

9. EMBRACE TECHNOLOGY

"I combine traditional networking with today's online networking because you have to do both," says Leake, who has attracted new clients with her profile on LinkedIn, a professional networking and social media site.

Overlock, meanwhile, taught himself QuickBooks, an accounting software program that is helpful in managing his own business but also something he helps set up for clients. You should seek out and use all avenues, including having your own professional website and blog while using Twitter and Facebook to gather an audience and promote your work.

Chapter 8

Save While Shopping

"IF YOU KNOW HOW TO SPEND LESS THAN YOU
GET, YOU HAVE THE PHILOSOPHER'S STONE."

The Best Months to
Buy Everything Cheaper

Timing is everything — especially when it comes to saving money. In an ideal world, you'd make all of your purchases only when the items are on sale. But how do you know when the best sales are for each purchase?

This calendar can help. Most purchases have seasonal spikes and dips. We've researched when 29 categories of items drop to their lowest prices and grouped them by month. You can still find deals anytime, but with this guide, you won't have to work as hard to do it.

JANUARY

- **Bedding and towels.** Since Wanamaker's started the tradition in 1878, retailers have offered January "white sales" in order to tempt customers to keep spending after the holiday season.
- **Fitness equipment.** Gym memberships tend to get all the attention, but treadmills and ellipticals can also help with exercise-related new year's resolutions, and they're attractively priced in January.

FEBRUARY

- **Snow blowers.** Most of winter has passed, and stores don't want to get stuck with too many of these bulky machines.
- **Mattresses.** Mattress sales tend to revolve around national holidays with long weekends, such as President's Day.

MARCH

- **Golf clubs.** New models hit the shelves in late winter, according to product review site CartTek.com, and when they do, last year's clubs will be steeply discounted.
- **Frozen items.** March is Frozen Food Month. Who knew? Watch your local grocery store circular (or its digital app equivalent) for coupons and discounts throughout the month.
- **Cruises.** The website DealNews.com says it tracks more cruise deals in March than in any other month.

APRIL

- **Cameras.** New camera models announced at the Consumer Electronics Show in January typically reach store shelves by April, making it a great month for deals on previous generations.
- **Outdoor power equipment.** If you're in the market for a chainsaw, lawn mower, leaf blower, pressure washer, or string trimmer, April is the time to buy, according to Consumer Reports. Both Home Depot and Lowe's offer a "Spring Black Friday" sale on everything to spiff up the outside of your home.
- **Vacuums.** Your home's interior also gets attention in April, with spring cleaning sales that discount the tools and supplies you'll need to clear out winter's grime.

MAY

- **Major appliances.** New models are released each May, and older models are available for less, especially around Memorial Day. And because fridges, washers, and dryers don't have radically different designs each year, you won't be missing much by buying an older model.
- **Small kitchen appliances.** Because May is the season for bridal showers, weddings, Mother's Day, and setting up new college grads in their own apartments, it is a prime time for discounts on blenders, irons, and the like.

JUNE

- **Tools.** Father's Day brings great sales on classic Dad gifts like cordless drills, ladders, and toolboxes.

JULY

- **Amazon devices.** For the past several years, Amazon has staged a blowout sale in July for Amazon Prime members. Every category sees discounts, but Amazon devices, such as the Echo Dot, Kindle Paperwhite, and Fire Tablet, are usually sure bets, with prices $20 less than during other sales, according to Tom's Guide.
- **Furniture.** According to sales tracked by ClarkDeals.com, furniture discounts peak in July.

August

- **Laptop computers.** Back-to-school sales on computers can rival those on Black Friday. Even if you aren't a student, it's a great time to shop.
- **Outdoor furniture and grills.** You'll see great end-of-season sales in August, and you might even get to use your spoils for months before storing them away.

September

- **A house.** According to a study by Realtor.com, the week of September 22-28 is the best time to buy a house in most markets. Homes for sale in this time frame have more price reductions, plus there is still plenty of inventory to choose from and less competition.
- **iPhones.** Apple announces its new phone models each September, and within days, major carriers offer deals for pre-orders as well as discounts on last year's models.
- **Holiday airfare.** Flight prices for Thanksgiving and Christmas steadily increase throughout the fall, according to CheapAir .com's Holiday Cheap Flights Report. Get your tickets in September to save.

October

- **Jeans.** The fall denim inventory has been in stores since August and September, and the back-to-school rush has come and gone. Expect to pocket big savings.
- **Bicycles.** Fall is the best time to look for deals on your new dream ride, according to the editors of Bicycling magazine. Manufacturers release new models in the fall, and bike shops heavily discount the previous year's stock.

November

- **Electronics.** No surprise here, but Black Friday and Cyber Monday sales are dominated by TVs, tablets, laptops, gaming systems, and activity trackers. There's no data showing this year will be any different.
- **Used cars.** November is the best month to get a deal on a pre-owned vehicle, according to car search engine iSeeCars.com. The best day is Black Friday, which offers 33% more deals than average.

- **Baby gear.** November brings a drop-off in families prepping for a new arrival (there are fewer births December through February), so baby stuff tends to go on sale.
- **Wedding dresses.** Lots of engagements happen at the holidays, so November is a great time to score a deal before others start looking. Also, brides who got married in September or October (now the most popular wedding months, according to WeddingWire .com) will start offering their dresses online at a discount.

DECEMBER

- **Pools and spas.** Installers hoping to maintain their cash flow during the slow winter months are willing to offer deep discounts to put you on their schedules now.
- **Holiday items.** The days immediately after Christmas have the most selection at the best prices. If you can shop a year ahead for your decorations, wrapping paper, ornaments, and artificial tree, you can save 50% or more.
- **A new car.** In four of the six years from 2013 to 2018, December topped the list for dealer incentives, according to vehicle data company Motor Intelligence.

Get Cash Back on Things You'd Buy Anyway

Think you can't get anything for free? Think again. Competition for consumer dollars is fierce, and retailers know that once you buy from them, you're likely to buy again. So they're willing to pay big bucks to advertising agencies and affiliate marketing companies to attract and keep customers.

What does it mean for you? There are lots of smart ways to get cash back for things you were already going to buy anyway.

TARGET REDCARD

For example, the Target REDcard is a store-branded debit card. It's a card that carries the store's distinctive logo, but is tied to your bank account, like a debit card.

Unlike a credit card, however, there's no credit check to get a REDcard, so there's no hard pull reported on your credit report. You can apply for a REDcard online, or just ask a Target cashier for an application.

When you use the card to make purchases at Target, you get an immediate 5% cash deduction on your total bill. And yes, it even includes 5% savings at in-store Starbucks locations. There are a few exclusions, such as prescriptions, most gift cards, and Target Optical eye exams, although optical products, like glasses and contact lenses, are eligible.

Unlike other rewards programs, you don't need to collect points or wait six weeks for a check to come in the mail. And when you shop at Target. com, you'll get free two-day shipping on eligible purchases.

In addition, having the REDcard means you get an extra 30 days past the usual 90 days to return merchandise. And you can get 15% off and free shipping for ongoing subscriptions for select brands of formula, diapers, and wipes.

TARGET CREDIT CARD

If you like the idea of Target's 5% discount debit card, but don't want to tie it to your bank account, you can also get a REDcard that's a credit card. You'll get the same 5% discounts and perks as with the regular REDcard, but you can also use it as a regular credit card, although the discounts and free shipping only apply to purchases at Target and Target.com.

Since most cash-back credit cards only offer 1.5% to 3% cash back, and many have hefty annual fees, this could be a good deal.

You may also receive an introductory bonus offer when you apply for this card, such as $25 off a future purchase of $100 or more. These promotional offers are not always available, and you may find different offers online versus in stores, so make sure you do an online search for sign-up bonuses before applying. And if you sign up for Target's email list, you'll receive exclusive offers, early access to special deals, and every year on your anniversary of signing up, you'll receive a 10% off coupon.

AMAZON.COM: EVERYTHING FROM A TO Z

Not only does Amazon sell everything from A to Z — including groceries — it also has a discount store card, too. And if you have an

Amazon Prime membership, you might want to get this card, which offers 5% cash back at Amazon and Whole Foods.

While there are no annual fees for the Amazon store card (or the Amazon credit card, which offers the same perks), applying for one will show up on your credit report. It's not a huge deal, but it's worth noting if you're trying to repair your credit or boost your credit score by not opening new accounts.

The good news is that you'll receive 5% cash back on nearly everything sold on Amazon, including groceries, which will get delivered to your doorstep in just two days. And when you use the card at Whole Foods, you can get an additional 10% off hundreds of sale items (the discounted items change weekly).

DISCOUNT SHOPPING SITES

There are a number of online shopping sites that offer you cash back for your purchases, too. These include Rakuten.com, BeFrugal.com, CashBackMonitor. com, ShopAtHome.com, UPromise.com, and CouponCabin.com.

These sites work in a similar way: You simply create a free account, and when you want to buy something at one of their affiliated retailers, you log into the shopping site and click on the link to your chosen retailer.

These sites are affiliate marketing businesses, which means they get paid by the retailers for directing customers to their sites. For instance, Rakuten.com has over 2,500 affiliate stores to choose from, including Target, Amazon, and Walmart. If you shop at Target by clicking on the link through Rakuten, Rakuten gets a fee from Target and passes some of that money on to you. Use your Target REDcard, and you'll receive another 5% off. BeFrugal.com has affiliate relationships with over 5,000 stores, including Amazon, Walmart, Home Depot, eBay, and Best Buy.

The beauty of these sites is that they are not only free, but the cash back offers are richer than you'd get from most cash back credit cards — sometimes 5% to 10% or more on every purchase. You'll get your earnings either by check, direct deposit, gift card, PayPal, or in the case of UPromise, by a deposit into a college savings account for your child.

Some of these sites also offer special coupons that aren't available anywhere else. And if you have a branded store card, like the Amazon card, you can double dip and get even more cash back!

SHOPPING EXTENSIONS FOR YOUR BROWSERS

Another way to get cash back when shopping online is to add a free extension to your web browser. Honey and Wikibuy are two such browser extensions.

Honey scours the Internet at checkout, tests every online coupon, and applies the one that offers the biggest discount. If you're shopping at Target.com or Amazon.com, you may find a juicy discount code waiting at checkout. Use your Target or Amazon cards for an additional 5% discount.

Wikibuy does the same thing, plus Wikibuy also alerts you when items you've viewed have gone on sale.

With so many no-cost cash-back options available, there's no reason not to use them!

5 Splurges That Are Worth It

The definition of a splurge is spending money on something extravagant or ostentatious. Some splurges are just for fun, but others are surprisingly a good value for their cost. In fact, just because something is non-essential doesn't mean that it's not beneficial or financially worth it. Consider the following five money splurges. If you do the math, you just may find they are worth the extra expenditure.

1. A PERSONAL TRAINER

How do we get ourselves to actually exercise? Gym memberships clearly don't work; 67% of them go unused. The key is accountability to another human being who's there to encourage and guide you.

Independent personal trainers charge $40 to $90 per hour, according to Thumbtack, an online marketplace for local service professionals. But that expenditure may end up saving you money in the long run.

Why it's worth it: A study published in the Journal of the American Heart Association found that people who get adequate physical activity each week save an average of $2,500 in healthcare expenses each year. What's more, people who exercise regularly earn more, according to the Journal of Labor Research. The bump is 6% for men and 10% for women.

2. AIRLINE CREDIT CARDS

Cash-back cards can seem preferable to airline points credit cards because the rewards are not only simpler to claim, you can use cash anywhere at any time. What's more, the most generous airline credit cards typically have annual fees, ranging from $95 to $550. However, if you tend to fly the same airline, you ought to check out its credit card perks — and not necessarily for the points.

Why they're worth it: One reason is because airline credit cards typically offer waived baggage fees as a perk. Those fees can run $30 per bag. And of course, there's the promise of free flights if you can accumulate the miles or meet the spending minimum to get the signup bonus.

3. QUALITY SHOES

These days, it's easy to find cheap footwear. Too easy, found from the likes of Amazon, Target, and DSW. One problem with buying bargain shoes online is that you're never getting your shoe size checked by a professional. One study found that 86% of older people are wearing an incorrect size! But quality shoes, such as those sold by a reputable brand from a full-service shoe store, can not only make your feet more comfortable, they can save you money, too.

Why they're worth it: Quality shoes provide appropriate arch support, heel cushioning, and shock absorption. That means you may be able to sidestep conditions like tendinitis, plantar fasciitis, or even a sprained ankle that cheap shoes can give you (not to mention the associated medical costs).

Some doctors claim that poor quality shoes can even change the way you walk, leading to long-term knee and hip issues. Plus, shoes with appropriate support may help you walk more, which can improve your health and happiness in myriad ways. The American Podiatric Medical Association has granted its Seal of Acceptance to brands like Carhartt, Chaco, Dansko, and Vionic in recognition of their quality.

4. APPLECARE

If you're planning to get a shiny new iPhone, iPad, iWatch or Mac computer anytime soon, you'll be asked if you want to add Apple's extended warranty and technical support program, called AppleCare. You can buy AppleCare when you buy your device or add it within 60 days of your purchase.

In general, AppleCare extends the built-in warranty from one year to two years (three years for computers), extends your access to free technical support from 90 days to two years, and gives you discounted repairs for two incidents of accidental damage. The cost is slightly different for each device and model; for iPhones, AppleCare starts at $129.

Why it's worth it: If you're not tech savvy, the two years of 24/7 technical support alone makes AppleCare worthwhile. In addition, the $29 repair fee for screen damage (which happens to two-thirds of smartphone owners) is a good price. It costs $75 and up to replace a screen at a non-Apple repair store, and going there does invalidate your warranty.

5. HIGH-END SUNGLASSES

Do you enjoy boating, sailing, hiking, or just relaxing on the beach? Sunglasses are a must. It's tempting to keep buying a few cheap pairs each season and tossing them as they break or get scratched. However, if you splurge on an expensive pair, such as from Unsinkable Polarized, your experience may completely change your outlook.

Why they're worth it: Higher-quality lenses don't scratch as easily, and some brands make sunglasses that float when dropped in the water. And some sunglass manufacturers will replace a lost pair once or twice for just a processing fee. (It's $35 for Unsinkable Polarized; others just charge shipping and handling.)

Best Apps for Saving Money on Groceries

You probably know that you can point-and-click your way to saving money on everything from vacations and clothes to dog beds, sneakers, and more. So it's no surprise that technology can help you trim your weekly grocery budget, too. And the best part is you can do it without having to sacrifice your family's favorite goodies or spend hours scouring the Sunday paper for coupons.

Here's a look at several apps you can downloaded to your cell phone or tablet to help you make the most of your time in the grocery store and keep your bank balance in good shape.

GROCERY PAL
Cost: Free

This handy tool points you toward weekly specials from stores such as Walgreens, CVS, Walmart, Target, RiteAid, Safeway, Family Dollar, Dollar General, Publix, Kmart, Food Lion, Albertsons, Aldi, Save-A-Lot, and many more.

It's a great app for anyone to use, but GroceryPal is particularly nice for coupon clippers because it lets you digitally store coupons and locate on-sale items in your local area. You can also create shopping lists, so you won't walk out of the store with more than you planned to buy.

IBOTTA
Cost: Free

Instead of storing weekly ads, this app highlights cashback offers or coupons available at major grocery stores. The app is easy to add to your phone, but there are multiple steps to take to make using Ibotta worthwhile.

Shoppers purchase select qualifying products, then take a picture of their receipts to provide Ibotta with proof of purchase. Then, after 48 hours, shoppers get the cash back in their Ibotta accounts.

Users have several ways to earn cash back, all found in the "Offers" section. Start by scanning products and offers.

If a store or item strikes your fancy, tap the "Earn $--" bar. Then you will see the tasks you'll need to complete in order to earn the cash back after buying the product. Those tasks might include reading a fact, taking a quick poll, watching a video, etc.

Most products have more than one way to earn cash. You can complete one or all of the tasks, but the more tasks you perform, the more cash you will get back. After completing at least one task per product offer, the product is automatically added to your "Checklist" on the app, so you can earn money for purchasing the item.

Users need either a PayPal or Venmo account to receive cash back or can cash in their rewards for gift cards from select retailers.

Checkout 51
Cost: Free

This app lets you choose from an assortment of cashback offers and discounts from various brands and stores each week.

Simply download Checkout 51, sign up, and scan the list of savings opportunities. When you find one you're interested in, add it to your shopping list. Then hit "redeem" after you buy items on your list, upload your receipt and get the cash back in your Checkout 51 account. When you've accumulated $20 in cash back, you can cash out.

Checkout 51 publishes new savings opportunities every Thursday.

Shopkick
Cost: Free

Structured much like Ibotta and Checkout 51, this tool gives cash back through proof of purchase (scanning your receipt). However, if you're not into submitting receipts, you can also scan items to earn points, or "Kicks," that you can use to earn cash as well.

You can earn Kicks for every dollar spent on a linked card at select partner stores. You can also scan barcodes of select products while in the store, visit certain online partners, watch videos, and make online purchases at partner merchant sites through the app to earn Kicks.

Flipp
Cost: Free

Driving from store to store to find the best deals on toilet paper, grapes, or milk is time-consuming and costly. Flipp's mission is to aggregate store ads and deals all in one place, so you can quickly find the best price on groceries from among the stores in your area before you head out the door.

Flipp matches local flyer deals with coupons available to bump up the savings.

You can also use the app to create a shopping list, and Flipp will highlight deals for items on your list to help you pinpoint savings faster. You can also link loyalty program cards, to then "clip" coupon deals to the card for instant savings when you check out.

YOUR FAVORITE SUPERMARKET APP
Cost: Typically Free

In many instances, the most common apps to save money or make the grocery shopping experience easier are those created by your favorite grocery store. Nearly all major supermarkets have apps that let you link loyalty programs, review sales, create lists, and review previous purchases.

The potential for savings comes when grocers allow you to stack their coupons located within the app with manufacturer coupons.

For example, say Albertson's is having a sale on cereal for $1.49 versus the usual retail price of $3.99, and the app features a special offer for $1 off any box of cereal. That box of cereal now costs just $0.49. If you happen to have a manufacturer coupon for $.50 off that box of cereal, it's now free.

Even better: If the store has a policy that gives customers a refund of a coupon overage, you could even get your supermarket to pay you $0.01!

THE BOTTOM LINE

Coupon apps do offer savings potential, but just like clipping coupons, you may have to make an effort to get the best deals.

Still, with a little planning and flexibility, you may be able to either reduce the amount you spend at the supermarket every week, or cultivate a digital savings account based on your shopping habits that ultimately offsets the price of your pickles, pears, or paper towels.

The 8 Best Things to Buy at a Thrift Store

You may not consider yourself a fan of thrift store shopping, but if you dip your toe into regular thrifting opportunities in your neighborhood, you might be pleasantly surprised at the deals you find. Your local church may operate a store on your very block. Or, your closest thrift store may be a national name such as Goodwill, The Salvation Army, or Savers. No matter the brand, there are certain categories of purchases at thrift stores that make the most sense financially.

BEST BUYS FROM THE THRIFT STORE

1. Clothing for short-term use.

Sometimes clothes are useful for only a defined period of time. Think of maternity outfits, children's clothes, and attire for a vacation in a vastly different climate. Why spend a lot of money on these things when you can get them for pennies or just a few dollars at the thrift store?

2. Solid wood anything.

Solid wood furniture is durable and meant to last. As such, the design is likely timeless, not trendy, which means it will match most styles of décor. And if you do crave a change, solid wood can be easily refinished or painted. However, solid wood furniture is substantially more expensive than other types. Purchasing it at a thrift store allows you to get a high quality product for much less.

3. Books.

Many thrift stores sell books that are in excellent condition for 50 cents to a few dollars. We recently came across a $40 home decorating book by HGTV personality Joanna Gaines from 2018 priced at just $3.

4. Tools.

Most hand tools are made of sturdy materials designed for decades of use. Even in used condition, most are durable enough to serve for many more years.

5. Curtain ties.

For a small strip of fabric, ties can be incredibly expensive. New ties from a department store can run as much as $70. Ties at many thrift stores (from some of the same brands, mind you) are $1 each.

6. Housewares.

Thrift stores should be your first stop when planning a new look for your home. Vases, mirrors, trays, baskets, and accent furniture are all plentiful at thrift stores and are priced at a fraction of what you'd pay elsewhere.

7. Jewelry.

Thrift stores can be an excellent source for items to mix and match with your higher-end pieces. From bangle bracelets to vintage necklaces, your local store might have some great finds for a fraction of what you'd pay for new jewelry, even from bargain stores.

8. Frames.

Thrift stores often sell discarded original art and prints. Even if the artwork isn't your style, there could be value to the frame around it. At a minimum, a beautiful or unique frame can be used to hold different art. If you get creative, you can make frames into chalkboard signs, bulletin boards, and jewelry holders for your home.

HOW TO SAVE EVEN MORE MONEY

You're already giving yourself huge discounts by shopping at thrift stores, but these tactics can make it pay off even more:

FIND OUT WHEN THE STORE MARKS DOWN PRICES.

Most thrift stores tag merchandise for discount when a new batch is displayed for sale. To keep inventory fresh, there are typically new discounts each week.

GO EARLY IN THE WEEK.

As you might expect, weekends are when most thrift stores receive the bulk of new donations. For the best selection, show up right after the racks are refreshed.

GET TO KNOW THE STAFF.

If you become a regular, the store employees get to know your tastes and could give you a heads-up when items come in that you might like — before they are offered for sale to the general public. This can be especially valuable if you like vintage toys, baseball memorabilia, or name brand clothing that is likely to get snapped up fast.

TRY ONLINE THRIFT STORES.

You never know what you're going to find at brick-and-mortar thrift stores, and that can be part of the fun. However, if you're looking for a specific brand or type of item, you may have better luck shopping at online thrift stores. Examples are ThredUp, Swap. com, reStitch, and GoodTwice. Prices will be a little higher than you'll see in person, but there's a better chance you'll find exactly what you're looking for.

When an Extended Warranty is Worth It

It's hard to buy anything from any retailer these days without a cashier or sales clerk asking if you'd like to purchase an extended service plan. You may be wondering if these promises to repair or replace items at no charge to the consumer are savvy financial protection or a waste of money.

For some items, it may be worth it. Think of a new washing machine that breaks down in the first few years of use. Having it replaced for only the cost of the warranty could save you a lot of money.

However, John Myers, the owner and broker of Myers & Myers Real Estate had a very different experience when he looked to his extended coverage following the death of his smartphone. He was told by the company that oversees and processes his smartphone warranty's claims that his issue was not covered by the warranty, despite the sales clerk assuring him at the time of purchase that "everything" would be covered under the insurance.

Lisa Schiller, director of Investigations and Media Relations for the Better Business Bureau (BBB), said she always recommends that consumers take their time and get all the details when deciding whether or not to buy an extended warranty. Here are some things to consider:

WHAT'S IN A NAME?

First, as a point of terminology, a warranty is a promise by the manufacturer to stand behind the product if something goes wrong. Some warranties are explicit, like when a manufacturer offers to repair or replace an item if it turns out to be defective.

Other warranties are implied, meaning that the manufacturer doesn't say anything, but is still on the hook when things go wrong. All states have laws in place that govern implied warranties.

Technically, only the manufacturer of a product can offer a "warranty." Other plans are protections that extend the coverage offered by a manufacturer's warranty, however, they are not literally warranties. This protection is offered by a third party (not the manufacturer) and may — or may not — have restrictions, limitations, and even coverages that are different from the original warranty.

BE PATIENT

You're standing in line and the cashier is giving you that "can you please make a decision" look. Don't give in to the pressure. Schiller assured us it's worth it to take a minute, five, or even a day or two to decide. In many instances, you can add an extended warranty within a certain number of days of the initial purchase.

If you haven't already done so, she suggests using that time to learn the life expectancy of the product and brand you are purchasing and make sure you understand what warranty is already offered plus what exactly is covered. Then think about the cost of the product. Is it a pricey item, such as a home appliance or a car, or is it an inexpensive television in the spare room?

The cost of the item will clearly affect your decision. If instead of paying for the warranty, it's cheaper to put that money aside to later cover repairs or a replacement if needed, that may be a better use of your money.

For instance, if the item typically lasts five years and has a built-in warranty for three years, are you willing — and financially prepared — to pay for a repair or replacement sometime during years four and five? If so, then it doesn't make sense to buy the extended coverage.

ASK QUESTIONS

Don't settle for sales lines like "everything is covered." Ask specifically what is covered with the free warranty and what is covered with the extended plan. And make sure you ask about all the nuances, including cost, coverage, length of time the warranty is good for, and the fine print.

Nicole Miller, a public relations representative for Asurion, which powers Home Depot's Protection Plan program, recommends that customers look at the details and terms and conditions to assess if the plan meets their needs.

For example, some protection plans are traditional extended warranties that simply extend the manufacturer's original warranty for defects, such as mechanical and electronic failures.

Other protection plans bundle an extended warranty with a service plan, so they provide more value to you if the device or appliance breaks. Likewise, some service plans may include accidental damage (such as a dropped TV or laptop) or even liquid damage. Take the time to understand what is covered.

HOW DID YOU PAY?

Nishank Khanna, chief marketing officer for Clarify Capital, told us consumers often don't realize that their credit cards offer extended coverage automatically at no additional charge. Several credit cards, including many offered by American Express and Citibank, offer free extended coverages that replicate the manufacturer's warranty when you use the credit card to buy the product.

On some American Express credit cards, the issuer will extend the original manufacturer's warranty by as long as two years. That means if you buy a product that has a five-year warranty, your Amex extends the protection period to seven years. Coverage is typically limited by occurrence and over time. And claims are filed with your card issuer, not the product manufacturer.

If your claim is approved, you'll typically receive a check or statement credit reimbursing you for repair costs, replacement costs, or the original purchase cost, depending on the claim details and coverage limits.

MasterCard goes the extra mile and, in many instances, covers wear and tear from normal use as well.

There are, of course, some restrictions. You have to hang on to your original receipt and the credit card statement that includes the charge plus documentation regarding the manufacturer's warranty.

Extended coverage offered by credit cards also doesn't apply to all purchases — only those deemed eligible in the fine print. And because it often replicates the manufacturer's coverage, if the original warranty covered only parts and labor, then the extended coverage does the same. Also, depending on the card issuer, you may have to register the item with the manufacturer.

Khanna told us that for lesser-priced items (typically those under $1,000), a credit card's coverage should suffice. But for more expensive purchases or those that have short manufacturer warranties (a $900 washing machine that has a warranty of less than a year), extended coverage offered by the retailer may be worth the money.

THE EXCEPTION TO THE COST RULE

Sonia Steinway, co-founder and president of Outside Financial, told us that her company thinks vehicle service contracts (VSCs) are always worthwhile because it's so expensive to repair cars. Like other extended warranties, VSCs typically offer the same repairs as the original manufacturer's warranty and kick in after that warranty has expired.

VSCs are best for car buyers who intend to own their vehicles beyond the manufacturer warranty period (frequently three or five years) and mileage limits, or for buyers who purchase a used car.

But she cautioned against purchasing this type of coverage at the dealership. Most of the time, there's not enough time to compare all of your options or fully understand what the dealer is offering when you're buying a new car. And some dealers offer service contracts that require you repair the vehicle only at that dealership, which limits your flexibility.

No matter if you're considering extended coverage for a new car, laptop, dishwasher or electronic gadget, the best policies are "exclusionary," meaning they cover everything except what's specified on a list of exclusions. Review that list before buying a policy.

Unlocking the Value of Amazon Prime

Despite often shopping online, you may have yet to spend the $119 a year (or opt to be charged $12.99 a month) to have items arrive at your door two days after ordering them. But with more and more people signing up to be Prime members, you may be considering if the service is worth its high price. We dove into the perks of Amazon Prime and also looked to see what comparable or better options are available.

PRIME PERKS:
SHIPPING, STREAMING, MUSIC, AND MORE

The shipping benefits of membership are perhaps the most well-known. But we were surprised to learn that along with free two-day shipping on eligible items to addresses in the contiguous U.S., the annual fee also provides free same-day delivery and free two-hour delivery on thousands of items in eligible zip codes. You can also score free release-date delivery on eligible pre-order items delivered on their release date to eligible zip codes.

Streaming benefits include free unlimited streaming of many movies and TV episodes. You can also order non-Prime movies and TV episodes for an extra fee. And you can subscribe to HBO, Showtime, and STARZ channels for $4.99 to $14.99 a month, much less than the price of these services for many cable or fiber optic service providers.

You can also get your groove on with unlimited, ad-free access to hundreds of Prime music songs or buy an Amazon Music Unlimited monthly plan or annual plan at a discount.

Got a gamer in the house? Twitch Prime offers exclusive discounts on physical games, pre-orders, and new releases.

Other benefits include Amazon Dash, which makes reordering certain products as easy as pushing a button (literally), while Prime Wardrobe lets you try-on up to three clothing items before you buy. Some areas can also offer Prime Pantry, which delivers groceries and household products, for an extra fee. In addition, there are early-bird deals on certain products and up to 20 percent off of diapers, baby food, and more, plus access to Amazon's own line of everyday essential products.

You can also borrow books, magazines, and more from the Prime Reading catalog for your Fire tablet, Kindle e-reader, or the Kindle reading apps and enjoy early access to a new book for free every month from the Amazon First Reads picks. Another benefit is secure unlimited photo storage through Prime Photos, which offers enhanced search and organization features.

Finally, you can get an Amazon credit card or store card and get 5 percent off on Amazon purchases, plus extra discounts at Whole Foods Market.

Depending on how much you buy, watch, or listen to online, the savings stemming from being a Prime member appear to potentially amount to hundreds of dollars.

PRIMARY ALTERNATIVES

Still not convinced that these services and offers are worth Prime's price? Shoppers can cobble together a Prime-like online shopping and entertainment experience that costs less (or nothing at all). But before trying to do that, you have to consider what your time is worth.

Do you want to take time surfing multiple online stores like Walmart, Target, Jet, and Overstock to take advantage of their free two-day shipping at low thresholds (around $35 to $40 on most sites)? If so, those options or shopping at stores like Walmart and Best Buy that offer free in-store pickup can be a great alternative. Those merchants allow you to take advantage of the convenience of ordering something online without having to wait two days for it to arrive at your doorstep. And with in-store pickup, you can go get the item in as little as a few hours. You do, however, have to factor in the cost of your time and gas to retrieve your purchases if you opt for the pick-up route.

Plenty of major retailers are also offering price-matching and price-adjustment policies to stay competitive with Amazon. In fact, eBay just launched a Best Price Guarantee program that gives you a coupon worth 110 percent of the price difference if you find a lower price on Amazon (and other online stores) within 48 hours of your eBay purchase. Other retailers, including Target, Bed Bath & Beyond, Best Buy, and Kohl's offer similar guarantees.

Prime perks such as free ebook borrows and audiobook, video, and music streaming can be swapped with public libraries, television, and video network apps, and free tiers on music services like Spotify and Pandora. However, seeking these out, setting up multiple accounts, downloading apps, and remembering user logins is not as turnkey as Prime's simple solution.

For regular consumers of streaming entertainment, the $119 an-nual Prime fee is slightly more than the basic Netflix fee of $7.99 per month, or $95.88 a year for one user/one screen.

And since Prime members can add up to two adults, four teens, and four children in the household to their Prime account, many of the benefits, including free shipping, Prime Video, Kindle borrows and sharing, and more can be shared with all household members under one $119 per year membership.

TRIMMING THE COST

If you want to take the plunge into Prime membership, there are some ways to slash the yearly fee. First, start out with a 30-day free trial to make sure it's the right fit for you.

If you're a student or have one in your household, you can use the student's .edu email and get the first six months free, plus 50 percent off your subscription after those first six months. And low-income shoppers with a valid Electronic Benefits Transfer Card can get a Prime membership for just $5.99 a month.

No matter what you pay for Prime, the key to making its fee eco-nomical is making a few purchases a month. Since most purchases come with free two-day shipping, you'll save money not having to pay for expensive rush shipping if you forgot your best friend's birthday or your own anniversary.

Plus, in certain areas, you can take advantage of Prime Now, Fresh, and Restaurant delivery services, saving you both time and gas money by getting your favorite groceries or meals delivered to your door the same day.

Buy Jewelry Online
Without Getting Ripped Off

Buying jewelry online has been growing in popularity recently. There are now dozens of websites like I Do Now I Don't, Rare Carat, Brilliant Earth, and FourMine.com that retail both loose and set diamonds and gemstones. They promise as much as 50 percent off retail prices, thanks to low overhead. But can you truly point and click your way to better pricing than what's found at brick and mortar locations?

To understand the benefits and risks of shopping online for sparkling baubles, we asked Erica Hirsch, a GIA-certified gemologist at RareCarat.com, for some insight. We found that price tags are definitely lower online. But there's more to web jewelry shopping than evaluating cost. Here are some things to consider.

GO FOR THE CERTIFICATION

The non-profit Gemological Institute of America (GIA) has a mission to "ensure the public trust in gems and jewelry by upholding the highest standards of integrity, academics, science, and professionalism through education, research, laboratory services, and instrument development." To support that, the GIA produces reports that assess the color, clarity, cut, and carat of diamonds and colored gemstones.

Each loose stone assessed by the GIA is assigned a report number, which is typically laser inscribed on the edge of the stone and can be researched using the GIA's website (gia.edu).

Anyone can physically bring — or send — a stone to be certified by the GIA. But typically, retailers or wholesalers do this for consumers. Many stores have a sticker in their window or advertise on their website that they work with GIA stones.

No matter where you're shopping, Hirsch recommends always looking for a GIA-certified stone. However, that will cost you. GIA diamonds and gemstones can cost 15 to 25 percent more than their non-GIA counterparts.

On the flip side, you'll have the assurance of gem quality. And if you resell, the GIA certification makes it easier because you can demonstrate the quality and value to a potential buyer. The GIA laser inscription also protects you in the event your stone is lost or stolen, as it acts as a serial number, uniquely identifying your stone.

LOOK FOR THE REFUND POLICY

Choose a site that offers a full refund return policy in case you want to send the item back for any reason including fit, change of mind, etc.

SIZE UP SHIPPING

To protect against theft or shipment swapping, shop on sites that ship jewelry to you through insured carriers. This reduces the chances you'll pay for something you never receive.

RESEARCH THE RETAILER

Brush up on the online retailer's ratings and reviews. These comments can provide an in-depth and behind-the-scenes look at other customers' experiences — both positive and negative — and clue you in to any problems with quality, authenticity, etc., that others have encountered along the way.

KNOW YOUR METALS

Along with the size, color, clarity, etc., of the stone, the metal in which those shining stars are set affects the price and value of an item.

ASK ABOUT ORIGIN OF THE STONE

Diamonds and gemstones can be either earth-grown (or mined) or lab-created. Both are "real" and display the same chemical and optical properties. However, lab-created stones cost about 30 percent less than mined stones of the same quality and durability.

While lab-created stones are a great alternative for environmentally conscious individuals who still want quality stones, some shoppers may prefer mined gemstones and diamonds. And it's important to inquire about the origin of all stones in a setting before committing to a purchase to know exactly what you're buying and if it's the deal you're looking for.

THE BOTTOM LINE

When it comes time to shop, first head to a brick and mortar store to explore shapes, cuts, sizes, possible settings, etc. Then peruse the web to see how online offerings stack up. If possible, you can purchase online to save money, but only after making sure you've done everything you can to ensure that you are enjoying significantly lower prices on exactly what you want — and have paid for.

Saving Time and Money
With Mail-Order Meals

According to the U.S. Department of Agriculture, the thriftiest of frugal shoppers can meet recommended nutritional guidelines and feed a family of four for $148.50 per week. Got a taste for something other than plain, boneless, skinless chicken breast? Crafting a grocery list considered "modest" by the USDA will almost double, costing $242.90 per week.

As hefty as they are, these figures don't take into account time spent shopping for groceries, or the cost of gas and wear and tear on your car. So you might be thinking about cooking dinner with the help of those handy meal kits that deliver all the ingredients right to your door, and wondering how their prices compare to in-person shopping.

Available for subscriptions of anywhere from two to six meals per week, companies like Plated, Blue Apron, Hello Fresh, and Green Chef provide a variety of meals that range from gluten-free and vegetarian to omnivore or carnivore.

Just about every plan allows subscribers to customize shipments depending on family size and/or how much food people typically eat. For example, you can opt for a larger plan that serves four hungry adults and teenagers. The food arrives packaged in containers designed to keep ingredients fresh for several hours on your delivery day, so you don't have to rush home.

And to assess the price of convenience versus taste, quality of food, and overall cost of meal kits, my family agreed to nosh on two meals each from Plated, Blue Apron, and Hello Fresh recently.

Here's what we learned about mail order meal kit subscription services.

THE PROS
Time Savings
Although you're not getting fully prepared meals delivered to your home like you could if you ordered Chinese takeout or a pizza and wings, you're still saving a ton of time you'd otherwise need searching for fresh, new recipes and pulling together shopping lists. Another time savings comes from not having to measure out all the ingredients. And some plans like Terra's Kitchen ships food washed and chopped, too.

Lastly, most plans advertise the ability for meals to be fully prepped in 15 to 30 minutes. In general, we found the six meals we sampled were prepared in about 30 minutes.

Waste not
With meal kit plans, there's little to no food waste. So there's no more purchasing an entire package of lentils when you only need a 1/4 cup or a large bundle of celery for just one or two stalks. And because ingredients are portioned to make the exact number of meals specified, there's no excess leftovers for your family to get sick of eating for the next four days.

Flexible timing
Don't worry if you're not in the mood for what's at your front door. In most instances, the culinary team recommends cooking seafood dishes within two days of receiving your box and all other dinners within five days, giving you flexibility in the timing of the meal.

The ease of experimenting
These services can be a way to experiment with unfamiliar ingredients. The cooking process is easy and stress-free, as all meals came with easy-to-follow step-by-step instructions that featured photos of the finished entrée. And in some instances, wine pairings for the meal are also included.

THE CONS
Your Magic Touch
You may prefer to choose the exact food your family is going to eat. While these meal kits provide the ingredients, they might not ship the exact variation you and your family are used to eating. That can decrease the likelihood everyone will dig into the meal, leaving you with leftovers you paid for and no one will eat, plus rumbling stomachs you still need to fill.

The Flavor
Let's face it, no two sets of taste buds are the same; however, the mail order meals are portioned and pre-prepped without individualization. So if your household likes a heavy hand when seasoning or likes to go extra light on the garlic, you still have to have those items on hand and make adjustments to the recipe. If that's the case, you lose a bit of the time, and cost saving.

Organic isn't always an option
Plans like Green Chef and Terra's Kitchen try to use 100 percent certified organic ingredients as much as possible. But others don't have — or state — the ability to order organic foods. If you generally cook with organic ingredients, meal kits might not be for you.

The bottom line
Most services offer an introductory rate that can trim as much as 50 percent of the cost of the shipment. And several offer free standard shipping for orders over a set amount. That meant the first box of meals (with each service) cost well below what you'd spend at a grocer.

However, after that special offer, subscription kit services cost anywhere from 5 to 15 percent more than meals an average person would shop for and fully prep (wash, chop, etc.).

However, the cost is equal to, or in some instances (such as seafood dishes) less than, eating at a restaurant. And while canceling the subscription is easy, you have to remember to actually do so, or you'll wind up with a surprise shipment.

How to Shop at a Warehouse Store Without a Membership

Do you have a wistful relationship with warehouse stores, like Costco, BJ's, and Sam's Club? The deals are impressive. But for many, the large quantities don't make economic sense. However, you can shop at them without a membership.

How? You could simply go with someone else who has a membership and reimburse them in cash.

But that isn't the only way to take advantage of warehouse deals. Some products are open to everyone because of state laws. Others deals are doled out freely as "test drives," with the hope you'll be convinced to join. Learn these rules, and you can get the benefits of shopping at warehouse clubs without paying the membership fee.

FILLING PRESCRIPTIONS

You don't need to be a member to fill prescriptions at Costco or Sam's Club. (BJ's locations no longer include pharmacies.) People often opt not to use health insurance for some prescriptions, whether it's because certain prescriptions aren't covered or it's the end of the year and they haven't met the deductible. If that's the case for you, shop around. Consumer Reports found that retail prices of drugs at Costco were consistently lower than large pharmacy chains.

BUYING ALCOHOL

State liquor laws vary widely, but most states make it illegal for a "private club" to sell alcohol. So you can buy beer, wine, and hard liquor at warehouse clubs, even if you're not a member. Declare your intentions at the door to gain entry. Prices at warehouse stores usually beat the grocery or liquor store by a few bucks.

USING A DAY PASS

Costco doesn't offer these, but BJ's and Sam's Club do.

At BJ's, it's called a One Day Shopping Pass, and you can get it from the Member Services desk in any store. At Sam's Club, it's called a Guest Membership Pass. You print it at home and bring it to a store. Go to help. samsclub.com and enter "guest membership" in the search field. Select the first result. Click the link under "Attachments" and print.

However, these aren't free rides. BJ's charges a 20 percent nonmember surcharge (which can be applied to a membership opened within seven days). A better bet is to shop at BJ's online (see below). At Sam's Club, nonmember shoppers pay a 10 percent service fee, except in California, South Carolina, and Elmsford, N.Y.

BEING A MEMBER'S GUEST

Have a friend you love to shop with? Only think you'd benefit from warehouse deals sporadically? Make a regular arrangement with them. At all three clubs mentioned here, members are allowed to bring two guests per visit (children don't count). Only members can purchase items without an extra fee, so your friend will need to buy your stuff, but if it's a big enough purchase, it may be worth the trouble. Who knows? Maybe your friend likes having company while shopping, too.

SHOPPING ONLINE

You can shop Costco.com as a nonmember, and it's pretty easy to do so. Click "Sign In/Register" in the upper right. Select the gray "Create Account" button. Fill out the form, leaving the "Membership Number" field blank. When you check out, you'll see a 5 percent surcharge for nonmembers (except if you're buying prescriptions). Some items on the website are designated "member only."

At Bjs.com it's a similar process. Click "My Account," then select the "I am not a BJ's Member" radio button, and click "Continue." Fill out the form. BJ's also has a 5 percent nonmember surcharge.

Nonmember shoppers at Samsclub.com pay a 10 percent fee (except in California, South Carolina, and Elmsford, N.Y). The easiest way to get set up is to add items to your cart first, then start the check process, and you'll be shown an option to "create a guest account."

USING A GIFT CARD

Costco is the clear winner here. If you can convince a member to buy you a Costco Cash Card, you can shop in-person as a nonmember with no extra fee. You can even get the balance back in cash if it's under $10, so you don't need to spend extra money just to use it up. Nonmembers can use Cash Cards online, too, albeit with the same 5 percent surcharge mentioned above.

A BJ's Gift Card can also be used by nonmembers, with the same 20 percent surcharge for in-person purchases mentioned above. Note that the cards can't be used at BJs.com. Also, members can't purchase BJ's Gift Cards online — only at a BJ's location or by emailing GiftCardRequest@bjs.com.

Sam's Club also offers gift cards that nonmembers can use — with the standard 10 percent nonmember service fee.

Wine and Spirits for Less $$ During the Holiday Season

Wine and spirits are frequently a part of parties and holiday celebrations and make great hostess gifts, too. Here's how to celebrate with wine and spirits — without the spirit-dampening costs!

USE A LEGAL LOOPHOLE TO BUY AT A WAREHOUSE CLUB.

State laws make it illegal for any "private club" to sell alcohol. The warehouse clubs get around these laws by opening up their liquor offerings to everyone, even nonmembers. At the door, just say you're there to buy booze, and you're in. (See page 5 for other ways to shop warehouse clubs without a membership.) Prices are usually $2 to $3 less per bottle than the grocery or liquor stores.

BUY IN BULK.

You can buy cases of wine for generally around 15 percent less than the cost of individual bottles. Your local winery may offer even sweeter deals. For example, a winery near me offers a 10 percent discount for three bottles. Discounts increase to 15 percent for six bottles, and 20 percent for 12.

DON'T GIVE STORE BRANDS THE BRUSH-OFF.

There is something of a renaissance for store-brand labels right now. Many are great for the price, and some are truly excellent. Kroger sells house brands of vodka and rum. We've also heard great things about Costco's house brand, Target's Wine Cube line, and Trader Joe's Charles Shaw Wines (known colloquially as "Two Buck Chuck"). And a rosé wine by grocery chain Aldi even earned top honors at the International Wine Challenge, a prestigious blind taste test.

CHECK OUT CASH-BACK GROCERY APPS.

You can get cash back on alcohol purchases by just taking a picture of your receipt with smartphone apps, Ibotta and Checkout 51. Downside: You have to accumulate $20 before you can cash out. But it doesn't take too long. Right now in my area, Ibotta is offering $1 to $4 back on selected individual wine bottles and $3 to $5 back on selected hard liquor.

SERVE A SIGNATURE DRINK.

For a holiday party, try serving a punch or special cocktail instead of buying lots of different kinds of alcohol. Signature drinks can be less expensive because ingredients are bought in bulk, and the alcohol, combined with other flavors, doesn't need to be top shelf. Mulled cider is a natural showpiece for winter gatherings; you can add wine at the beginning or rum, bourbon, cognac, or scotch at the end.

HAVE A BYOB PARTY.

It's not as tacky as it sounds, especially if you make a theme of it. Hold a party with a "beers around the world" theme, for example. You can mount a large wall map for each person to insert a pin for the origin of his or her contribution. It was fun and interactive — and probably a money-saver for her, though it didn't feel that way to guests.

BUY ONLINE.

It's so easy to compare prices this way. Wine.com and WineExpress.com both run specials constantly, including free shipping if you buy a certain amount. And they have helpful features: Wine.com has experts available by chat to guide you in selecting a bottle. WineExpress.com has hundreds of virtual "video tastings" by its wine director. If you order wine online, be aware that you will need to be present for the delivery so you can show identification to prove your age.

Don't Waste Money:
How to Eliminate Impulse Buys

Have you ever walked into a store to buy milk and walked out with two bags of groceries? You're not alone. In fact, three out of four Americans have made impulse purchases, according to a survey by CreditCards.com. But don't be so quick to blame your own willpower.

"There is a psychology behind impulse buys — we are highly impressionable and easily manipulated," says Ildiko Tabori, Ph.D., a practicing licensed psychologist and neuropsychologist since 2004. "Marketers have made a science out of that vulnerability. We make a temporal connection between objects and perceived needs, and marketers exploit this. An example of this is the well-known practice of designing department stores so the consumer becomes lost and disoriented. At this point, the consumer is most open to impression and impulse buys."

Tabori offers four tips on how to eliminate or at the least control those impulse buys that manage to creep into your credit card bill each month:

1. SEPARATE NEED FROM WANT.

Decide in advance the items you need versus ones you want. You may want a Ferrari, but a simple Ford may make more sense. Marketers design impulse buys to be easy and seductive. Don't fall for it.

2. REMEMBER THAT IT ALL ADDS UP.

Marketers design brick-and-mortar and online stores to make impulse purchases fast and easy. One latte every day is $4.25. That is $1,500 a year. Over the course of 10 years, that's $15,000. If you extend that to all the impulse purchases you make, you have now paid for your child's private college education with lattes and the junk in your garage. We work hard and deserve to reward ourselves from time to time, but know your financial limitations and plan for your future.

3. ALWAYS CONSIDER UTILITY IN DECISION-MAKING.

Can your three kids and large dog fit into the aforementioned Ferrari? No? Stick with a minivan. Utility always trumps impulse. It's old advice but it holds — budgeting is a powerful tool. And to scratch that occasional itch for an impulse buy, allow yourself a small amount of "fun money" within that budget.

4. ASK THE KEY QUESTION WITH EVERY SINGLE PURCHASE.

When we walk into an electronics store, we start doing mental gymnastics to justify, say, a new big-screen TV. Before making an impulse buy, ask yourself, "How will this really improve my life?" Stop for a moment to play devil's advocate, and come up with at least three reasons why someone might tell you it's not a good idea to make the purchase.

"Marketing experts are trained to tease a 'yes' from a consumer," Tabori says. "No is not a dirty word. We all need to learn how to say no, mean it, and use it effectively. The goal is to only purchase what we need despite the pressures of the salesperson, the allure of seductive photography, or the promise of a better life."

Buy Gold and Silver Without Getting Ripped Off

Opinion is often sharply divided when it comes to the topic of gold investment: Proponents make impassioned arguments in favor, while naysayers do the same against it.

We are immediately skeptical of anything someone is trying really hard to sell us on, no matter which side of the fence they fall. This skepticism is natural, and, frankly, healthy.

So, we were initially reluctant to make that leap from understanding gold could be a good investment to actually buying some. But gold does have a mysterious draw all the same.

You see, gold connects us to our past in a fundamental way. The very first coins containing gold were struck around 600 B.C. in Asia Minor, and it has been a medium of exchange ever since. In addition to its use as money and jewelry, it also has been administered as medicine, used in industry, and has played a role throughout history. The pinnacle of human physical achievement is rewarded with an Olympic gold medal.

Of course, just as emotions should not be a barrier to investing in gold, or any other asset, nor should they be the sole motivation to invest, either. There are sound, logical reasons for owning gold that go far beyond the attachment we might feel to it.

GOLD AS MONEY

Gold is the one object that has best functioned as a trusted medium of exchange throughout history. But while gold can be described as many things, it is not the same thing as money. Try trading a gold coin for dinner at a fancy restaurant or for a shopping cart full of food. The idea is laughable in today's America.

Gold's value lies in its properties. Unlike dollars, gold is difficult to produce — it cannot simply be created; it has to be mined, which puts a natural limit on its supply. As an element, it is practically indestructible. To the extent that anything can have value, gold has it in spades.

But while gold is not money in any practical sense today, its value in dollars is a reflection of the supply of dollars versus the supply of gold, as well as our confidence in the dollar as a medium of exchange and a store of value. It is, ultimately, a reflection of the confidence we have in our political leadership. But that confidence is failing rapidly . . . and is the main reason we think everyone should own some gold.

THE END OF THE DOLLAR RESERVE STANDARD

The U.S. dollar is the world's reserve currency, which means that dollars, and debt that pays in dollars, are held as reserves by other countries, protecting their own currencies from speculative outflows.

The dollar can function this way because it is used to settle a significant portion of international trade, specifically the multi-billion-dollar-per-day trade in energy, primarily oil. This is the so-called "petrodollar" system, which dates back to the 1970s, when major oil producer Saudi Arabia agreed to accept only dollars for its oil.

In recent years, though, the rise of Russia and the United States as major oil and gas producers has changed the focus of this policy. Then there's Iran, which has been subverting the petrodollar since 2012. Cut out of the international banking system by the United States, Iran was reduced to barter for its oil.

And this is where it begins to get interesting. Gold was smuggled through Turkey into Iran to pay for oil exports after sanctions were imposed. Once a country can bypass the system, it lays the foundation for a larger shift away from dollars when the time is right.

Now let's turn to Russia. Because Russia supplies Europe with nearly 40 percent of its natural gas, it acts from a position of strength. And Russia, like the Chinese, has been buying gold by the hundreds of tons. Every ton of gold bought by Russian and Chinese central banks increases the effective gold backing of the ruble and yuan. At some point, we believe Russia and China will dump the dollar as a settlement currency, which will send the dollar price of gold skyrocketing.

How to Buy Gold

Now we know why we should buy gold, let's look at how. The most obvious method, buying gold in the form of stock, is complicated. Not only do you have to time the gold market right, but you also have to pick the right companies or exchange-traded funds.

Yet buying gold need be no more complicated or risky than buying food at the local grocer or ordering a book on Amazon. Gold coin shops, be they brick and mortar or online, are merchants just like anyone else. You walk in, you chat with the clerk, and you offer to buy a coin or two. He quotes a price that will be 3 to 10 percent over the current spot price (for reasons I explain a little later). If you agree, you exchange dollars for the coins and you get a receipt. You don't have to fill out forms or sign any papers. The transaction doesn't need to be reported to any governmental agency.

But here's the No. 1 (main) rule when buying gold as wealth insurance: Get the most metal for the dollar that you can.

To do this, you'll need to know the gold content of foreign coins, like British Sovereigns or French Roosters, which don't have weights stamped on them. Modern bullion coins are issued in standard sizes from 1 ounce to 1/20 of an ounce. Older coins have specific weights, easily found on the Internet. Smaller denominations of these coins will all be perfect fractions of these weights based on their face value. For example, a Mexican 20 peso coin, which weighs 1.2057 ounces, will have 0.4823 ounces of gold in it, which is 40 percent of its weight, just as 20 pesos is 40 percent of 50 pesos. The coins will be quoted to you as a price per coin.

A little math will reveal the price per ounce — simply divide the price by the weight.

WHAT TYPES OF COINS?

We recommend buying coins issued by a national mint. The main reason is that there is little to no worry about weight and quality (known as "fineness"). They're also easier to deal with when it comes time to sell them.

For the most part, U.S. bullion is attractive because of a good combination of liquidity, tax-reporting exemptions, and price. U.S. Gold and Silver Eagles are in ready supply and can be found at reasonably low premiums to the current price of the metal for new coins.

The most common denomination for these coins is 1 troy ounce; this is the most popular size bought by consumers and where the premiums on the coins over the spot price are lowest. New coins will always cost more than the price you see quoted on the Internet or CNBC. The reason is simple. The spot price is the current price for 1,000 ounces of gold or 5,000 ounces of silver delivered from an exchange. That price does not include the cost of transporting that bar to a mint, turning it into stacks of coins, packaging them up, and then shipping those coins to dealers around the country. That's where the premium comes from.

For a 1 troy-ounce coin, you can expect to pay between 3 and 10 percent over spot. For smaller weights, the premium goes up as a percentage of the total price because all those other costs — transportation, minting, and packaging — are similar.

Reputable dealers alter their prices with each tick of the gold and silver price on international markets. Gold and silver trade nearly all day between Sunday evening and Friday afternoon. It should be no problem for a dealer to quote you a retail price based on that spot price up to the moment you commit to the purchase.

UNDERSTANDING A BULLION DEALER

Bullion dealers really don't care whether the price of the metals rises or falls. In general, they buy stock — either from you, a wholesaler, or a mint — at a shallow discount and sell it to their customers at a small markup.

One-ounce Gold Eagles are the same the world over, like D batteries or Snickers bars, so the buy and sell margins are pretty consistent.

Avoid any online dealer that tries to charge you a lot for shipping. Shipping rates are based purely on weight and size, and insurance is cheap. As a good rule of thumb, compare final costs.

In general, a dealer will buy your coins from you for a few percent below spot price and sell them back to you for a few percent above spot price for popular, liquid coins. It's a good rule of thumb to expect a 10 to 15 percent spread between the buy and sell price from a vendor. Now, high-volume dealers like the American Precious Metals Exchange will have tighter spreads than that. APMEX, for example, is laudable for its pricing transparency.

Some coins, like American Eagles, are in such high demand and so liquid that the buy/sell spread is very shallow. Since April 2013, after the huge plunge in gold prices, APMEX has been buying U.S. Gold Eagles for a few percent above spot and marking them up just $25 to $30 per ounce, which is less than a 3 percent profit.

DEAL LOCALLY

We recommend getting to know your local coin-shop dealer, too, even if you can get better deals online. Dealing with a person you can trust is important when you go to sell. He'll give you a slightly better price if you have coins that he sells more of. And if you need to raise cash quickly, a trusted dealer will be your best resource.

Get to know what the local market likes and build a supply of that. But don't do so at the cost of the main rule of getting the most metal you can per dollar. If there's a deal to be had on old Mexican pesos or British Sovereigns, go for it. If not, buy what the locals like.

A NOTE ABOUT CONFISCATION

Some people are leery of buying gold because they fear government confiscation. The likelihood of this is minuscule. Still, some worry about "know your customer" laws and that the government will find out who bought gold from the dealers and come after them. If that is a worry, buy locally with cash, even if it means paying a bit more for that privacy. Local pawnshops, coin shops, and flea markets are places where you can buy precious metals in near anonymity.

The more likely scenario is that the government will change the tax laws and try to tax away your profits. Like all investments, this is something you will have to keep tabs on, in the same way that you monitor your stock and bond investments.

FRACTIONAL EDUCATION

Coins smaller than 1 troy ounce are called "fractionals" because they are a fraction of an ounce. As noted earlier, they will cost more per ounce than 1 troy-ounce coins because the minting process is a fixed cost that is spread out over less metal.

When we don't have the luxury of being able to afford a full ounce of gold, though, buying fractionals can still fulfill the main rule.

If you see a dip in gold prices and can afford a Sovereign but not a 1 troy-ounce Eagle, buy the Sovereign. You fulfilled the main rule by getting the most gold you could for your dollar because one 0.2354-ounce Sovereign is greater than zero 1 troy-ounce Eagles.

Fractionals also are more easily traded. If you're buying gold because you think you may have to use it in the case of a currency collapse, then having a supply of 1/10-ounce gold and 1/2-ounce silver won't hurt you.

GOLD OR SILVER?

If you're wondering whether to buy gold or silver, the short answer is own both. The gold-to-silver price ratio is a good indicator of the relative value of one versus the other. This ratio has been declining since the top of the last precious metals bull market in 1992. (See the chart below.)

The declining trend line tells us that silver has been slowly appreciating versus gold for decades. It has dropped from a 71-to-1 ratio to about 52-to-1, a 40 percent relative outperformance. Will this trend continue? I don't know, but one thing you do not argue with in markets are ultra-long trends. They filter out day-to-day noise and reveal big investment themes that investors can use to gain an edge.

The ratio is very volatile, but the guideline is simple. When the gold-to-silver ratio is above the trend line on the chart, buy more silver than gold, and when it is below it, do the opposite. This way you are taking advantage of overcorrections in both metals.

The key is to see value where others don't. When everyone is crowded into gold, buy silver, and vice versa. This ensures that over the long term, you are satisfying the main rule, thereby getting the most portfolio protection possible for your dollar without having to constantly stay abreast of what the metals are doing right now.

JUNK SILVER

You also might consider junk silver. This is pre-1965 U.S. coinage that still had silver content, either 40 or 90 percent depending on the coin and the year. It usually sells in bags or rolls for something close to the spot price of silver. Bags are sold with a known "face value," say $100. This means the junk silver bag contains $100 in coins at their face value.

Junk silver bags are cheaper because the coins are well-used and in various states of disrepair — nicked, scratched, worn, etc. Like fractionals, they are useful for small purchases in the case of a local currency crisis.

SPECULATIVE CONSIDERATIONS

Some gold and silver issues from the national mints are simply beautiful items. Chinese Pandas and the offerings from the Perth Mint in Australia are gorgeous coins whose designs change every year.

While these are more expensive per ounce than U.S. Eagles are, thus violating the main rule, they have the potential for long-term price appreciation as collectibles. The supply of them is tight so, at times, their prices can spike strongly and can make you some extra money if you own them and decide to sell during those spikes.

Another consideration is pre-1933 U.S. coinage: 1907-33 St. Gaudens and 1850-1907 Double Eagles, for example. They can be found for a small premium over new Eagles and carry with them some history. If you can find them at or close to spot, they are a bargain at that price.

All these coins tend to see faster price appreciation during bull runs than the new issues do. But the best way to look at them is being worth no more than a U.S. Eagle would be worth. Any premium they generate over time should be considered "found money."

HOW MUCH GOLD AND SILVER SHOULD YOU HOLD?

As a rule, we suggest having a minimum of 10 percent of your savings in gold and silver. In other words, for every $100,000 you have saved for retirement, $10,000 should be in the form of gold and silver coins.

To start with, however, you should consider cash to be a vital part of your defensive strategy. Cash gives you options and allows you to sleep better knowing you have enough to pay the bills and buy food if something horrible were to happen. My recommendation is a minimum of four months' cash for all basic expenses — food, utilities, housing (mortgage/rent), child care, and insurance.

Add to that another one to two years in gold and silver, on hand. If your monthly expenses are $2,000, then you need $24,000 to $48,000 in gold and silver in a safe in your house, along with ready access to $8,000 cash. Now, this gold and silver will double as your portfolio protection. But it's there to keep you solvent if things are bad and stay that way for a long time.

WRAPPING IT ALL UP

The primary reason to own gold (and silver) is to protect your hard-earned wealth from the depredations of inflation and geopolitical upheaval. It is a hedge against uncertainty. Think of your precious metals as part of your savings, not as part of your investment portfolio. They are like cash.

Because they have no counterparty risk, gold and silver is better than modern digital cash. Gold and silver provide you with a foundation to build a solid wealth edifice that cannot be taken from you through expedient political means like inflation, bank bail-ins, and bond market collapses.

Keep your early priorities simple. Build the walls first — the most metal for your dollar that will keep a roof over your head. Then add trim in the form of coins with collectible potential, and after that, make yourself happy. After all, that's the ultimate goal of life anyway, isn't it?

Save Big on Big-Ticket Purchases

By researching sales, clipping coupons, and using price-comparison smartphone apps, you can save on groceries and other daily essentials. But what about more expensive items of $1,000 or more, like computers, cars, appliances, or furniture? We asked two top consumer experts to share their best tips on big-ticket savings. They came up with these five favorites:

1. ASK FOR THE OUTDATED SALE.

"My rule of thumb is that any sale price you have seen in the past year can be suggested for an item that is no longer on sale," says Rick

Doble of Savvy-Discounts.com and author of *Cheaper: Insiders' Tips for Saving on Everything*. "Big-ticket items can be haggled."

2. NEGOTIATION ISN'T JUST ABOUT MONEY.

So maybe the retailer isn't going to budge as much as you wanted it to on price. Haggle for something else. "Ask for free delivery or installation of furniture or a refrigerator, or get the company to cart away your old one for free," Doble suggests. You'll still be saving money in the long run.

3. SLASH THE PRICE WITH A GIFT CARD.

In the Franklin Prosperity Report, we've told you about websites where you can sell your unwanted gift cards, such as Cardpool.com — you get less than face value for it, but it's cash in your pocket versus a card you may never use. There's a flip side to that transaction, however, which you can take advantage of when buying a big-ticket item. If you know what store you're buying from in advance, you can buy one of those discarded gift cards for less than face value.

Michelle Madhok, shopping expert and the founder of SheFinds.com, says she renovated her whole house using GiftCardGranny.com and saved more than 20 percent. Say you're going to a store like Best Buy for a new $500 TV — if you can pick up five $100 gift cards for $90 apiece, that's like getting another 10 percent off your purchase.

4. JUST SAY 'NO' TO THE UPSELL.

"No matter what amount you want to spend, salespeople will try to get you to spend just a bit more, saying that you will be getting more for your money," Doble says. Stick to your guns. Most likely, their upsell is something that won't benefit you but will benefit their commission. You can buy the batteries cheaper elsewhere, he says, and extended warranties are a waste of money and time. "Most electronic devices that fail will fail within the standard warranty [period]," he says.

5. BUY WHEN OTHERS AREN'T.

Avoid the highly advertised sales days like Black Friday and Labor Day, Madhok says, because chances are, the items that are for sale are the substandard models you don't really want. Go in when sales are slow and retailers are more likely to make a deal.

Shop Smart by Avoiding Rip-Offs and Scoring the Best Deals

Online research, comparison shopping, cutting through the marketing hype, turning the tables on salespeople, and deftly maneuvering through throngs of aggressive shoppers — these are all skills of the world's best shoppers, whose goal is to ensure they hunt down the deal of the century every time they make a purchase.

Why do they do it? Well, to save money for one, but there's more, too. Let's face it, it's a very satisfying feeling to know you've played the shopping game well and scored an incredible deal on something you really wanted.

To better arm readers of The Franklin Prosperity Report in the quest for deals, Christopher Elliott, consumer advocate, personal finance columnist for Tribune Media Services, and author of *Scammed: How to Save Your Money and Find Better Service in a World of Schemes, Swindles, and Shady Deals*, shared seven key shopping strategies, on everything from the art of negotiation to the surprising truth about loyalty programs.

1. DEVELOP A NOSE FOR SNIFFING OUT A STORE'S TRICKS

If you've ever walked out of a store the proud owner of items that weren't even on your radar to buy, then you've fallen victim to one of the oldest tricks in the book: impulse buying.

But it's not really your fault — blame the masterminds behind the enticing store displays. "Stores have their displays down to a science," Elliott says. "They study lighting and smells to try to figure out which are going to encourage people to buy. So from the moment you walk through the door, your every sense is being manipulated to make a purchasing decision."

And yes, they also happily trigger those embarrassing, epic child meltdowns in the candy aisle and the checkout counters. "The candy is at eye level for your kids, which encourages impulse buys," he says.

Now that you know you're being influenced, you have to take conscious steps to outsmart these ploys. Be aware of the environment when you walk in. Start trying to pick out the manipulative efforts of the stores you frequent — with a little practice, you'll be able to spot them instantly.

If you struggle with impulse buying, you may want to recruit a friend to shop with you for at least a few trips, someone who's no-nonsense and has been instructed to stop such purchases in their tracks.

Other ideas: Make a list of needed items before you leave the house and stick to it, leave your young children at home, and never go to the grocery store on an empty stomach (an old but very effective idea).

2. KNOW A TRUE 'SALE' VS. THE MARKUP/MARKDOWN GAME

On sale. No other phrase is so meaningful to shoppers. The words hit consumers from all angles — commercials, signage, and sales associates — yet they never seem to lose their attraction.

But what is a sale, really? "Price is just an illusion," Elliott warns. "Ever since there have been stores, people have been marking things up to mark them down. When I see something that says 20 percent off or 30 percent off, I just ignore it. With other people, though, it sets off alarm bells. I've got to buy this! It's 50 percent off! But they marked it up 200 percent to mark it down, and it's still probably more expensive than it should be."

Of course, that doesn't mean you shouldn't track pricing and try to buy low. If you can time your shopping excursions to the major holidays — Memorial Day, Labor Day, Fourth of July, Thanksgiving/ Black Friday — you'll find better prices. In the case of purchasing a car, proper timing can yield you very aggressive savings.

"The truly informed consumers try to find out how much the car actually cost the dealership," Elliott says. "Then they allow for a reasonable profit, and they try to negotiate themselves as close to that number as they possibly can. When the model year changes in September and October, that's when you want to be out there negotiating for a new car. At that point, they're just trying to move the car off the lot and they're willing to do so without making a profit at all. So you can get a car at dealer cost."

3. LEARN TO RECOGNIZE A SALES PITCH

"How can I help you?" Some people divulge their entire shopping list and bank account when a salesperson asks this question. Others mumble an "I'm just looking" and avoid eye contact. Is there a right, or wrong, answer?

According to Elliott, it comes down to knowing which kinds of businesses pay commissions and which don't. Salespeople who don't earn a commission are really just there to help you. For example, the produce guy at the grocery store is just trying to help you find cilantro and gains nothing other than the satisfaction of doing his job well. But employees of many clothing or furniture stores work on commission and have a vested interest in getting you to make a purchase.

For aggressive pitches on big-ticket items: "Let's take a time-share presentation, for instance," Elliott says. "There's a lot of training for people who are selling those types of items. The sales pitch and the responses are scripted to a certain extent, making it even more difficult for you to say no. But your firm 'no' is always your most effective bargaining chip."

Elliott strongly advises that if you're going into a situation in which you're being sold a big-ticket item, your best defense against the pitch is always being willing to say no and walk away — right up until the end. "Your best negotiating tactic is to say, 'I need time to think about it.'" Elliott points out that 90 percent of the people who say that never come back; sales-people know this, so using it may prod them into desperation mode.

"Once you say you need time to think about it, walk out and watch what happens," he says. "I did that when I was looking for a new car. I test-drove it, went through pricing and financing, and we got down to the very end of the negotiating process and I just felt that the sales guy was being intransigent. So we walked out. A manager actually followed us into the parking lot."

4. NEGOTIATE LIKE A PRO

When on vacation in the Caribbean or Mexico, it's commonplace to negotiate with vendors for treasured trinkets, and they are usually amenable. But have you ever tried to bargain with the sales associate at a department store for a sweater? Probably not.

Then again, at a car dealership, bargaining is not only acceptable but also expected. So when is a price tag fixed and when is it OK to use it as a jumping-off point for negotiations? "It's just a matter of knowing when and where to negotiate," Elliott says.

"At a farmers market or an arts and crafts fair, you absolutely can and should try. Ask for a two-for-one deal or offer 10 bucks for a $12 item."

That doesn't mean you can't give it a shot in a store, especially a non-chain, locally owned establishment. Buy a television at a Best Buy, and you'll likely have little luck in negotiating a price (unless on a slightly used or damaged floor model, which the store sometimes clears out). A local business owner, though, who has total leeway over the pricing and no home office looking over his or her shoulder, may be more amenable to wheeling and dealing, within reason.

Don't just limit your negotiations to the retail establishment, either. "I don't have dental insurance," Elliott says. "So when I go to the dentist to get my teeth cleaned, I ask for a non-insurance rate. They knock 20 percent off right there. Doctors love getting paid cash upfront."

5. DON'T BE TEMPTED BY AN EXTENDED WARRANTY OFFER

It's the question you face at the cash register of any electronics store, the one designed to trigger anxiety: "Would you like to buy the extended warranty protection?"

You're about to shell out a fair amount of cash, and worst-case thoughts start to cascade through your head. "If this product breaks down, I don't want to have to replace it." And anyone who's tried to redeem a manufacturer's warranty knows that's an often-unpleasant experience, just as it's designed to be. (After all, the companies who offer them want to put up as many hurdles as possible to a consumer actually being able to make a claim on one.)

So the extended warranty becomes, in essence, a price to pay for peace of mind. But not a small price. "They can add 10 to 20 percent to the cost of the item," Elliott says. It's a cash grab by companies who know that (a) they are making a smart bet on a product that's likely going to decrease in value over the time of the warranty, (b) the majority of warranties will expire with no claims submitted, and (c) their fine print, such as limiting the types of damages that will trigger the protections, will likely protect them from a future payout.

"A lot of the warranties that are offered are almost pure profit to the company," Elliott says. "So it's like over-insuring yourself, in a way." As Elliott also points out, "If you use almost any type of credit card to make your purchase, your warranty may already be extended. So I would recommend looking at your credit card member agreement before you make a major purchase to see if you're covered."

Most technology these days is disposable anyway, making an extended warranty on such products even less appealing. "If you really think about it, the average computer lasts 24 months at most and then it's obsolete," he says. "So do you really want to extend it beyond 24 months? Probably not. People like the peace of mind that comes with an extended warranty. But as a practical matter, to make a gambling analogy, the house is going to win again."

6. DON'T LET LOYALTY PROGRAMS SKEW YOUR ABILITY TO FIND THE BEST PRICE

Many shoppers brag about their status with various loyalty programs — a platinum-level this, a diamond-level that, a triple gold card carrier of whatever. Sure, it sounds impressive, but they haven't revealed to you what they had to give up to earn (and maintain) that status. And in some cases, it may be their ability to notice a better deal with a competitor.

"There's almost an orthodoxy that participating in a loyalty program is good for you — that you should give your loyalty to one business and they'll repay you by giving you upgrades and free product," Elliott says. "But over the years, I have really come to believe that is a false assumption. Loyalty programs are actually there for the benefit of the company offering them but rarely are there for the benefit of the average consumer."

Once you get involved with a company's loyalty program, it's easy to put blinders on regarding how good a deal you're really getting because you're so focused on attaining a certain goal. And that affects your purchasing decisions because you want to earn points with company A even though company B may offer a better price or more convenient option.

"Whether or not you earn points or miles should be the last consideration, not the first," Elliott explains. "This also applies to credit cards. A lot of people will get a card that has an annual fee just so they can earn miles. They're spending more on their credit cards just to get these miles. Sure, there are people who say they flew to Hawaii for free, but when you break it down, you realize they actually paid more for their tickets than if they'd gone out into the (open) market and purchased (them)."

7. GET THE BEST RESOLUTION OUT OF A BAD EXPERIENCE

You've just purchased that new tablet you've been eyeing, but when you get to the parking lot, you realize they failed to apply the instant rebate. Do you head back inside or figure you'll just call the store for an adjustment when you get home?

"You always want to see if you can resolve a problem in real time," Elliott suggests. "If you think you've been taken advantage of, say something right then and there because that is the absolute best time to resolve something. If you wait too long, then you're going to have to deal with the customer service department, and that department isn't usually focused on service; it's focused on making you go away."

If you don't realize a mistake has been made until you're already home or you find the product is shoddy the first time you go to use it, it's time to contact the customer service department — armed with these tips. "Your best bet is to send a brief email to the business explaining what happened, outline your disappointment, and ask for a specific resolution," Elliott says. "They usually will respond with a form letter, and that's the beginning of your paper trail. So if they say no to your resolution — and they probably will say no — you can then appeal to a supervisor in writing and keep the paper trail. At some point, you may have to hand that paper trail off to an attorney or an investigator."

Another option, if you made the purchase with your credit card, is to dispute the charge. If you didn't get what you paid for, your credit card company will give you a provisional credit. If the merchant does not respond to the investigation, then your provisional credit becomes permanent.

Elliott suggests following the "three p's" of getting the resolution you want from a bad transaction. "Your most effective tactics are persistence (not taking no for an answer), patience (waiting long enough to get a meaningful response because sometimes it takes a while to get an answer), and politeness (if you can be polite even when you're upset, then you can accomplish so much more).

Read This Before You
Rely on Other People's Reviews

Do you check TripAdvisor to see the hotel ratings when planning an out-of-town excursion? Before you go out to eat, do you pull out your Zagat guide to see which restaurants received more than three stars? And if you're looking for five-star ratings for a local cabinet maker to redo my kitchen, do you first check out Yelp to see which craftsmen placed at the top of the scale?

Star ratings are available for almost everything today, and they can frequently help you find the best products and services in a bevy of categories. But do they ensure you're going to get your money's worth? What does a five-star rating really mean?

A TALE OF TWO RATINGS SYSTEMS

A Lufthansa press release got us interested in these questions. It said Lufthansa had become the first European airline to be awarded a 2018 five-star rating from Skytrax, the international airline rating organization.

When we investigated further, we found that only 10 airlines in the entire world achieved this distinction. And Skytrax doesn't skimp on the process of formulating its "certified" ratings: It uses professional inspectors to check every aspect of an airline's service — from seats and in-flight food to the performance of cabin and ground crews.

But Skytrax has competition. The Airline Passenger Experience Association (APEX) issues its own "official" five-star ratings. This year, it awarded them to 22 global airlines, 19 major regional airlines, and nine low-cost carriers!

Unlike Skytrax, the APEX ratings reflect information obtained from thousands of airline passengers. Using an app, these passengers rated the service they received on a half-million flights. (APEX says it took steps to verify that these people really flew on these flights.)

So getting five stars doesn't always indicate a single standard of quality. And the disparity between Skytrax and APEX shows that the method used to determine a star rating can make a big difference.

CROWD-BASED SYSTEMS: PLUSES AND MINUSES

When star ratings began in the 1920s, only experts judged the quality of a product or service. Now it's easier and cheaper to let ordinary consumers do that online. The average level of their responses then determines the number of stars awarded.

And the wisdom of the crowd brings credibility; it's widely believed that "a million people can't be wrong."

However, there are growing questions about the accuracy of crowd-based ratings systems. One problem: They may not reflect a complete range of consumers. Consumer data expert Ori Reshef of Clicktale.com says most people express opinions about a product or service only when they either "love it or hate it." That often pushes star ratings higher or lower than they should be.

In addition, businesses often try to manipulate the results. For example, one bed and breakfast owner in California began asking his guests not to rate any aspect of their stay below the highest level. As he put it, "anything below five stars tells people you would not recommend staying with us and is equal to warning people to stay away."

THE CONTROVERSY OVER HOSPITAL RATINGS

It's one thing to select a B&B on the basis of a five-star rating when the worst that can happen is you have a less-than-perfect vacation. But should you depend on ratings for a life-or-death matter, like choosing a doctor or hospital for a major operation? Here's why you may want to think twice about that:

Four years ago, the government's Center for Medicare and Medicaid Services (CMS) decided to award star ratings to hospitals. The idea was to give patients an easy way to compare the overall quality of in-patient care at various institutions.

To come up with the stars, the organization set up a rating system based on 57 quality measures divided into seven groups: mortality, safety of care, readmissions, patient experience, effectiveness of care, timeliness of care, and efficient use of medical imaging.

The composite score from these groups would be ranked against the composite scores of other hospitals and would result in an overall star rating for the hospital, from 1 for worst to 5 for best. It seemed to be a very scientific formula. However, when the first hospital ratings were rolled out in the summer of 2016, the medical community was shocked. The results were the exact opposite of what everyone expected.

The biggest surprise: Large hospitals, including those affiliated with medical schools, generally did poorly. Even many of the most renowned institutions received one-star ratings. On the other hand, the top five-star category (including only 83 hospitals nationwide) was dominated by small hospitals. It was clear that something was amiss.

WHAT WENT WRONG?

The Bloomberg news organization spotted one clue: hospitals that got the five-star ratings were mainly located in expensive neighborhoods, while those with the one-star ratings were mostly in rundown urban areas.

One theory: Since large hospitals tend to be located near the centers of major cities, they serve a disproportionate number of low-income patients. Unfortunately, after being discharged, many poor people can't afford to continue medications they were given in the hospital or are unable to travel to their doctors for follow-up visits. That makes them likely to quickly land back in the hospital. The CMS formula didn't account for this. Instead, it penalized hospitals with frequent patient readmissions.

Another possible error: Because large hospitals often perform the most complex and high-risk surgeries, their death rates often exceed those of hospitals in wealthy neighborhoods that perform limited procedures. This also may have hurt their ratings. And making matters worse, scores for that (and readmissions) counted far more than other measures. That may have further skewed the results.

There are other ways to compare hospitals and doctors. Yelp, Healthgrades.com, and RateMDs.com have ratings for both hospitals and doctors.

And recently, the Manhattan Institute, a respected research group, gave Yelp a vote of confidence for its hospital ratings. It said, "We find that higher Yelp ratings are correlated with better-quality hospitals (in New York State) and that they provide a useful, clear, and reliable tool for comparing the quality of different facilities."

But many doctors strongly disagree. They claim that patients and their families aren't in a position to know what's going on behind the scenes or how to evaluate a hospital in terms of its medical outcomes. That's true. A quick perusal of these websites shows that consumers do tend to review doctors and hospitals based on the service they get, the congeniality of the office staff, or the expense of the procedures rather than medical expertise or outcomes.

THE RIGHT (AND WRONG) WAY TO USE RATINGS

Clearly, there can be problems with ratings systems. And unless you're an expert in statistics or methodology, those problems may not be easy to detect. But here are some guidelines to help you use five-star ratings wisely:

Crowd-based ratings:

- **Look at the number of people who gave their opinions.** If only a few hundred people rated something, that skews the overall star rating for that business. Also, be skeptical of an extreme rating (one or five) unless it came from a large group of people.
- **Be sure that a rating is current.** Look for the period when the survey was conducted. If it was done years ago, it's possible that the problem with the product or service no longer exists.
- **Know what the rating covers.** Is the product or service being rated in the context of a limited group (U.S. budget airlines) or against the entire universe (all airlines)?
- **Have steps been taken to prevent manipulation?** How do they ensure that raters have actually purchased or used the product or service? Or that individuals have not registered their opinions more than once?
- **Look closely at what the rating covers.** Are reviewers angry because they had to wait a long time for a service or because the receptionist was rude? Those things may be important when choosing a nail salon, but not so much when choosing a cancer surgeon.

Formula-based ratings:

- **Is the data reliable?** If statistics are used in putting together a rating, what is the source? Do they come from a third party with no stake in the outcome or from the company being rated?
- **Are the ratings based on past experiences that may not be repeated?** For example, Morningstar, which rates mutual funds, has come under fire for using past performance as a key factor in its ratings.
- **Have provisions been made to ensure a level playing field?** A small hotel may not have the same facilities as a large one, but may have better customer service. A good ratings system needs to balance various factors in coming up with an overall rating.

Regardless of what ratings system is used, it's important to keep in mind that all ratings are subjective. Even if a product or service gets five stars, you may still end up hating it. And if something has attained a certain number of stars, that doesn't necessarily tell you everything you need to know. For example, a lot of people may hate a heart surgeon's bedside manner, but if she is the best in her field, wouldn't you still want her operating on you?

The bottom line is: Looking at a star rating is a good way to start your research, but it's no substitute for doing a more thorough investigation.

Words to the Wise

BONUS TIP!
Before You Make a Large Purchase, Do This ...
Planning to make a large purchase, such as a new washing machine or computer? Make sure you buy it with a credit card that offers purchase protection. Some cards, like the Chase Sapphire card, offer protection against theft or accidental damage for items you buy with the card. Typically, all American Express, MasterCard and Visa cards offer some type of purchase protection (not so with Discover cards). There may, however, be limits as to how much is covered and how damaged items are handled (e.g., repaired, replaced or reimbursed for the cost). Check with your issuing bank before buying anything big.

BONUS TIP!
Score Free Grocery Delivery
Amazon's Whole Foods free delivery deal for Prime members is likely to kick the grocery delivery business into high gear. Already, major chains are planning to expand into so-called "dark" stores in some areas just to develop faster delivery options. A dark store has no customer entrance and exists only to pick and pack online orders.

Meanwhile, discounters, such as Walmart and Target, are also working to attract pickup orders. Typically, pickup is free.

BONUS TIP!
Almost-New Mobile Tech Can Save You Hundreds

If it's time to upgrade your cellphone, but you don't want to change carriers (to get that fancy new iPhone or Samsung for free), it might be time to buy one used instead. The internet is crawling with second-hand technology resellers that act as trusted marketplaces between far-flung buyers and sellers.

Besides old standbys Amazon and eBay, you can try Swappa and Gazelle to find phones, laptops, gaming devices, and more handheld tech from a variety of individual sellers across the nation. The sites track prices across the web and give you a very good idea of whether a given offer is reasonable or too high before deciding to buy. If you agree on a price, the seller ships you the phone directly. Before buying, make sure to get an unlocked phone or that the model you seek is set up to work on your carrier.

Chapter 9

Protect Your Financial Privacy

"FOR WANT OF A NAIL THE SHOE WAS LOST;
FOR WANT OF A SHOE THE HORSE WAS LOST,
AND FOR WANT OF A HORSE THE RIDER WAS LOST,
BEING OVERTAKEN AND SLAIN BY THE ENEMY,
ALL FOR WANT OF CARE ABOUT A HORSE-SHOE NAIL."

The 4 Best Ways to
Guard Your Digital Data

When outlaw Willie Sutton was asked why he robbed banks in 1952, he said, "Because that's where the money is." Things are different today. More money is stolen with the stroke of a pen or keyboard than by the guns and masked men of the Wild West. But the motive for taking Social Security numbers, birth certificates, and credit profiles is the same: Because that's where the money is.

Most people would agree that new technology has made us far better off, but there are always tradeoffs. Today, money isn't only stored in steel bank vaults, but also as zeros and ones on a cloud computer. If cybercriminals can access your data, it can easily be used — or sold — to create fake passports, poach tax returns (and refunds), open new lines of credit, start new cellphone services, or transfer bank funds.

In 2017, there were 829 data breaches in the U.S., with nearly 17 million Americans losing $17 billion. Top breaches occurred at Equifax, Uber, and Verizon.

In 2018, British Airways, T-Mobile, Saks Fifth Avenue, and Lord & Taylor joined the list of major companies with data breaches.

And in 2019 saw the worst year of data breaches ever, with 100 million Capital One credit card applications already hacked.

Clearly, this isn't a problem that's going away soon. No matter how strong someone makes a system, there's always a thief who can find a way to break into it.

For instance, in 2007, personal data security company LifeLock's co-founder, Todd Davis, ran a series of television campaigns where his actual Social Security number was painted across the side a truck and driven through large cities as if to taunt would-be thieves. The intent was to show that LifeLock was so secure, it was foolproof. It was a brilliant marketing strategy — until it backfired. Between 2007 and 2008, Davis was a victim of 13 cases of identity theft.

What can you do to guard your identity? The best defense is to take steps to protect your data and not expect others to do it for you. Cybersecurity experts agree on these top ways to protect your identity.

1. FREEZE YOUR CREDIT.

A credit freeze is a voluntary way of not allowing anyone access to your credit reports. If someone has your Social Security number and is trying to open a new line of credit, it simply won't happen if you have a credit freeze on your account.

All you have to do is contact the three major credit reporting agencies — Equifax, TransUnion, and Experian — and tell them to freeze your credit. It's easy and can done by phone or online, and it won't impact your credit score. Once you make the request, the agencies must comply within one business day.

There used to be a nominal charge to freeze credit, but federal law now makes it free. Once in place, most states allow the freezes to last indefinitely. According to the Federal Trade Commission (FTC), if you wish to unfreeze or "thaw" your credit, just contact the bureaus, and the freeze must be lifted within one hour.

It's also important to note that in addition to the big three credit bureaus, there are others. Innovis is a distant fourth, but hackers often attack this site if they run into trouble with the other three.

For added protection, it's a good idea to contact the National Consumer Telecommunications and Utilities Exchange (NCTUE), which was founded by AT&T in 1997 to maintain payment and account histories for telecommunications, pay TV, and utility service providers. Even though Equifax is the contractor that manages the NCTUE database, you'll still need to contact NCTUE to freeze any credit reports provided by them. However, understand that you'll need to unfreeze this report before applying for new cell service.

One final reporting agency to contact about a freeze is ChexSystems, which is primarily used by banks and credit unions. Its reports show things like check overdrafts or unpaid fees over the past five years.

Despite the hassles of having to freeze credit, there are some upsides. First, it will keep you from impulsively opening a new account. Second, it prevents bureaus and banks from selling your information. Most of those unwanted credit card solicitations that clutter up your mailbox will stop.

Finally, it's important to understand that while freezing your credit is good step, it only prevents new accounts from being opened. The more common problem is current credit card or bank accounts getting hacked, and a credit freeze isn't going to prevent that.

2. SIGN UP FOR CREDIT MONITORING.

The best way to stop current accounts from being hacked is to monitor your credit. There are many credit monitoring services out there, but Privacy Guard is one of the top rated. It runs $9.99 per month to actively monitor your credit report at the big three bureaus and send you texts or email alerts if there are any changes, including attempts to open new accounts.

The company also advertises to scan the "dark web" for signs of your social security number, passport, medical records, or other data that may be up for sale. However, dark web scans usually have little value because if your information is there, it'll be hiding behind a paywall run by tech-savvy cybercriminals. It's OK if dark web monitoring is included in a monthly fee, but be cautious about paying addition fees just for dark web scans. In nearly all cases, they'll produce nothing.

Other top pay services include Identity Guard, which costs between $7.50 and $20.83 per month, depending on the service you choose, and Identity Force, which runs between $17.95 and $23.95 per month.

There's also a free credit monitoring service: Credit Karma, which provides free credit updates each week along with free texts and e-mails of any changes to your report, including immediate alerts for any new credit applications. The only downside is that Credit Karma only includes information from two bureaus — Equifax and TransUnion.

Nerd Wallet is also free and provides similar information, but it only includes data from TransUnion.

However, there is a possible way to get better credit monitoring for free. After the Equifax breach that affected 147 million people, the credit bureau reached a settlement with the FTC, agreeing to pay those impacted up to $700 million.

If you've been affected, you can register for a one-time check, which will be up to $125, or at least four years of free credit monitoring from Equifax. After that time, you may enroll in free credit monitoring for an additional six years, but it will only be from one of the big three bureaus. To see if you qualify, check eligibility.equifaxbreachsettlement.com.

Because of the huge response, experts say that the settlement is likely to be far less than the maximum $125 per person, with some saying it may amount to pennies. So opting for the free credit monitoring is probably a better choice, worth closer to $1,200 or even as much as $3,600.

3. USE A PASSWORD MANAGER

A password manager is software that stores all of your passwords and allows you to access them with one master password. And if you use a password manager app on your phone, you can access passwords with your fingerprint or face ID. The benefit is that you can construct long, complex passwords without having to memorize them.

For example, once you've logged into your password manager, if you go to your banking website, it'll automatically fill in your username and password.

This also reduces the chance that a cyberhacker can grab your passwords by "keylogging," which is done by through Trojan software that sneaks onto your computer through legitimate software. With keylogging software, cyberhackers can monitor your keyboard strokes.

For instance, if you've typed "BankofAmerica.com" followed by "Fido123" thieves would know it's your password. But because password managers don't use a keyboard, those prompts are never seen by keylogger software.

More importantly, many of these password managers will generate random passwords of any length you choose. Despite continued warnings, people still use their children's names, home address, or cellphone number as passwords. Nobody likes to use long random passwords they can't remember. For example, in the Equifax breach, one of its databases in Argentina used "admin" as the username and password.

4. DON'T GIVE OUT SENSITIVE INFORMATION OVER EMAIL.

Another way that criminals get important data about you is through "phishing" or "spoofing," which can take many forms. One of the most common is when hackers send email using official company logos and fonts. They're perfect replicas and very convincing. The email will ask you to log into your account for an "important message" and provide a link.

Don't ever click on the links in an email. Typically, they'll direct you to a fake website, and once you've entered your username and password, you'll get a page saying the site is currently down and to try back later. By then it's too late, as the cyberhackers now have your information and can withdraw money, make purchases, or just steal your information for other scams.

How to spot a phishing or spoofing email? Oftentimes, they won't use your name, saying "Dear Customer" instead of "Dear Sam Smith." By contrast, most reputable companies will address you by the name listed on the account.

Other scams are more sophisticated. The best rule: When contacted by email or phone, no matter how official it seems, don't provide any information. Instead, hang up and call the company yourself or type in the company's website yourself (not by clicking through a link in an email).

And if you do find that you're a victim of identity theft, visit identityTheft.gov, operated by the FTC, or Identity Theft Resource Center (idTheftCenter.org), a nonprofit that provides free help for victims.

Protect Your Business Against ID Theft

Small businesses are especially vulnerable to identity theft, says John Sileo, a privacy expert and CEO of The Sileo Group (thinklikeaspy .com). "Entrepreneurs are targeted more than others because they tend to have more liquid assets than individual consumers, yet have fewer protections than large corporations," Sileo says. "Small businesses are the real sweet spot for hackers." Here are four ways to protect your organization from theft:

1. Lock Your Mobile Device

A survey by mobile security firm Confident Technologies found that more than half of respondents do not protect their mobile devices with passcodes, and nearly two-thirds use these phones to access business email and networks.

"That is like walking around with an open business computer for anyone to use," Sileo says. Set the auto-lock function, which shuts off a laptop, smartphone, or tablet after a set amount of time and can only be opened by a passcode. Most devices allow for advanced passcodes of more than the usual four digits, Sileo says.

2. LIMIT NETWORK ACCESS

"The advent of 'bring your own device to work' policies at companies severely weakens network security," Sileo says. To combat this, require that all devices in the office be protected with malware software (including yours).

Also, consider setting up two networks: one limited to business-sanctioned devices and a second for guest access, which employees can use for their personal phones and tablets.

3. RETHINK MOBILE BANKING

"I'm all for online banking on computers, but if you're making financial transactions with a mobile device, that is the same as using an unsecured computer — which is very risky," Sileo says. When it comes to paying bills, depositing checks, and transferring money, stick with a computer with a secured connection, or traipse down to the bank in person and handle your transaction the old-fashioned way.

4. EDUCATE EMPLOYEES

"When it comes to business identity theft, data breach is the biggest risk — and personal social media accounts being used on work computers is the top culprit," Sileo says.

The most effective way to combat this is to train workers what not to click on, which includes any link that they are not 100 percent positive came from a reputable source. Sileo says the message should be: "Even if the link says it comes from your mother but it promises a free iPad, assume it's baloney."

Why You Should Freeze
Your Kid's Credit Now

Years of publicity on the dangers of identity theft has led to an unintended consequence: Scammers are now targeting kids instead of adults. More than 1 million children were targeted in 2017, reports Javelin Strategy & Research, two-thirds of them age 7 or younger.

The average theft using a child's identity was $2,303 in 2017 — double the adult average — and costing $540 million to correct.

Identity thieves are after kids not for their savings accounts or credit card numbers since they have none. Instead, the bad guys look for Social Security numbers that are not already in the credit system.

A clean number can be used to apply for credit, and the parents and child are unlikely to realize there's a problem for years. The solution, besides being vigilant with your data online, is to freeze your child's credit.

You might want to do this to protect them from fraud, but, frankly, also to protect them from themselves. Imagine your kids as freshmen on college campuses and strapped for cash. When they get to college, far from home, they will find themselves outgunned when it comes to pocket money. Their friends may have credit cards and spending money, new cars, fancier clothes, and gadgets — all the usual claptrap that spendthrift parents shower on distant kids.

And your kids will be tempted to open credit card accounts.

Tell them, "Some good-looking kid in fancy shoes will get paid $50 to talk you into filling out an application, and just like that, you'll have a $1,000 credit line. And you'll spend it, but have no income to pay it down. That's how you'll get on the credit treadmill."

GETTING IT DONE CAN BE TRICKY

We went to the websites for Equifax, Experian, and TransUnion for instructions on how to freeze a minor's credit. We also went, on the advice of a financial adviser, to a lesser-known fourth credit agency, Innovis.

Thanks to the big Equifax breach, it's now free nationwide to freeze your credit, but you have to do so by mail for a minor. Moreover, you can't just sign up with an aggregator service to freeze your child's credit at all the bureaus at once.

Generally speaking, you will need a copy of your driver's license, a copy of the child's birth certificate and Social Security card, and your basic identification information (Social Security number, address, name, etc.).

THE DETAILS ARE IMPORTANT

If you want to freeze your child's credit, the process is different for a minor who is over and under age 16.

It's slightly different at each credit bureau, as well, but you'll generally need the same information. I'll use Equifax as an example. For a minor age 16 or older, Equifax asks for: complete name and all suffixes, complete address, Social Security number, and date of birth. To validate the parent's identity, you'll also need a copy of one of the following: a driver's license, Social Security card, or birth certificate, plus a pay stub with address, a W-2 or 1099 tax form, passport, or a state or military ID.

Finally, to validate your address, the bureaus will want one of these as well: a valid state driver's license, a utility bill with the correct address, a cell or residential phone bill, a pay stub, a W2 or 1099, a lease agreement or house deed, or a mortgage or bank statement.

For a minor under 16, Equifax wants both a birth certificate and Social Security card for the child, a copy of a parent's valid ID (Social Security card or birth certificate), and, to validate the parent's relationship with the child, a birth certificate with the parent's name on it, a court order, a power of attorney, or a foster care certificate.

You can find more details on the credit bureaus' websites:

- TransUnion: https://www.transunion.com/credit-freeze/ credit-freeze-faq#freeze-other
- Equifax: https://www.equifax.com/personal/education/ identity-theft/child-identity-theft/
- Experian: https://www.experian.com/freeze/center.html
- Innovis: https://www.innovis.com/personal/lc_minorsProtected

The Hidden Problem With Gift Cards

Gift cards are becoming increasingly popular, but they have a hidden trap, and you may not discover it until it's too late.

THE PRICE OF CONVENIENCE

It all has to do with where you buy the gift card. If you buy it at a grocery store or other retailer, it may say "Amazon" or "Apple" on it, and it can be used at those merchants' stores/websites, but it isn't issued by those merchants. Instead, these gift cards are likely produced and serviced by Blackhawk Network, one of the largest gift card servicers in the world.

Why does it matter? Because unlike a gift card purchased directly from a merchant, you could find yourself out of luck if the card is lost, misplaced, or stolen.

Blackhawk Network's advice for us? Contact the merchant. However, many merchants consider their gift cards to be like cash, meaning there is no refund if the cards are lost or stolen. Other merchants will replace a lost or stolen card if the cardholder can provide sufficient information about the card, prove that he or she was the owner, and that a balance remains.

We learned that Amazon, like many merchants, doesn't provide customer support for gift cards purchased outside of its website. Amazon suggested contacting Blackhawk, and Blackhawk suggested I contact the merchant where the card was purchased (a local grocery chain). The grocery chain said it doesn't handle lost/stolen cards and that I needed to contact Amazon.

GETTING OFF THE CAROUSEL

Blackhawk Networks' advice for avoiding this circle of chaos was to use an electronic wallet to store the card number, PIN, and other details.

If you are the gift-giver, include the receipt and/or activation slip for the card with your gift. If you are the recipient, keep the receipt/activation slip in a safe place. The receipt/activation slip will have the information necessary to find the card and prove who purchased it.

It's also a good idea to treat the card like you would cash — consider entering the card info into an electronic wallet, and if possible, register the card.

An even easier way to avoid this problem: Buy gift cards directly from the merchant or retailer where the card will be used.

16 Ways to Protect Your Financial Information Online

It's a scary world out there. Data breaches and hacks have become such routine news events that you might think getting your personal information stolen is inevitable. However, it's not.

In fact, it's much less likely if you follow one key principle: Don't be an easy target. The quickest way to become low-hanging fruit for a thief is choosing weak passwords such as "12345," "qwerty," or "password." (These always top the lists of most-commonly-hacked pass-words each year.)

So choosing a stronger password is a start, but there are other things you can do to keep your information safe, or at the very least, minimize the damage if someone does infiltrate some part of your digital financial life. I've compiled a list of 18 simple habits that any-one can (and should) take to protect their finances from attack.

SAFEGUARD YOUR EMAIL
1. Turn on two-step verification.
Your email is a gateway to your finances, with valuable information about what banks, credit cards and investment companies you use. Two-step verification is a way to shut out would-be thieves.

It's pretty simple: When anyone tries to log into your account from a new computer or device, your email service asks for a pass-word, but also sends a numeric code to your phone via text message. If the criminal has your email password but not your phone, they're out of luck.

2. Don't click links in suspicious emails.
If you receive an email from a friend, and it says something non-spe-cific such as "I thought you'd like this" followed by a clickable link, be careful It could be a trick to get you to download software or fill out a form to give up personal information. Don't fall for it.

Even in legitimate-looking emails, avoid clicking links. For exam-ple, when you get an email from a bank saying that your statement is ready, it might be real, or it might be a lookalike. Better to type in your bank's website yourself rather than using a link.

3. Act on red flags right away.
If someone tells you he or she got a suspicious email message from you, change your password immediately.

SAFEGUARD YOUR CREDIT
4. Freeze your credit file.
If aren't taking out a new loan or credit card anytime soon, it's a good idea to put a security freeze on your credit file with each of the three credit bureaus (Experian, Equifax, TransUnion). Doing this can pre-vent thieves from opening accounts in your name.

5. Review your credit report regularly.
By law, you are entitled to one free credit report every year from annualcreditreport.com.

6. Review your credit card statements regularly.
Review them at least every month before you pay them, but ideally once a week to catch malicious activity sooner.

SAFEGUARD YOUR COMPUTER
7. Install anti-virus and anti-malware software.
Without this protection, your computer can be infected with harmful programs. One example is keystroke loggers, which record what you type on the keyboard. They can look for website addresses you type (say, Fidelity.com) and what you type in immediately after (usually a username and password).

8. Keep your computer's operating system up-to-date.
Do the updates when your computer prompts you, or consider allowing automatic updates. Usually they include security patches that will protect you from the newest threats.

9. Put a password on your home Wi-Fi network.
Otherwise anyone who drives by your home can use your internet and try to access your files.

10. Don't perform financial transactions on public Wi-Fi networks.
It's easy to quickly check your bank balance while at a coffee shop, but there's a chance your information could be intercepted.

SAFEGUARD YOUR PASSWORDS
11. Change your passwords every so often.
Once or twice a year is good, and of course, every time an account is compromised.

12. Don't use the same password for every account.
Once criminals have one valid password of yours, they are likely to see if it works elsewhere.

13. Try a password manager.

These services can generate random, hard-to-crack passwords for every account you have. They also automatically log you onto websites so you don't need to remember any crazy long passwords. Dashlane and Keeper are two services recommended by PCMag.

DON'T SHARE YOUR PASSWORDS WITH ANYONE.
14. Don't leave your passwords out in the open.

A cheat sheet is ok, but keep it well-hidden. Even better: Instead of listing your actual passwords, give yourself a hint.

15. Choose passwords that aren't guessable.

For example, don't use your favorite sports team, a child's name, or a pet's name — anything that everyone knows about you or can find out from a quick scan of your Facebook page.

16. THINK PASS PHRASE INSTEAD OF PASSWORD.

One trick to inventing complex passwords that are easy to remember: Base it on a phrase — perhaps a favorite song lyric, a quote from a movie you like, or something funny your kid once said. Then create your password by taking the first letter of each word of the phrase or substituting numbers or symbols for some of the words.

IRS at Your Door?
How to Tell If It's a Scam

To most Americans, the acronym "IRS" conjures fearful visions of audits and penalties. So when someone from the IRS contacts them, they take it seriously and do whatever the person asks.

However, often the person on the other line isn't a government employee at all, but a criminal. When well-meaning taxpayers are taken advantage of this way, the results can be disastrous. Since 2013, over 10,000 taxpayers have been tricked into paying scam artists more than $54 million.

Fortunately, there are telling signs an IRS impersonator isn't the real deal. Keep reading to learn our warning signs, as well as what to do if you've been contacted by a scammer.

FIVE CLUES TO FOLLOW

Criminals often change their scripts and tactics, but IRS representatives have standard ways of conducting their work, such as:

A legitimate IRS representative initiates contact through paper mail. Nearly all IRS communication begins with a mailed notice. After sending the notice, an IRS rep may contact you by phone to set up an appointment, but he or she will never ask for personal financial information (credit or debit card numbers, account passwords, Social Security numbers) over the phone.

Moreover, the IRS does not use email, text messages, or social media to discuss individual tax situations. Most scams are perpetrated via email and phone, so be particularly suspicious of anyone using those methods.

A legitimate IRS representative shows identification. In-person scams are less common, but if you have any doubt, ask to see identification. There are two forms of ID that all IRS reps are required to provide: a pocket commission, which outlines the specific authority and responsibilities of the holder, and a Personal Identity Verification (PIV). A true IRS representative willingly shares these items.

A legitimate IRS representative does not threaten you in any way. Often scammers try to scare innocent people into thinking they are in a lot of trouble. The scammers might threaten to revoke your driver's license or have you arrested. This is not how the real IRS operates. IRS reps are required by law to treat you with professionalism and courtesy. Remember, true IRS representatives are accountants trying to balance the books — not make a bust.

A scammer might also try the opposite approach, saying you are due a huge refund. Don't fall for it. The old adage still holds: If it sounds too good to be true, it probably is.

A legitimate IRS representative won't demand immediate payment. A real IRS inquiry is a drawn-out process, where you have the opportunity to question or appeal the amount you owe. (It's one rare situation where administrative bureaucracy works in your favor.) Beware of anyone insisting you can resolve a tax matter within a few minutes.

A legitimate IRS representative doesn't dictate how you pay your taxes. Some scammers convince victims to pay them via prepaid debit cards, gift cards, or wire transfers. The IRS doesn't specify payment methods and asks for payments to be made only to the U.S. Treasury.

How to Protect Yourself From IRS Scams

Scrutinize any request for your personal information. Anytime someone asks you for financial information — no matter where the person claims to be from — be very suspicious. Never give this information to anyone you haven't contacted on your own.

Verify a rep's identity with the IRS. The agency can confirm the legitimacy of any communication if you call 1-800-366-4484. If someone claiming to be from the IRS calls you, simply ask for the person's name, badge number, and a callback number, and say you will return the call after you've confirmed their legitimacy. Should the person get angry or aggressive, that's a sure sign he or she doesn't work for the IRS.

If it's not legit, report it. Report any scams to the Treasury Inspector General for Tax Administration at treasury.gov/tigta. Use the red button that says "IRS Impersonation Scam Reporting." If you receive a suspicious email, forward it to phishing@irs.gov.

Know your own tax situation. It's a lot easier to tell a potential scammer to buzz off if you're certain you don't owe the IRS money. If you do owe taxes or think you might, call the IRS at 1-800-829-1040 to get a handle on the situation and work out a payment plan.

Familiarize yourself with typical scams. The IRS publishes examples of current scams on its website at irs.gov/newsroom. Click on "Tax Scams/ Consumer Alerts" in the left column.

5 Myths You Need to Know About Charities

How many charitable organizations have asked you for money in the past week? From hurricane victims to the local field hockey team, you want to offer support. But how do you know which organizations are legitimate before you hand over your hard-earned money?

To find out the right way to check out charities, we spoke to Stephanie Kalivas, an analyst at CharityWatch, a review site that grades charities on an A to F scale. She clued us in to a few persistent myths about charities:

MYTH #1: ALL CHARITIES USE THEIR FUNDS WISELY.

While many of the 1 million charities in the United States are responsible stewards of contributions, a number are not. Basic research should uncover if a charity is poorly run, but few people do the legwork to find out.

Kalivas recommends being particularly vigilant with charities tied to emotional causes, such as support for cancer patients, veterans, and police and firefighters. "There are some bad actors out there that are just taking advantage of people," she says.

MYTH #2: IT'S TOO COMPLICATED TO RESEARCH A CHARITY.

Charity watchdogs sites — such as Kalivas' CharityWatch, as well as Charity Navigator and the Better Business Bureau's Wise Giving Alliance — make it easier than ever to check a charity's standing.

If you're considering one that isn't reviewed online, it's possible to use the watchdogs' methodology to do your own research. "In general, we're using publicly available documents to do our work," Kalivas explains.

Start with the charity's own website. Is there information posted about its staff and board of directors? Are details shared about its past successes and future goals? Does a donor privacy policy exist?

Next, get your hands on the charity's IRS Form 990 and its audited financial statements. Oftentimes, these documents are posted to the charity's website. If not, they can be obtained at GuideStar.org or your state attorney general's website, or you could also ask the charity to share them. (If they won't, that's a red flag.)

Look for: how much of the organization's funding goes to program costs vs. administrative costs? (Programs should be 75 percent or higher.) Is executive compensation reasonable, given the size and impact of the organization? (Compensation in the low-to-mid six figures is average.)

Kalivas says the "notes" section of the audited financial statements can be a treasure trove, too. "A lot of times those notes have interesting disclosures about what the charity is doing," she says.

MYTH #3: ALL THAT MATTERS IS THE PERCENTAGE A CHARITY SPENDS ON PROGRAM COSTS.

Program spending is important, but charities have flexibility in how they report that number. For example, fundraising materials can be counted as program costs if they include an educational message. (Imagine a solicitation from a cancer charity that includes a tip about eating vegetables.)

"It's favorable for [charities] because it will inflate their program spending, and most people will focus in on that," Kalivas says. But CharityWatch assumes donors would not consider these legitimate program costs and adjusts them out.

For a charity you evaluate on your own, consult page 10, line 26, column B ("Joint Costs") of the charity's Form 990 to find out if it uses this methodology.

MYTH #4: IF YOU DON'T HAVE TIME TO RESEARCH A CHARITY, GIVE A SMALL AMOUNT.

Listen, we've all been there. The person representing the charity is persistent, and sometimes you just want to end the encounter. The solution is never to donate over the phone or on the street. Instead, ask to be contacted by mail. That way you can research the charity at your leisure.

"Never feel pressured to give on the spur of the moment without knowing anything about the charity," Kalivas says. "Your donation is meaningful. You should take some time."

Another reason not to donate over the phone: Many charities hire professional fundraisers to do telemarketing, according to Kalivas. These pros may keep as much as 90 percent of your donation before it reaches the charity!

MYTH #5: IT'S BEST TO DONATE TO A CHARITY WHOSE NAME YOU RECOGNIZE.

Most people prefer to give to well-known organizations. However, many charities have "sound-alike" names that are easily confused.

Double-check the name to be sure you're giving to the charity you think you are.

Furthermore, name recognition isn't a guarantee of quality. It surprised me to learn that the American Cancer Society has a grade of "C" from CharityWatch and a two-star rating from Charity Navigator.

For every charity with a poor grade, Kalivas says there are plenty of well-run charities in the same category. "Just redirect your donation to one of those instead," she recommends.

Words to the Wise

BONUS TIP!
Privacy Help for People With Smart Speakers

Feel like you've already said too much online? It probably won't make you feel better to know that your Alexa device has kept recordings of your voice for as long as you've been talking to it. Fortunate, there is a way to get rid of your recordings. It's as simple as saying, "Alexa, delete what I said today."

If you want to erase recordings that are older than a day, you have to go into Alexa's settings to access your entire voice history. Google has a similar option in its account settings to delete voice recordings.

BONUS TIP!
An Alternative to Closing That Missing Card Account

Losing a credit or debit card can be a big hassle. You probably will have the urge to close the card as soon as you realize it's missing, but in many cases it's just in a pair of pants in the laundry or under a car seat. If you think the card is recoverable, consider locking the card temporarily instead. Most of the big card issuers and banks now offer this service, including American Express, Bank of America, Capital One, Chase, Citibank, Discover, and Wells Fargo. New purchases and cash advances will be stopped, but recurring payments you set up prior to losing the card will continue.

BONUS TIP!
Veterans Beware: Scams on the Rise

If you are a veteran or have a veteran in the family, be especially cautious about responding to unsolicited phone calls and emails. Elder abuse scams that are aimed at vets are on the rise. According to an AARP study, 80% of veterans say they have encountered a veteran-specific scam. Sixteen percent of veterans have lost money on them, twice the rate of the general public.

One way this happens is when callers pose as charities to collect money to benefit other vets or claim that a government benefits program for which the veteran qualifies requires an initial payment. The U.S. Postal Inspection Service and AARP have launched a campaign called Operation Protect Veterans to raise awareness of these cons. In general, never give money or personal information to strangers who contact you by email or phone.

BONUS TIP!
Education ID Theft Increasing

Hackers are increasingly targeting students for identity theft. Email and data security firm Mimecast reported that in the first quarter of 2019, schools received more malicious email traffic than any other type of organization. Many education websites — such as lending information, scholarship databases, and college application aggregators — lack proper security.

Experts recommend that parents and students avoid clicking links and opening attachments to emails offering assistance with school funding and acceptance. Those links could result in downloads to your computer or phone that can expose your identity or otherwise compromise your information.

Chapter 10

College Savings

"AN INVESTMENT IN KNOWLEDGE
ALWAYS PAYS THE BEST INTEREST."

Best Ways Grandparents Can Help Pay for College

Chipping in to pay for higher education is a goal for many of today's grandparents, with one in five specifically saving for their grandchildren's college expenses, according to a survey from TD Ameritrade. The average amount set aside is $2,460 each year.

But simply writing a check to your grandchild may not be the smartest financial move to make — for you or for them.

For starters, it may harm his or her chances of getting financial aid, including free money, like grants. That's because 20% of the money held in the student's name is considered available to pay for college, whereas only 5.6% of money in the parents' names is considered available to pay for college, according to federal financial aid formulas.

You may think that doesn't matter if you assume your grandchild won't qualify for aid. But that would be a mistake. According to the National Center for Education Statistics, 85% of undergraduate students qualified for aid in 2015.

The tips below will show you how you can help your grandkids, without jeopardizing any possible financial aid opportunities.

SAFELY CONTRIBUTE TO GRANDKIDS' COLLEGE COSTS
1. Contribute to a 529 education savings plan.

A 529 plan is a great place to park and grow college savings for your grandchild. You can contribute to a 529 account owned by the parents, or you can set up one of your own.

The benefits of 529 plans are many:

- There are no income limits for you that would phase out your ability to contribute.
- There are no income taxes on any earnings.
- Some states offer income tax deductions for contributions to a 529 plan.
- There are no annual contribution limits, though you may want to give less than $15,000 per year to steer clear of gift taxes. (Contributions to a 529 savings plan count as a gift to the beneficiary — your grandchild — in the year you contribute to the 529, not the year you withdraw it to pay their college expenses.)

- The accumulated funds can be used for tuition and fees, plus other expenses, such as textbooks, computer equipment, software and internet access, special needs expenses, and room and board (if the student is enrolled at least half-time).

And the downsides? If you, as a grandparent, own the 529 plan, withdrawing the money and using it for your grandchild's benefit will count as income to the student in the year it is withdrawn, which could lower the child's eligibility for financial aid.

However, if you give to a parent-owned 529 plan instead (or transfer the ownership of your 529 plan to the parent), there is less of a financial aid impact. Any money in a parent-owned 529 plan is considered a parental asset, and only around 5% of parents' assets are considered available to pay for college.

2. Tilt your support to the latter part of their schooling.

There are ways for grandparents to chip in for college costs without affecting financial aid at all. You just have to time it right — specifically to the last five semesters of the student's college career (spring of sophomore year and later, if the students is on the standard four-year track).

Here's why: When a family applies for federal student aid, they must share their financial information, of course. However, it's not information from the previous year, as you might expect; it's from the year before that.

For example, a student beginning college this fall (the 2019-2020 school year) would apply with family financials from the year 2017. You have to reapply every year, so the reported years will end up being 2017, 2018, 2019 and 2020. So in this example, as long as a grandparent's support comes in calendar year 2021 or later, it won't affect the student's ability to get financial aid.

This applies to contributions to a grandparent-owned 529 plan as well as regular cash gifts. Remember, even if you don't need to report the gifts to the IRS, your grandchild must declare money held in a 529 as untaxed income on his or her financial aid applications.

3. Gift your grandchild money to pay down (or pay off) student loans after he or she graduates from college.

This one might be best of all. It doesn't interfere with financial aid, and it rewards the true goal: the completion of college. Plus, you retain control over your money that much longer, which comes in handy if the student decides not to go to college or drops out. And it gives your grandchild an incentive to work hard and be responsible.

KEY INFORMATION ABOUT SAVINGS BONDS

If we were writing this article 30 years ago, government-issued savings bonds (specifically Series EE and I bonds) would have figured prominently in the recommendations. The interest you earn on these savings bonds is tax-free when they are used toward certain educational expenses. For decades, thousands of students were sent to college using savings bonds, and they are still available today.

However, since federal legislation created 529 plans in 1996, they have been considered a superior investment. That's because savings bonds:

- historically have not kept pace with dramatic increases in college costs;
- have income limitations that prevent some bond holders from claiming the tax-free interest benefit;
- can only be used for tuition and fees (so no textbooks, computer equipment, software, internet access, special needs expenses, or room and board).

The newer 529 plans address all of these drawbacks and more.

If you've already invested in savings bonds, not to worry. You can roll over the funds to a 529 tax free (provided you haven't exceeded the income limits for getting tax-free interest on the bonds. The phaseout starts at $79,550 for single filers and $119,300 for married filers. Using the bond proceeds to fund a 529 plan is considered a "qualified education expense" — same as making a payment to a university would be.

Unlocking the Value of College Counseling Services

I n 2019, 50 people, including celebrities Lori Loughlin and Felicity Huffman, were indicted for bribing their children's way into elite colleges. The actresses used a private college counseling service called

The Key, which promises to get children of the wealthiest families in the U.S. into top schools.

When the news broke, some parents were cynical and assumed that's how it's always been done. Others wondered if their children could have gotten into those elite schools had their spots not been taken by the undeserving children of ultra wealthy who cheated the system. And clearly, the reputations of for-profit college counseling services took a hit after the fallout.

But there are legitimate educational consulting services that don't use bribery to help their clients with the college admissions process. Could there be some benefit to using one?

The fact is getting into college is harder than ever. Acceptance rates across the board are down, with rates for the more competitive colleges being down the most.

For example, according to BusinessStudent.com, the average acceptance rate for a school in the top 10 percent of colleges was 16 percent in 2006. Today, it's just 6.4 percent. Even mid-range schools are harder to get into. Case Western Reserve University, for example, accepted 67 percent of applicants in 2006; in 2018, it accepted just 35 percent.

No wonder parents are dropping hundreds — sometimes thousands — of dollars for college admissions help from one-on-one advisers. Rates typically run around $200 an hour, with some services costing north of $16,000 for a package that helps students get into an Ivy League school.

WHAT EDUCATIONAL CONSULTANTS OFFER

So is a private personalized college admissions advice worth the money?

Start by considering what you're actually buying. Educational consultants can offer students a wide variety of services, including everything from helping students select appropriate schools and organize the application process to providing advice on essay topics, helping students prepare for admissions interviews, and providing strategies for boosting standardized test scores.

These services can be useful for parents who either don't have the time or the expertise to help their children navigate the brave new world of higher education.

For example, Fiona Haynes of Seattle, Washington, used Prep-Northwest, a test-preparation service in Bellevue, Washington, to help her daughter boost her standardized test scores.

"Despite having a 3.9 GPA in math, my daughter attained a lower-than-expected score in the math portion of the SAT," Haynes said. "She needed to figure out how to take the test.

"I enrolled her in a six-hour review session, paying just under $300 ($3,000 buys 30 hours of one-on-one time plus eight practice tests). She then practiced some more at home. When she took the SAT a second time, her math score improved by 90 points, and she got into her desired college. So yes, it was money well spent."

COMPREHENSIVE COLLEGE PREP AND PLANNING

Other services are more comprehensive. College Coach, for instance, is a nationwide service that offers students help with finding the right colleges, writing admissions resumes, scheduling and preparing for admissions interviews, and applying for financial aid, scholarships, and loans.

College Coach will also arrange campus tours and work with international and transfer students. The level of service generally falls into two tiers, either an hourly fee or an all-inclusive package price.

Another service is Collegewise, which provides students with an individual counselor who will help them develop a balanced list of colleges to apply to, organize a timeline for submitting and managing applications, help students solicit letters of recommendation, brainstorm essay topics, arrange campus visits, find tutoring help if necessary, prepare for college interviews and auditions (for music or theater majors, for example), and help with standardized test preparation.

Collegewise also has a pay-as-you-go counseling system and an early "jumpstart" program for pre-high-school-age students. Collegewise claims that 95 percent of its 2018 seniors got into one of their top three college choices and received in total more than $54 million in merit-based financial aid.

Again, this sounds great, but it could be the case that a professional college counseling service simply makes sure that its clients apply to schools where they are likely to get accepted and offered scholarships. That in itself might be worth paying for; just be sure you know what you're getting before shelling out big bucks.

According to one public high school guidance counselor in Maryland, these services seem to be most useful for parents who either never went to college, don't have the time to help their students navigate the application process, or who don't understand how the process works. The trick is to find a legitimate service that can identify where the student needs help and provide that help at a reasonable cost.

THE FREE ROUTE

But many of the services offered by private college admissions consultants can be duplicated by parents and students for free or at a low cost.

For example, most high schools offer online college search tools free to students, and many are quite sophisticated, offering charts, for example, that show a student's likelihood of being admitted to a particular college based on his or her GPA, courses, and test scores.

The College Board's BigFuture service (bigfuture.collegeboard .org) and College Niche (www.niche.com) also offer myriad ways for students to search for colleges based on majors, size of the schools, locations, GPAs, test scores, and more. College Niche also has rankings lists for everything from best dorms to safest campuses and offers Yelp-like student reviews to give insights into what college life is really like at a particular school.

FastWeb.com and Unigo.com offer search services for scholarships, and PrincetonReview.com provides help with preparing a college essay. (Note: Princeton Review charges $39.99 per month for one hour of consulting, but it has a free trial.)

Finally, if you plan to get financial aid, you'll need to fill out the Free Application for Federal Student Aid (FAFSA.gov). This is required by all schools in order to qualify for federal grants, student loans, and work study programs.

And even if you don't think you'll qualify, it's worth filling out. Schools consider student loans a form of aid, for example, and in order to get a student loan, you will need to fill out the FAFSA.

If your student is bound for a private school, you will also have to fill out the CSS Profile. It is available at CollegeBoard.org.

Determining the Value
of an SAT/ACT Prep Class

Every year, the latest crop of high school students begins gearing up to take the SAT and/or ACT tests for college admission. And whether to combat test anxiety or increase attractiveness to a "reach" school, many register for college exam test preparation courses.

These courses claim to significantly increase students' scores, but they can come with a sometimes hefty price tag. Depending on the depth of the prep, length of the course, and instruction manner, this promised advantage could cost anywhere from free for online courses, books, and practice tests, to $300 to $2,000 for group classes, to $50 to $350 an hour for individualized tutoring, depending on the location and subject matter.

Online, on-demand video, and group classes are more economical than one-on-one tutoring. However, it also makes sense to ask about sliding scale fees at private tutoring companies.

But aside from the question of cost, is an SAT/ACT prepping class really worth the money? We put that question to Ben Bernstein, Ph.D., a psychologist specializing in performance enhancement. He is the author of three books on how stress affects performance: *Crush Your Test Anxiety; Stressed Out! For Teens; Stressed Out! For Parents*.

According to Bernstein, solid test prep has four parts:

1. Orientation to the SAT or ACT test itself. This includes covering how it is structured and scored, as well as the time requirements and other basics. Bernstein calls this the "lay of the land."
2. Orientation to material on the test, including vocabulary, reading comprehension, math, and any specific subject matter.
3. Practice. Good test prep should include practice leading to mastery.
4. Performance skills. Students should learn to be calm, confident, and focused in the test environment. However, Bernstein says this is the least attended to in the test prep industry.

DETERMINE YOUR NEEDS

The biggest reason to plunk down cash for a prep class is if a child's test score isn't in line with what teachers, report cards, and guidance counselors indicate is his or her potential. And the only way to determine that is having your child actually take the SAT or ACT test at least once before any outside prep.

Having your child's score, along with the average score range of schools he or she wants to apply to, is the first step to determining if your family needs to explore test prep courses or not.

PREP COURSES AREN'T FOR EVERYONE

If your child is a confident test taker and a strong student who has scored up to her or his potential, Bernstein can alleviate a wave of guilt you may have about not signing your child up for an SAT prep course in high school. Bernstein said kids of this profile typically have nothing to benefit from these courses.

However, test prep educators frequently say that every student can benefit from test prep because it offers a review of not only material, but how to weed out false answers to multiple choice questions or remain calm as the clock ticks off precious minutes during a section of an exam.

Bernstein counters that logic saying that for kids whose PSAT/PACT and/or first round of SAT/ACT scores are within their potential range, a prep course might not generously bump up test scores.

ALL PREP COURSES ARE NOT EQUAL

The number of test prep options is dizzying! Online classroom settings, online guided testing and practice material (without an instructor leading the session), on-demand videos, in-person tutoring, group in-person instruction, and flipping through books are some of the ways a high-schooler can try to tack on valuable points to their score.

But which one is best for your child? The answer depends on your child and his/her needs.

In-person tutoring allows for disorganized students to have a tutor sit with them and help them focus. It can also help kids with learning issues and students who are performing well in all but one area by zeroing in on the content of that section.

Kids who routinely underperform on tests or have test anxiety are best served by individual coaching (for instance breathing techniques, imagery, etc.) that is customized for the child instead of straight review of course material.

MAKE SURE YOUR CHILD IS COACHABLE

Regardless of the type of student, his/her potential, or type of prep you're considering, educators and test prep administrators agree that the one "must have" for considering test prep is coachability.

A coachable student is one who will take on the work, show up to sessions, and do the follow-up homework. Those without their own goals (think or say, "My mom wants me to get higher SAT scores") or rely on parental nagging to complete practice assessments or attend the prep class are also not likely to receive much benefit from the investment.

10 Ways to Make College More Affordable

Is your family is gearing up for a child's senior year of college? Along the path to Pomp and Circumstance, we've learned a few lessons about trimming the costs of college that no admissions counselor ever even eluded to, from considering off-campus housing to sending your kid back with home-cooked meals. Here are nine college money savers:

1. CONSIDER COMMUNITY COLLEGE.

A Georgetown University study found that nearly 30 percent of Americans with associate's degrees make more than those with bachelor's degrees. And even if four years in hallowed halls is on the horizon, community college can be a great starting place to collect credits for general education classes at a fraction of the price they would cost at four-year universities.

2. CHOOSE A TUITION-STABLE SCHOOL.

Schools like George Washington University and Miami University in Oxford, Ohio, have taken the guesswork out of predicting how high college costs will soar throughout your child's academic experience. With their Tuition Promise programs, these schools offer all first-time undergrads the certainty that tuition, room and board, special purpose fees, and course fees will be frozen over the four years of a student's four-year tenure.

3. PICK A TUITION-FREE SCHOOL.

A few schools provide free tuition for all students. The Curtis Institute of Music in Philadelphia covers all tuition costs for each admitted student.

Barclay College, a four-year Bible college, also provides a full tuition scholarship to every accepted student who enrolls at its Haviland, Kansas, campus.

The armed forces academies — air force, coast guard and naval academies — don't charge tuition either, however, they do all have service requirements for all graduates. The length of service varies by school and degree program.

And The Cooper Union college in Manhattan, awards every admitted student a half-tuition scholarship valued at $21,000 per academic year.

4. LOOK FOR TUITION WAIVERS.

There are a variety of ways students can either forgo paying college tuition or pay greatly reduced rates. These include signing up for the military, Peace Corps, or AmeriCorps. Veterans and teachers can also receive these benefits, as well as dependents of higher education employees and students whose parents work in civil service (i.e., firefighters, police or academia).

5. ASK FOR A TUITION DISCOUNT.

To attract the best and brightest students to their campuses, many U.S. colleges, especially private schools, offer grants and scholarships to cover tuition. This free money or merit aid doesn't have to be repaid.

And many colleges — especially private schools — are quite generous. A survey from the National Association of College and University Business Officers (NACUBO), found that 89 percent of freshmen entering private colleges received an institutional grant or scholarship, which covered 54.3 percent of tuition and fees.

6. DON'T BE SHY ABOUT ASKING FOR MORE.

After two years of residing on the Dean's List, my clever son popped into the admissions office to request a review of his scholarship and merit aid. He figured it couldn't hurt to ask for a little more moolah since he's proven himself to be committed to his studies. His college agreed and coughed up an additional $2,500 per year!

7. GRADUATE EARLY.

Consider colleges that offer accelerated learning programs aimed at cutting out a semester or year of undergraduate work, thus reducing the cost of a degree by up to 25 percent. Some college programs designed for accelerated graduating include Ball State

University's Degree in Three, Hartwick College's three-year degree program, Manchester University's Fast Forward, and the University of North Carolina at Greensboro's UNCGin3, which even offers priority registration to highly motivated freshmen, transfer and returning students who want to complete their degrees in three years.

Alternatively, consider having your student take mid-semester and summer courses to accelerate graduation. These classes can be cheaper than regular classes. For example, the University of Texas at Austin's tuition for summer classes is 15 percent less than classes taken during the fall or spring terms.

Bonus: If your child takes a mid-semester class or two or lives at home while taking a summer class, you won't have to pay extra for room and board during that time.

8. BRAG ABOUT ALUMNI.

Make sure your child's application mentions if you or your parents graduated from a school he or she is applying to. Being a legacy can sometimes give an applicant an edge in the admissions process along with big tuition breaks and scholarships.

For instance Pittsburg State University's Legacy Program helps students save about $7,500 by shaving out-of-state tuition expenses. Kansas University's Jayhawks Generation Scholarship Program gives attractive tuition discounts to out-of-state legacy freshmen whose parents or grandparents graduated from the university.

9. STAY IN-STATE.

It may seem obvious but bears mentioning that attending an in-state public college can yield significant savings over similar institutions just a state or two away. On average, in-state residents pay one-third to one-half of the tuition that nonresidents pay for the same education.

10. DO YOUR HOMEWORK.

Perhaps the most important nugget is to ask questions. No two experiences are the same. And even if you've already put one child through college, opportunities can change. Make sure to probe every counselor, info session and recruiter for information specific to your student and the school he or she is interested in attending.

Words to the Wise

BONUS TIP!
Beware of Some Loan Programs

A small number of colleges are moving away from student loans and toward an innovative financing program, but consumer advocates are not so sure it's an improvement for borrowers. Called "income sharing agreements," or ISAs, these programs are backed by investors, who get a percentage of the student's future income in place of loan repayments.

It sounds attractive at first because the student pays nothing until he or she gets a job after graduation. With a normal student loan, the student is on the hook within months of graduation, job or not.

However, critics warn that the devil is very much in the details. For instance, a student who borrows $30,000 might agree to pay back 12% of her income over 10 years. If she gets a job paying $50,000 and gets a 2% raise each year, that's the equivalent of paying 18.4% — essentially a credit card rate. On the other hand, if the student earns below a specific salary, he or she pays back nothing. If the student "defaults," the school is liable for the loan instead. A bill in Congress would allow ISAs to charge up to 20% of student income.

Chapter 11

Travel

"DOST THOU LOVE LIFE? THEN DO NOT SQUANDER
TIME, FOR THAT IS THE STUFF LIFE IS MADE OF . . ."

Save Money While
Traveling in Europe

Dreaming of a European vacation, and assuming it's too expensive to actually go? It's not as bad as you think. To be sure, flights to Europe can be costly if you aren't careful. But once you're on the ground, you quickly find that European cities have many natural qualities that keep other costs down.

Here are seven ways to save on your expenses while traveling in Europe.

1. SAVE ON LODGING (AND EVERYTHING ELSE) WITH AIRBNB.

There are many sentimental reasons people love Airbnb: stylish spaces, charming neighborhoods. For me, it's purely practical. Airbnb presents an opportunity to pay less money for a better product. You can rent an entire apartment on Airbnb for less than a single hotel room.

In fact, travel website BusBud.com compared average Airbnb rates to average hotel rates in nine popular European cities. In eight of them, renting through Airbnb was cheaper, some by over $100 a night.

In Dubrovnik, Croatia, you can enjoy a one-bedroom apartment with breathtaking views of the Adriatic Sea from your balcony, not to mention a full kitchen and a washing machine. The cost? Just $140 a night.

2. SKIP THE CAR RENTAL.

If your European plans are mostly in cities, you likely won't need to rent a car. Public transit is generally excellent. Some cities are even connected to Google Transit, so you can see real-time transit schedules, same as in the U.S. If you use Uber to get around in the U.S., you'll likely be able to use it in Europe, too. Uber operates in most European countries, except Denmark, Hungary, and Bulgaria.

3. LOOK CAREFULLY AT ALL-IN-ONE CITY PASSES.

As in the U.S., many European cities offer a city pass for tourists with discounts on attractions and restaurants. Sometimes it will also act as your public transportation fare card. You can buy the cards in advance online to save even more money (as much as 10%).

4. CHOOSE SOUVENIRS STRATEGICALLY TO AVOID BAGGAGE FEES.

That thick cookbook of recipes from the Dalmatian Coast might be the perfect gift for the home chef in your life, but it'll be heavy and awkward to pack around. Think about buying smaller items like belts, chocolate bars, delicate jewelry — all much easier to tuck into suitcases.

Another strategy: As you pack, leave space for future purchases. Or pack an extra collapsible bag to hold your goodies. You'll only pay the baggage fee one-way, and you won't overpay for a new piece of luggage abroad.

5. AVOID FOREIGN CREDIT CARD FEES.

Call your credit card companies in advance to find which of your cards don't charge foreign transaction fees and consider getting a new card if you can't get free foreign transactions on any of your existing cards.

There's one other pesky credit card fee you need to be aware of in Europe: When you use your card, some vendors will ask whether to process the charge in dollars or the local currency. Always choose local currency. If you don't, you'll likely receive a poor exchange rate, plus a 3% currency conversion fee for the privilege of seeing your cost in U.S. dollars. Not worth it.

6. DON'T TIP LIKE AN AMERICAN.

Sure, you're used to tipping 15% to 20%, but that's not how it's done in Europe. Before adding on a tip, look up the tipping customs in the country you're visiting (your guidebook will certainly cover it, or just Google the question).

For example, in Spain, tipping is not customary. And Croatians and Italians typically leave 5% to 10% for outstanding service.

7. GET COMPENSATED FOR ANY FLIGHT DELAYS.

The European Union has laws that require cash payments to passengers if their flights are delayed. Imagine that!

Here's the deal: If your flight on an EU-based airline is delayed by at least three hours or is canceled within 14 days of departure, you may be entitled to nearly $700! It also applies to any airline flying out of (but not into) Europe. For flights within Europe, you can get between $285 and $455.

The catch is that it's not automatic; you have to file a claim with the airline to be compensated. If you can't get traction, services like AirHelp, FlightRight, and EU Flight Delay can advocate for you in exchange for 25% of whatever proceeds they obtain.

Best Apps and Sites for Slashing Travel Costs

You've probably used Travelocity or Hotels.com to get a lower air-fare or hotel rate, but there are dozens (maybe hundreds) of web-sites and apps that can help you snag the lowest price on all of your travel expenses. Here are some of the best.

AIR TRAVEL
Fareness (Fareness.com)
This flight comparison app helps you search for the least expensive airfare with one click.

How it works: Unlike other sites, you don't enter specific dates and destinations and then compare fares. Instead, you put in your location, the month(s) you'd like to travel, and where in general you'd like to go (e.g., beach, Europe, U.S. cities, etc.). Fareness then reveals the travel dates and places with the lowest-priced trips in a single, one-second search.

And Fareness has interactive map and calendar that lets you see and compare fares across hundreds of dates at once, making it easy to make informed decisions about when to book.

If you have a specific destination already in mind, Fareness can help you slash your airfare by showing round-trip ticket prices for each day of the week for over 190 departure dates at once.

Scott's Cheap Flights (Scottscheapflights.com)
This site sends members information on discounted international flights.

How it works: You can sign up for a free email newsletter or the premium version that costs $39 per year. Then enter your nearest air-port (or multiple airports for premium members) and Scott's search-es 24/7 to find international flights at up to 90 percent off normal ticket prices. Once the site finds a deal, it'll show up in your email newsletter, including the travel location, which airports you can fly from, travel dates, and if there are extra costs, like baggage fees. Discounts are typically hundreds of dollars off regular fares.

The free membership only offers international deals; however, premium members receive deal alerts for fares to Hawaii and Alaska, as well as mistake fare alerts (when an airline or online travel agency mistakenly offers a deeply-discounted fare, usually because of human or computer error). The site does not sell tickets or work with the airlines.

Yapta (Yapta.com)
This is a free website that tracks airfares and issues price-drop alerts.

How it works: Yapta is not a booking platform. The site only tracks the prices of flights, but it can do so for specific flights both before and after a ticket is purchased, and it will alert you when the price of your seat drops.

Simply enter your flight details into Yapta, and the site will constantly monitor your fare for price decreases. When a drop is found, you will receive an email that explains how to call the airline and re-book your ticket at the lower available price and be credited for the difference.

Most airlines charge a fee to re-book a ticket at a lower price (unless you purchased a ticket that allows this at no additional charge). However, Yapta takes all re-booking fees into account before issuing an alert, and prices can fluctuate enough to warrant high savings above these fees. Yapta can also track the price of the flights you haven't booked yet, if you prefer to watch the price before shelling out money for a ticket.

LugLess (Lugless.com)
This is a cost-competitive alternative to checking bags with the airline.

How it works: LugLess cuts baggage fees by leveraging existing logistics networks to make shipping luggage easier and cheaper than using an airline.

The shipping search engine finds and compares the lowest UPS and FedEx rates to generate the cheapest shipping label for any travel itinerary. If that's all you need, there is no other cost to using the platform. If you need more help with your shipment, for an additional fee, you can add additional coverage or a doorstep pickup.

Rates start at $15 per bag. Prices are based on distance, size, and speed of delivery. On average, people pay $28 to ship one bag or $54 to ship two bags. LugLess provides service to and from every zip code in the United States.

WATER EXPERIENCES
SamBoat (samboat.com)
This service lets you rent a boat, anywhere in the world (think Airbnb for boats) at discounts of around 40 percent off usual rates.

How it works: There is no fee to join, and SamBoat has more than 30,000 boats available all over the world, ranging from a simple sea vessel to a luxurious yacht. Once you find a boat you like, you can make a booking request to the boat owner and then chat with him/her. Prices start at $50/ day with insurance provided, and you can rent a boat with or without a skipper, depending on your nautical skills.

GetMyBoat (getmyboat.com)
This is a boat rental and water experience marketplace with 130,000 listings in 9,300 cities in 184 countries.

How it works: GetMyBoat is a handy tool for saving money on booking water activities. It enables you to comparison shop among various marinas and tour companies, as well as private/individual boat owners. The site has something in just about every hot spot, whether it's boat rentals or water sports like windsurfing, kayaks, or parasailing.

CAMPING/RVING
BoondockersWelcome (boondockerswelcome.com)
This web platform helps RV travelers save hundreds per week on camping fees.

How it works: For a $30 subscription, you'll have a year of unlimited access to over 1,600 hosts across North America (most of them RVers themselves) who welcome travelers to camp for FREE on their private property. Perfect for short en route stops and meeting local people with common interests.

Pitchup (Pitchup.com)
Recently launched in the U.S., this site allows travelers to choose from nearly 3,300 campsites, cabins, and glamping sites to book around the world.

How it works: Some of these private sites start at just $10 a night. There is no fee associated with using this website (think of it as a Hotels.com for campsites). The one restriction is that only private parks are listed in Pitchup's data-base (in the United States). National and/or state parks are not searchable.

ACCOMMODATIONS
Pruvo (Pruvo.net)
This is a free app and web service that tracks price drops for existing hotel reservations.

How it works: Just book a refundable hotel reservation on any website (80 percent of hotel reservations worldwide are done with a free cancellation policy). Then forward the email confirmation of the hotel reservation to save@pruvo.com.

Once received, Pruvo tracks the reservation and notifies you when a lower rate is discovered. You can review the offer sent, then rebook the cheaper offer and cancel the original reservation.

ATTRACTIONS
GetYourGuide (GetYourGuide.com)
This is a destination where you can shop for and compare the prices of tours, attractions, and more.

How it works: Browse the site's international (Paris, the Vatican, Barcelona, etc.) and domestic (New York City, Miami, Las Vegas, etc.) destinations and book tours, admission tickets, etc., at deeply discounted rates.

For instance, the "Paris in 1 Day" tour is $102.76 per person. It includes a local guide, an entrance ticket to the Eiffel Tower second or top floor, a guided tour of the Eiffel Tower, a Seine River cruise ticket, a Louvre Museum skip-the-line ticket, a guided tour of Notre Dame Cathedral, and a bus RATP ticket. The "Skip-the-Line Vatican, Sistine Chapel, St. Peter's" tour is $67.05 and includes a live guide and no-wait entrances to all of these attractions.

MISCELLANEOUS DISCOUNTS
Raise (Raise.com)
This is a gift card marketplace where you can buy discounted gift cards or sell unwanted gift cards for cash.

How it works: You can save money on restaurants, airfares, hotels, etc., by purchasing someone else's unwanted travel gift card.

For instance, here are a few of the current travel-related deals on the site:

Southwest Airlines: up to 3 percent off (a $500 gift card for $482) Hotels.com: up to 6.5 percent off (a $1,000 gift card for $935) American Airlines: up to 4 percent off (a $100 gift card for $96) Airbnb: up to 3 percent off (a $500 gift card for $485)

Raise is available on iOS, Android, and desktop, and offers a one-year money back guarantee on all purchases.

BUYER BEWARE

It is always a good idea to read ALL the fine print, exclusions, and restrictions any time you're booking any component of your vacation. And if you're not sure about a detail, send an email or phone the company, hotel, or airline for clarification before paying. That way you can sidestep booking — and paying for — a mistaken vacation.

Terms, conditions and prices are subject to change.

10 Travel Hacks That Save a Bundle

The spring and summer travel seasons are right around the corner. And whether you're eyeing a quick weekend getaway or a week-long tropical retreat, you want to land the best deal. Here's how to ensure you nab the best value for your money on all your excursions.

1. KNOW WHEN TO BOOK

Third-party travel site Priceline recently crunched numbers to find the best times to book holiday-timed travel this spring and summer. If your Memorial Day, Fourth of July, or Labor Day plans include travel, here's how to score big savings on hotels and flights, per Priceline's data:

Memorial Day
When to book: Hotels and flights hold steady pricing until about 12 days prior to Memorial Day weekend (May 25 this year). At that point, airfares start to rise. You can feel confident booking a hotel at

any point between now and Memorial Day weekend, but for flights, it's best to book more than 12 days out.

What you'll pay: An average Memorial Day weekend flight costs $239 if bought 12 days in advance, but then prices begin to rise.

The average price for a flight booked one day prior to Memorial Day weekend is $313 per ticket, about 31 percent more expensive.

Fourth of July
When to book: Hotel and airfare prices hold steady until about 16 days before July 4. After that, airfares rise.

What you'll pay: An average Fourth of July flight costs approximately $214 per ticket 16 days prior, but the average price for a flight booked one day in advance is approximately $304 per ticket, about 42 percent more expensive.

Prime Summer Travel
When to book: August 4-11 is the busiest travel week in the summer (outside of holiday weeks). Hotels and flights tend to hold steady until about 14 days prior to August 4.

What you'll pay: An average early August flight costs approximately $216 per ticket if purchased 14 days in advance, but the average price for a flight booked one day prior to August 4 is approximately $369 per ticket, about 71 percent more expensive.

Labor Day
When to book: Flight prices start to soar about 10 days before the start of Labor Day weekend. An average Labor Day weekend flight costs approximately $252 per ticket 10 days prior, but the average price for a flight booked after that is about 44 percent higher, approximately $364 per ticket if bought one day in advance. Hotel prices typically hold steady right up until Labor Day weekend.

2. CONTACT THE PROPERTY
Before booking a room online, make a call to the property, suggests Raphael Marchand, manager at the Fairmont San Francisco hotel. "There are often special offers and exclusive deals available only through the hotel," he explains.

For instance, Fairmont San Francisco recently introduced its Spring Break "Save or Splurge" deals, which are only available through the hotel, not travel sites like Priceline or Travelocity.

And if you do find a better price on a third-party booking site like Booking.com, ask the hotel to price match the deal. Andrea Woroch, consumer money-saving expert, says ultimately, it's often best to book through the hotel. "You often have more flexibility for making changes to the reservation or getting a free upgrade or other freebies," she notes.

3. PARK AT AN OFFSITE LOT

A lot of people spend time shopping around for airfares, but overlook the cost of parking at the airport, which can negate any savings you scored on your flight! Use sites like AirportParkingReservations.com to review parking lot options that are near, but not at, the airport.

These tools list various parking locations, distance to the airport, available shuttles, and reviews, plus daily prices. Some also offer coupon codes to help you save on their service fees. When we checked, we were able to find a parking lot for a flight out of LAX for $5.99 per day.

4. STAY OUTSIDE OF THE CITY CENTER

Most major cities have plenty of hotel options outside of the city center. For example, when planning a trip to the Big Apple, consider staying in an outer borough versus Manhattan. This allows you to spend more on experiences than lodging.

5. GET ON THEIR EMAIL LISTS OR FOLLOW ON SOCIAL MEDIA

Hotels, airlines, and travel sites often highlight special travel deals for email subscribers. Priceline, for example, offers exclusive deals to Twitter followers and newsletter subscribers. Priceline also offers mobile-only deals if you search for hotel accommodations via its app.

6. PURCHASE ADMISSION TICKETS IN ADVANCE

Woroch says you can often pay less for activities and entertainment by pre-booking tickets in advance. For example, you can save up to $25 per person at Six Flags by purchasing passes online. You can even do this from your hotel room the night before.

7. Negotiate on Home Rentals

If you're booking accommodations at the last minute, you may be able to negotiate the rate for a home rental through sites like VRBO, since the homeowner may be eager to get the space filled.

8. Bundle Up

Bundle or package deals that include airfare, hotel, and/or a car, can yield hundreds of dollars in savings. On Priceline, the average traveler saves $240 per transaction when booking a bundle.

9. Consider Booking "Express Deals"

Hotels (even some luxury ones) will often offer steep discounts (50 percent or more) on third-party sites when you book blind — just choose the hotel based on its star rating, location, and reviews without knowing its specific name. Once you complete the reservation, you'll learn the name of the hotel. Such deals are often only available for last-minute travel, but can also sometimes be found weeks in advance.

10. Embrace Flexibility

If your schedule allows, try to plan a vacation for a mid-week stay, rather than one that spans a weekend. The rates will likely be cheaper, while the amenities and experience are the same. Or choose your destination, then price out the cost of the hotel for the length of your trip over multiple different time frames to spot the lowest rates. The savings may be considerable.

Best Way to Exchange Currency

You've got your grand tour all lined up, your new, uncreased passport in hand (with that new passport smell!), and a smartphone loaded with boarding passes.

Now all you need is cash. Money for baggage handlers, money for snacks and drinks, taxis and trinkets. So what's the best way to get the euros, yen, and pesos you will need to smooth the way?

The clear consensus, experts agree, is not to change money at the airport. Those little foreign-exchange wagons you see parked in concourses? A ripoff, just like that dried-up chicken sandwich at the gate that costs $15.

"It is best to avoid these if you wish to save money. Their virtual monopoly means you're unlikely to get a good exchange rate, so it is best to get your currency exchanged elsewhere, such as at your domestic bank before you leave for your trip," suggests Melita DeHazes, marketing director, North America, for cross-border payments provider OFX.

That leaves three ways to get the cash you need abroad.

USE A CREDIT CARD

Plastic is the easy choice, and global payment networks make it easy to just pretend that sliding your card across the counter or slipping in the chip at the checkout is no different from buying groceries back home.

But it's very different. Every institution that touches your transaction takes a little piece of the deal. You just can't always tell who's taking what and how much they're taking.

There are foreign transaction fees charged by the payment network, typically Visa or Mastercard, then more fees charged by the issuing back, plus a margin of between 3 percent and 5 percent on the actual exchange rate. That means you could be paying a 6 percent premium or more on your purchase by using a credit card.

The way around some of these fees is to choose a card that doesn't charge them. A recent CreditCards.com survey identified 39 out of 100 cards that did not charge foreign transaction fees. However, you may still be subject to fees from the credit card payment networks (Visa and Mastercard).

GET CASH FROM AN ATM

You've successfully avoided the foreign exchange booths in the airport, but you still need some walking-around money. Why not just hit up a bank ATM in town?

Because the fees there can be just as bad as with credit cards. Foreign bank fees can range from flat surcharges to percentage-based fees plus a fee for using the ATM itself.

The way to avoid this is by doing the homework before you leave, says DeHazes. Does your bank have foreign branches or foreign partners? Is it in a global ATM network?

"You just have to be sure that you can find and use partner ATMs; otherwise, you will be hit with high fees for using an ATM that is outside of the network," she says.

EXCHANGE MONEY IN CASH

You can exchange cash in-country at a bank — one far from the airport — and do OK. If you prefer to have money in hand before you leave, though, it pays to educate yourself on current foreign exchange rates, says Chris Gaffney, president of world markets at EverBank.

Check with your local bank branch and compare their exchange rate to the rates you see on Travelex.com. "Travelex is the leader in physical currency exchange and operates a majority of the airport kiosks and also has a very easy-to-use website," says Gaffney.

Know the spot rate in the market, says Gaffney, and make sure you understand what exchange rate you are looking at.

For instance, most currencies are quoted in what is called the "European" style: 18.53 Mexican pesos to 1 U.S. dollar, that is, that you can buy 18.53 Mexican pesos with every dollar, he explains.

But a few currencies quoted in what is called the "American" style: 1 euro / $1.2364, meaning that each euro costs $1.2364. "You have to know which way you are being quoted to understand which rate is better for you," says Gaffney.

For example, one ATM that shows an exchange rate of 17.5 MEX/USD and the other shows a rate of 18 MEX/USD. "You would want to pull funds out of the one at 18 MEX/USD since you will receive more MEX for every $1," Gaffney explains.

But, if you are in Europe, an ATM showing an exchange rate of 1.25 USD/EUR is a better offer than one which shows 1.27 USD/EUR, Gaffney says.

"Unfortunately, the foreign exchange markets can certainly be confusing to newcomers," Gaffney says. "But before traveling you should definitely try to do your homework and understand how the currency works in the country you are headed to."

A Cheaper Alternative to Europe

When panning your summer travel you have so many options. Where to this year? Europe? Perhaps, but how about a place that is reminiscent of old France, but you can get there without a long and expensive transatlantic flight?

I'm talking about French Canada. In fact, when you cross the border into the province of Quebec, it's easy to forget that France lost control of this region more than 250 years ago. French is still the prevailing language spoken here. French cuisine is alive and well. And across its picturesque rural areas, many residents still do what their ancestors did in the 1700s: farming or fishing.

There are compelling reasons to visit French Canada in the summer. A big one is that fears of terrorism aren't as prevalent in Canada as they are in Europe.

Also, there is the strong U.S. dollar, which usually trades at a premium to the Canadian dollar. For Americans, that means the price of everything is effectively marked down by a large percentage. (Of course, the exchange rate fluctuates daily.) An added benefit is that the U.S. dollar's strength more than offsets Quebec's stiff 15 percent sales tax.

MONTREAL AND QUEBEC CITY

The obvious starting point for a visit to French Canada is Montreal. For one thing, it's easy to get to. From New York, it is just six-and-a-half hours away (from Boston, the drive is an hour shorter).

That's similar to the distance between London to Paris. And as the world's second-largest French-speaking city, Montreal has a lot in common with its Parisian sister.

You'll find that Montreal has plenty to see and do. Here are some highlights:

- Mount Royal, the city's namesake mountain, offers great views of the busy downtown area below and the St. Lawrence River in the distance.
- Old Montreal is where the city was established in 1642. You can explore everything from archaeological sites to ultramodern art galleries.
- There is outstanding architecture throughout the city; among the note-worthy buildings are the Notre-Dame Basilica and the Biosphere, home to an excellent environmental museum.
- If you get tired of French food, there are plenty of restaurants with other menus reflecting the city's varied ethnic population.

Once you've had a taste of Montreal, move on to Quebec City, about three hours away. This historic and impressive walled city, located at the point where the St. Lawrence River narrows, was founded in 1608.

In view of its strategic importance, Quebec City became the capital of New France (France's territories in the Western Hemisphere) and held that title until it fell to the British in 1759.

Even while under British rule, the original French residents of Quebec City and their descendants stayed put and vowed to never give up their traditions. They also managed to keep the old city of Quebec intact over the centuries.

Today, when you enter Quebec City's gates, it's like stepping into a medieval French town right out of the storybooks. You'll find stone buildings and cobblestoned streets (most are too narrow for cars, so put on your walking shoes). Along the alleys are art galleries, churches, patisseries, bistros, and restaurants with some of the best French food around.

Quebec City is also a great place to get a firsthand lesson in military history. The battle that cost France its Canadian territories occurred just outside the walls. And Canada might be part of the United States today had it not been for the fact that Quebec City withstood an attack and siege by American forces at the Battle of Quebec in 1775.

CAPE BRETON ISLAND AND LOUISBOURG

If you'd like to see how people lived in French Canada during the 1700s, continue driving eastward through Quebec province and New Brunswick until you reach Nova Scotia's beautiful Cape Breton Island (originally known as Isle Royale). On its northeast corner is the site of the Fortress of Louisbourg National Historic Site.

Louisbourg was a thriving French port and guarded the entrance to the St. Lawrence River until it fell to the British in 1754. Although it was destroyed in the 1760s, Louisbourg has been reconstructed from its original blueprints.

Like its American counterpart of Williamsburg, Virginia, Louisbourg operates as a living history museum that depicts life in French Canada during colonial times and is well worth a visit.

Last-Minute Holiday Travel Tips

The holiday season officially arrives in November, and you've decided — late — to take a trip. Are there still good deals to be had? "When it comes to holiday travel, the early bird gets the worm," admits Gabe Saglie, senior editor of Travelzoo. "However, big cities, Caribbean destinations with a lot of inventory like The Bahamas, Jamaica, and Mexico, national parks, and cruises often offer solid deals." Here are a few insider ideas to plan a trip for less than full price.

TIP NO. 1: CONSIDER A ROAD TRIP.

"On airfare, last-minute bargains are rare," Saglie says. "Hotels are more likely to offer last-minute bargains, although popular holiday destinations like Orlando and ski resorts will be charging premium pricing this time of year." Instead, pick a neighboring state to yours and explore all it has to offer — even if the weather isn't much different, the scenery and activities can provide for a new adventure on the cheap.

TIP NO. 2: STAY FLEXIBLE WHEN FINALIZING TRAVEL PLANS.

"Those pigeonholed into flying on specific dates and to specific destinations are the least likely to find a deal; the more flexible you are with your travel dates, the better the odds you'll nab a bargain," Saglie says. "And the further away from the holiday you travel, the better the deals. For example, avoid flying back home the Sunday after Thanksgiving. Instead, come back the following Tuesday or Wednesday for better availability and better pricing."

TIP NO. 3: TRY THE MAJOR METROPOLISES.

"If you're looking to vacation during the holidays, look at big cities — popular destinations like New York City often see better availability, and travel slows during the holidays," Saglie says.

TIP NO. 4: EXTEND YOUR VACATION.

Adding days to your vacation can lower your average per-night costs. "For example, December 31st in Las Vegas or NYC will mean paying a premium, but by extending your stay to January 3rd or 4th, you will see your average nightly rates drop dramatically in many cases, and thereby make your per-night hotel costs more manageable overall," Saglie points out.

Avoid These Costly
Last-Minute Travel Blunders

You work hard to save up for a vacation. But whether you're planning a weekend getaway or a dream trip, there are a few common errors that could turn a stress-relieving holiday into a budget-busting headache. Here is some expert guidance to help you avoid these nine money missteps:

1. LEAVING YOUR LODGING TO THE LAST MINUTE.

Booking flights late in the game can sometimes score you a great deal on a seat a carrier wants to fill. Yet that's not always the case when it comes to securing a soft place to land after a long day of traveling.

Booking a hotel in the eleventh hour can severely limit your options, cost you more, and steer you into a location much farther from the attractions you're in town to see, says Eric Boromisa, a travel expert who founded a company that prepared Arrival Kits for international travelers and groups going to Europe and the U.S. That is, if you can find a room at all — you also could find yourself completely out of luck if a large conference or event is scheduled at the same time of your trip.

2. BEING UNAWARE OF BASIC SCAMS AND TRAPS.

Sometimes in the haste of planning a last-minute trip, you skimp on research and fall right into the hands of scammers at the airport or in the touristy center of town, Boromisa says. Get on the Internet to search scams common to the area you're visiting (especially if you're headed out of the country), so you're a little more street smart upon arrival.

3. NOT ALERTING YOUR BANKER OF YOUR PLANS.

Forgetting to tell your financial institutions you're headed off to remote places — or even those in another state — can trigger a fraud flag on debit/credit cards, meaning your card stops working. And once you're out of the country, or even your home state, it can be tougher to convince the card issuer you're the one using your card.

"I've also had an ATM eat up and not return my debit card in mainland China because I forgot to notify my bank," says Cameron Postelwait, former marketing director at SewellDirect.com. The cost to have a new card overnighted to you can soar into the hundreds if you're overseas or on the other side of the country from your home.

4. BUYING BOOKS AND MAGAZINES AT THE AIRPORT.

If you prefer the tactile experience of flipping paper pages rather than reading e-books and digital versions of magazines, buy those items near your home, not the airport, Postelwait suggests. Newsstands in airports and hotel lobbies charge more for these items than local grocers or bookstores. And if you run out of reading material, skip hotel gift shops and instead purchase those items at a local grocery store or drugstore. That goes for snacks, gum, etc., as well, Postelwait says.

5. EXPECTING THE AIRLINE TO FEED YOU.

Make sure to eat before boarding the plane. Discount carriers might not offer much more than a bag of peanuts. Other airlines have taken to charging for what used to be a perk; yes, meals will cost you extra onboard, and worse yet, they're small portions, meaning that feeding a famished family could turn into a big, unexpected cost.

6. MAKING USE OF THE MINI-BAR.

Raiding the mini-bar or frequenting the hotel vending machine is never a good idea. Instead, even pre-trip you'll want to pinpoint the nearest drug or grocery store to your hotel via the Web. You also can ask the hotel concierge or front-desk staff to point you in the right direction. Even with prices that are somewhat higher than discount merchants or standard grocery stores, as a last resort, a mini-mart usually will be cheaper than a hotel on things like bottled water, gum, or other incidentals, Postelwait says.

7. OVERDOING IT ON THE DATA.

If you travel with a smartphone or other electronics with a data plan, check to see how you'll be billed for Internet usage. Although international telephone charges are higher than domestic calls, it's actually the data usage to surf the Web, check email, etc., that generates much steeper bills.

If traveling internationally, ask your wireless carrier about a short-term discounted data contract for a particular country. Alternatively, check to see how to turn off your roaming capability because you may be billed for any use, including unsolicited incoming emails that are not opened or are immediately deleted. As a result, you could unknowingly run up a huge bill in just a week or two.

8. FORGETTING ABOUT VACCINATIONS.

"I once arrived in the Seychelles and heard a couple ahead of us in immigration be asked for their vaccination card; we didn't bring ours and had to convince them we hadn't been to particular countries and had had a recent medical visit," Boromisa recalls.

Immunize yourself from a costly delay — or even a denial of entry to a country or resort — by asking your primary care providers for an electronic version of your vaccination record you can access via your phone or tablet. "It can't hurt to print out a copy, too, as some countries won't take a confirmation on your iPad," Boromisa warns.

9. UNDERESTIMATING AMENITIES.

Extras like lift tickets for ski vacations can be pricey if not purchased in advance, says Peter Reeburgh, the operator of SummitCove.com, a vacation rental lodging company in Keystone Resort, Colorado. "It's always on people's wish lists to have the perfect winter ski resort experience that might include a gondola ride to the top of the mountain to a fancy dinner or sleigh rides to dinner," he says. "But often, if these are not booked three or more months in advance, guests pay a higher price or miss out altogether due to no availability."

Words to the Wise

BONUS TIP!
The Downside of Using a Debit Card to Rent a Car

It used to be that using a debit card to pay for a rental car was a risky way to try to make the transaction. Automatic holds on debit cards were high — $350 or more — and rental agencies would sometimes run a credit check or demand additional ID besides your driver's license. Even worse: The holds could last until well after you got home, tying up cash in your account. That's going away, thanks to more widespread use of debit cards and to plain old competition.

Dollar and Thrifty will now rent to debit cardholders who book 24 hours in advance using just a driver's license, and they reserve just $200 on the card during the rental. Remember, though, that credit cards often provide extra protection, such as collision coverage, roadside service, and travel insurance, while debit cards do not. Review the terms of your cards before deciding which to use.

BONUS TIP!
Watch for Hidden Resort Fees

Planning a vacation at a resort? You might get a bit of sticker shock once you see your bill. Like airlines and their confusing baggage fees, getaway hotels are trying to compete on lowest room rates online, and to do so, they're loading up guests with hidden fees on the final bill — things like breakfast fees, early check-in fees, and daily pet fees. Attorneys general in Washington, D.C., and Nebraska have sued some of the big chains, including Marriott and Hilton, on the grounds that the fees are illegal because you can't avoid them. In the meantime, you can research potential fees at sites such as ResortFeeChecker.com. Also, if you are a frequent guest, hotels often will waive fees just for asking.

BONUS TIP!
Travel Insurance That's Worth Considering

Considering travel insurance to protect yourself in case your trip gets canceled? If you're going to buy a policy, be sure to understand what's covered. Generally, most travel insurance policies are designed to help you recoup your costs if your trip gets canceled, or you are stranded and need a place to stay. That can mean a lot of things, such as your ill health, the bankruptcy of the airline, unusually dangerous weather, and unexpected events arising, such as jury duty or a work assignment you cannot refuse.

Not every policy covers the same risks, so read the fine print before buying one. For extra peace of mind, ask for "cancel for any reason" coverage. It will be more expensive, but the policy means you will be reimbursed for 50 percent to 100 percent and even 150 percent of your prepaid costs if you simply decide not to go. Policies typically cost between 4 percent and 10 percent of your trip cost.

BONUS TIP!
Watch Out for Fake Travel Sites

When you go to book that cheap-o hotel, make sure you buy from a legitimate operator. An astonishing 55 billion bookings valued at $4 billion were taken by third-party web sites posing as popular hotels or resorts.

I'm not referring to real third-party travel sites such as Expedia or Travelocity, but to fake sites made to look big name hotels, that, in fact, are fraudulent. Use a trusted, well-known site (like Expedia), check carefully if you are redirected by an ad straight to a hotel site, and always use a credit card whose issuer will block the transaction if you get taken.

Chapter 12

Small Business

"DRIVE THY BUSINESS, LET NOT THAT DRIVE THEE;
AND EARLY TO BED, AND EARLY TO RISE, MAKES
A MAN HEALTHY, WEALTHY, AND WISE . . ."

The Best Retirement Plan for Your Microbusiness

Striking out on your own to start a business? Don't mourn the loss of your company-sponsored 401(k) plan too much. There are many retirement plans that can work well for one-person business owners.

The best part: Establishing one of these plans doesn't interfere with your contributions to IRA accounts — either traditional or Roth. You can still set aside a combined $6,000 per year (or $7,000 if you're over 50) in a Roth or Traditional IRA even if you set up one of the following retirement plans for your small business.

(As you probably already know, traditional IRAs are funded with pre-tax dollars, and Roth IRAs are funded with after-tax dollars.) The following retirement plans are all funded with pre-tax dollars.

Here are the basic retirement plan options for small businesses:

SEP IRA

Whether you're a one-person business or you have additional employees, you can set up a Simplified Employee Pension (SEP) IRA. If you are a one-person business, in essence, you are the sole employee of your company, and you are making a SEP contribution as the employer.

You decide what percentage of your income you want to contribute to the SEP each year. You can set aside up to 25% of your net income. However, because the contribution is made on net income rather than gross income, the maximum allowed percentage for sole proprietors works out to be more like 20% because of the way the calculation flows through on a Schedule C.

The maximum dollar amount you can contribute to a SEP IRA was $56,000 for 2019. And you have until the date your tax return is filed (including extensions) to set up your SEP IRA. Contributions can be deducted as a business expense.

One of the nice things about a SEP IRA is that if you have plans to add employees in the future, it can accommodate that growth. However, keep in mind that you will have to contribute the same percentage of compensation to all employee accounts in the SEP every year.

SIMPLE IRA
(SAVINGS INCENTIVE MATCH PLAN FOR EMPLOYEES)

Like a SEP IRA, a SIMPLE IRA is a retirement plan for small businesses that allows you to contribute both as the employee and the employer.

As the employee, you can contribute up to 100% of your income, to a maximum dollar amount of $13,000 per year or $16,000 if you're over 50. Additionally, as the employer, you can choose to either match your employee contribution dollar-for-dollar up to 3% of your salary (and your employees' salaries if you have employees) or contribute a flat 2% of salary.

A SIMPLE IRA is a good choice if you're just starting out and your business is a side job because you can use it to basically bank all of what you make from your business for retirement and just live off of what you make in your main job.

A SIMPLE IRA is also a good option if you plan to add employees in the future. Employees like SIMPLE IRAs because 100% of the employer contributions are vested from day one.

SOLO 401(K)

The solo 401(k) plan is tailor-made for single-person businesses. It's just like a regular 401(k), except it's designed for one person business or businesses that have one person and a spouse if both are working in the business.

Typically, solo 401(k)s are used by self-employed consultants, free-lancers, and other independent contractors. I first heard about the solo 401(k) from my friend Dan, a healthcare IT consultant who uses one.

Self-employed people like solo 401(k)s because they have very high contribution limits and are easy to set up.

Solo 401(k)s allow you to invest up to $56,000 a year (and another $6,00 per year if you're over 50) from your self-employment income for retirement. That is considered your "employee contribution.

These plans are relatively simple to operate. Many financial institutions offer solo 401(k) plans with no setup fees and low annual investment fees, but you are required to file Form 5500 with the IRS when your balance reaches $250,000.

ROTH SOLO 401(K)

You can also add a Roth component to your solo 401(k) account if your 401(k) provider allows it. (Not all providers do, so be sure to ask yours if this is available.) You'll want to open a Roth Solo 401(k) in addition to — not instead of — a regular solo 401(k).

You can make employee contributions to either account, but only the regular solo 401(k) can accept your contributions as the employer. And of course, your employee contributions to a Roth solo 401(k) are not currently tax-deductible, but as with a regular Roth IRA, the earnings grow tax-free and are not taxed even when you withdraw.

Another nice thing about a solo Roth 401(k) is that there are no income limits for being able to make contributions — another advantage over Roth IRAs.

DEFINED BENEFIT PLAN

If you're making big bucks (perhaps as a physician, dentist, or lawyer), you may be able to establish this type of plan, which allows you to make massive pre-tax contributions.

The limits for defined benefit plans increase with age, such that someone over 60 can put away more than $200,000 every year. These plans are quite complex to set up and administer, so you'll need to work through a financial advisor or CPA.

NEXT STEPS

To set up one of these plans, you can work with a bank, such as Wells Fargo, or a financial services firm, such as Fidelity. There are also retirement plan providers geared to small businesses, including ForUs-All, Guideline, Spark 401k, and Ubiquity. Even payroll providers such as ADP and Paychex are getting in the game.

As with any big financial decision, it's smart to collect quotes from several of these sources and compare their fees and offerings.

Get Corporate Sponsors for Your Business

You're probably used to thinking of corporate sponsors as something sports figures get after winning an Olympic medal, or perhaps something nonprofits use to fund charity events. But an increasing number of for-profit businesses are procuring funding from

SMALL BUSINESS | 359

corporations, and this money can be not just for special events, but ongoing, dependable revenue.

Walking the World (WalkingtheWorld.com) is one small business that uses corporate sponsors to provide cash for its operations. Founded by Ward Luthi, the company offers guided walking tours all over the globe. The tours are designed for people age 50 and older (or "50 and better," as its website says).

Luthi obtained one major sponsorship from a vitamin company that was launching a new supplement line for seniors. Other sponsors have included companies that sell outdoor clothing and other equipment.

Luthi makes his sponsors a priority; he has mentioned them on his website, spoken about them at public events, and worn one brand's gear during a walking tour. He's even appeared on 9 million boxes of a new cereal launched by Quaker Oats.

The revenue from such sponsorships has helped his company grow: Walking the World recently celebrated 30 years in business, and Luthi has 13 tours planned for 2019.

Would he recommend sponsorship to others? Absolutely. "There is so much money out there, and a lot of companies don't spend all their sponsorship money," he says.

Carolyn Gross has also found success with corporate sponsorships. Her company, Creative Life Solutions (CreativeLifeSolutions.com), has been in business for more than 22 years. Gross is a professional speaker on topics related to health and wellness, and she is the author of four books, including *Rise Above the Chaos*.

Her sponsors have included supplement companies, tea makers, a health resort, and a manufacturer of ionic foot baths for detoxification. In exchange for their support, Gross has mentioned these sponsors in her talks and books, given out their literature at events, and highlighted them in social media posts.

Her advice to other businesses considering getting corporate sponsors: "Ask and ye shall receive!"

To score these opportunities, Luthi and Gross received assistance from Linda Hollander, author of *Corporate Sponsorship in 3 Easy Steps* and founder of Sponsor Concierge, which helps small businesses and other organizations get corporate sponsorship (SponsorConcierge.com).

We called on Hollander to learn the ins and outs of getting corporate sponsorship, and how other small businesses can do it.

HOW TO GET A CORPORATE SPONSOR
Step 1: Identify Your Audience

"The number one reason that companies want to sponsor a for-profit business is what's called influence," Hollander says. Your business has influence with your audience (your clients or customers), and that influence is the most important thing you have to offer a corporate sponsor.

That's because they know that if you recommend a certain product or service, people in your audience are more likely to buy it.

Step 2: Research Potential Corporate Targets

Hollander suggests starting with businesses that are similar to yours. Go to their websites and social media pages to see if they have sponsors. (How can you tell? Sponsors will likely be listed on the home page or on a separate sponsors page. They may be mentioned in blog posts or social media posts that are marked as sponsored. They may also figure prominently in giveaways the business does.)

"That's a cool thing, because you don't have to educate them about sponsorship if they're already sponsoring a business that's close to yours," Hollander notes.

Once you have a starting list of companies that already do sponsorships, brainstorm to find other corporations in the same industry to contact. Add to your target list any companies you can think of with audience demographics that overlap with your own.

Finally, add to your target list any companies whose products or services you already use and love. "I never have had a sponsor where I didn't use the product and believe in it," Gross says, noting that she has turned down sponsorship offers for products that didn't work for her.

Step 3: Make Contact

Once you have a list of target corporations, Hollander recommends going to LinkedIn.com to find specific company contacts.

"Look for someone who is in the marketing department," she says. "Every company has marketing, and they have a good budget."

Reach out via email first, Hollander suggests. "A lot of sponsors have told me they don't want to be surprised by a phone call." If the contact shows interest by email, move to a phone or in-person conversation as soon as possible.

"Sponsorship is a relationship business," Hollander says. "You build relationships and rapport with conversations."

Step 4: Write a Proposal

Successful proposals follow a basic template, according to Hollander. First, include a description of your business and what it does. You want to make an emotional connection — tell the story behind your business or the story of someone your business has helped.

"It's not a faceless corporation that's going to sponsor you. It is a human being," Hollander says.

Then, write a benefits section, listing as many benefits of partnering with you as possible. "If the sponsors don't see benefits, they will not fund you," Hollander says.

Next, provide information on your audience demographics. Include your typical customer's age, sex, income, education level, occupation, and marital status. Include as much detail as you can on your audience's spending habits, especially compared to other groups. In Luthi's case, he included the statistic that people age 50-plus still outspend millennials 2 to 1.

It might also make sense to share what cars they drive, neighborhoods they live in, and magazines and websites they read regularly. "Your demographics are your destiny in sponsorships," Hollander says.

The next section should be your marketing plan. Share how you will get the word out about what you do. Potential sponsors want to see a robust plan for marketing, branding, and promotion that they can be a part of.

Finally, a clear menu of prices is essential. You'll want to include pricing for common sponsorship options, including blog posts, videos, social media posts, a mention in your e-newsletter, a mention in your public talks, or the sponsor's logo on your website.

Unique ideas tailored to the sponsor's goals are even better, so don't be afraid to include any other creative options you devise. To give you a sense of prices, the latest "State of Sponsored Social" report from IZEA found that sponsors expect to pay an average of $411 per sponsored blog post and $244 per sponsored Facebook post.

Step 5: Consider Getting an Expert's Second Opinion on Your Proposal

Any document can benefit from a second set of eyes, but if you're new to sponsorship, it's even more important. When Luthi was first approached to participate in a national media tour for one company, they asked what his fee was.

"I had no idea at the time," he says. He and Hollander worked on a proposal and a suggested fee. "It was a lot higher than I would have asked," he says. The company came back with an offer very close to their proposed number, so Luthi was thrilled.

"You can do it on your own," he says. "It's just helpful to have somebody who's been through the process and understands sponsors."

Prepare Your Small Business for a Natural Disaster

Anyone with a television would agree that 2017 was a doozy for natural disasters. Floods, wildfires, and major hurricanes battered regions of the U.S., and millions of homes and businesses were affected. Watching all the devastation may have you wondering: How ready is my business for a natural disaster?

Take these first steps to fortify your business against whatever Mother Nature might send your way.

9 WAYS TO BE READY

1. Call your insurance agent. Property insurance may not be enough to protect your business after a natural disaster. Other expenses and lost revenue resulting from the downtime can do serious damage to your company's bottom line. Ask your agent about business interruption and extra expense insurance to deal with these situations.

2. Secure your place of business. A natural disaster could happen while you and your employees are present. To prepare for that scenario, ensure there are clear evacuation routes, marked exits, and proper emergency lighting in case of a power loss. Identify spaces in your building that could serve as shelters during an emergency if needed. Make sure they are easy to access. Consider having a qualified contractor tour your facility to discuss risk mitigation construction techniques.

3. And if a natural disaster were to destroy your business location, think about possible places you could relocate your operation temporarily. Are there other businesses in the area that might

allow you to operate at their location? Can any employees work from their homes?

Make an inventory of your business equipment. An up-to-date list makes the insurance claims process easier after a disaster. Photos or video of the equipment can help, too. Store these items at a location that's separate from your place of business.

4. Back up key documents so they are accessible from multiple locations. Modern online backup services make it easy and automatic to back up your data in the cloud (basically on the internet). Examples of services include IDrive, Acronis True Image, and SOS Online Backup. For essential paper documentation, consider a fire-rated safe at your business location or a safe deposit box at your bank or credit union. (It can't hurt to scan these items digitally as well.)

5. Maintain a list of important contacts. If your work location is destroyed or inaccessible, you'll need a way to inform key people of your business' status. Make a list of names and contact information for your suppliers, creditors, customers, employees, and insurance agents. Store this list off-site or in the cloud for easy access from elsewhere.

6. Make a communication plan. If your business serves the general public, you'll need to share your status in a broader way. Make a list of all the ways customers may reach you or search for your business; these are places you'll want to update after a disaster. The list should include:

   - Your business listing on Google
   - Any social media accounts you have (Facebook, Pinterest, LinkedIn)
   - Review sites such as Yelp (there's a setting for "temporarily closed")
   - Your outgoing phone message
   - Signage at your business location
   - Your website (urgent updates can be shown as an announcement bar or notification bar)

When you're back in business, consider a grand re-opening celebration, and notify your local media to spread the word.

7. Give yourself a financial buffer. Just like an emergency fund for your personal finances, a stash of money for unexpected business expenses is essential. Your bills still need to be paid even

when your business is on hiatus, of course. An emergency fund can allow you to cover payroll, debt obligations, and other essential expenses while you are in limbo.

8. Add any region-specific preparations. If your area is prone to flooding, you'll want to store important items as far from the basement or ground floor as possible. Those in wildfire zones should provide ample fire extinguishers and train employees how to use them. Find detailed checklists for specific natural disasters at preparemybusiness.org/planning.

9. Consider a turn-key disaster recovery service. If all this sounds like more work than you have time for as a small business owner, there are turnkey services that can help you formulate a disaster preparedness plan and activate it if needed. Check out Agility Recovery Solutions (agilityrecovery.com), which partners with the SBA to educate small businesses about disaster preparedness.

The Power of a Customer Email List

True or false: Nobody wants more emails, so businesses should refrain from sending them to customers.

False! It turns out that most U.S. adults prefer email over any other form of communication from businesses, according to a study commissioned by MarketingSherpa. Email was far and away the winner, with 72 percent saying they like when companies use it to contact them.

That's great news for business owners, because email is one of the simplest tools at your disposal to communicate with customers. It's low-cost but has enormous reach. It's intimate, connecting with people in their homes and on their phones. Best of all, it's a level playing field. In your customer's email inbox, your message is displayed right next to the big brands with huge marketing budgets.

So how can you start an email marketing program, and what should you say? Let's start with the basics.

HOW TO GET EMAIL ADDRESSES

In order to start communicating with your customers via email, first you need their email addresses. Depending on your type of business, you may already have them, or you may need to start collecting them.

To store that trove of important data, you'll find it easiest to use a service, such as Constant Contact or MailChimp. These email marketing platforms allow you to build a list of email addresses as well as organize and segment your list, plus format, send, and preschedule emails.

These services also provide support and advice for businesses that are just starting out with email marketing.

Once you have an email system set up, start gathering customer emails from:

Your existing email program.

Follow the email marketing software's instructions for exporting names from your current email program (Outlook, Gmail, Yahoo) and uploading them into the email program software.

At checkout.

Check your payment processor or point-of-sale software to see if you can collect customer email addresses. Ideally, choose one that automatically transmits that information to your email marketing software. Alternatively, post a clipboard at your register to ask for email addresses, then enter them into your email software manually.

On your website.

Add an email newsletter signup box to your website. This lets you easily capture existing customers as well as potential new ones that are checking you out online and adds those email addresses to your list automatically.

To encourage people to share their emails, try offering something of value in exchange — perhaps a small discount off a purchase or an e-book that complements your products or services. And make sure you request first names as well as email addresses so you can personalize your email messages.

WHEN TO EMAIL YOUR LIST

I follow two rules when it comes to email frequency:

Rule No. 1: Email your customers regularly.

Create a schedule that works for you and that you can follow through with. Daily, weekly, monthly, or quarterly are all legitimate choices depending on your business and customers.

If you communicate frequently, it's no big deal if your customers miss one email; they'll likely see another. On the other hand, with less frequent communication, people take note when you do contact them. Either way, map out a calendar of what to communicate when.

Rule No. 2: Email your customers when you have something to say.

Above all, don't waste anyone's time. Don't email every week if you only have something to say once a month. However, it's OK to email outside your normal schedule for special circumstances.

For example, if there is a big story in the news that relates to your industry or expertise, by all means share your thoughts about it! If your business is announcing an expansion, a new product launch, or another major change that's important to communicate immediately, definitely let your customers know.

WHAT TO SAY

Email your customers like you would a friend. Greet them by first name. (Your email program can handle this.) Use your unique, authentic voice. Most importantly, make it all about them.

People only open emails because they anticipate something of value inside. It can be monetary savings or free information they can use to get ahead in their own lives or careers.

Even news that's about you should be made about them. For example, if you're emailing on the occasion of your business's five-year anniversary, thank your customers by offering 5 percent off all orders booked during the anniversary month.

Get the idea? Now give it a try!

Are You Paying Your Employees the Right Amount?

Sweating salary isn't just for job candidates; employers worry about getting it right too. Many small companies have only one of a given position, making it difficult for an owner to know what the market rate is. And many jobs at small businesses are hybrids of several positions, so it's hard to compare them with positions at other companies.

The good news is that there are more resources than ever to determine the market rates for your staff. If you can afford to shell out for someone else to do the legwork, you could hire a compensation consultant for an analysis that is customized to your business. There are also services such as Salary.com or Payscale.com that provide access to detailed compensation databases and custom reports for a fee or by subscription.

If you'd prefer to bootstrap the information from other resources, we'll show you how. The first step is to conduct a market survey.

PERFORMING A MARKET SURVEY

Here are some ways to collect salary information for a given position:

Look at job postings for the same position that include salary to see what others are offering right now for the same roles (Indeed .com and CareerBuilder.com show this information when available). Be sure to compare job descriptions, not just titles. A certain job title at your company might carry very different responsibilities at another business.

Check out your competition at Glassdoor.com. This site allows workers to report their compensation anonymously. So you can see what companies in your region or your industry are paying even if they don't have open positions.

Consult industry guides or compensation surveys. The more localized, the better. Organizations that conduct salary surveys include compensation consulting firms, industry associations, educational institutions, and state and federal governments. Try Googling the job title with the phrase "salary range" to find these surveys.

Talk to others, especially fellow business owners, about compensation. Recruiters and job placement agencies are resources, too. They may give you a sense of what local candidates expect salary-wise. As you go, put the data into a spreadsheet. For salaries from other parts of the country, use a cost of living calculator to figure the equivalent amount in your location. This will give you a salary range for each position you research.

WHAT SHOULD YOU PAY?
Next, take these steps to tailor salaries to your company:

1. Consider Your Payment Philosophy
Where do you want to fall on the spectrum? Some companies pay in the 90th percentile of the market in a conscious effort to attract and retain the best people. Others pay at the low end to keep costs down and try to manage the resulting high turnover.

Consider these two scenarios. Dan is an IT consultant working in healthcare. He relied on his past experience as an employee to arrive at his payment philosophy. Since he always felt most valued in prior jobs when he was well compensated, he feels it's essential to pay them very well to inspire the best work, now that he's in a position to employ others.

On the other end of the spectrum is Gabe, who runs a small tech startup. He starts employees off on the lower end of the range and lets them earn more as they perform. His priority is to hire people who are excited about his business concept, then reward them with large increases to keep them on board.

2. Take Other Perks Into Account
Does your business offer generous or unusual perks that may offset a slightly lower salary? For example, a flexible schedule, the ability to telecommute, weekly free lunches, or unlimited time off are valuable perks to workers today.

As a consulting firm, Dan's company can offer employees a flexible schedule and remote work on some projects. In addition to a flexible schedule and unlimited time off, Gabe's startup offers equity in the business as part of compensation, which he takes into account when making pay decisions.

If you're setting a salary for an open position, you don't need to pinpoint a salary to the dollar. In fact, you want to have a range, so you can adjust your offer based on a candidate's education, skills, and experience.

TRACKING MARKET RATES OVER TIME

Let's say you bring someone on at just the right salary. Because the market changes constantly, you may run into trouble if you fail to adjust your employee salaries regularly.

On the flip side, if you give someone a large raise every year, you risk paying the person outside the appropriate range. Perform these market surveys every so often to see where salaries stand in your area and industry, and where you might be paying more or less than you should.

The Right Way to Keep Business Receipts

M ost people are not fans of paper clutter. More and more we set up bills online, get our news from the radio, and when a cashier offers a receipt, we typically decline.

But when it comes to your business, you may need to change that way of thinking, at least regarding receipts.

The IRS allows — and frankly, expects — a great deal of expenses from a new business, and you shouldn't minimize them by not getting receipts. (Also, keep in mind that expenses for meals and entertainment are some of the least scrutinized.)

You could lose several hundred dollars in deductions for want of a few slips of paper. "Receipts are important. You've got to keep them," says Mark J. Kohler, a CPA, lawyer, and the author of *The Tax and Legal Playbook*. Here's why:

YOU HAVE AUDIT PROTECTION

You probably know this already, but it's only wise to deduct expenses on your tax return that you could back up with a receipt if you had to. Credit card or bank statements won't cut it. "The IRS still wants to see the detailed receipt of what you actually purchased," Kohler says. (Digital receipts, such as you would receive after an online purchase, are just fine.)

You Can Take Higher Deductions

In some cases, there are two methods available to calculate a tax deduction, and having receipts allows you to choose the better one, says Linda Pinson, an author of 11 books on entrepreneurship, including *Keeping the Books: Basic Recordkeeping* and *Accounting for the Successful Small Business*.

For example, she says, "you can keep a mileage log and get so much per mile that you or your employees traveled for the business, or you can use the actual expenses plus the depreciation of the vehicle." If gas prices in your area are high, calculating actual expenses may be the better deal. But without a receipt, you'll never know.

You Can Make Better Business Decisions

"Numbers are the only thing you can evaluate a business by," Pinson says. Receipts are part of proper bookkeeping and allow you to create profit and loss statements, budgets, cash flow analysis, and financial projections. If you aren't familiar enough with accounting principles to create these reports, start with keeping track of your spending.

"It's really good to get some kind of course or read some kind of book," Pinson says. "Understand what this whole thing is all about and why you need [receipts]." You don't have to do your bookkeeping yourself, she notes, but as a responsible business owner, you should at least know the concepts.

How to File and Store Receipts

Here's welcome news: The way to file and store your receipts is totally up to you. That's right, you can choose whatever system you like — hard copies in a folder, scanned versions on your computer, pictures in a mobile app — as long as you actually use it.

"Use an app if it works best for you," Kohler says. "If you're not tech-savvy, have a shoebox or a drawer [to collect paper receipts]." The only rule is that records must be organized by year.

There are receipt-specific mobile apps (search "receipts" in your smartphone's app store for options), as well as general document storage programs, such as Evernote and Dropbox. Some of the receipt-specific apps also have mileage trackers, which can help keep deductible travel expenses tidy as well.

If you digitize paper receipts by scanning or taking pictures via an app, you can toss the originals. "The IRS will take a copy of a receipt," Kohler says.

Not into digital solutions? That's OK.

"Lots of people still do paper," Pinson says. "For instance, the business that I'm in, if I took every receipt and scanned it, I'd be spending a lot more time than I'd spend just putting it in a file somewhere. 'Online everything' isn't always the most effective thing."

Your company itself may also determine how to set things up. "You have to figure out what system is best suited to your business," Pinson says. The smaller the business, the less complex the recordkeeping will need to be.

If you have an accountant or bookkeeper, whether on staff or outsourced, that person or their firm may have preferences. "Some businesses save everything they've got and they just pile it over to their bookkeeping service and it's up to them what they do," Pinson says.

If you go the digital route, there's the matter of keeping your data intact if your computer or smartphone malfunctions or is damaged. Many apps sync with the Cloud automatically for hassle-free, secure storage. If you scan and save receipts on your computer, you'll want to back up the data regularly.

No matter what solution you choose, Kohler suggests saving the documents for six years or more.

In the end, you want a system that's effective but manageable. "Receipts shouldn't be a huge part of your bookkeeping," Kohler notes. "Just keep them by year, in one area, for at least six years, and don't stress about it."

6 Tips to Launch an Online Business

Products are bought and sold online more than ever, and that's not changing anytime soon. If you've thought about tapping into the power of the Internet to start a virtual business, you're onto something. "It's to the point where anybody can do this," according to Joel Comm, author of *KaChing: How to Run an Online Business that Pays and Pays*.

Follow Comm's quick-hit tips as you plan the launch of your online venture:

DETERMINE WHAT YOU HAVE TO SELL.

Evaluate your particular passions, talents, skills, and abilities. Comm says to ask yourself: "How do I leverage what I know to help others and get paid?" The more unique and specific, the better. "You have a much better chance of rising to the front of the pack in your particular niche if you're micro-targeted than if you're going broad."

SHARE YOUR KNOWLEDGE WITH A BLOG.

Comm calls this "the low-hanging" fruit of making money online. Best of all, it's practically free, using tools such as Wordpress, Blogger or Tumblr. "As you grow [your blog] and begin to get readers, you can place advertisements," Comm says. In time, your website can advance to selling informational products, private coaching, and subscriptions to exclusive content and resources.

CRAFT A PROFESSIONAL-LOOKING WEBSITE.

Unless you are operating your business through a platform such as eBay, Etsy, or Amazon, you'll need to have a website. And it should be high quality, Comm insists. "You can have an incredible product that brings immense value," he says, "but if the presentation is amateur, people might not be able to get past that."

BUILD A FOLLOWING WITH MARKETING TOOLS.

"Once you've got great content and a beautiful site up, you have to get customers to it," Comm says. You can market it using social media, by sending out press releases, or creating ad campaigns via Google Adwords or Facebook to help drive traffic.

BECOME AN AFFILIATE.

In this situation, you advertise someone else's product on your site. When people buy it, you earn a commission. "If you target your promotions to your audience, you can make money off that," Comm says.

DON'T SPEND ALL YOUR TIME AT THE COMPUTER.
To open more doors, Comm recommends finding a good mentor and attending industry events. "No matter what you sell, you're in the people business," he says. "The best way to facilitate fast-track growth is to get face to face."

The Worst Advice Given to Small Business Owners

If you're an entrepreneur, you probably don't look to others for approval very often. But you likely do seek out counsel and input from others frequently. Most of the time, that's a good thing.

However, we've noticed that a lot of oft-repeated business advice can be misleading or outright harmful to entrepreneurs.

Carol Roth, author of *The Entrepreneur Equation: Evaluating the Realities, Risks, and Rewards of Having Your Own Business* and on-air contributor for CNBC, helped us identify the worst offenders. From her tough-love approach, you'll learn to avoid these bogus business recommendations:

"FOLLOW YOUR PASSION"

This common refrain is the No. 1 worst piece of advice out there, according to Roth. She argues that other qualities are much more important to long-lasting success. "Passion may be enough to get you started in business, but it's not going to be enough to sustain you in business," she says.

What do you need even more? "Determination and a willingness to grind it out every day," Roth says. "Passion burns out pretty quickly when you get into the thick of business."

After all, once you establish a company around an activity you love, your time is taken up by operating the business and all it entails, such as properly training your staff, managing the finances, booking appointments, and dealing with all the tax and legal issues that are part and parcel of commerce.

Other times, turning a hobby into a profession can change your attitude toward it, dampening your enthusiasm — a problem which will eventually hamper success. "Sometimes pursuing what it is you love so much as a business — and being dependent on that to earn a living — actually kills your love for that particular something," Roth warns.

You also have to possess the financial resources to sustain yourself in the beginning; you can't depend on immediate cash flow, because that often doesn't happen. Roth recommends having about three years of working capital on hand before you start a business. "Until passion is taken as currency in banks and supermarkets, I'm pretty sure you can't just live off your passion," she says.

Then there's the endeavor itself. "You need the right business opportunity, which is driven by the customer, not by what you would like to be doing," Roth says.

"STRIVE FOR BALANCE"

"Balance is a myth," Roth asserts. "To have everything at the same level at all times is not realistic."

Instead, she recommends focusing on priorities that can be re-ordered when needed. "In the early stage, your business is going to be your priority, sometimes even more so than your family if you want to succeed," Roth says. She acknowledges that pace isn't sustainable forever, though. "Over time, you have to find a way to take care of yourself."

"NEVER TURN DOWN AN OPPORTUNITY"

There may be times you won't have the luxury of being picky, Roth says. However, try to avoid taking on clients who don't make sense financially or who keep you from pursuing better opportunities because of the time commitment they require.

Clients to stay away from: those who don't pay you in a timely manner (or friends looking for freebies), those who take up far more of your time than they are actually paying for, those who are emotionally damaging to you or your employees, and those who could get you into legal trouble.

"Think about what kind of clients and customers you want to be doing business with," Roth says. "Realize that sometimes you're being penny-wise and pound foolish."

"BIGGER IS BETTER"

Entrepreneurs often hear that they should be continually growing their business. That's misleading, Roth notes.

"You want to grow smartly and in a way that makes sense," she says. "Just because you're pursuing growth doesn't mean it's going to be profitable growth and that it's the right thing." A business may increase its revenue but be less profitable when all costs are considered. Roth cautions against growth for the sake of growth.

Take Your Business Online and Make More Money

So you own a successful business. You enjoy a great reputation and a devoted client base. Have you finally "made it"? Or is there more you can do to maximize your earning potential?

The answer to that last question is "of course," says Joel Comm, author of *KaChing: How to Run an Online Business that Pays and Pays*. "You want to find a way that you can serve your customers with your knowledge and generate a greater return on investment," he says. Expanding into online opportunities is a way to do just that. And since you already have an established following, you're that much ahead in the online game. Consider this proven progression:

STEP 1. SELL INFORMATION PRODUCTS.

"Take the knowledge that you have and package it," Comm explains. The format can be anything from an e-book or audio download to a full webinar series or video course. After creating the product once, you deliver it digitally to people who pay to consume it on demand. Think you don't have anything new to say? Don't worry, if it's great information that you want to share. "It's the reason you see a brand-new book on fitness every other month," Comm says. "The topic is universal, but there's something about the proof that person has created in his or her own life. People want to know what others are doing that's working."

STEP 2. START A MEMBERSHIP SITE.

Establishing a virtual community around your expertise provides continuity. "People pay every month to have ongoing access to you, your community or your information," Comm says. Typical offerings include something like an e-book as part of the initial registration, plus regular webinars, a weekly coaching call, and an online forum where you interact and answer questions. "The goal is to deliver content and value in an ongoing process and build your tribe," he adds.

STEP 3. OFFER COACHING.

Assuming you've cultivated your audience through the steps above — people are going to want more of you. Through coaching, you can offer them personalized and focused attention. Whether one-on-one or with a mastermind group, coaching can be primarily conducted online (and in person if you wish to do so). The best part? It's the perfect opportunity for older adults. "People who are middle-aged already have a lot of experience," Comm says. "They have a lot to say and a lot to teach."

Comm says many people will pay top dollar for this expertise, and there's no ceiling to your earning potential. "Over time, as you demonstrate value, help people and get testimonials, you can raise your prices," he adds.

Best Big-Business Moves for a Small-Business CEO

Large and small, all businesses have one thing in common: someone in charge. And that leader's performance — good, bad, or mediocre — has an outsized and lasting effect on the organization's success. Large companies know this and cultivate their top talent through leadership training at each career stage.

As a small-business CEO, you might not have had those opportunities. Like so many other things, you figured it out as you went along. But in a marketplace where you compete against the behemoths, wouldn't it be nice to know their secrets?

To find out what the big players do to ensure their businesses grow and succeed, we spoke to David Rohlander, author of *The CEO Code: Create a Great Company and Inspire People to Greatness With Practical Advice From an Experienced Executive*. He shares these common mindsets and tactics used by large-business leaders that can translate to the small-business CEO's needs:

UNPLUG FROM YOUR BUSINESS.

Rohlander notes that many small-business owners tend to become "obsessed" with their companies, thinking about them 24/7. "A typical large company doesn't have the same type of emotional involvement," he says. "It's more of a job."

Of course, a small-business owner's passion can inspire excellent work and drive innovation, but it also can backfire. If a leader burns out and loses his or her enthusiasm for the work, it'll certainly hold a company back. "No matter how intensely they love their business, they need to figure out ways to back off, relax, get some exercise, and work on their spiritual life, family life, and hobbies," Rohlander says.

DON'T NEGLECT THE PLANNING ASPECT OF YOUR JOB.

"Every leader has four primary functions: planning, communicating, managing, and execution," Rohlander explains. "Larger companies tend to spend a lot of time on plans, and entrepreneurs spend all their time on execution." Improve your performance by setting aside time to plan and strategize.

MEET WITH EMPLOYEES ONE-ON-ONE.

The yearly performance review is a hallmark of big-business culture, and Rohlander says it also can be useful in small companies for tracking employee progress. However, touching base just once a year can leave you open to unpleasant surprises.

Because most problems are communication related at their core, he says the solution is to have regular, one-on-one meetings with your reports — with no agenda. Just ask what's going on and how you can help and celebrate their successes. "It's what you would call with your significant other a 'date night,'" he says. Not having these regular, low-stress meet-ups spells trouble in a business relationship.

INCORPORATE ONE KEY METRIC.

Large companies measure their workers' productivity obsessively. We're not saying you have to go that far. Instead, identify your biggest challenge and brainstorm ways to measure progress on addressing it. "If you can't measure it, you can't manage it," Rohlander says. "Every day people have to know whether they have won or lost."

GET QUOTED.

It's common for CEOs of large companies to be interviewed by national newspapers and magazines. As your business becomes more and more successful, you may need to do the same. To get comfortable with the process now, connect with local writers who cover your industry and offer yourself as a source. Or, if your writing is high quality, consider penning a book, magazine article, or blog post to cultivate a reputation as an expert in your field. When it comes to the media, Rohlander says, "the more you give, the more you get."

SOLICIT REGULAR FEEDBACK FROM CLIENTS.

Have you noticed that every receipt from a retail store these days asks you to take a customer satisfaction survey? It's uncommon for small businesses to request such feedback, so you may only hear from clients when there is a complaint — and that's a missed opportunity. "Many minds are better than one mind," Rohlander says. Find out what your customers want from you so your business can grow and change with their needs.

TRY EXPORTING.

According to the Small Business Administration, two-thirds of the world's purchasing power is in foreign countries. And because of the Internet, reaching them is easier than ever. Rohlander has experienced this firsthand. "I have sold more of my books in Brazil and India than in this country," he says. If your product or service can be exported, you owe it to your business to investigate if it's a smart move. Explore opportunities and resources available at www.export.gov.

BE A CONTINUAL LEARNER.

A lifelong commitment to education is a common trait of many big-business leaders. But we're not talking about obtaining advanced degrees here. "Some of the most successful people are self-educated,"

Rohlander says. What matters more is building the habit of learning, in whatever format works for you. "You never arrive," he says. "You're continually trying to improve."

These 4 Mistakes May Be Squeezing Your Profits

You'd never ignore uncontrolled bleeding in your body. But your small business? It may be hemorrhaging right now without you even noticing. Blame it on your big-picture outlook, which prevents some entrepreneurs from spotting their biggest profit drains, according to Brad Farris, principal adviser at Anchor Advisors and former executive editor at EnMast.com. "The mindset of the business owner is to look for more opportunities," he says, rather than worrying about small amounts lost through the back door. But those costs can be significant, especially when they compound over months or years. Here are four of the most common business bleeders:

1. CARRYING HIGH-INTEREST DEBT.

Credit cards are easy to obtain, but Farris says applying for a business loan is the better option when you need capital. "You're going to carry the balance longer than you think," he says. If you've already accumulated high-interest debt, pay it off as soon as possible or consolidate it into a business or home equity loan.

2. NOT REVIEWING YOUR STATEMENTS.

"There are so many subscription services that we put on a credit card and then forget about," Farris says. "Have you reviewed all your bills to make sure you are really using this stuff?" He suggests taking a close look every six months at money spent on professional organizations, online tools, and communication services. Be on the lookout for unused services, extra licenses you don't need anymore, or overage charges that can be avoided.

3. UNDERPAYING TALENTED EMPLOYEES.

This may sound counterintuitive but underpaying top employees could eventually get out of your workforce — i.e., you'll spend money on employees for less and less return over time. "What happens is you lose the good ones and keep the lousy ones," Farris says. Because their skills are often increasing more rapidly than their salaries, employees who excel are likely to be underpaid in relation to their contributions to the business.

4. Overpaying longtime employees.

It happens easily: When an employee is loyal and works hard, you want to reward him or her with a yearly raise. Over time, compensation edges way outside the appropriate range. To combat this effect, do a market survey every couple of years so you know what the standard ranges are, even if you're not hiring. "There's no reason to go above the market salary," Farris says. And after a banner year, give bonuses instead of pay raises.

7 Ways to Outsmart Card Processing Fees

"**P**aper or plastic?" It's a decision consumers make every day, but not about grocery bags. We're referring to payment methods, and plastic (in the form of credit and debit cards) is increasing in appeal for shoppers. Less so for retailers, who must pay fees with each transaction (a flat fee for debit and a percentage of the purchase for credit).

It's enough to make some businesses opt out altogether and go cash only. But retail consultant James Dion, co-author of *Start & Run a Retail Business*, says that's unwise.

Aside from the substantial inconvenience to customers, he says that the more cash you have on hand, the more of a target your business is for criminals. Plus, credit and debit cards offer a psychological advantage. "The customer doesn't perceive that as real money, so the amount of impulse purchases and overbuying ... is still pretty substantial," Dion says.

So cutting out cards isn't the ideal answer. But these options for dealing with processing fees can lessen their bite:

1. JOIN A TRADE ORGANIZATION.

Mega-retailers such as Walmart and Target can negotiate hefty discounts on processing services because of their volume. "If you're a smaller retailer, you're paying what you'd call in a hotel a 'rack rate,'" Dion says.

One way around the rack rate is to join your trade association, which may have negotiated a more advantageous rate with a particular processor. Some retailers have access to an association but choose not to join because of annual fees, he says. "If they did the math, they'd pay for that [annual fee] in the first two months."

2. LEARN WHAT YOUR RATE REALLY MEANS.

Ben Dwyer, founder of CardFellow.com, a credit card processor comparison website, says the best thing a business owner can do is understand what makes up the charges. "There's no magic to credit card processing," Dwyer says. "There's a fixed component and there's a markup component, and that's what a business is really shopping for."

The fixed component includes an interchange fee, which is paid to issuing banks, and an assessment fee, which goes to the card brands such as Visa and MasterCard. It's the same no matter what processor you use. The markup component is made up of the card processor's fees.

3. REQUEST ONLY TRUE PASS-THROUGH (OR INTERCHANGE-PLUS) PRICING.

In this structure, interchange and assessment fees are passed along at cost, and the processor's markup is clear. Dwyer says this is the only format in which you can compare processing costs accurately. The alternative is called tiered (or bundled) pricing, in which interchange and assessment fees are not passed through at cost and the breakdown is obscured. "The No. 1 mistake that businesses tend to make when they're shopping for processors is asking 'What's your rate?' It's not really the rate that matters," Dwyer says. "In fact, the rate is a [distant] second to the pricing model and the terms that it uses."

4. LOCK IN COMPETITIVE RATES FOR LIFE.

If you don't get this protection, Dwyer says "processors can quote whatever they want because they know they can adjust that pricing down the road."

He explains that "portfolio reviews," in which processors periodically evaluate your account and can apply a rate increase, are typical. A simple notification is printed on the first page of your statement, and if you miss it, the increase takes effect. Dwyer says all processors available through CardFellow lock in their markup rates for the life of the account.

5. DON'T BE FLEECED BY EQUIPMENT LEASES.

Many small businesses lease their processing terminals, but Dwyer says purchasing a terminal is better. It involves a small upfront cost of a few hundred dollars, but it usually pays off with savings many times that amount. "There is no good reason to lease equipment," he says. "It never makes financial sense."

6. ENSURE FUTURE FLEXIBILITY WITH THE RIGHT HARDWARE.

In addition to owning, you want processing equipment that's universally compatible, meaning it can be reprogrammed to work on another processor's network should you decide to switch later. "Universal equipment is at or near the cost of proprietary equipment, so there's no reason to limit your options," Dwyer says. He recommends purchasing these terminals from the processor directly so you'll know it's compliant. "Most offer a year warranty or more."

7. KEEP YOUR PRIMARY FOCUS ON GROWING THE BUSINESS.

It's true that every penny counts, but retail consultant Dion cautions against obsessing over fees when finding new ways to please customers is ultimately more profitable. "It's always better to have more sales and grow your business than to take that defensive position and cut costs," he says.

First, make sure you offer the right product, a wonderful atmosphere, great employees and phenomenal service. "If all that stuff is running perfectly and you've got some time," he says, "see what your operational savings can be on changing your credit card processing."

Collect Every Penny You're Owed

One problem can derail a small business pretty quickly — a cash-flow crunch. In exchange for the goods or services you provide, you need money, plain and simple. But some business owners tend to struggle with this side of the equation. It can be particularly pronounced in businesses where you provide services upfront for payment after completion or you're providing goods in bulk on an invoice rather than using a cash-and-carry system.

So if you're having issues getting paid, what can you do? First, figure out whether something is wrong in your approach. One of the biggest reasons invoices don't get paid in a timely manner is that payment terms aren't clearly defined upfront, says Craig Antico, former president of The Collection Authority in Paramus, N.J. "Be clear in the beginning about what your expectations are," he says. "They'll tell you right away if the terms you need are possible or not."

Next, create your own collection process. Antico advises asking how long processing will take once you've delivered the services or goods and getting the name of the person who will process your bills. "Get a credit card number you can use if necessary," he adds.

Antico recommends thorough research, as well. Does the company have a good credit rating and track record of paying within your terms of sale? If not, figure out the most risk you are willing to take or the longest number of days you can afford to go without payment. "If the customer is unable or unwilling to pay within the [time frame], you must be willing to walk away," Antico says.

Invoice at the time you deliver the goods or services and specify the number of days the recipient has to pay you, Antico advises. Ask for an acknowledgment of the invoice, and call if you don't get one. For big invoices, contact both the person who approves it and who processes it to make sure payment is scheduled for the date you need to be paid. If payment problems arise, contact higher-ups of the person who ordinarily approves your invoices, explain that you have done the work and the agreed-on terms for payment, and ask for help in getting paid.

All that said, the unfortunate fact is that many small businesses just aren't very good about getting their bills sent out, says Gary W. Patterson, CPA, MBA, author of *Million Dollar Blind Spots: 20/20 Vision for Financial Growth*. "The two best ways to collect overdue invoices are to send statements and call creditors asking for your money when payment isn't received, which far too many companies do not do," Patterson says. "A lot of people dislike having to call and say, 'You owe me money. Please pay it.' They let their receivables balances get far too high before they act."

Chapter 13

Bonus Chapter!

"DILIGENCE IS THE MOTHER OF GOOD LUCK."

13 Ways to Get the Most Out of Your Smartphone

Smartphones have become almost as ubiquitous as cars. A whopping 77 percent of Americans have a smartphone. And like cars, smartphones are a substantial investment. In addition to the phone itself, the average household spends over $1,000 a year for cellphone service.

Yet many people buy these pricey devices and only use them for calling and texting. That's a shame because smartphones are built to do so much more (and by more, I don't mean silly cat videos). Here are 13 ways to make the most of your smartphone.

WHAT YOUR SMARTPHONE CAN DO FOR YOU

1. Be your personal navigator.

Remember dedicated GPS devices? You don't need a GPS anymore, because your smartphone has a GPS built in. You can download navigation apps, such as Waze and Google Maps, to get turn-by-turn directions read aloud to you as you drive. And these navigators will update your route according to traffic conditions.

2. Let you always have a shopping list handy.

Ever realize you need something at the store, but you've forgotten what it is when you get to your paper shopping list? No longer, if you use your smartphone's list feature. I also use mine for listing gift ideas as soon as I think of them.

3. Save a trip to the bank.

Most major banks (and increasingly, smaller banks and credit unions, too) have smartphone apps with the ability to deposit checks by just taking a picture of the front and back.

4. Quickly make a last-minute dinner reservation.

Going out to dinner on short notice? You could call all the restaurants in your area to see who has availability and when, or you could just download the OpenTable app. It shows you at a glance all the restaurants that have reservations for your preferred time.

5. Get to bed earlier.

You have an alarm to wake up, but what about one to go to sleep? On the iPhone, the Bedtime feature (part of the Clock app) lets you determine what time you should head to bed each night to get the amount of sleep you want. Then it gives you a gentle reminder when it's time. And you no longer need to stay up to catch the evening news or see a late-night show. You can see the clips on the YouTube app the next day.

6. Save you money while shopping.

With your smartphone, you can easily check the online price of anything while shopping in person. Check the website of the store you're in (sometimes online prices are lower) as well as prices from competitors. If you find a lower price, ask the store if they will match it. If not, order the item right from your phone.

7. Reveal your grocery store's best deals.

Grocery store apps show their specials and let you digitally "clip" both store and manufacturer coupons. All you have to do is swipe your grocery store card or type in your phone number at checkout; the savings are then automatically deducted. No fumbling with scissors at home or with flimsy slips of paper at checkout.

8. See where people are in real time.

Smartphones can show you where you are on a map, and also where others are. If friends are en route, the navigation app Waze can tell you how soon they'll arrive. When you use Uber or Lyft to call for a ride, you can see how far away the driver is. And there are numerous apps that allow parents to keep an eye on kids' whereabouts via their phone locations.

9. Dictate instead of type.

Think typing on a phone or computer is a pain? Smartphones now have speech recognition, which means you can dictate almost anything you'd otherwise type: emails, text messages, Google searches. It's as easy as tapping the little microphone icon within an app.

10. Screen calls from unknown numbers.

When you receive a call, the Hiya app can compare the number to its database and display whether the number is suspected to be a scammer, telemarketer, or debt collector.

11. Keep tabs on your activity level.

The pedometer is another device that smartphones have made obsolete. Your smartphone will count every step you take, making it easy to see if you should take that extra walk after dinner.

12. Manage your health conditions with ease.

If you are experiencing a strange symptom, you can look it up immediately on the smartphone's web browser. If you have a chronic condition, there's most likely an app to help you manage it. Many hospital systems even have apps that allow you to video chat with a physician on demand.

13. Keep your mind sharp.

Download an app to play your favorite card game or word puzzle, or try apps specifically for brain health, such as Lumosity. Plus, the act of learning new things will challenge your brain and keep it working better as you age!

The Hidden Costs of Zero Commissions

The best things in life are free. Apparently, stock commissions are among them.

When Interactive Brokers announced it would offer commissions at an unbelievably low rate: free, the news sent competitors' stock prices tumbling. That is, until shortly after when Charles Schwab, TD Ameritrade, E-Trade, and Bank of America announced they would follow suit. A single news announcement nearly thrust the entire industry into a race to the bottom.

Why would any brokerage allow free trading? Well, they don't. It just appears that way.

Brokerage firms have always made money in four main ways: commissions, stock loans, margin interest, and interest on cash balances.

Stock loans are made to traders who wish to short a stock, hoping to make a profit if the stock's price falls. For a short sale, traders must borrow shares from the broker and return those shares to the broker at a later date. This is done by purchasing the stock on the open market at what the investor hopes will be a lower price.

For example, if you short a stock at $100 and buy it back at $95, you'll earn a profit of $5 (the difference) per share.

For this service, brokers often charge a "stock loan" fee and additionally charge interest on the amount borrowed, which is called "margin interest."

Lastly, while some brokers pay you small amounts of interest on your cash balances, they're also loaning out that money at higher rates and earning the difference, just like banks do.

So why would brokers willingly eliminate one of their income sources? In short, because they think doing so will earn them more money from the other revenue streams. By offering no commissions, traders will increase the number of transactions they do, which will result in more back-end fees.

Of course, commissions made up the bulk of a broker's income probably 75%. But now that commissions are being eliminated, brokers are turning to a new twist on an old tactic to make money.

HIDDEN COMMISSIONS: PAYMENT FOR ORDER FLOW

Although payment for order flow began in the 1980s, it's an unknown practice to most investors. Exchanges or third-party execution systems, such as electronic communication networks (ECNs), offer payments to brokers as an incentive for the brokers to route orders to their exchanges.

These payments are usually small, perhaps a penny per share, but they add up when multiplied by millions of shares per day. That's why firms are now in a heated competition to attract a whole bunch of new investors. Commission-free trading is a powerful incentive.

Receiving payments for order flow raises eyebrows. Add that it was pioneered by Ponzi-scheme king Bernie Madoff, and it goes from raising eyebrows to raising red flags. Is the broker going to act in my best interest? Or am I going to pay $50.10 per share when the stock is trading for $50 on all other exchanges?

Well, the SEC only allows a broker to accept payment for order flow if no other exchange is offering a better price. By having your orders routed, you may do better, but you can't do worse. Essentially, routing orders appears to be a benefit. Indeed, in many cases, it could very well be. However, there are other places where fees can hide.

Liquidity Fees and Rebates When trading through ECNs, you may be charged a fee removing liquidity. What is that? It's a fee for removing shares from the available pool.

Basically, if you place a "market order" to buy or sell shares, you could be charged this fee because market orders are guaranteed to execute. So you're automatically taking shares away from the available pool.

However, it's possible to earn credits by adding liquidity. In this case, the broker could give you a credit when you place a buy limit at any price below the current asking price, or a sell limit at any price above the current bid. In those instances, you'd be adding liquidity, and if those orders fill, you could earn a rebate for providing liquidity to the markets.

But there's a catch. Many of the commission-free brokers will pass the fees on to clients for removing liquidity — but keep the rebates for themselves when their clients add liquidity.

Fair? No. But that's the way brokers can make money without charging commissions.

BOTTOM LINE

So will you be better off using a zero commission broker?

It's hard to say. You could be better off. Or it may not affect you at all.

The biggest concern is that your broker may route your orders to exchanges with low liquidity just because these exchanges offer rebates, but your orders don't get filled because these exchanges aren't liquid enough.

If your order never fills — and the stock price rises — was it worth paying no commission? It's difficult to decipher the true "cost" to investors.

What can you do? Since it's hard to tell how this will shake out for investors, it's best not to switch to a no-commission broker just because it seems like a good deal.

And if your broker is now offering zero commissions, the best way to avoid high hidden fees is to avoid engaging in frequent trading just because commissions are "free." Don't change your investing style in an attempt to capitalize on free commissions. Stay with your plan, and let any potential savings be a bonus.

One thing is for sure: Brokers that receive the highest rebates can afford to charge the lowest commissions because they're making up for it with other fees.

Perhaps designer Coco Chanel summed it up best: "The best things in life are free. The second best things are very, very expensive." Commission-free trading may turn out to be great, but if you aren't careful, it may just end up being very expensive.

4 Ways to Teach Kids About Money

The easiest thing to do with money is give it away to your kids. The hardest thing to do is transfer your values along with that cash. Here are four ways to ensure you teach your kids the right lessons about money.

TRUTH NO. 1: THE WAY YOU TALK ABOUT MONEY MATTERS.

One mistake parents commonly make is telling their kids "we can't afford that" when their kids ask for something, even if that isn't quite true, says Elizabeth Odders-White, former associate professor of finance and former Kuechenmeister Bascom professor in business at the Wisconsin School of Business.

"For example, if your child says, 'Let's go to Disney World over spring break' and you actually could come up with money to pay for the trip but it's not a priority, saying 'We can't afford it,' is not only a cop out, it's also a missed opportunity to teach your kids about trade-offs," says Odders-White.

It's much more productive to say something like, "We're not choosing to spend our money on that," or "If we spend money on a trip to Disney World, then we won't have the money we need for summer camp," Odders-White explains. Couching it this way makes it clear to kids that financial decisions typically involve trade-offs.

TRUTH NO. 2: SPENDING IS A HABIT.

Everyone lives on a paycheck. Even the independently wealthy have a set income. The regularity of money is the key to creating financially conscious kids, says James Kassam, creator of allowance and chore tracking app, RoosterMoney.

"We believe an allowance routine is one of the best ways to teach young children money skills that will last a lifetime," says Kassam. Kassam also suggests encouraging positive conversations about money when kids are young, so money is seen as a tool, not a taboo. This allows kids to adopt the right mindset about savings and delayed gratification early on.

TRUTH NO. 3: INVEST EARLY FOR BEST RESULTS.

Prudently invested money compounds. It doubles every 10 years. For kids to grasp this, the best strategy is to set them up with an investment account in their teen years, says Robert Cucchiaro, a certified financial planner.

"I advise my clients to set up a brokerage account for each of their teenage or 20-something kids," says Cucchiaro. "They have to present to their parents what they want to purchase and why, and all dividend checks get sent to the kid instead of being reinvested." This gets kids interested in investing and shows them that their money has the power to grow.

TRUTH NO. 4: DIFFERENTIATE WANTS AND NEEDS.

Kids between the ages of eight and 12 can begin to understand the difference between spending for a good reason vs. just spending to spend, says financial security expert Pamela Yellen, a two-time New York Times bestselling author.

"Kids much younger than eight will have trouble grasping this lesson — as do some adults I know! But it's important to help your kids understand the distinction. A need is more connected to survival. A want is a desire that we can survive without," says Yellen.

She suggests that you make a list of items that you commonly purchase, everything from bread to comic books. Have your child rank each on a scale of 1 (just nice to have) to 10 (need to have), then discuss their rankings without making them wrong.

Using that same list, ask, "What's the worst that could happen if we don't get this?" Yellen suggests.

Then make a list of all of your personal "wants" that you are delaying for other priorities. "Share the list with your child and explain your reasoning," she says. "Encourage them to make their own list."

Donate to Charity Without Spending Any Money

It sounds impossible, but you really can donate thousands to charity without putting in a dime of your own money. This isn't about donating your time, skills, or household goods. This is about seven underused ways to get cold, hard cash to your favorite charity — with none of it coming from your own wallet.

STAGE A PERSONAL FUNDRAISER

Sure, you could just ask others to contribute to a charity, but it's more effective to up the ante by undertaking an impressive (or wacky) personal feat. The traditional option is something physical, such as running a race. But other creative ideas have come on the scene, such as men growing moustaches or people dumping buckets of ice water on their heads.

You'll want to set a fundraising goal and track its progress. Try the Fundraisers app on Facebook.com (look for it in the left-hand column, or type "Fundraisers" into the search bar at the top). Or use CrowdRise (crowdrise.com/online-fundraising). These sites make it easy to post regular updates to keep people engaged and donating to your cause.

CHOOSE FINANCIAL MANAGEMENT TOOLS THAT DONATE FOR YOU

When you open an account with online bank ableBanking, the bank will donate $25 to a charity you choose and another $25 for people you refer.

There are credit cards with rewards tied to charity, too. The Charity Charge World MasterCard funnels 1 percent of what you spend to a nonprofit of your choice. Plus, it gives a $10 bonus donation after your first purchase. There is no annual fee, and you can choose up to three charities.

DONATE YOUR POINTS

If you've accumulated a stash of credit card rewards points, you can donate them. For example, American Express lets you transfer points to a charity through its Members Give portal at amex.justgive.org. And as a bonus, Amex will kick in $10 for every 1,000 points you donate. Airline miles can also be gifted to charity. Go to your airline's loyalty program website for instructions.

DONATE WHILE YOU SHOP

Web behemoth Amazon offers a program called AmazonSmile, where 0.5 percent of your purchases is funneled to a charity you select, as long as you access the site through smile.amazon.com.

Another option, GoodShop (goodshop.com), is a site that displays current sales and coupon codes from online retailers. If you use the links on GoodShop's site to visit these stores, it will donate a percentage of your purchase (it's a different percentage with each store) to the charity of your choice.

Bonus tip: GoodSearch, another feature on the same site, donates a penny to charity every time you perform a web search.

ASK FOR CHARITY DONATIONS IN LIEU OF GIFTS

Celebrations are a great opportunity to support your favorite charity. When someone asks you for gift ideas (say, for your upcoming birthday, wedding, or anniversary), it's easy to say: "Even more than a physical gift, I would so appreciate a donation made to charity." If your loved one is open to it, suggest a few charities to consider, so he or she can have the satisfaction of making the selection.

SWAP PRICEY COMMERCIAL GREETING CARDS FOR CHARITY-SPONSORED ONES

Some charities sell cards to support their operations. While many focus on holiday cards, a few offer greeting cards, such as birthday cards and thank you notes, that you can use all year long.

Examples are UNICEF (market.unicefusa.org), MD Andersen Cancer Center (childrensartproject.org/cards.html), and National Wildlife Federation (shopnwf.org). You're not spending any extra money if you would have bought the greeting cards anyway. In fact, you'll likely save: When you buy card sets from these charities, often the cost is around $1 per card. And the designs have come a long way in recent years — many are on-par with commercial cards.

DONATE TO CHARITY IN YOUR WILL

OK, so this money technically does come from your wallet — but not right away. Donating in your will can be a great option if you want to donate a large amount to charity but are worried about having enough assets to last through your golden years.

The next time you update your will (experts recommend doing it every few years and after any major life changes), work with a lawyer or estate planner to include a charitable donation plan. It's also a good idea to notify the charities you've selected about your intentions. Most organizations say that they greatly appreciate knowing about these arrangements in advance.

Discover Even More Ways to _Save_ Money Every Month!

The _Franklin Prosperity Report_ is dedicated to helping its readers save money each month with creative ways to cut your costs on groceries, insurance, travel, and everyday expenses so you can save more and spend less this year. Named after one of our Founding Fathers, **Benjamin Franklin**, the newsletter follows Franklin's centuries-old wisdom and his principles of building wealth. After all, it was Franklin who said "A Penny Saved Is a Penny Earned," and it is the motto we have adopted for the newsletter.

Each month _The Franklin Prosperity Report_ follows in its namesake's footsteps and gives readers invaluable advice from a host of top-shelf, expert contributors on how to properly manage and maximize your money. Recent issues have included topics such as:

- Cut Your Tax Bill in Retirement! 6 Proven Financial Strategies to Keep More of Your Hard-Earned Cash
- Stop Overpaying for Health Insurance! 8 Ways to Put Your Money to Work for You in a Health Savings Account
- Baby Boomer Guide to a Fully Funded Retirement

If you would like to learn more about joining _The Franklin Prosperity Report_ and how it can help you keep more money in your pocket each month, go to:

www.Newsmax.com/Secrets